PENGUIN BOOKS

CHE GUEVARA

Chie Shimano is a manga artist in Japan. She published her first manga, titled *Mimi ni nokoru wa*, in *Big Comic Magazine* in 2003. Her recent works are found in many illustrated reference books on animals and insects.

Kiyoshi Konno is an experienced editor and writer in Japan and writes primarily about the history of wars. *Che Guevara: A Manga Biography* is his first manga script.

CHE GUEVARA

A Manga Biography

ILLUSTRATION BY
CHIE SHIMANO

STORY BY
KIYOSHI KONNO

PENGUIN BOOKS

PENGUIN BOOKS

Published by the Penguin Group

Penguin Group (USA) Inc., 375 Hudson Street, New York, New York 10014, U.S.A.
Penguin Group (Canada), 90 Eglinton Avenue East, Suite 700, Toronto,
Ontario, Canada M4P 2Y3 (a division of Pearson Penguin Canada Inc.)
Penguin Books Ltd, 80 Strand, London WC2R 0RL, England
Penguin Ireland, 25 St Stephen's Green, Dublin 2, Ireland (a division of Penguin Books Ltd)
Penguin Group (Australia), 250 Camberwell Road, Camberwell,
Victoria 3124, Australia (a division of Pearson Australia Group Pty Ltd)
Penguin Books India Pvt Ltd, 11 Community Centre, Panchsheel Park, New Delhi – 110 017, India
Penguin Group (NZ), 67 Apollo Drive, Rosedale, North Shore 0632,
New Zealand (a division of Pearson New Zealand Ltd)
Penguin Books (South Africa) (Pty) Ltd, 24 Sturdee Avenue,
Rosebank, Johannesburg 2196, South Africa

Penguin Books Ltd, Registered Offices:
80 Strand, London WC2R 0RL, England

First published in the United States of America by Emotional Content LLC 2008
Published in Penguin Books 2010

1   3   5   7   9   10   8   6   4   2

Copyright © Chie Shimano, 2008
English translation copyright © Emotional Content LLC, 2008
All rights reserved

Illustrations by Chie Shimano
Story by Kiyoshi Konno

LIBRARY OF CONGRESS CATALOGING-IN-PUBLICATION DATA
Shimano, Chie.
Che Guevara : a manga biography / illustration by Chie Shimano ; story by Kiyoshi Konno.
    p.   cm.
"First published in the United States of America by Emotional Content . . . 2008"—T.p. verso.
Includes bibliographical references.
ISBN 978-0-9817543-2-1 (Emotional Content pbk.)
ISBN 978-0-14-311816-9 (Penguin pbk.)
1. Guevara, Ernesto, 1928–1967—Comic books, strips, etc.   2. Revolutionaries—Latin America—
Biography—Comic books, strips, etc.   3. Guerrillas—Latin America—Biography—Comic books,
strips, etc.   4. Latin America—History—1948–1980—Comic books, strips, etc.   5. Cuba—History—
Revolution, 1959—Comic books, strips, etc.   6. Argentina—Biography—Comic books, strips, etc.
I. Konno, Kiyoshi.   II. Title.
F2849.22.G85S44   2010
980.03'5092—dc22
    [B]   2010019284

Printed in the United States of America

If you tremble indignation
at every injustice
then you are a comrade of mine.

—Ernesto "Che" Guevara

CONTENT

CHE GUEVARA

CHAPTER 1

EXPLORER
1928 - 1952

*I knew that the moment the great governing spirit strikes
the blow to divide all humanity into just two opposing factions,
I would be on the side of the common people.*

PROLOGUE

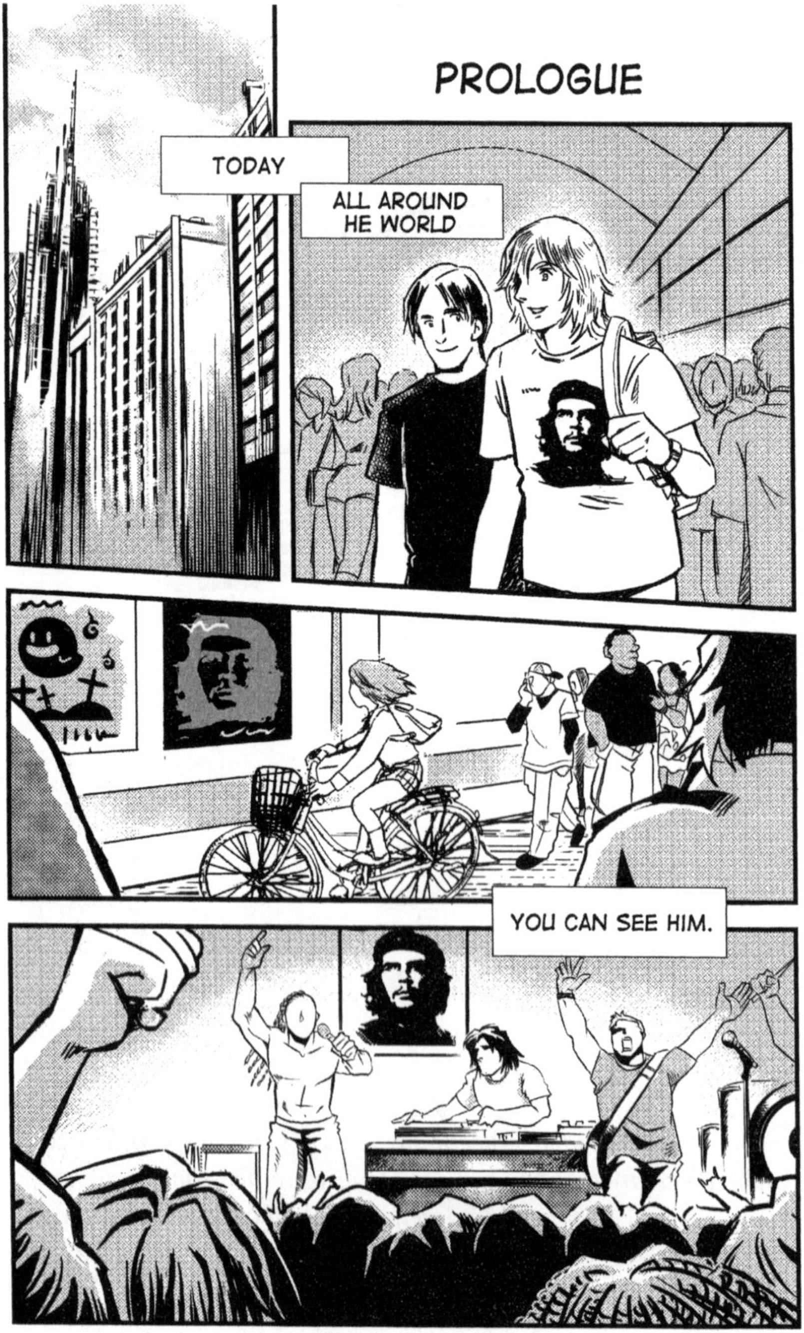
TODAY
ALL AROUND HE WORLD
YOU CAN SEE HIM.

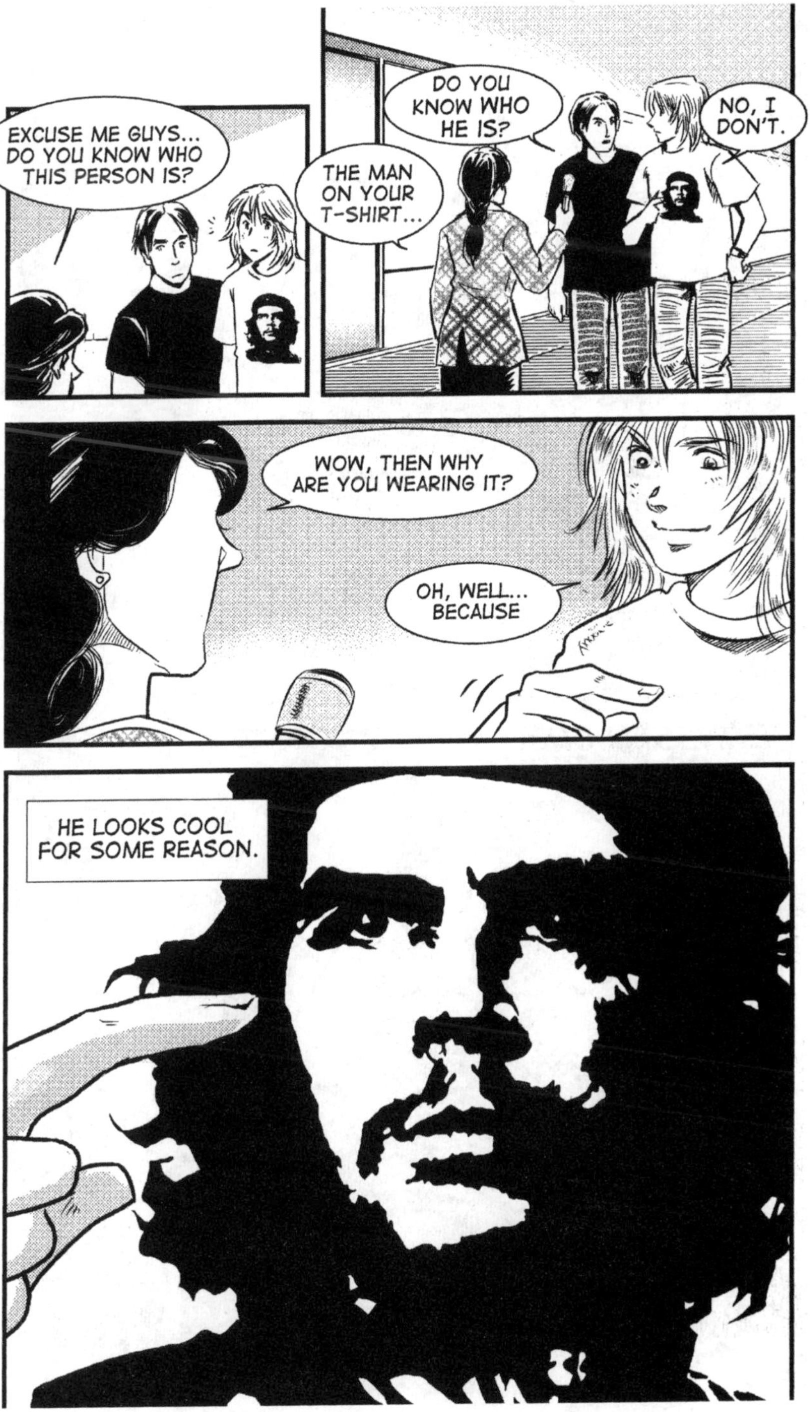
EXCUSE ME GUYS... DO YOU KNOW WHO THIS PERSON IS?
THE MAN ON YOUR T-SHIRT...
DO YOU KNOW WHO HE IS?
NO, I DON'T.
WOW, THEN WHY ARE YOU WEARING IT?
OH, WELL... BECAUSE
HE LOOKS COOL FOR SOME REASON.

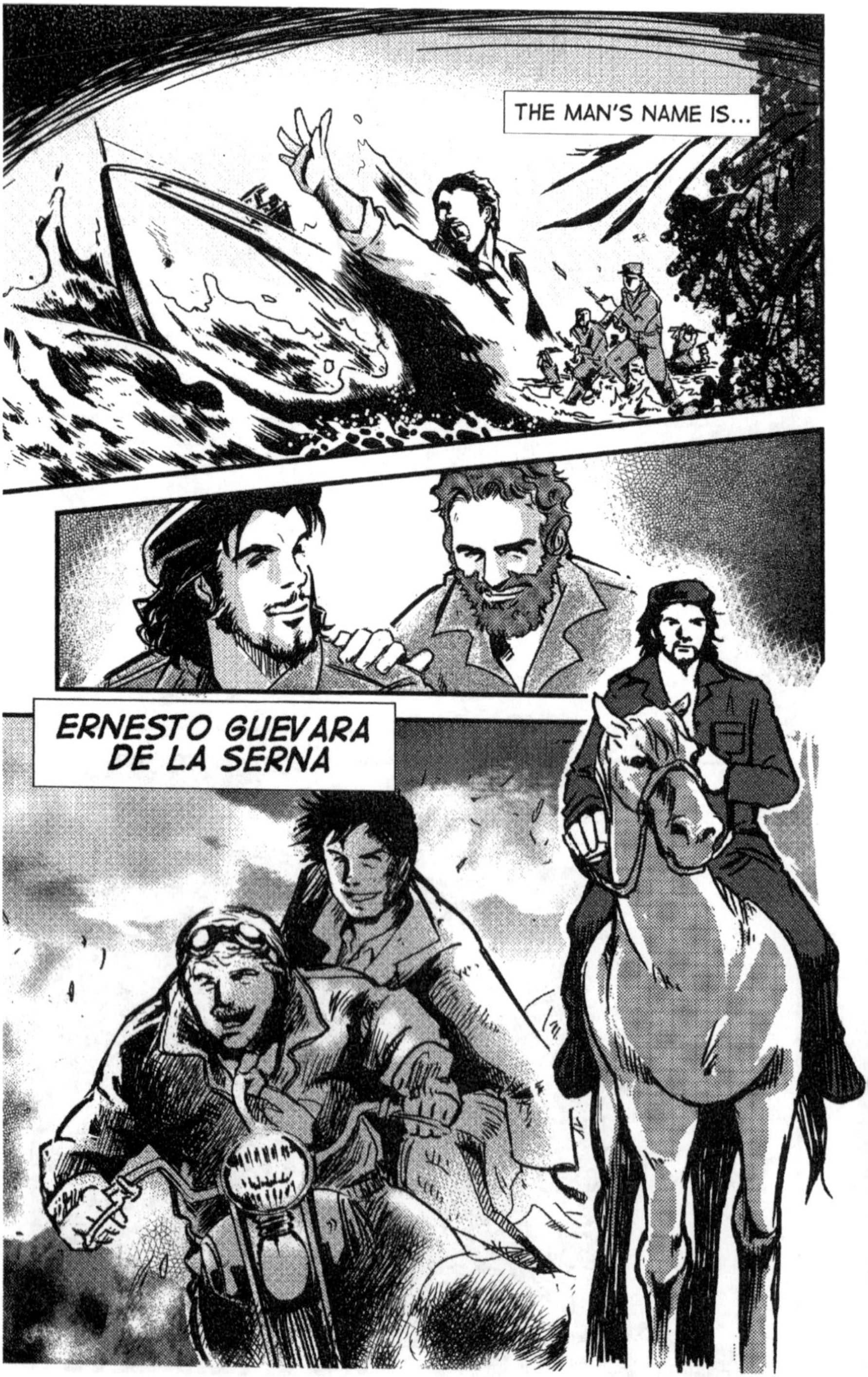
THE MAN'S NAME IS...
ERNESTO GUEVARA DE LA SERNA

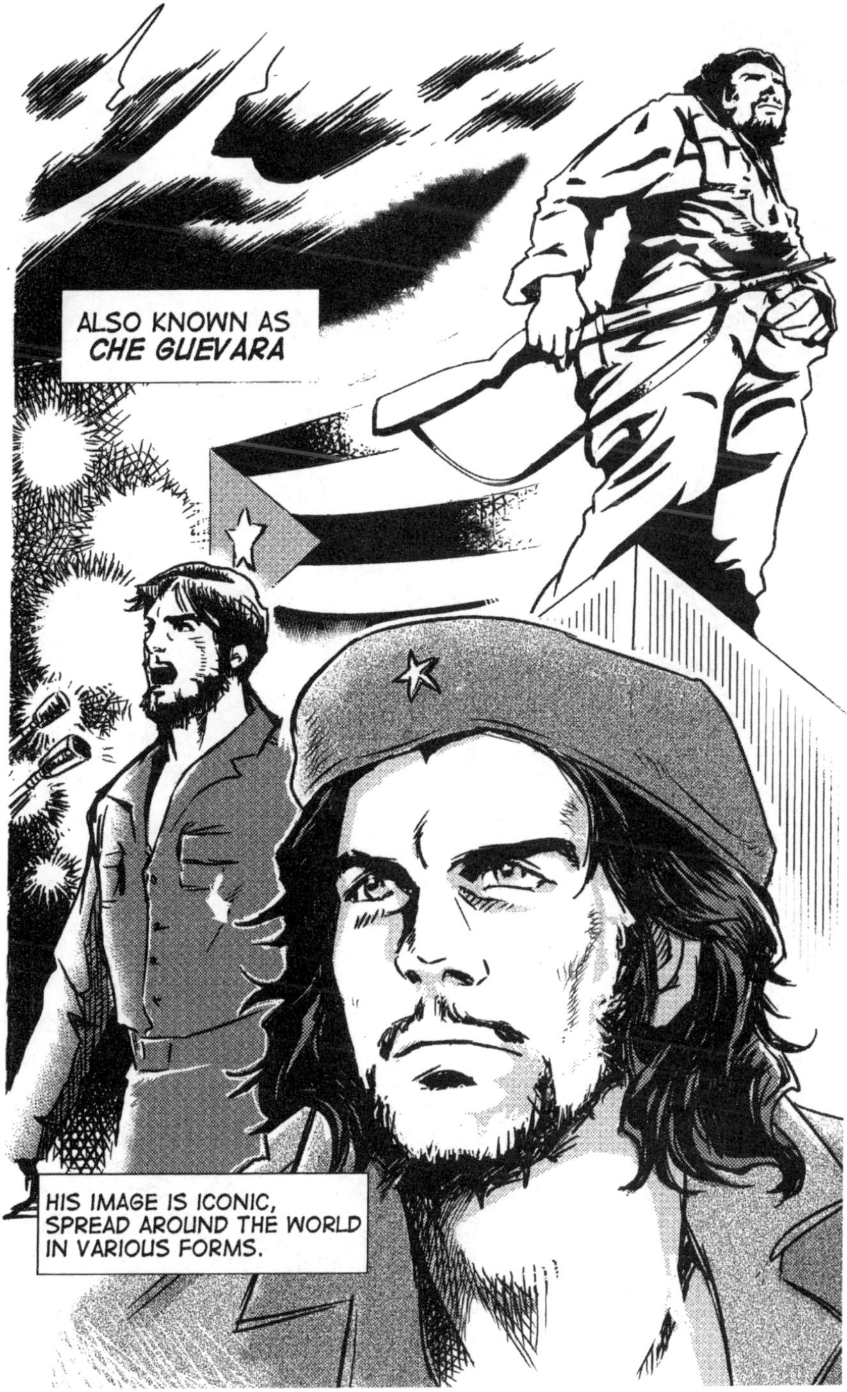
ALSO KNOWN AS *CHE GUEVARA*
HIS IMAGE IS ICONIC, SPREAD AROUND THE WORLD IN VARIOUS FORMS.

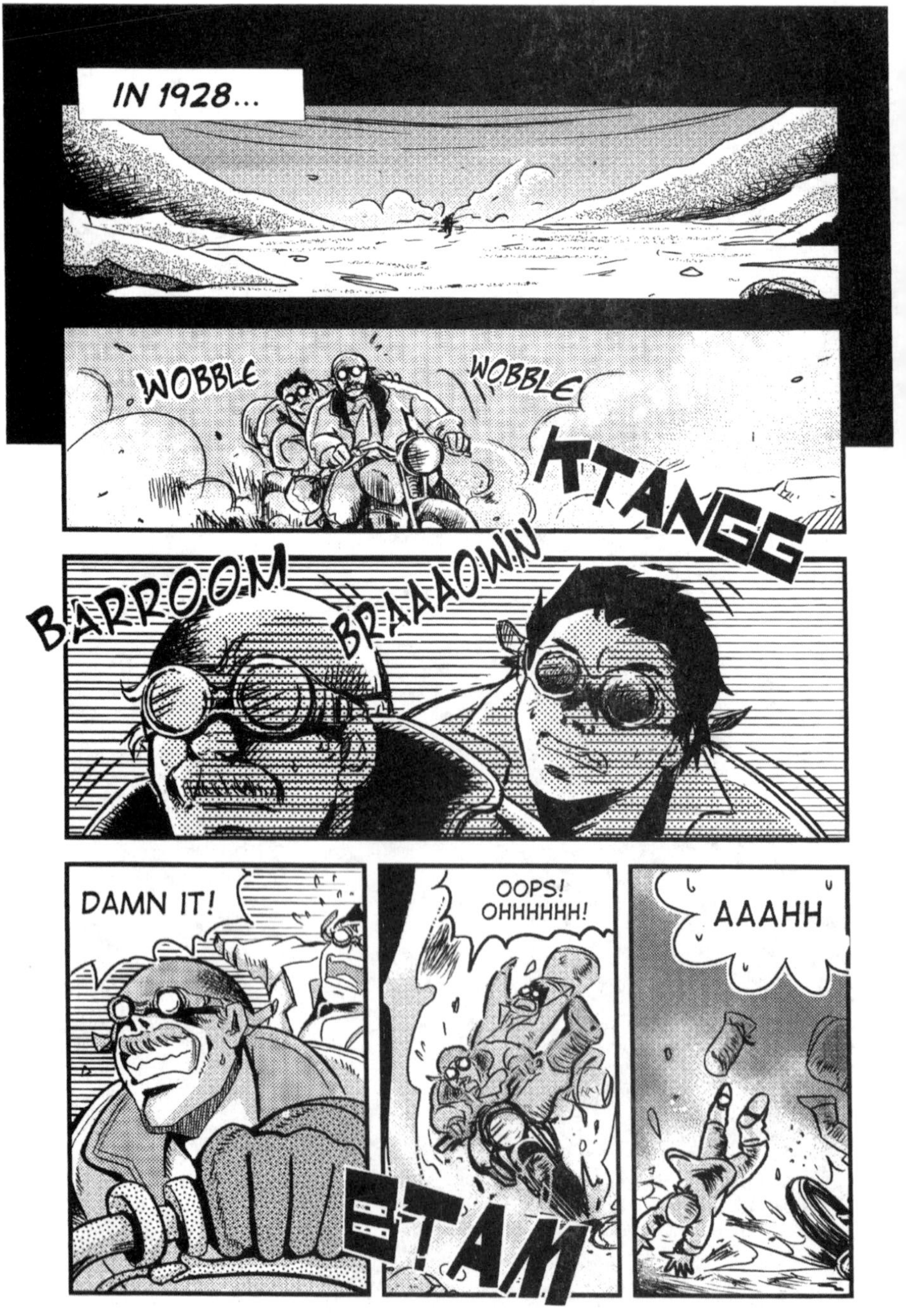
IN 1928...
WOBBLE
WOBBLE
KTANGG
BARROOM
BRAAAOWN
DAMN IT!
OOPS!
OHHHHHH!
BTAM
AAAHH

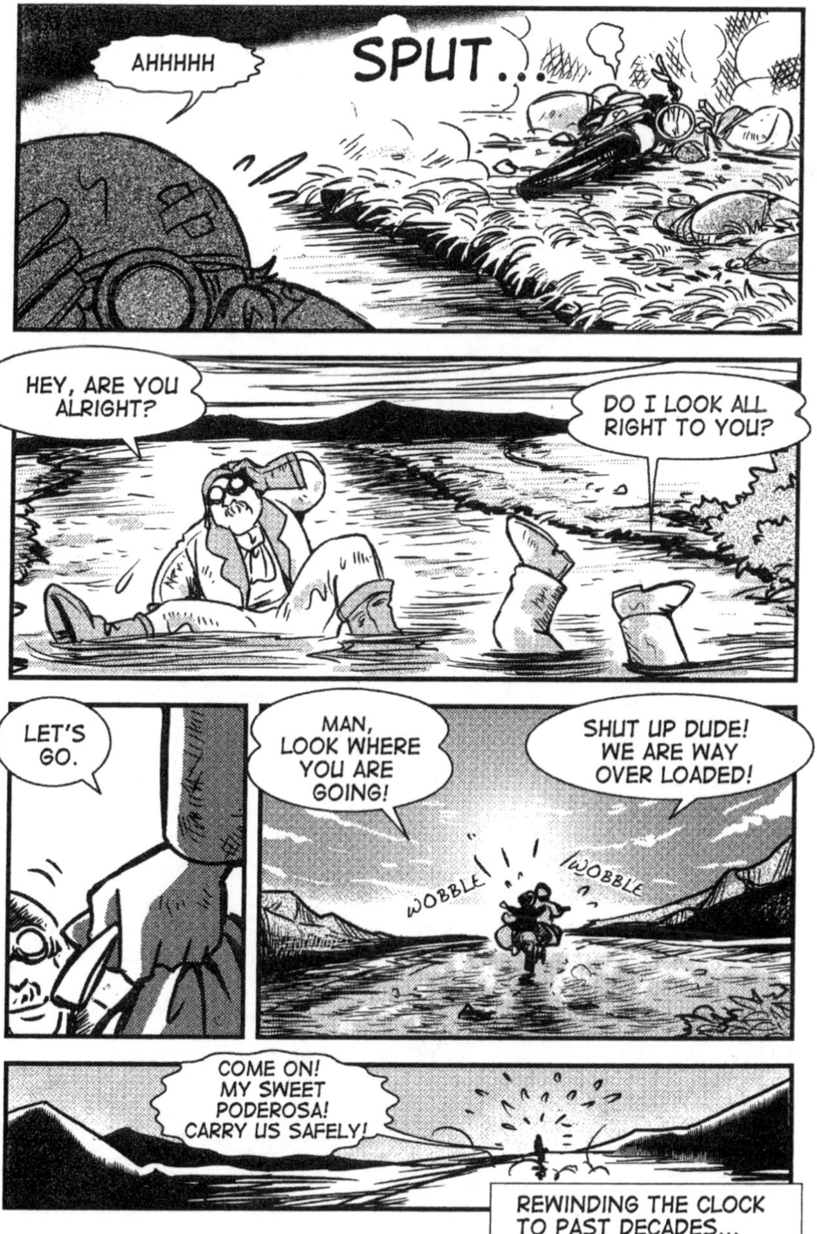
AHHHHH
SPUT...
HEY, ARE YOU ALRIGHT?
DO I LOOK ALL RIGHT TO YOU?
LET'S GO.
MAN, LOOK WHERE YOU ARE GOING!
SHUT UP DUDE! WE ARE WAY OVER LOADED!
WOBBLE
WOBBLE
COME ON! MY SWEET PODEROSA! CARRY US SAFELY!
REWINDING THE CLOCK TO PAST DECADES...

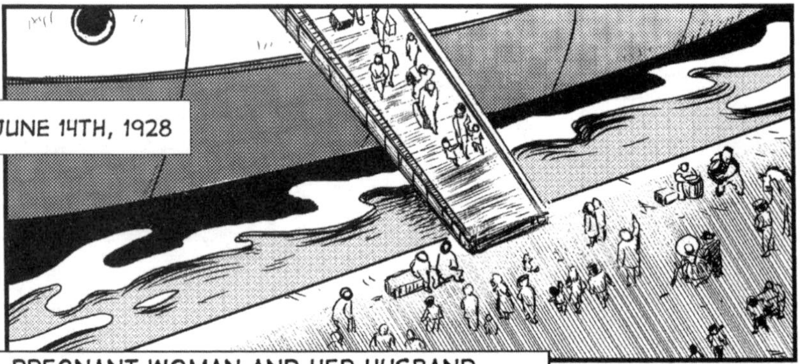
JUNE 14TH, 1928

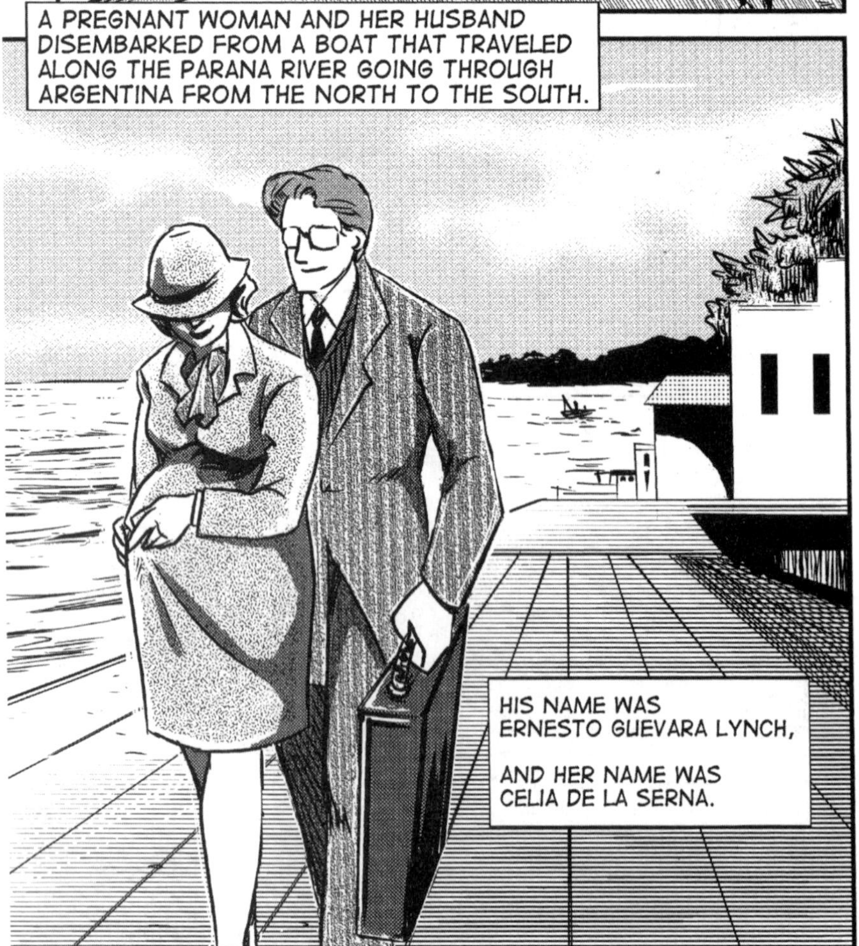
A PREGNANT WOMAN AND HER HUSBAND DISEMBARKED FROM A BOAT THAT TRAVELED ALONG THE PARANA RIVER GOING THROUGH ARGENTINA FROM THE NORTH TO THE SOUTH.
HIS NAME WAS ERNESTO GUEVARA LYNCH,
AND HER NAME WAS CELIA DE LA SERNA.

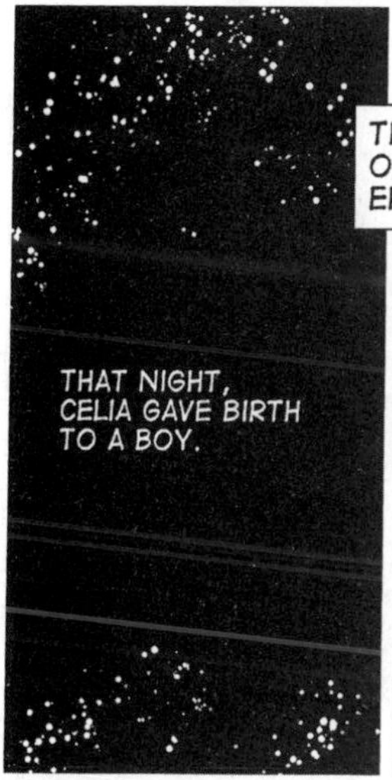
THAT NIGHT, CELIA GAVE BIRTH TO A BOY.

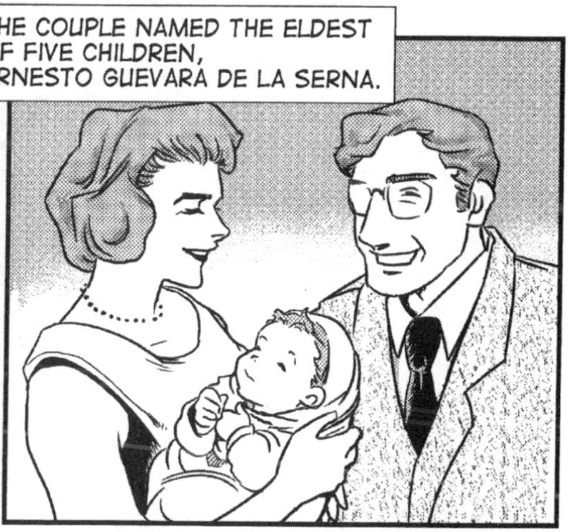
THE COUPLE NAMED THE ELDEST OF FIVE CHILDREN, ERNESTO GUEVARA DE LA SERNA.

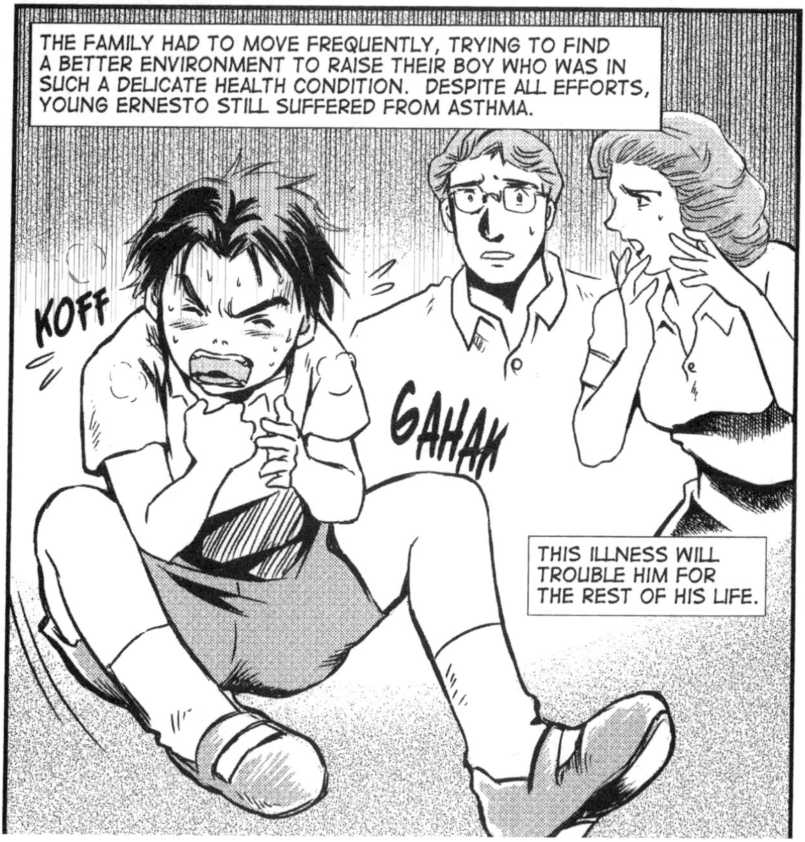
THE FAMILY HAD TO MOVE FREQUENTLY, TRYING TO FIND A BETTER ENVIRONMENT TO RAISE THEIR BOY WHO WAS IN SUCH A DELICATE HEALTH CONDITION. DESPITE ALL EFFORTS, YOUNG ERNESTO STILL SUFFERED FROM ASTHMA.
KOFF
GAHAK
THIS ILLNESS WILL TROUBLE HIM FOR THE REST OF HIS LIFE.

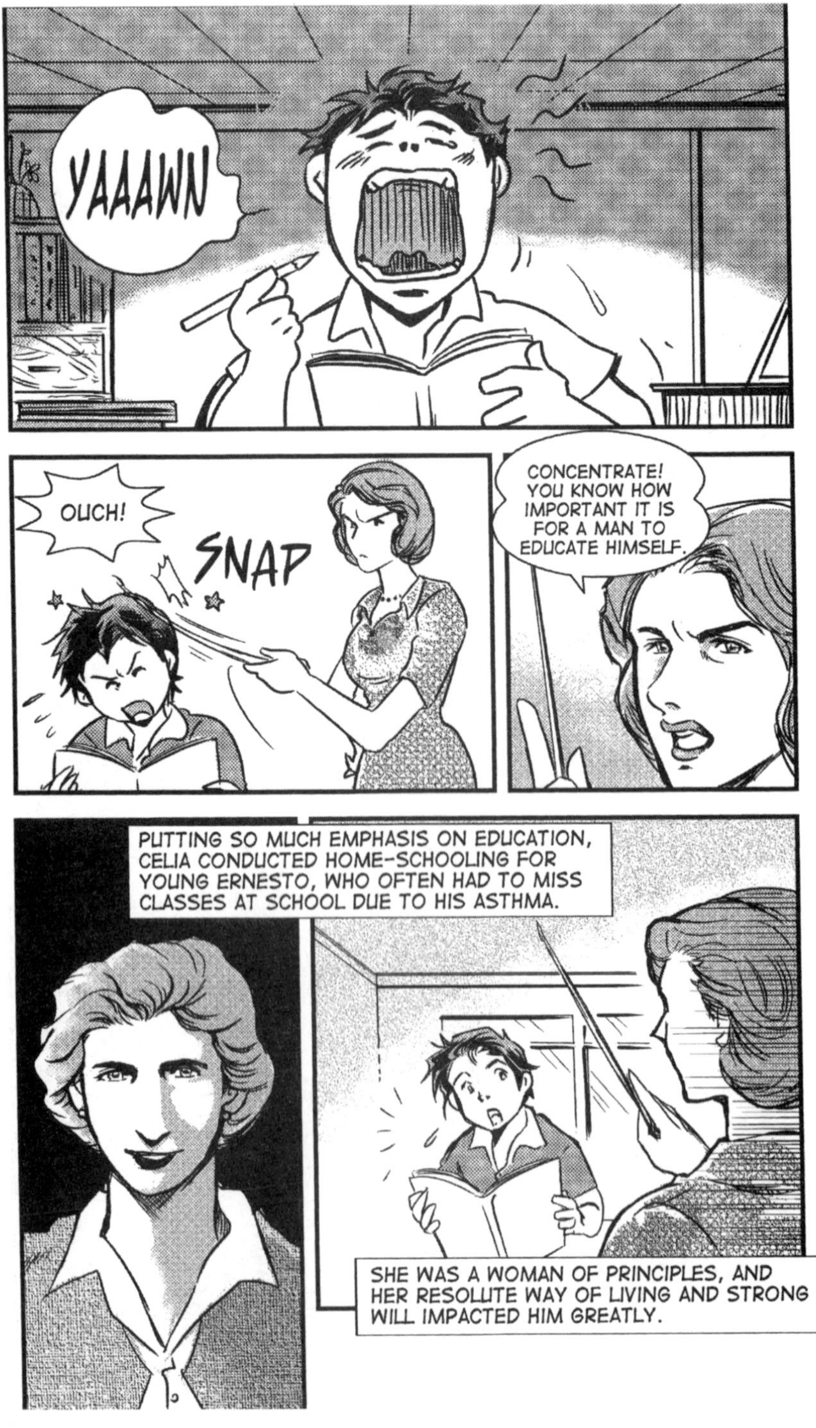
YAAAWN
OUCH!
SNAP
CONCENTRATE! YOU KNOW HOW IMPORTANT IT IS FOR A MAN TO EDUCATE HIMSELF.
PUTTING SO MUCH EMPHASIS ON EDUCATION, CELIA CONDUCTED HOME-SCHOOLING FOR YOUNG ERNESTO, WHO OFTEN HAD TO MISS CLASSES AT SCHOOL DUE TO HIS ASTHMA.
SHE WAS A WOMAN OF PRINCIPLES, AND HER RESOLUTE WAY OF LIVING AND STRONG WILL IMPACTED HIM GREATLY.

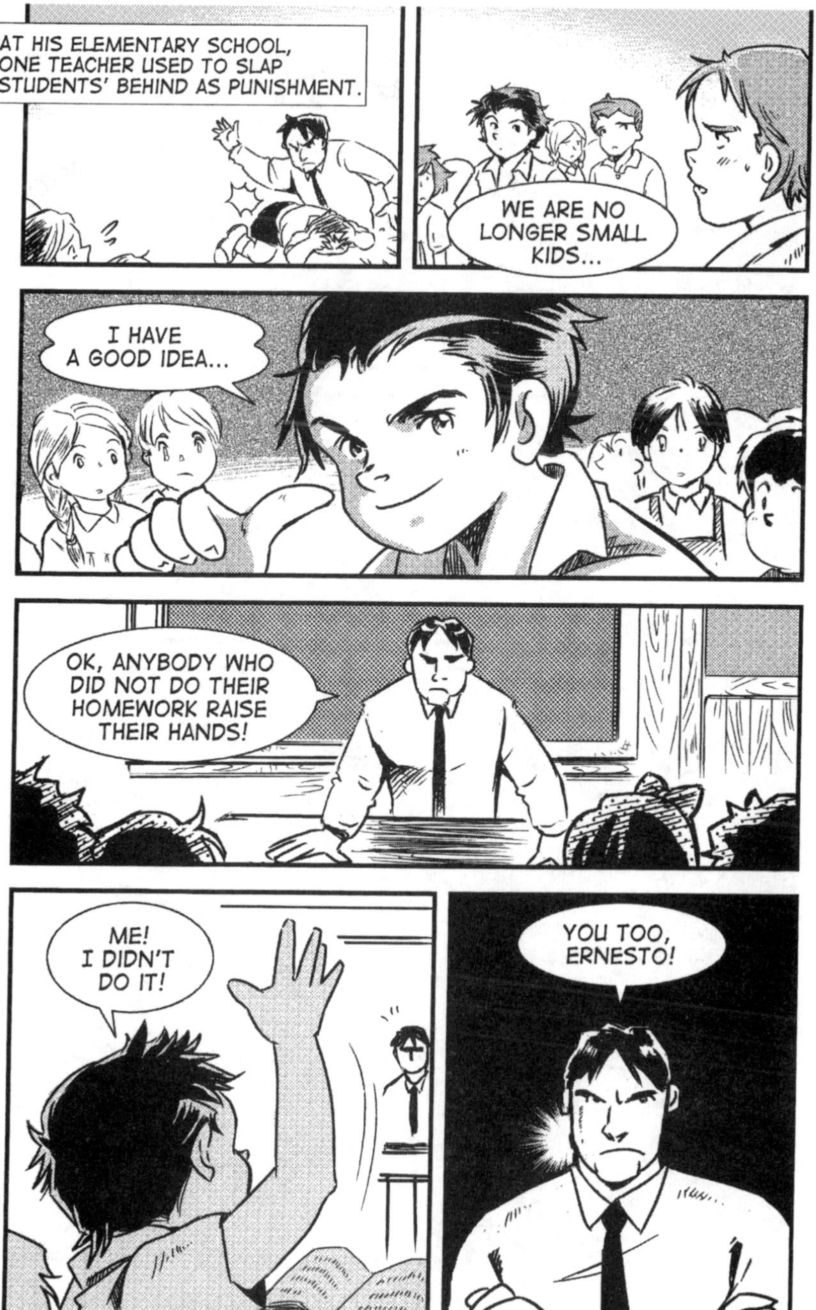
AT HIS ELEMENTARY SCHOOL, ONE TEACHER USED TO SLAP STUDENTS' BEHIND AS PUNISHMENT.
WE ARE NO LONGER SMALL KIDS...
I HAVE A GOOD IDEA...
OK, ANYBODY WHO DID NOT DO THEIR HOMEWORK RAISE THEIR HANDS!
ME! I DIDN'T DO IT!
YOU TOO, ERNESTO!

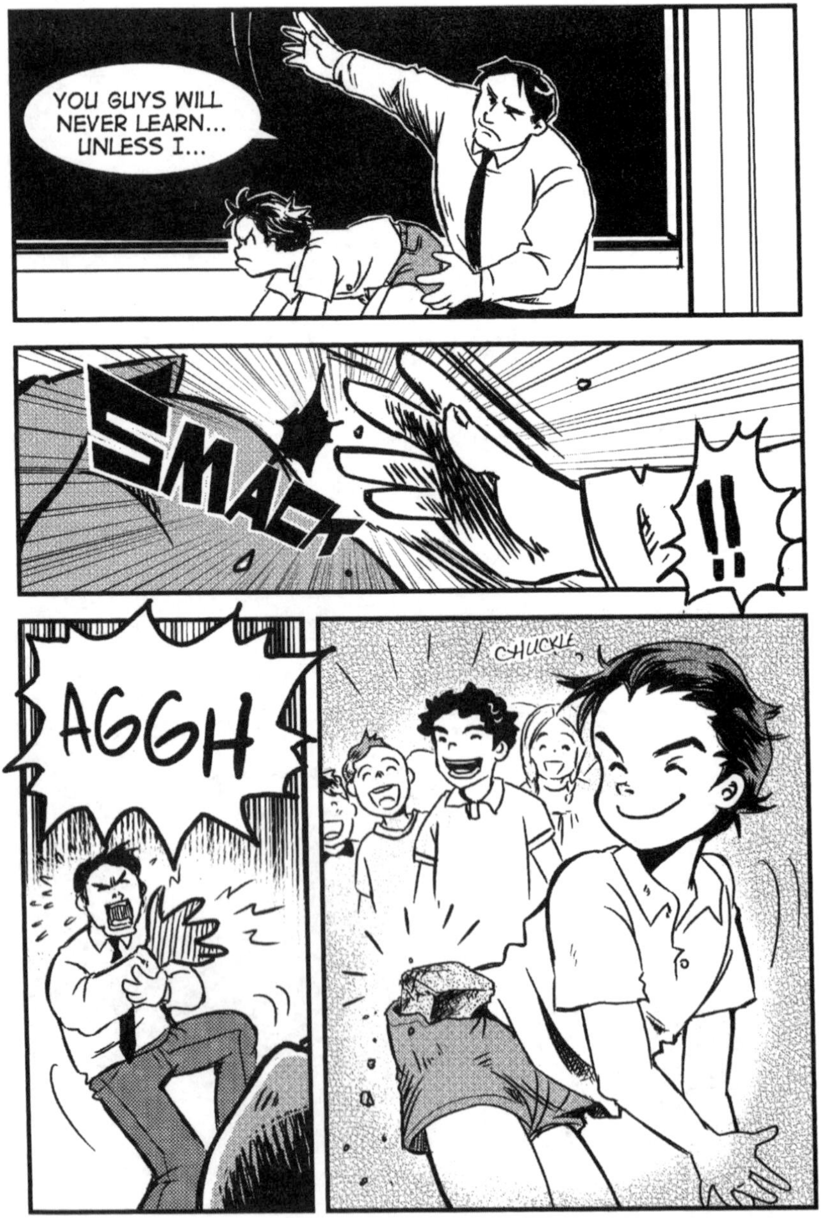
YOU GUYS WILL NEVER LEARN... UNLESS I...
SMACK
!!
AGGH
CHUCKLE

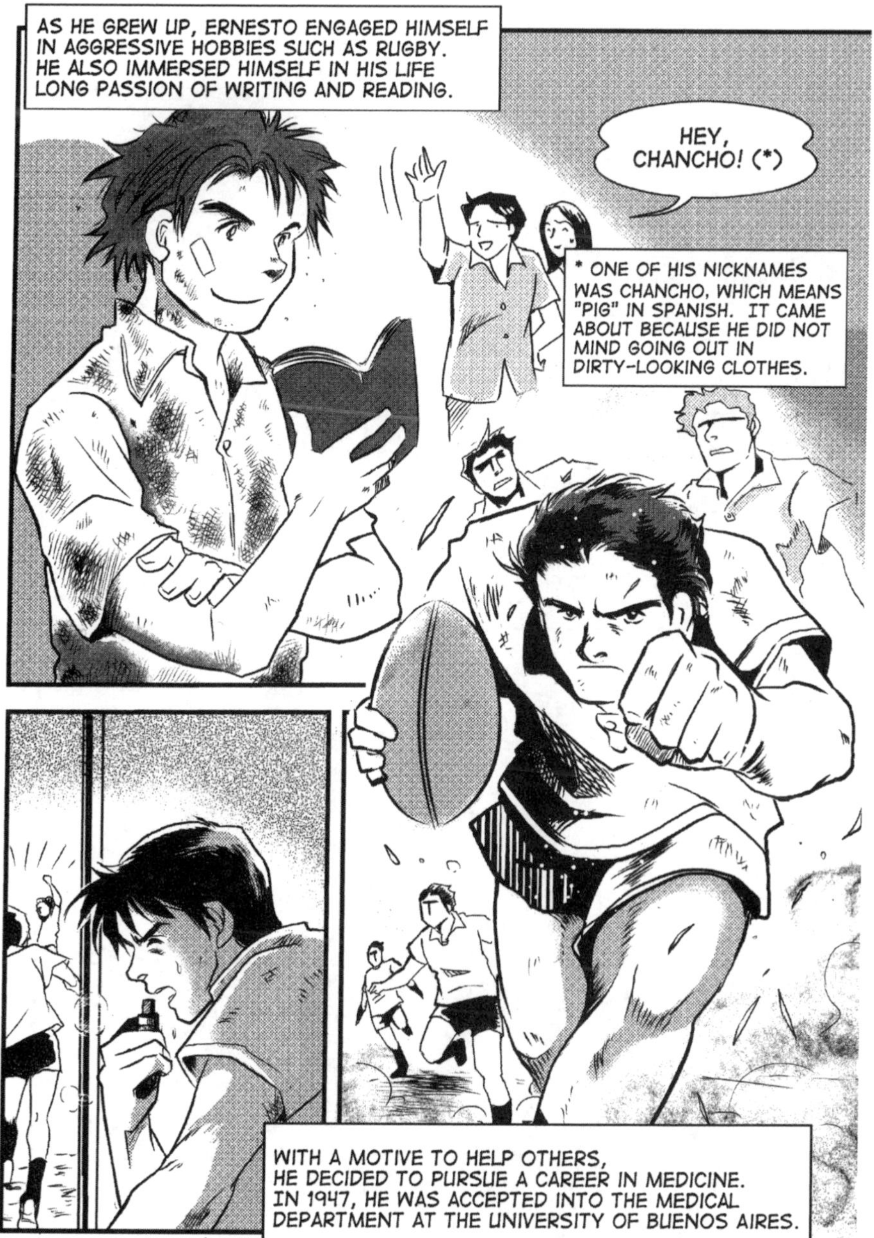
AS HE GREW UP, ERNESTO ENGAGED HIMSELF IN AGGRESSIVE HOBBIES SUCH AS RUGBY. HE ALSO IMMERSED HIMSELF IN HIS LIFE LONG PASSION OF WRITING AND READING.
HEY, CHANCHO! (*)
* ONE OF HIS NICKNAMES WAS CHANCHO, WHICH MEANS "PIG" IN SPANISH. IT CAME ABOUT BECAUSE HE DID NOT MIND GOING OUT IN DIRTY-LOOKING CLOTHES.
WITH A MOTIVE TO HELP OTHERS, HE DECIDED TO PURSUE A CAREER IN MEDICINE. IN 1947, HE WAS ACCEPTED INTO THE MEDICAL DEPARTMENT AT THE UNIVERSITY OF BUENOS AIRES.

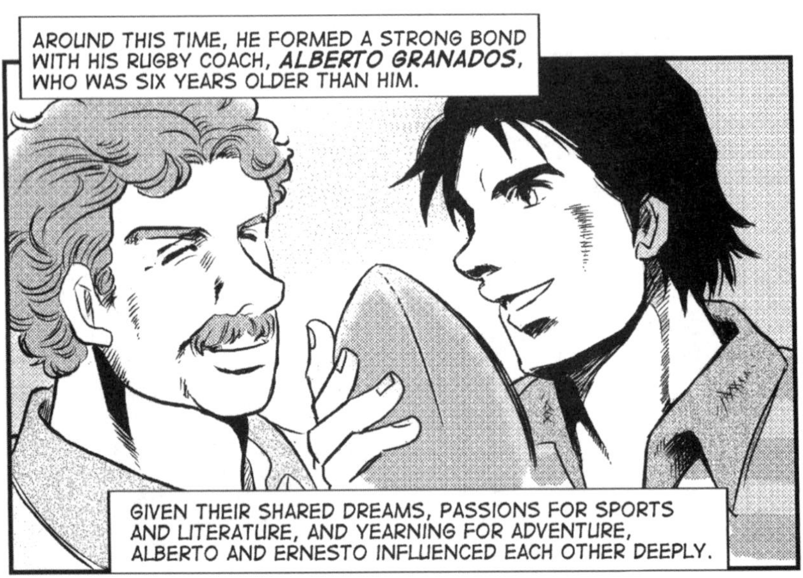
AROUND THIS TIME, HE FORMED A STRONG BOND WITH HIS RUGBY COACH, ***ALBERTO GRANADOS***, WHO WAS SIX YEARS OLDER THAN HIM.
GIVEN THEIR SHARED DREAMS, PASSIONS FOR SPORTS AND LITERATURE, AND YEARNING FOR ADVENTURE, ALBERTO AND ERNESTO INFLUENCED EACH OTHER DEEPLY.

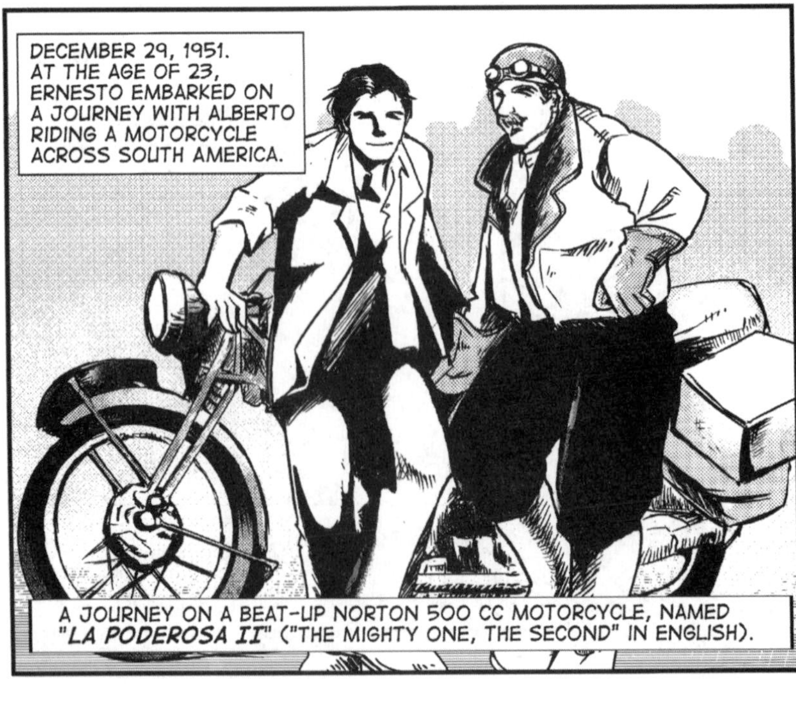
DECEMBER 29, 1951. AT THE AGE OF 23, ERNESTO EMBARKED ON A JOURNEY WITH ALBERTO RIDING A MOTORCYCLE ACROSS SOUTH AMERICA.
A JOURNEY ON A BEAT-UP NORTON 500 CC MOTORCYCLE, NAMED "***LA PODEROSA II***" ("THE MIGHTY ONE, THE SECOND" IN ENGLISH).

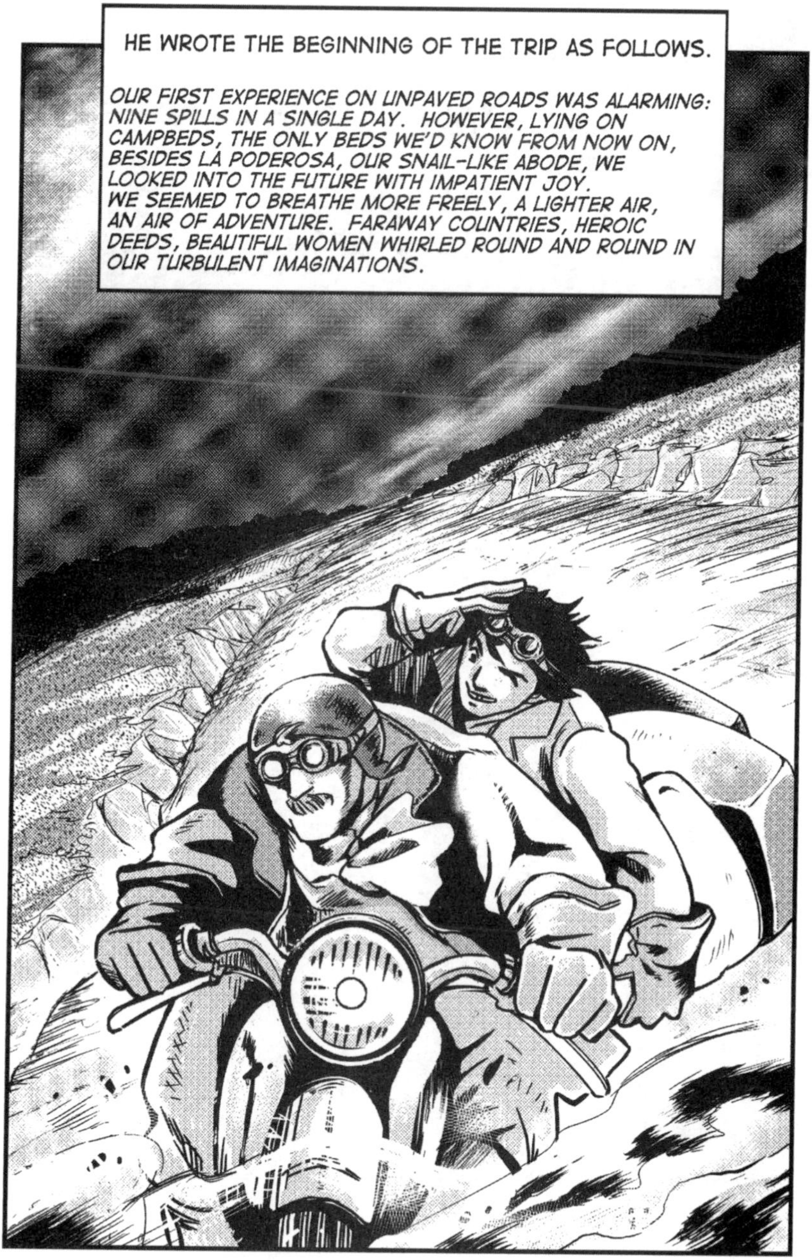
HE WROTE THE BEGINNING OF THE TRIP AS FOLLOWS.
OUR FIRST EXPERIENCE ON UNPAVED ROADS WAS ALARMING: NINE SPILLS IN A SINGLE DAY. HOWEVER, LYING ON CAMPBEDS, THE ONLY BEDS WE'D KNOW FROM NOW ON, BESIDES LA PODEROSA, OUR SNAIL-LIKE ABODE, WE LOOKED INTO THE FUTURE WITH IMPATIENT JOY. WE SEEMED TO BREATHE MORE FREELY, A LIGHTER AIR, AN AIR OF ADVENTURE. FARAWAY COUNTRIES, HEROIC DEEDS, BEAUTIFUL WOMEN WHIRLED ROUND AND ROUND IN OUR TURBULENT IMAGINATIONS.

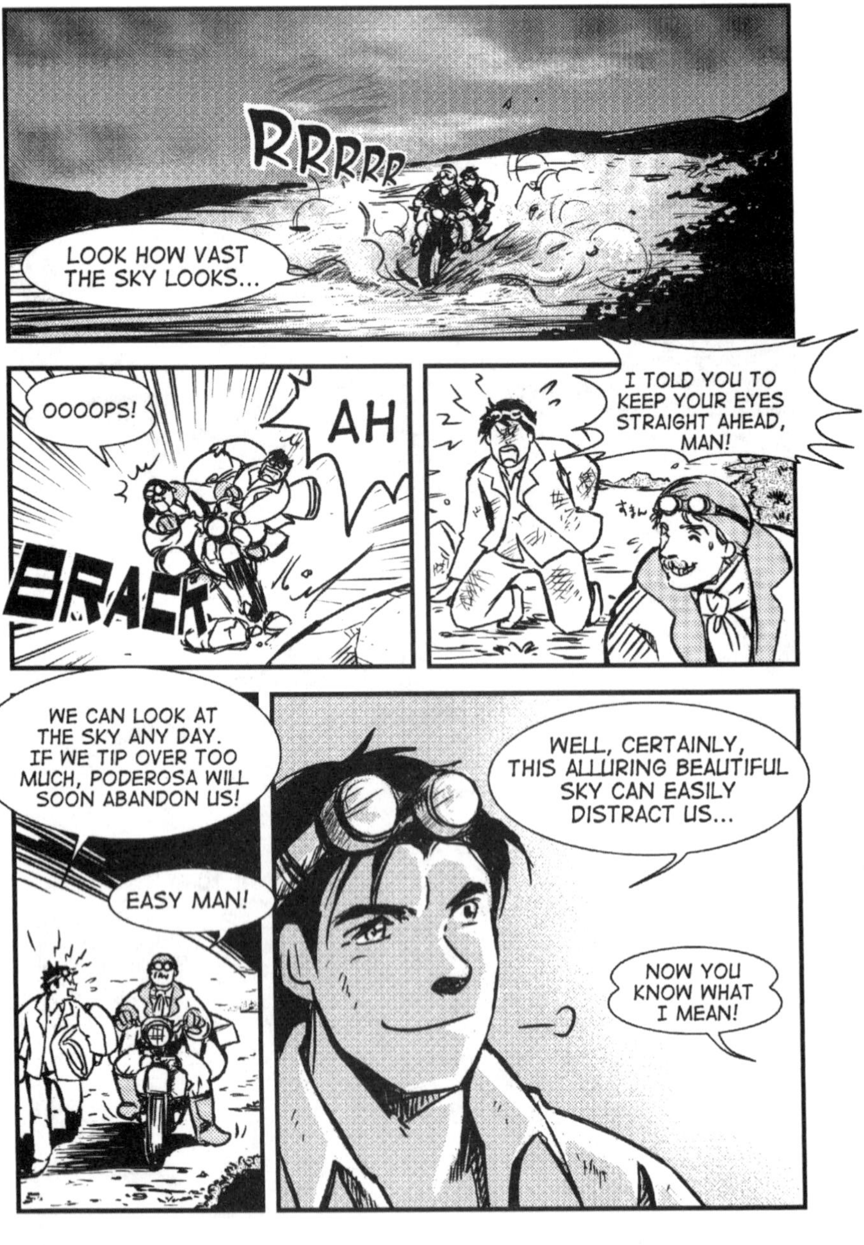
RRRRR
LOOK HOW VAST THE SKY LOOKS...
OOOOPS!
AH
BRACT
I TOLD YOU TO KEEP YOUR EYES STRAIGHT AHEAD, MAN!
すまん
WE CAN LOOK AT THE SKY ANY DAY. IF WE TIP OVER TOO MUCH, PODEROSA WILL SOON ABANDON US!
EASY MAN!
WELL, CERTAINLY, THIS ALLURING BEAUTIFUL SKY CAN EASILY DISTRACT US...
NOW YOU KNOW WHAT I MEAN!

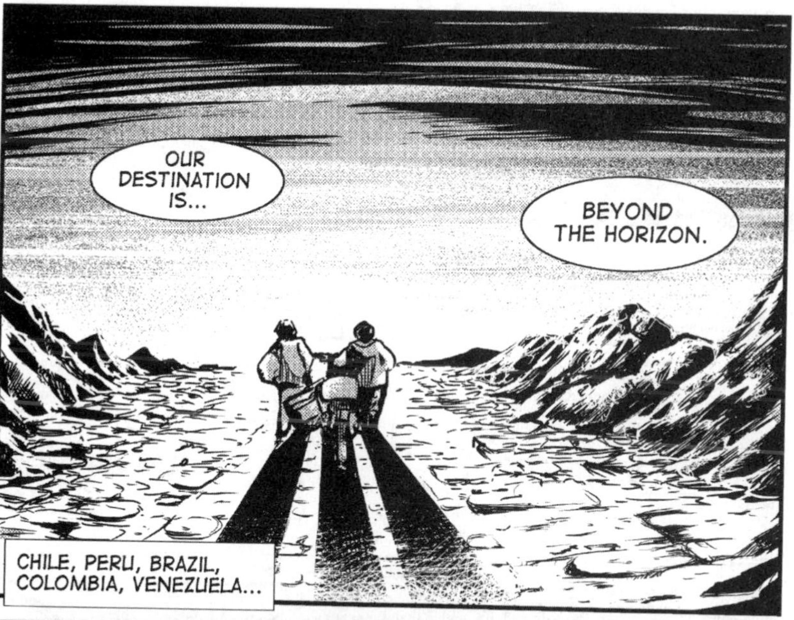
OUR DESTINATION IS...
BEYOND THE HORIZON.
CHILE, PERU, BRAZIL, COLOMBIA, VENEZUELA...

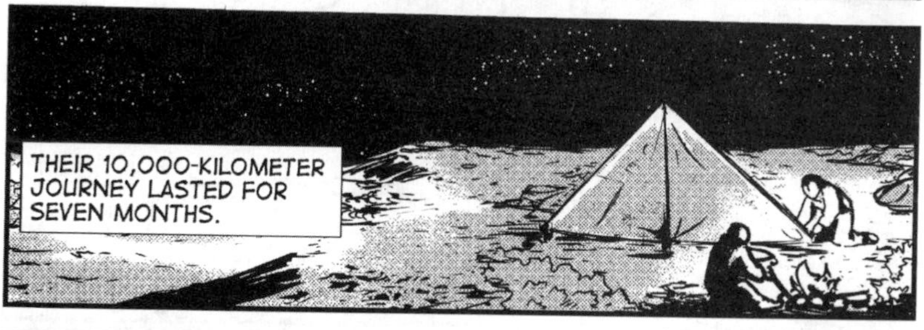
THEIR 10,000-KILOMETER JOURNEY LASTED FOR SEVEN MONTHS.

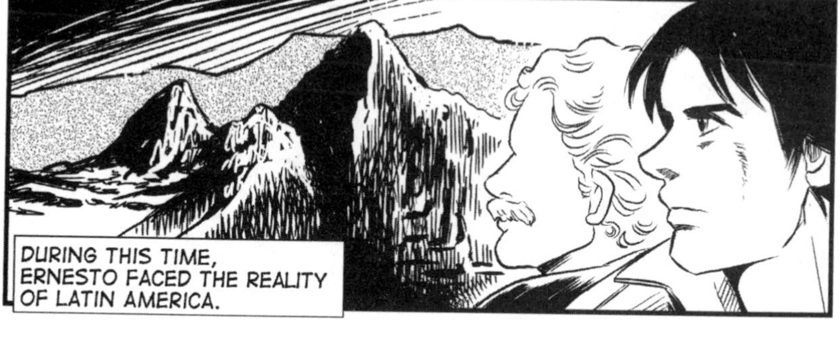
DURING THIS TIME, ERNESTO FACED THE REALITY OF LATIN AMERICA.

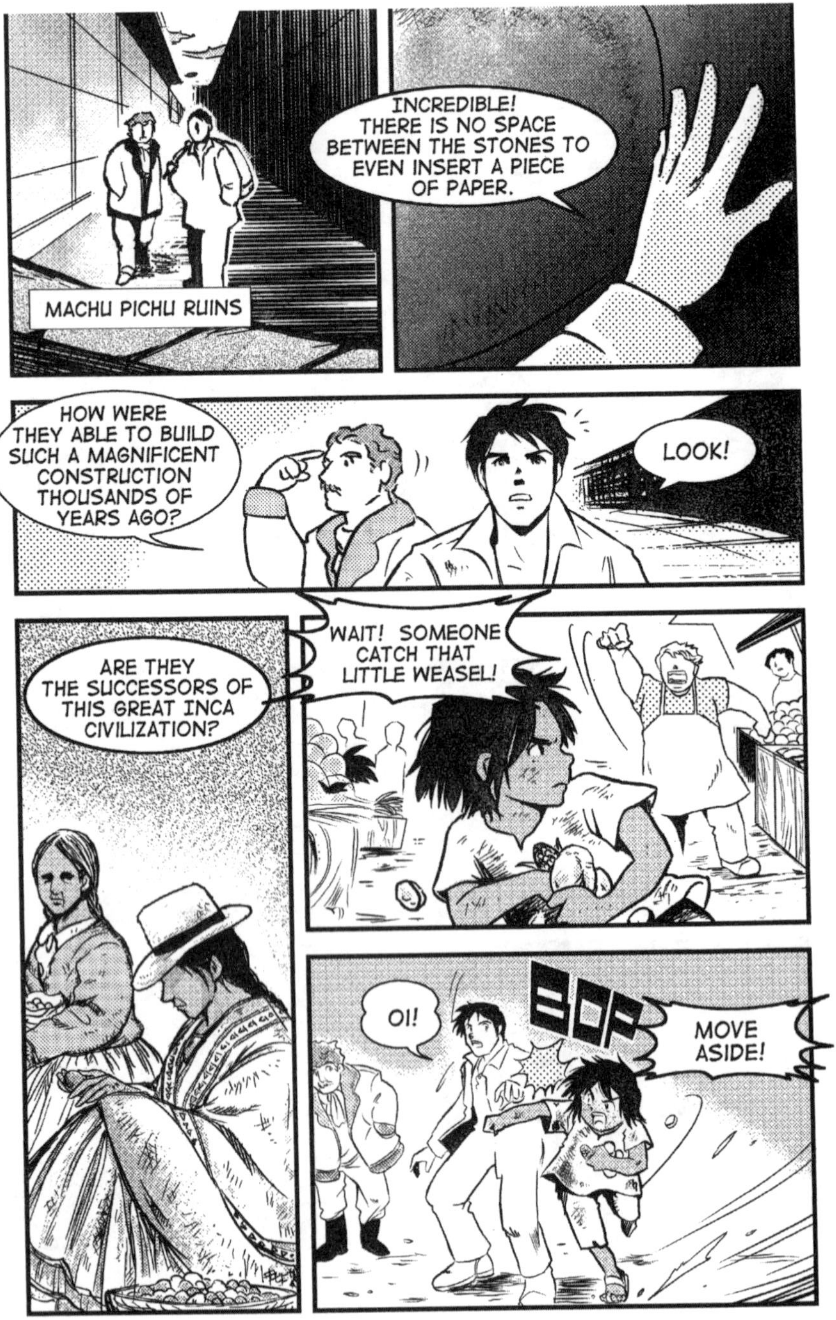
MACHU PICHU RUINS
INCREDIBLE! THERE IS NO SPACE BETWEEN THE STONES TO EVEN INSERT A PIECE OF PAPER.
HOW WERE THEY ABLE TO BUILD SUCH A MAGNIFICENT CONSTRUCTION THOUSANDS OF YEARS AGO?
LOOK!
ARE THEY THE SUCCESSORS OF THIS GREAT INCA CIVILIZATION?
WAIT! SOMEONE CATCH THAT LITTLE WEASEL!
OI!
BOP
MOVE ASIDE!

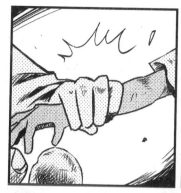

STEALING IS BAD, RIGHT?

LET ME GO! MY YOUNGER SISTER IS DYING!

DAMN THIEF! THAT IS WHY YOU INDIOS ARE...

SMAK

YOU GUYS ARE THE WORST ROBBERS!

WHAT!

I WILL BEAT...

OOOPS, EXCUSE ME.

THAKT

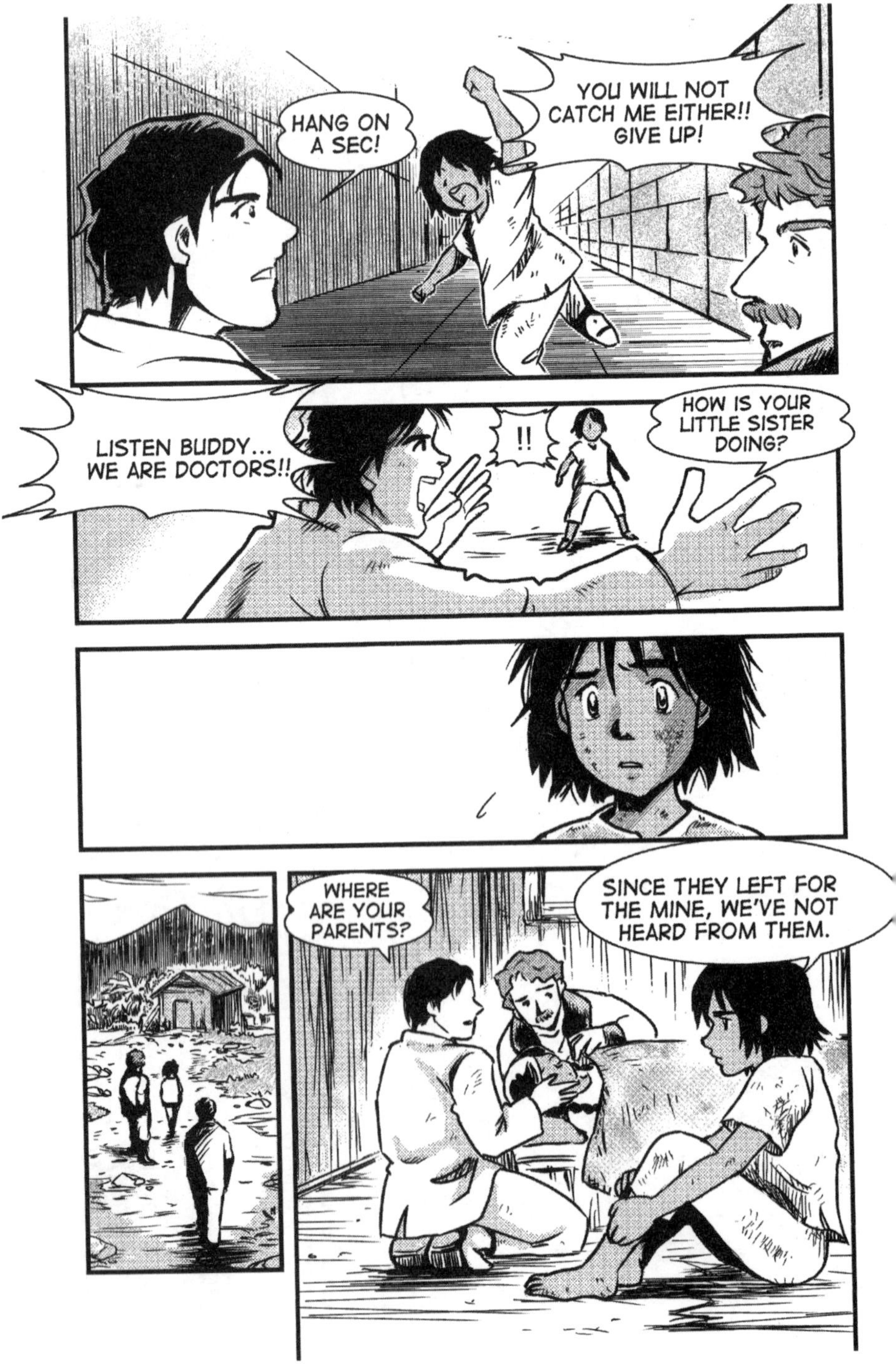
HANG ON A SEC!
YOU WILL NOT CATCH ME EITHER!! GIVE UP!
LISTEN BUDDY... WE ARE DOCTORS!!
!!
HOW IS YOUR LITTLE SISTER DOING?
WHERE ARE YOUR PARENTS?
SINCE THEY LEFT FOR THE MINE, WE'VE NOT HEARD FROM THEM.

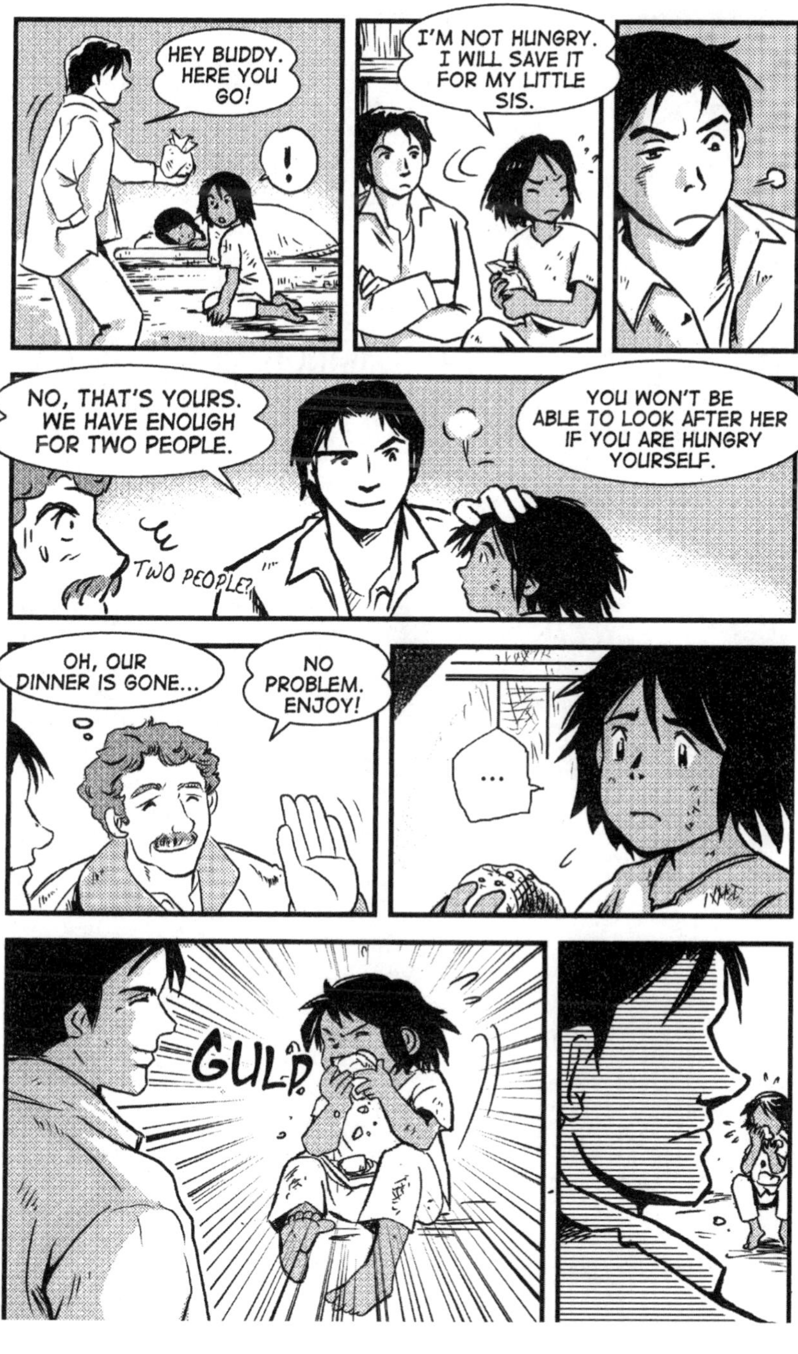
HEY BUDDY. HERE YOU GO!
!
I'M NOT HUNGRY. I WILL SAVE IT FOR MY LITTLE SIS.
NO, THAT'S YOURS. WE HAVE ENOUGH FOR TWO PEOPLE.
TWO PEOPLE?
YOU WON'T BE ABLE TO LOOK AFTER HER IF YOU ARE HUNGRY YOURSELF.
OH, OUR DINNER IS GONE...
NO PROBLEM. ENJOY!
...
GULP

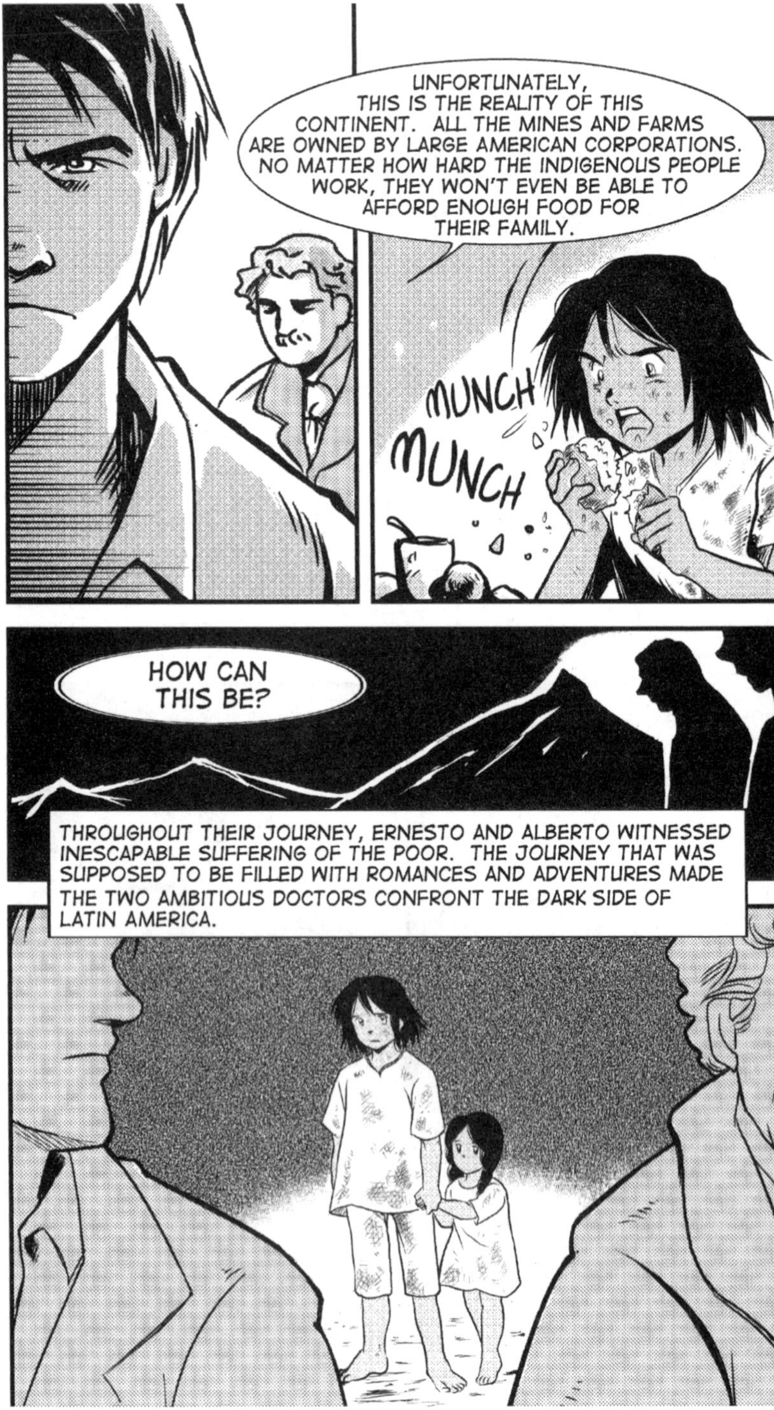
UNFORTUNATELY, THIS IS THE REALITY OF THIS CONTINENT. ALL THE MINES AND FARMS ARE OWNED BY LARGE AMERICAN CORPORATIONS. NO MATTER HOW HARD THE INDIGENOUS PEOPLE WORK, THEY WON'T EVEN BE ABLE TO AFFORD ENOUGH FOOD FOR THEIR FAMILY.
MUNCH MUNCH
HOW CAN THIS BE?
THROUGHOUT THEIR JOURNEY, ERNESTO AND ALBERTO WITNESSED INESCAPABLE SUFFERING OF THE POOR. THE JOURNEY THAT WAS SUPPOSED TO BE FILLED WITH ROMANCES AND ADVENTURES MADE THE TWO AMBITIOUS DOCTORS CONFRONT THE DARK SIDE OF LATIN AMERICA.

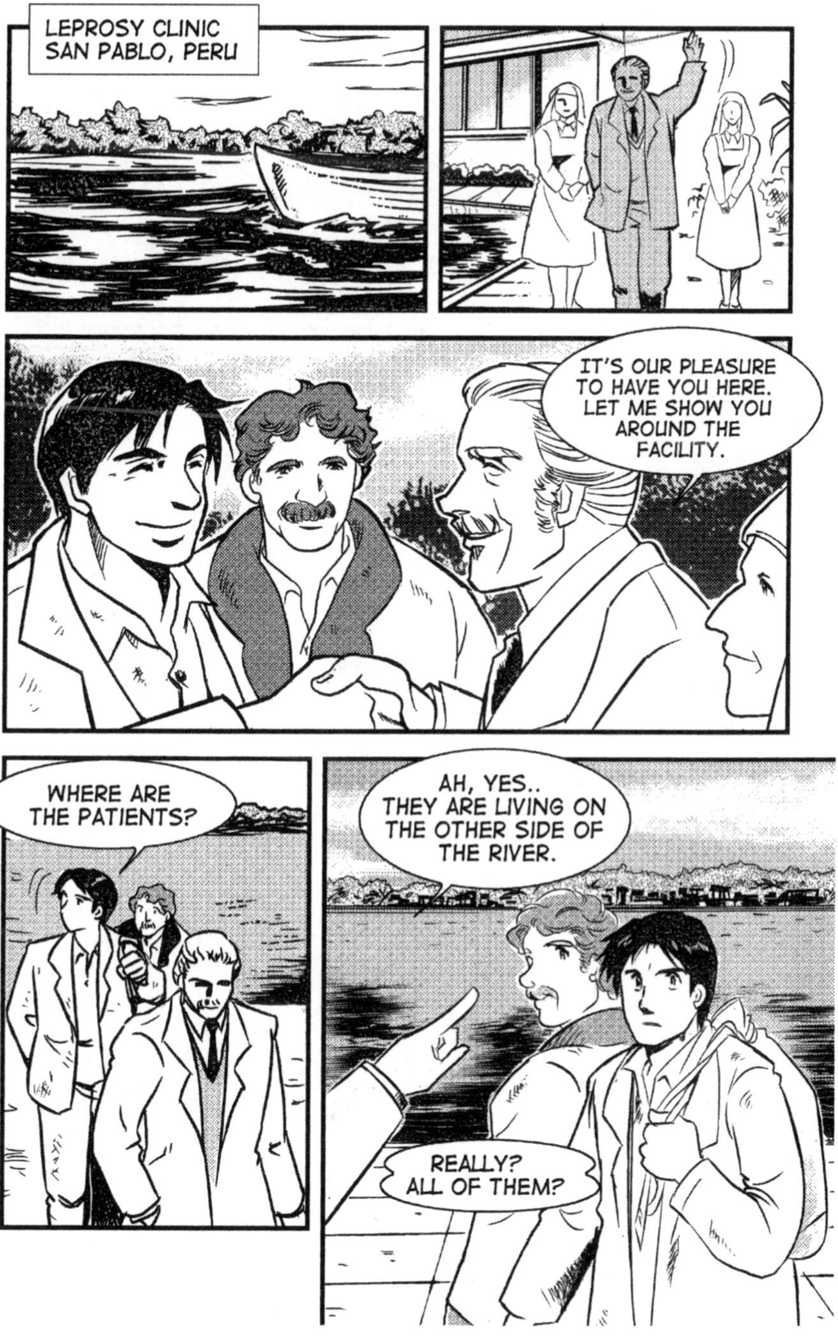
LEPROSY CLINIC SAN PABLO, PERU
IT'S OUR PLEASURE TO HAVE YOU HERE. LET ME SHOW YOU AROUND THE FACILITY.
WHERE ARE THE PATIENTS?
AH, YES.. THEY ARE LIVING ON THE OTHER SIDE OF THE RIVER.
REALLY? ALL OF THEM?

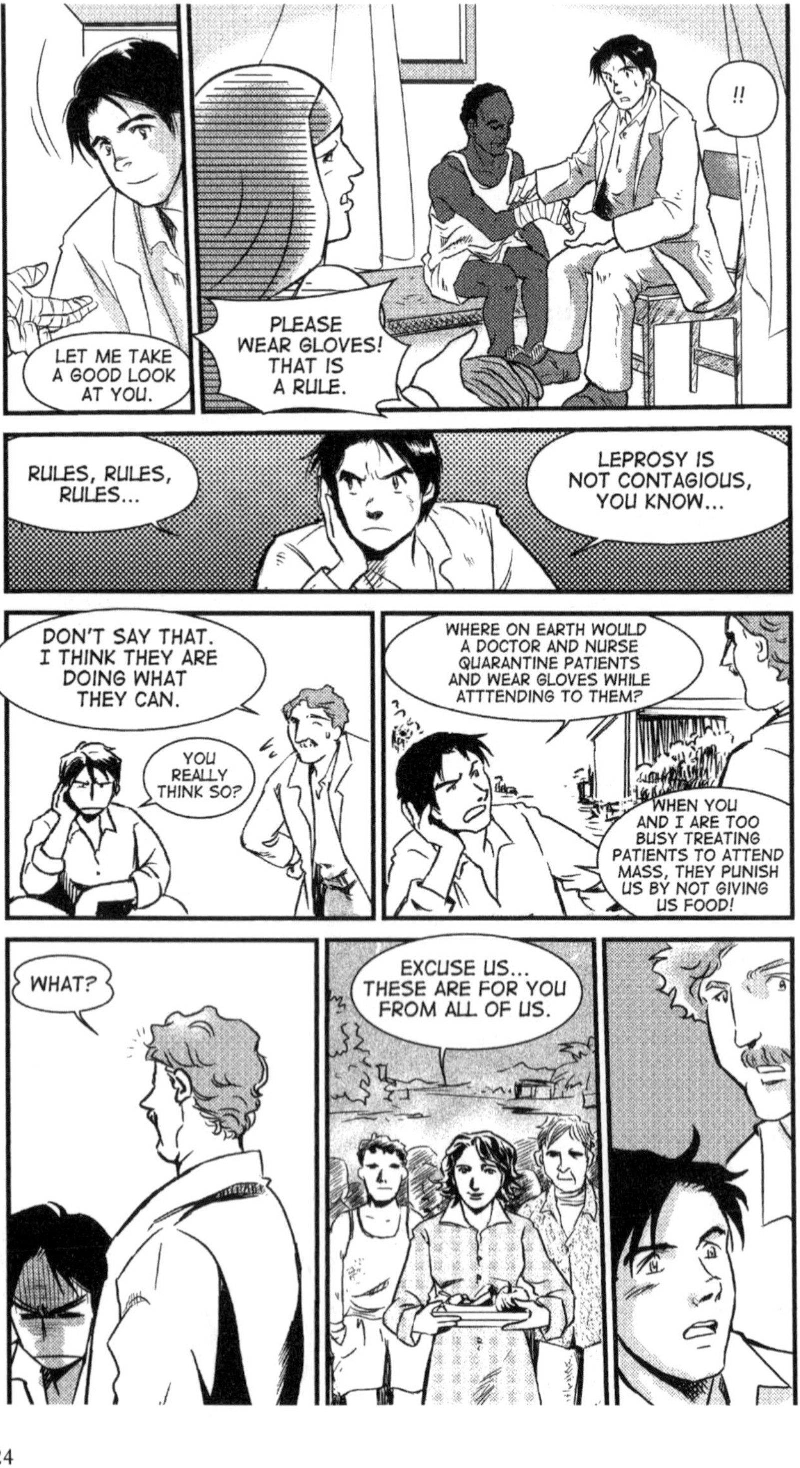
LET ME TAKE A GOOD LOOK AT YOU.
PLEASE WEAR GLOVES! THAT IS A RULE.
!!
RULES, RULES, RULES...
LEPROSY IS NOT CONTAGIOUS, YOU KNOW...
DON'T SAY THAT. I THINK THEY ARE DOING WHAT THEY CAN.
YOU REALLY THINK SO?
WHERE ON EARTH WOULD A DOCTOR AND NURSE QUARANTINE PATIENTS AND WEAR GLOVES WHILE ATTTENDING TO THEM?
WHEN YOU AND I ARE TOO BUSY TREATING PATIENTS TO ATTEND MASS, THEY PUNISH US BY NOT GIVING US FOOD!
WHAT?
EXCUSE US... THESE ARE FOR YOU FROM ALL OF US.

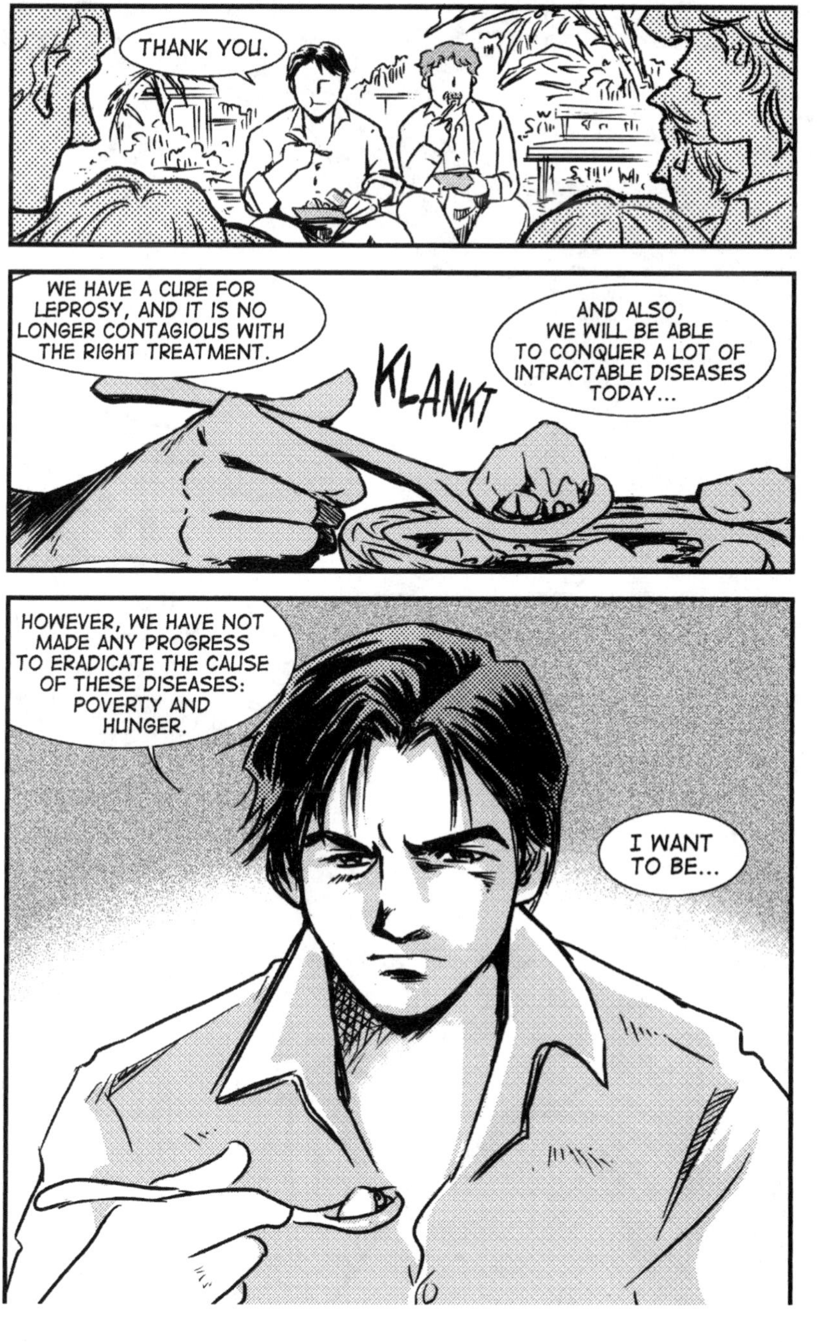
THANK YOU.
WE HAVE A CURE FOR LEPROSY, AND IT IS NO LONGER CONTAGIOUS WITH THE RIGHT TREATMENT.
KLANKT
AND ALSO, WE WILL BE ABLE TO CONQUER A LOT OF INTRACTABLE DISEASES TODAY...
HOWEVER, WE HAVE NOT MADE ANY PROGRESS TO ERADICATE THE CAUSE OF THESE DISEASES: POVERTY AND HUNGER.
I WANT TO BE...

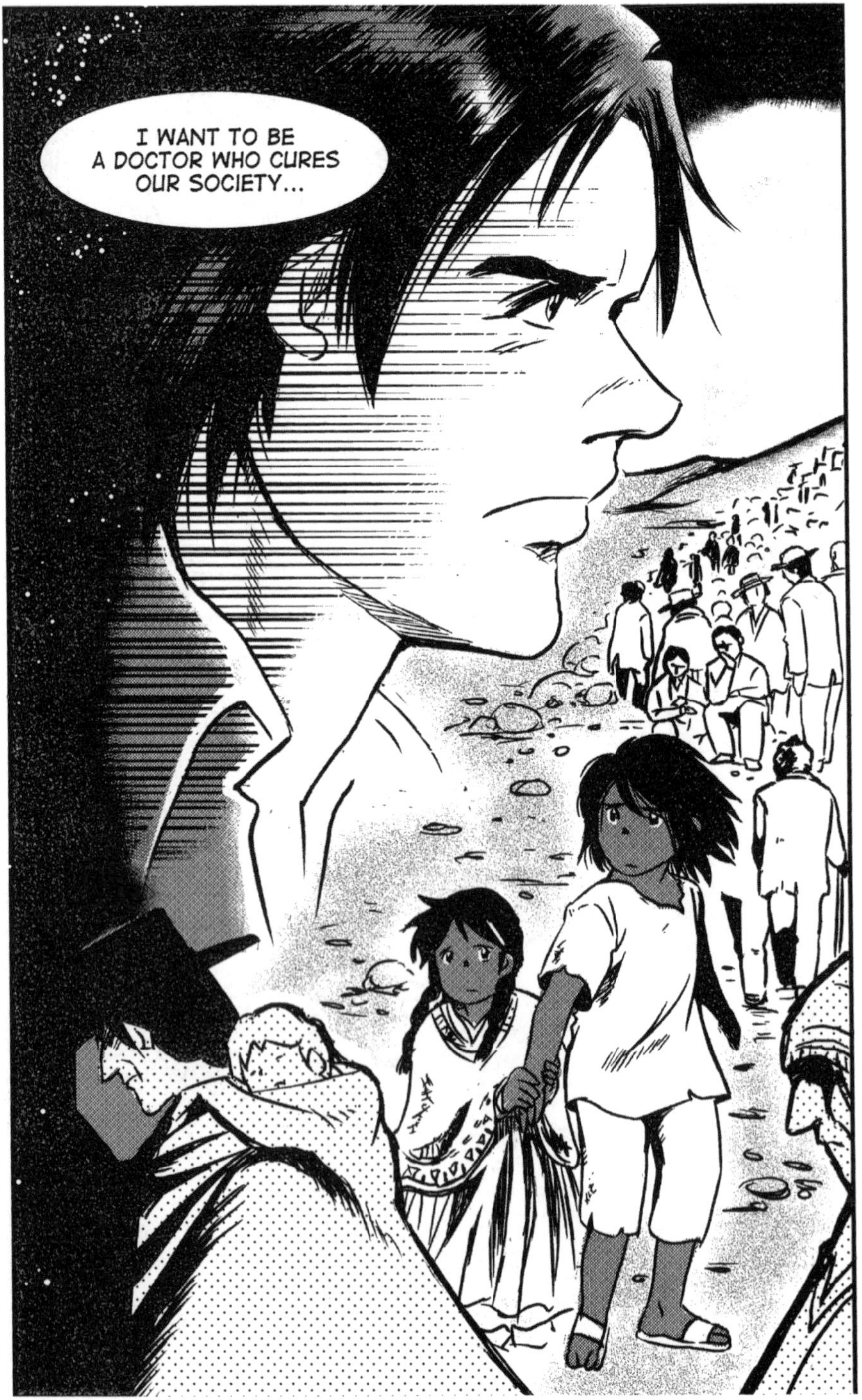
I WANT TO BE A DOCTOR WHO CURES OUR SOCIETY...

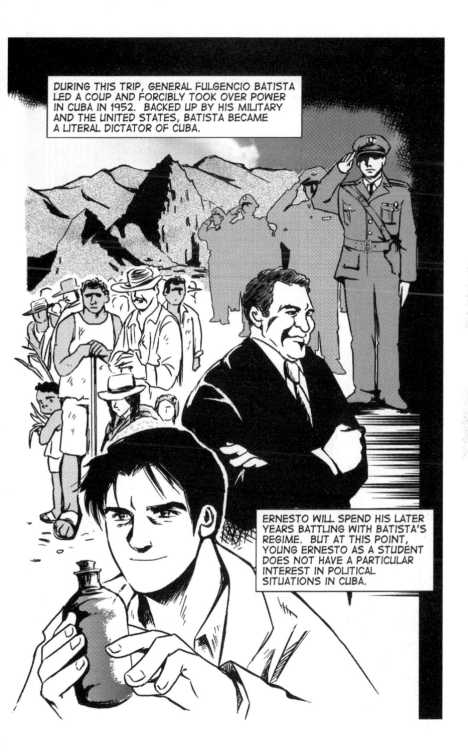

DURING THIS TRIP, GENERAL FULGENCIO BATISTA LED A COUP AND FORCIBLY TOOK OVER POWER IN CUBA IN 1952. BACKED UP BY HIS MILITARY AND THE UNITED STATES, BATISTA BECAME A LITERAL DICTATOR OF CUBA.

ERNESTO WILL SPEND HIS LATER YEARS BATTLING WITH BATISTA'S REGIME. BUT AT THIS POINT, YOUNG ERNESTO AS A STUDENT DOES NOT HAVE A PARTICULAR INTEREST IN POLITICAL SITUATIONS IN CUBA.

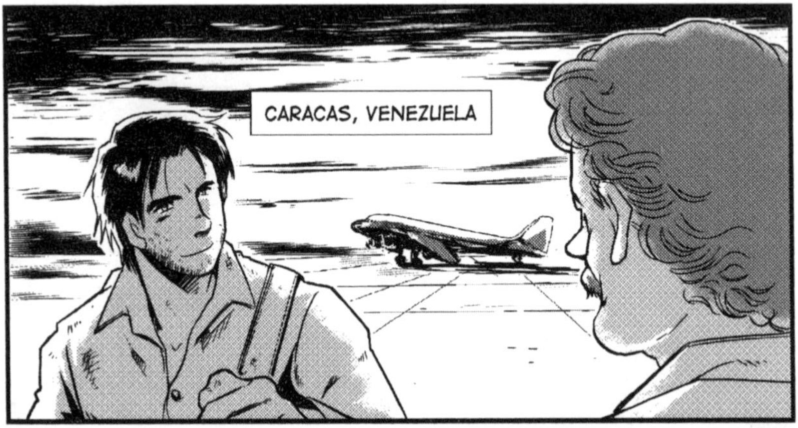
CARACAS, VENEZUELA
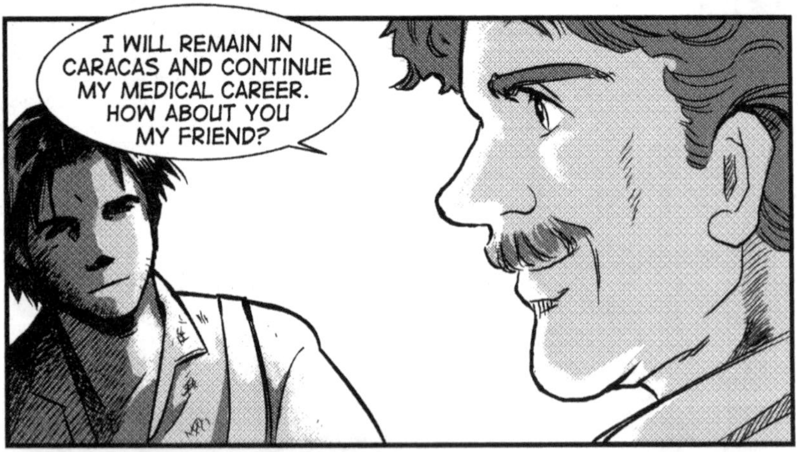
I WILL REMAIN IN CARACAS AND CONTINUE MY MEDICAL CAREER. HOW ABOUT YOU MY FRIEND?
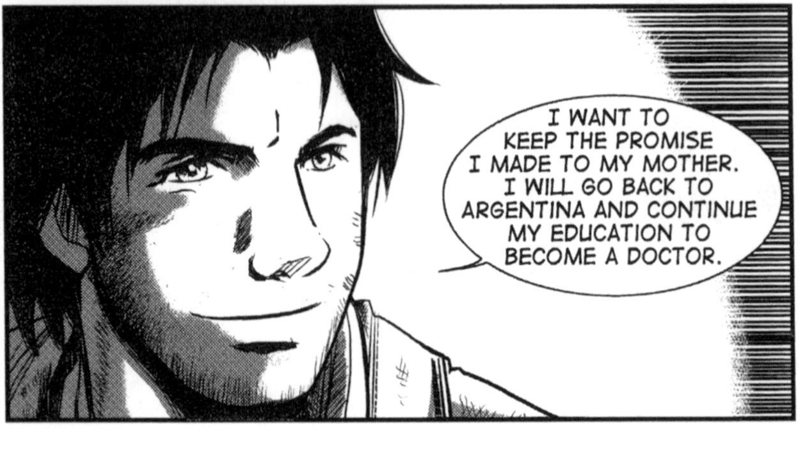
I WANT TO KEEP THE PROMISE I MADE TO MY MOTHER. I WILL GO BACK TO ARGENTINA AND CONTINUE MY EDUCATION TO BECOME A DOCTOR.

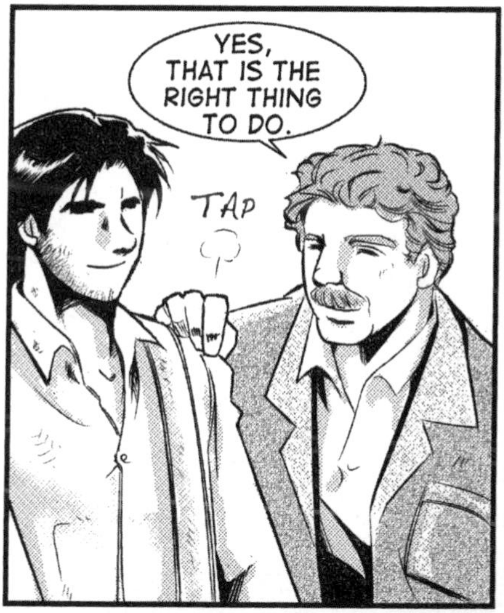
YES, THAT IS THE RIGHT THING TO DO.
TAP

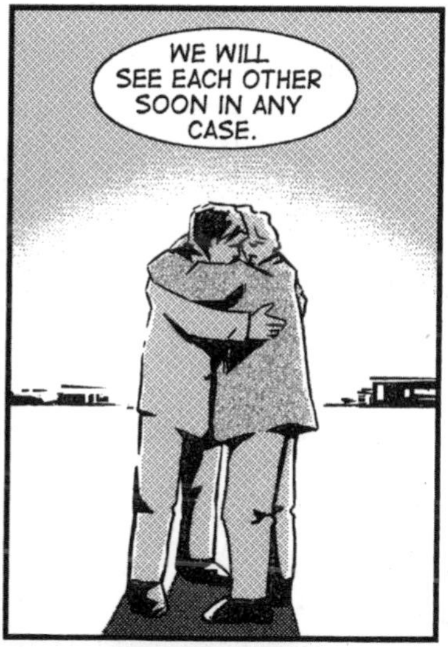
WE WILL SEE EACH OTHER SOON IN ANY CASE.

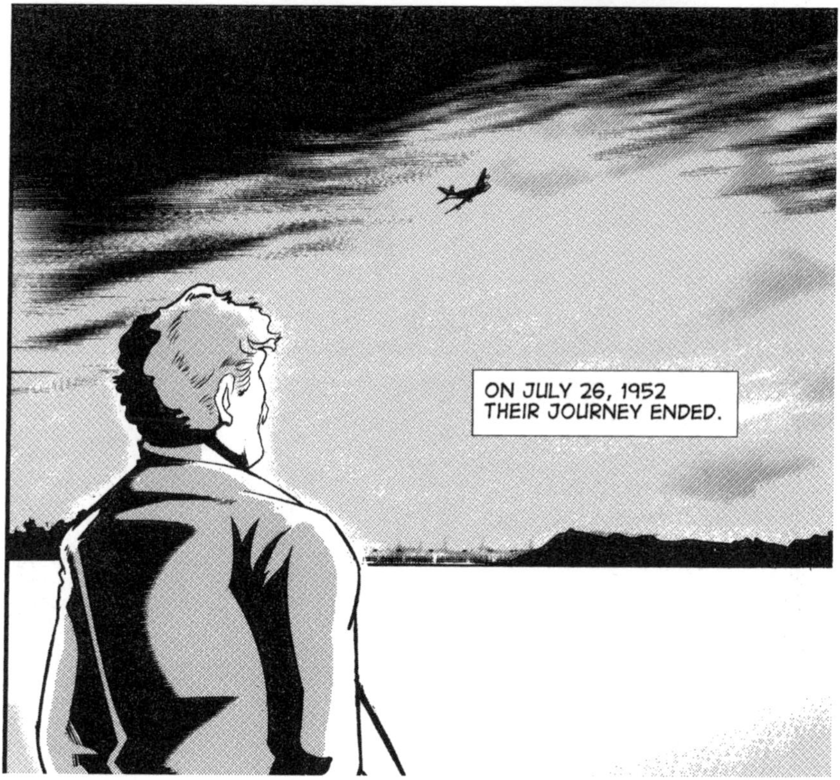
ON JULY 26, 1952 THEIR JOURNEY ENDED.

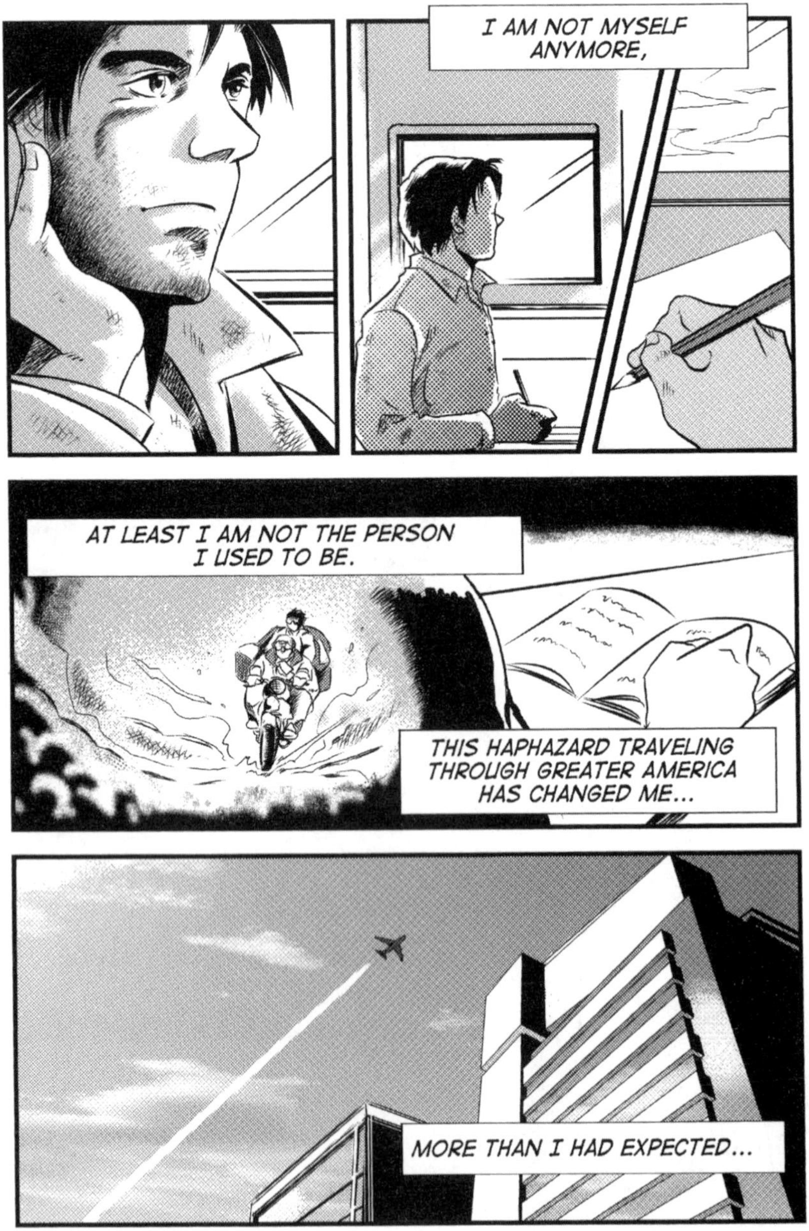
I AM NOT MYSELF ANYMORE,
AT LEAST I AM NOT THE PERSON I USED TO BE.
THIS HAPHAZARD TRAVELING THROUGH GREATER AMERICA HAS CHANGED ME...
MORE THAN I HAD EXPECTED...

CHAPTER 2 OUTSIDER

1953 - 1956

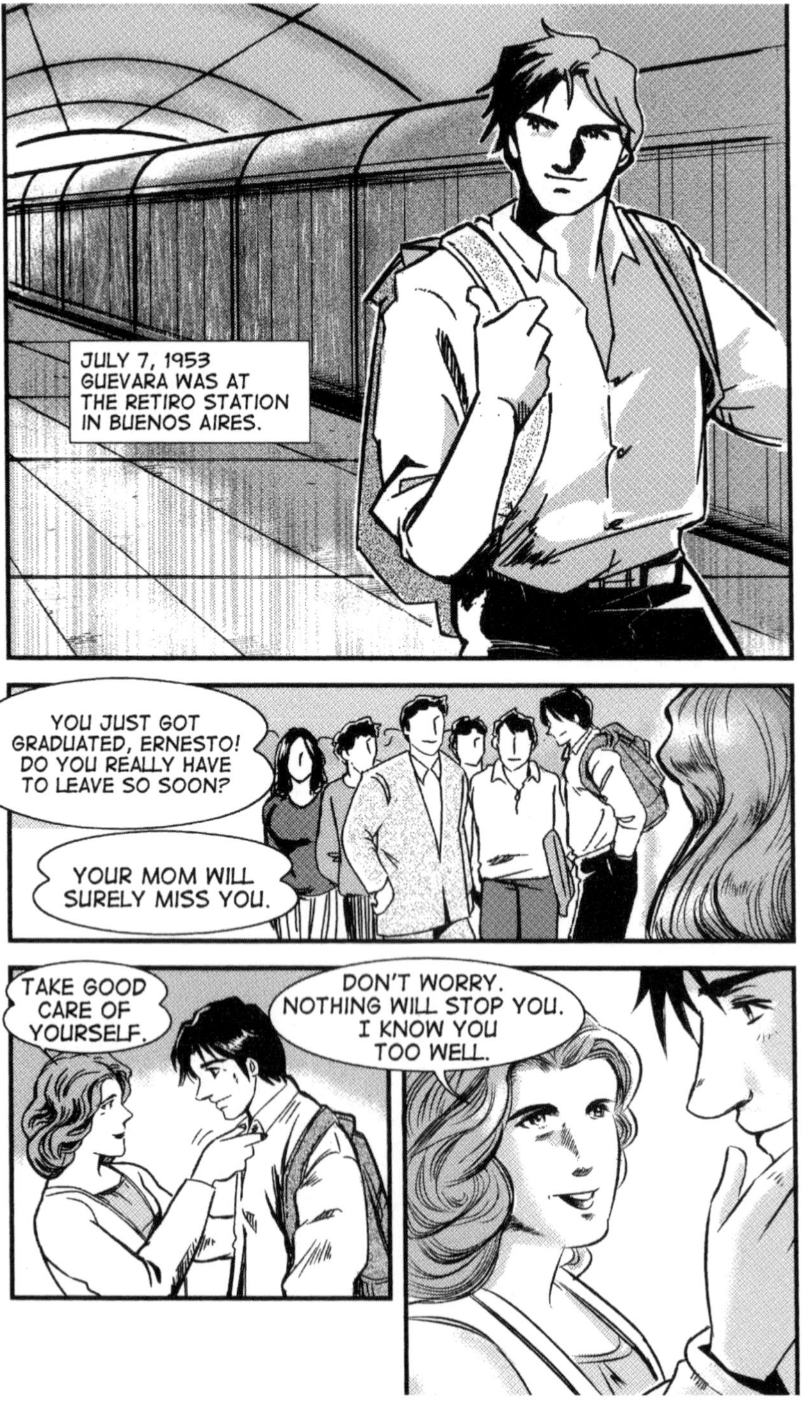
JULY 7, 1953 GUEVARA WAS AT THE RETIRO STATION IN BUENOS AIRES.
YOU JUST GOT GRADUATED, ERNESTO! DO YOU REALLY HAVE TO LEAVE SO SOON?
YOUR MOM WILL SURELY MISS YOU.
TAKE GOOD CARE OF YOURSELF.
DON'T WORRY. NOTHING WILL STOP YOU. I KNOW YOU TOO WELL.

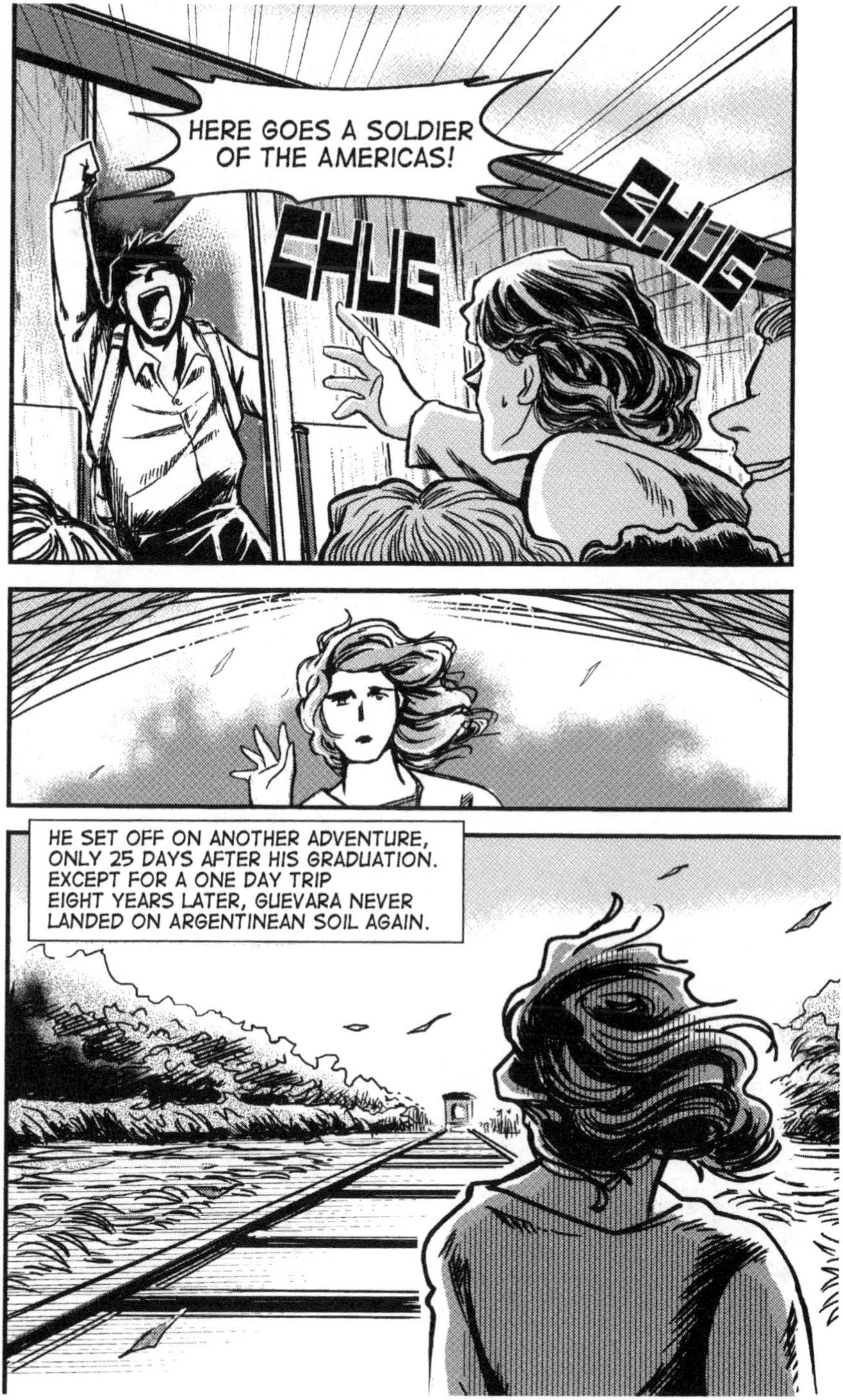
HERE GOES A SOLDIER OF THE AMERICAS!
CHUG
CHUG
HE SET OFF ON ANOTHER ADVENTURE, ONLY 25 DAYS AFTER HIS GRADUATION. EXCEPT FOR A ONE DAY TRIP EIGHT YEARS LATER, GUEVARA NEVER LANDED ON ARGENTINEAN SOIL AGAIN.

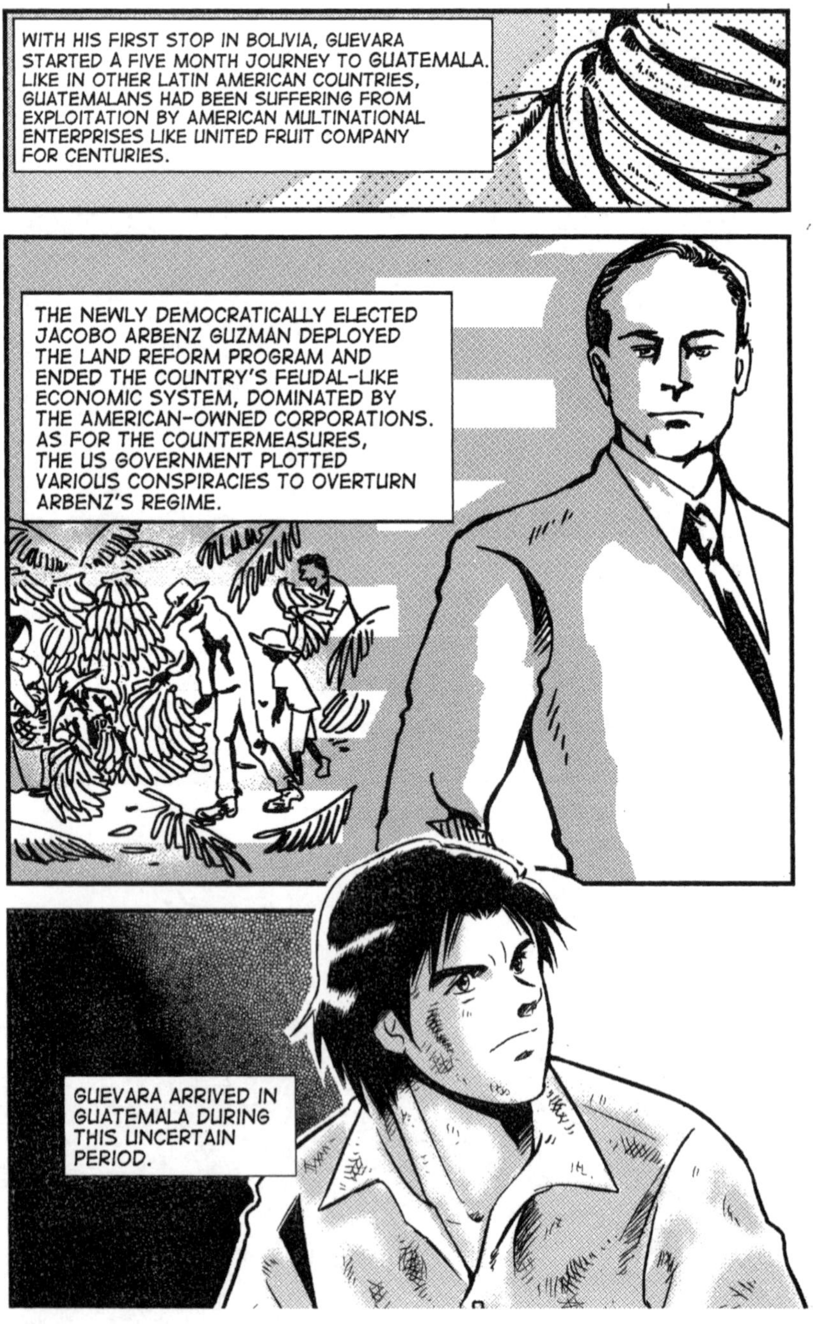
WITH HIS FIRST STOP IN BOLIVIA, GUEVARA STARTED A FIVE MONTH JOURNEY TO GUATEMALA. LIKE IN OTHER LATIN AMERICAN COUNTRIES, GUATEMALANS HAD BEEN SUFFERING FROM EXPLOITATION BY AMERICAN MULTINATIONAL ENTERPRISES LIKE UNITED FRUIT COMPANY FOR CENTURIES.
THE NEWLY DEMOCRATICALLY ELECTED JACOBO ARBENZ GUZMAN DEPLOYED THE LAND REFORM PROGRAM AND ENDED THE COUNTRY'S FEUDAL-LIKE ECONOMIC SYSTEM, DOMINATED BY THE AMERICAN-OWNED CORPORATIONS. AS FOR THE COUNTERMEASURES, THE US GOVERNMENT PLOTTED VARIOUS CONSPIRACIES TO OVERTURN ARBENZ'S REGIME.
GUEVARA ARRIVED IN GUATEMALA DURING THIS UNCERTAIN PERIOD.

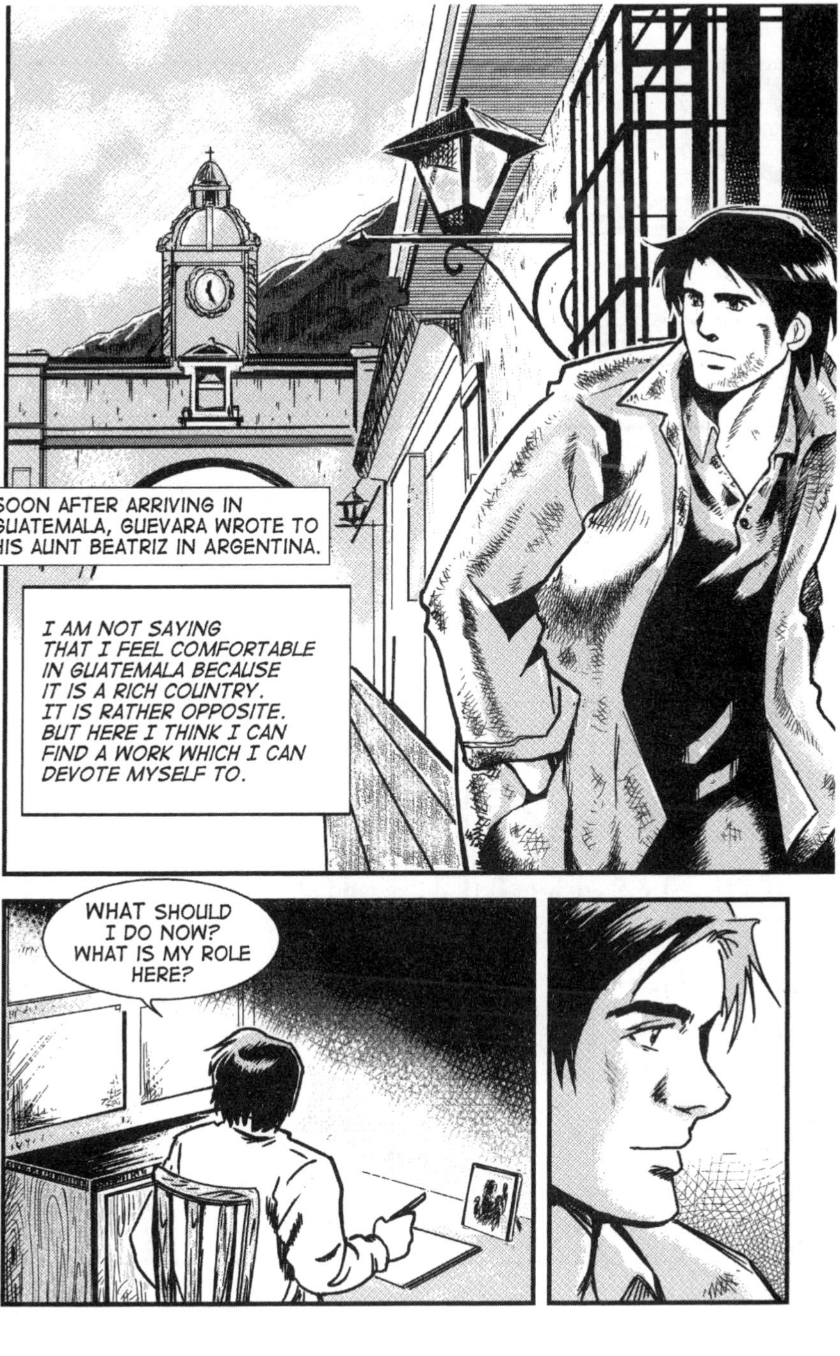
SOON AFTER ARRIVING IN GUATEMALA, GUEVARA WROTE TO HIS AUNT BEATRIZ IN ARGENTINA.
I AM NOT SAYING THAT I FEEL COMFORTABLE IN GUATEMALA BECAUSE IT IS A RICH COUNTRY. IT IS RATHER OPPOSITE. BUT HERE I THINK I CAN FIND A WORK WHICH I CAN DEVOTE MYSELF TO.
WHAT SHOULD I DO NOW? WHAT IS MY ROLE HERE?

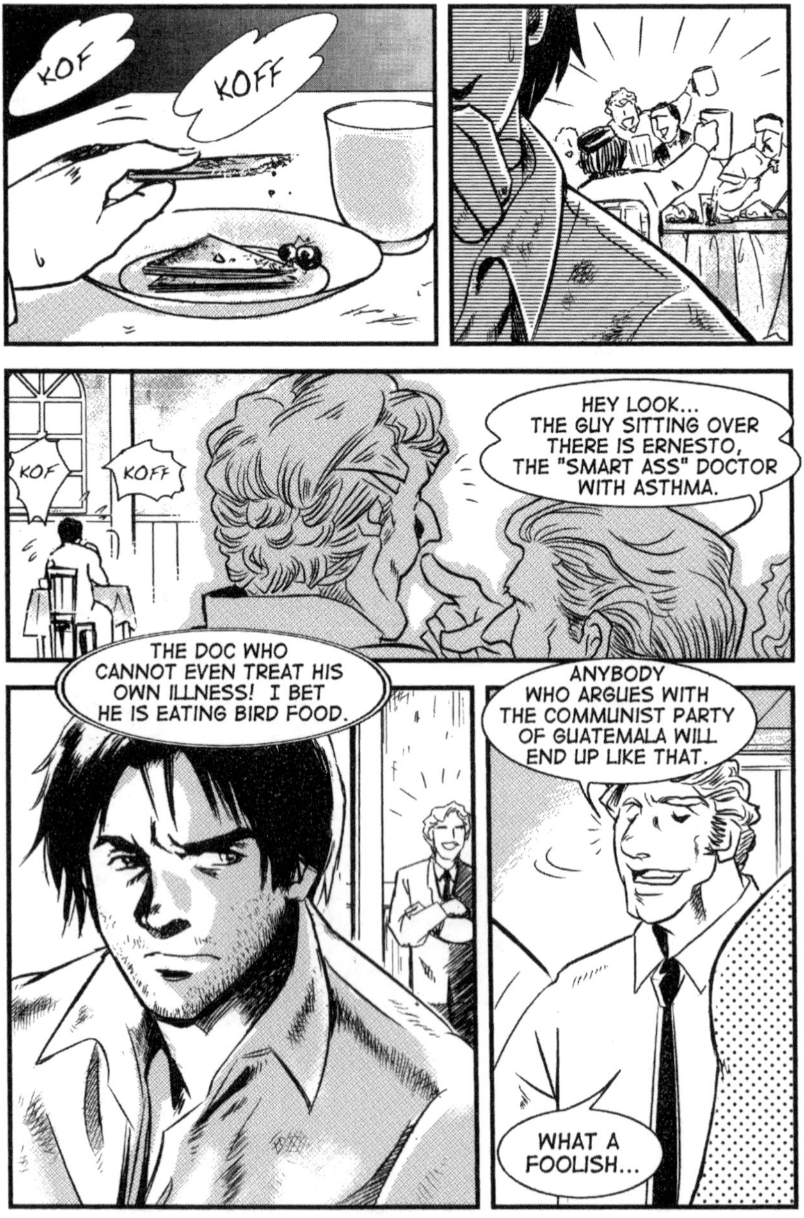
KOF
KOFF
KOF
KOFF
HEY LOOK... THE GUY SITTING OVER THERE IS ERNESTO, THE "SMART ASS" DOCTOR WITH ASTHMA.
THE DOC WHO CANNOT EVEN TREAT HIS OWN ILLNESS! I BET HE IS EATING BIRD FOOD.
ANYBODY WHO ARGUES WITH THE COMMUNIST PARTY OF GUATEMALA WILL END UP LIKE THAT.
WHAT A FOOLISH...

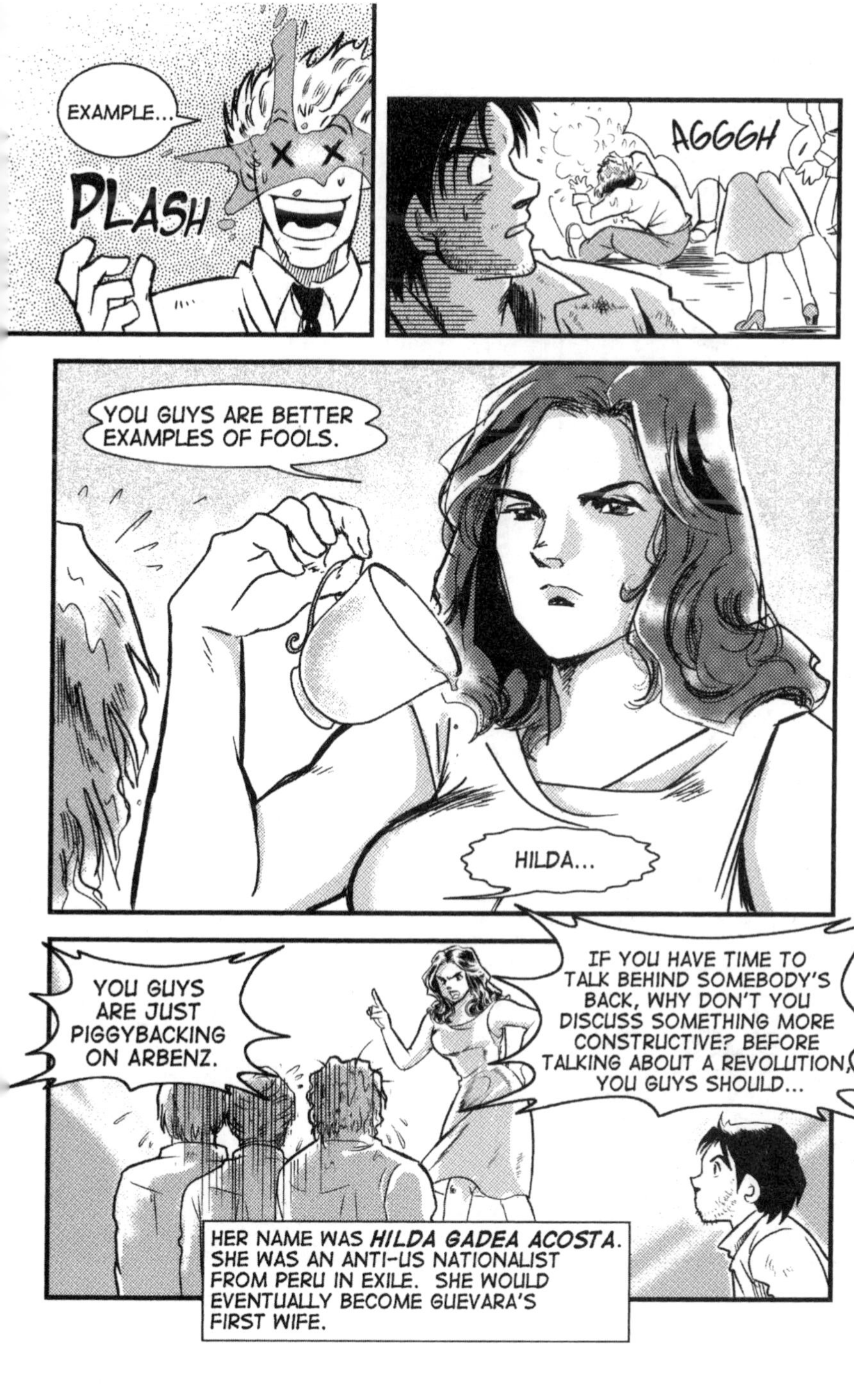
EXAMPLE...
PLASH
AGGGH
YOU GUYS ARE BETTER EXAMPLES OF FOOLS.
HILDA...
YOU GUYS ARE JUST PIGGYBACKING ON ARBENZ.
IF YOU HAVE TIME TO TALK BEHIND SOMEBODY'S BACK, WHY DON'T YOU DISCUSS SOMETHING MORE CONSTRUCTIVE? BEFORE TALKING ABOUT A REVOLUTION, YOU GUYS SHOULD...
HER NAME WAS *HILDA GADEA ACOSTA*. SHE WAS AN ANTI-US NATIONALIST FROM PERU IN EXILE. SHE WOULD EVENTUALLY BECOME GUEVARA'S FIRST WIFE.

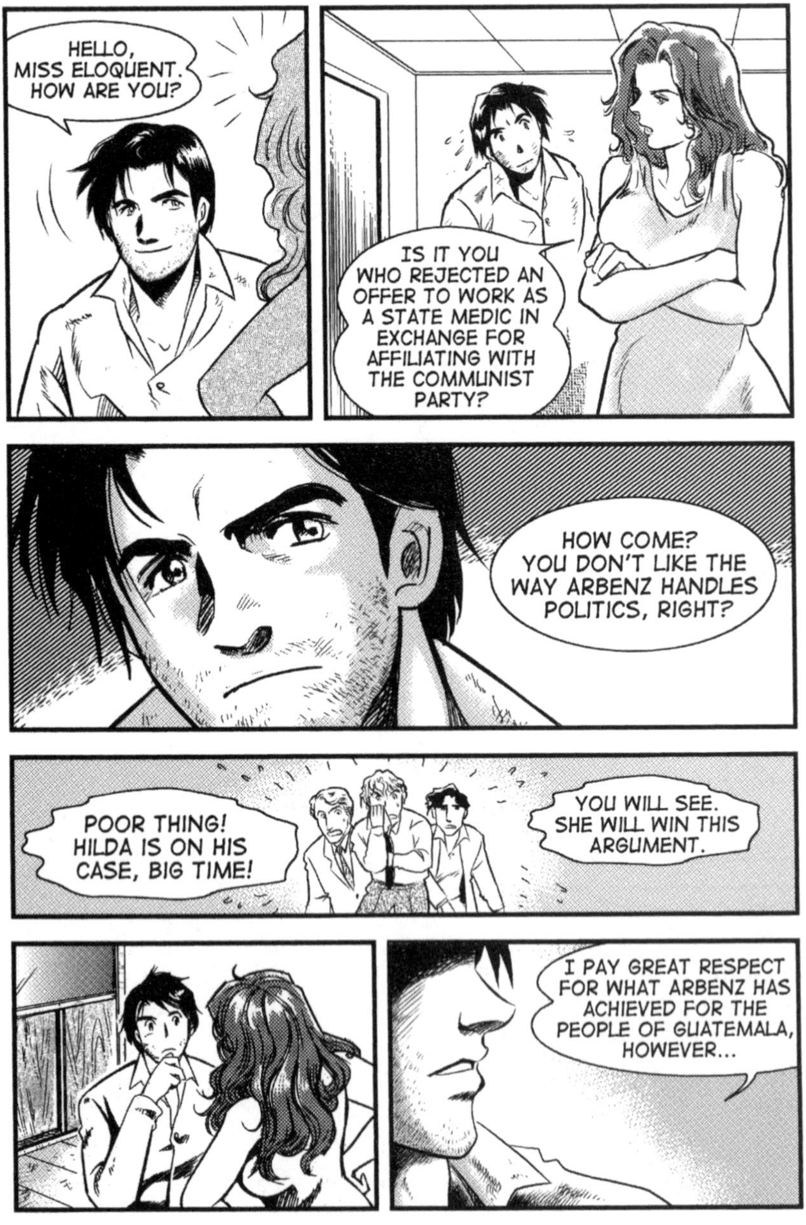
HELLO, MISS ELOQUENT. HOW ARE YOU?
IS IT YOU WHO REJECTED AN OFFER TO WORK AS A STATE MEDIC IN EXCHANGE FOR AFFILIATING WITH THE COMMUNIST PARTY?
HOW COME? YOU DON'T LIKE THE WAY ARBENZ HANDLES POLITICS, RIGHT?
POOR THING! HILDA IS ON HIS CASE, BIG TIME!
YOU WILL SEE. SHE WILL WIN THIS ARGUMENT.
I PAY GREAT RESPECT FOR WHAT ARBENZ HAS ACHIEVED FOR THE PEOPLE OF GUATEMALA, HOWEVER...

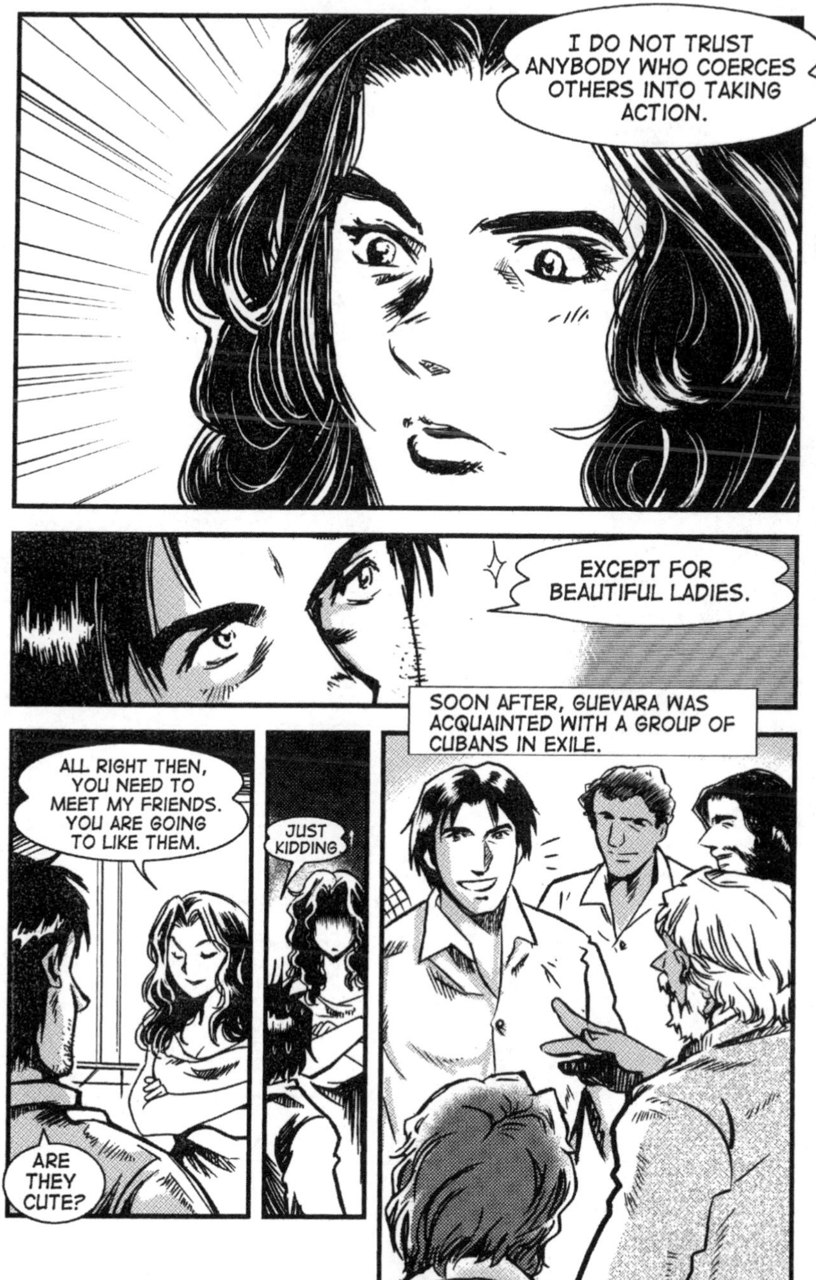
I DO NOT TRUST ANYBODY WHO COERCES OTHERS INTO TAKING ACTION.
EXCEPT FOR BEAUTIFUL LADIES.
ALL RIGHT THEN, YOU NEED TO MEET MY FRIENDS. YOU ARE GOING TO LIKE THEM.
ARE THEY CUTE?
JUST KIDDING.
SOON AFTER, GUEVARA WAS ACQUAINTED WITH A GROUP OF CUBANS IN EXILE.

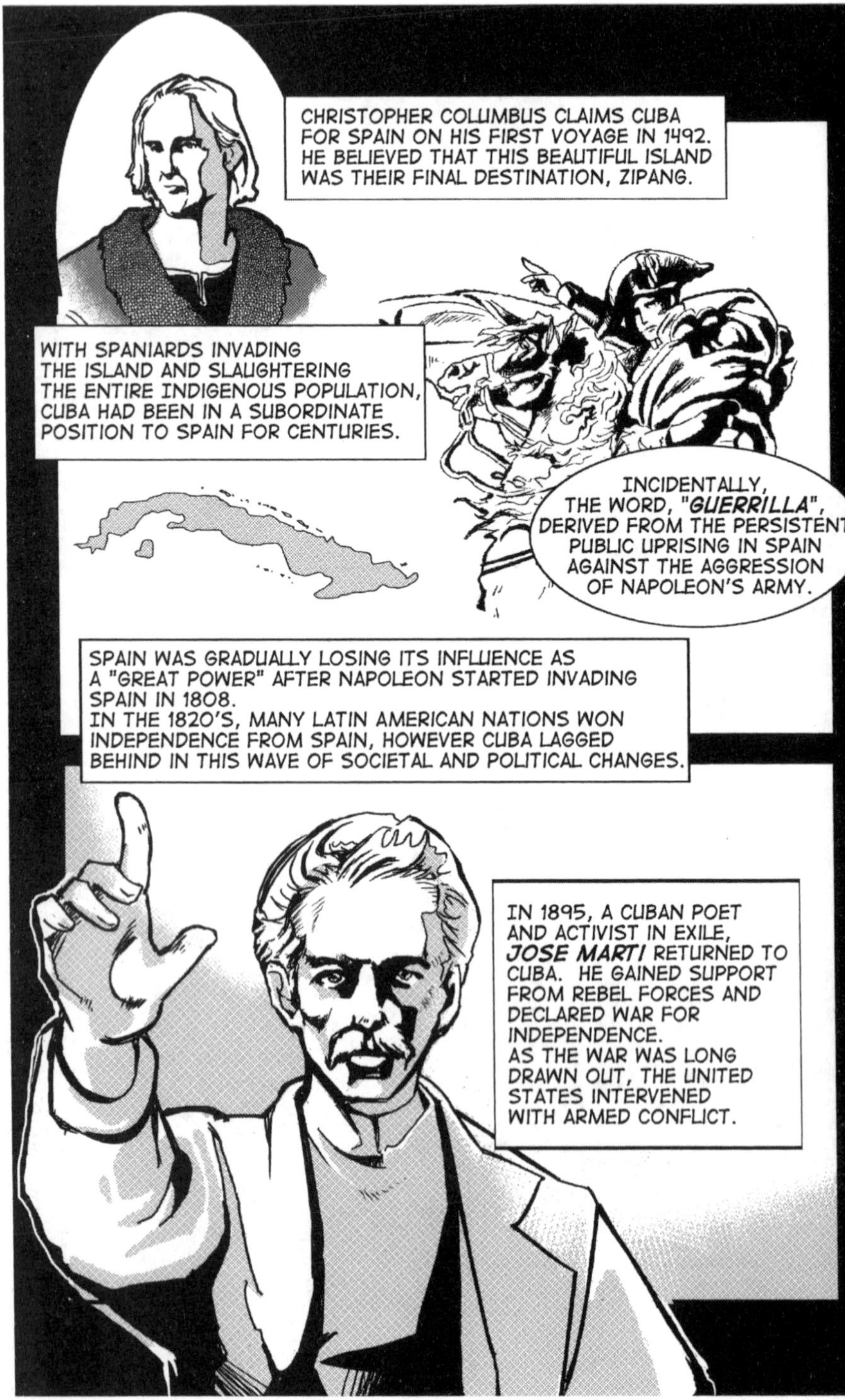
CHRISTOPHER COLUMBUS CLAIMS CUBA FOR SPAIN ON HIS FIRST VOYAGE IN 1492. HE BELIEVED THAT THIS BEAUTIFUL ISLAND WAS THEIR FINAL DESTINATION, ZIPANG.
WITH SPANIARDS INVADING THE ISLAND AND SLAUGHTERING THE ENTIRE INDIGENOUS POPULATION, CUBA HAD BEEN IN A SUBORDINATE POSITION TO SPAIN FOR CENTURIES.
INCIDENTALLY, THE WORD, "GUERRILLA", DERIVED FROM THE PERSISTENT PUBLIC UPRISING IN SPAIN AGAINST THE AGGRESSION OF NAPOLEON'S ARMY.
SPAIN WAS GRADUALLY LOSING ITS INFLUENCE AS A "GREAT POWER" AFTER NAPOLEON STARTED INVADING SPAIN IN 1808.
IN THE 1820'S, MANY LATIN AMERICAN NATIONS WON INDEPENDENCE FROM SPAIN, HOWEVER CUBA LAGGED BEHIND IN THIS WAVE OF SOCIETAL AND POLITICAL CHANGES.
IN 1895, A CUBAN POET AND ACTIVIST IN EXILE, JOSE MARTI RETURNED TO CUBA. HE GAINED SUPPORT FROM REBEL FORCES AND DECLARED WAR FOR INDEPENDENCE.
AS THE WAR WAS LONG DRAWN OUT, THE UNITED STATES INTERVENED WITH ARMED CONFLICT.

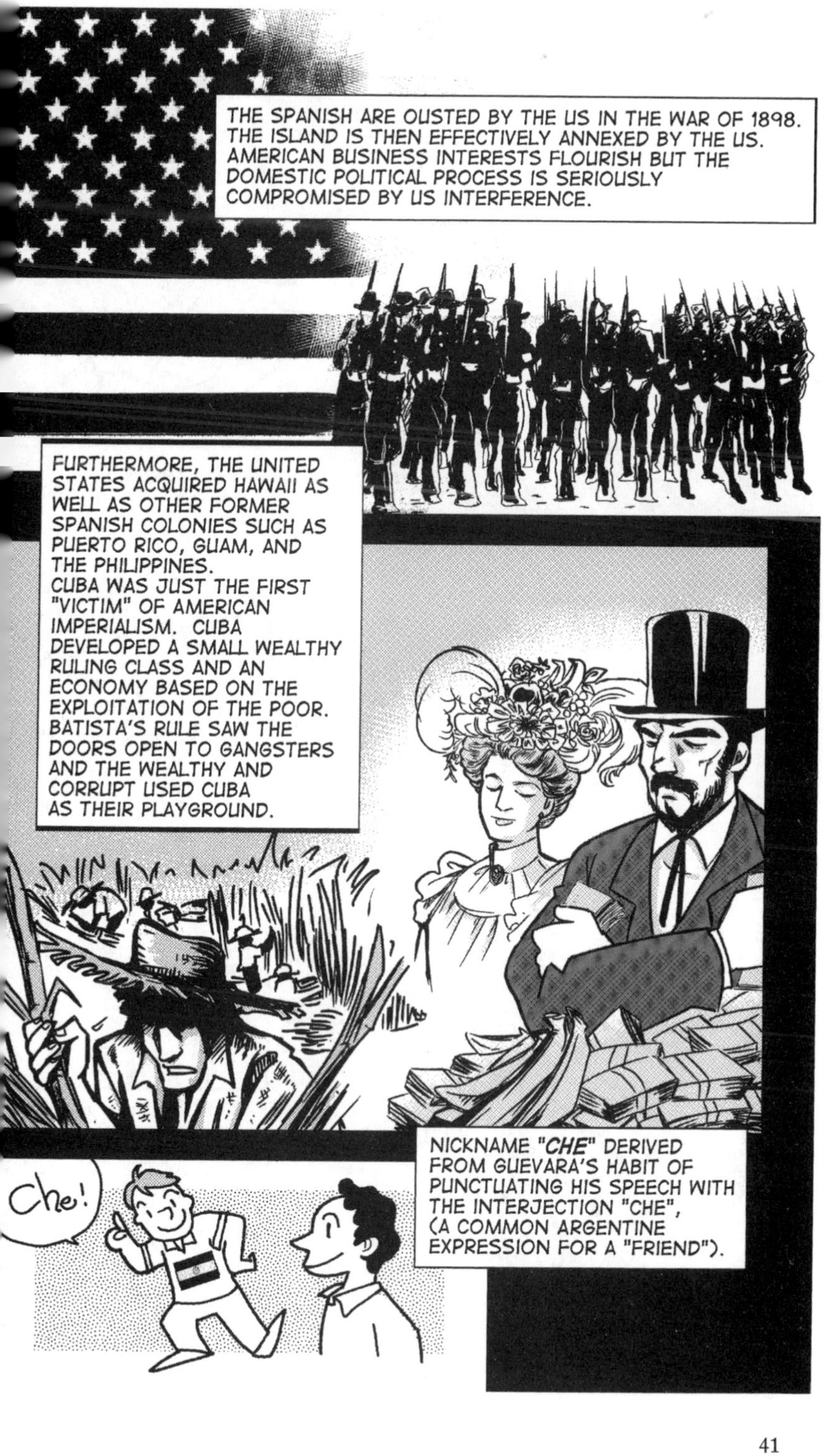
THE SPANISH ARE OUSTED BY THE US IN THE WAR OF 1898. THE ISLAND IS THEN EFFECTIVELY ANNEXED BY THE US. AMERICAN BUSINESS INTERESTS FLOURISH BUT THE DOMESTIC POLITICAL PROCESS IS SERIOUSLY COMPROMISED BY US INTERFERENCE.
FURTHERMORE, THE UNITED STATES ACQUIRED HAWAII AS WELL AS OTHER FORMER SPANISH COLONIES SUCH AS PUERTO RICO, GUAM, AND THE PHILIPPINES. CUBA WAS JUST THE FIRST "VICTIM" OF AMERICAN IMPERIALISM. CUBA DEVELOPED A SMALL WEALTHY RULING CLASS AND AN ECONOMY BASED ON THE EXPLOITATION OF THE POOR. BATISTA'S RULE SAW THE DOORS OPEN TO GANGSTERS AND THE WEALTHY AND CORRUPT USED CUBA AS THEIR PLAYGROUND.
Che!
NICKNAME "***CHE***" DERIVED FROM GUEVARA'S HABIT OF PUNCTUATING HIS SPEECH WITH THE INTERJECTION "CHE", (A COMMON ARGENTINE EXPRESSION FOR A "FRIEND").

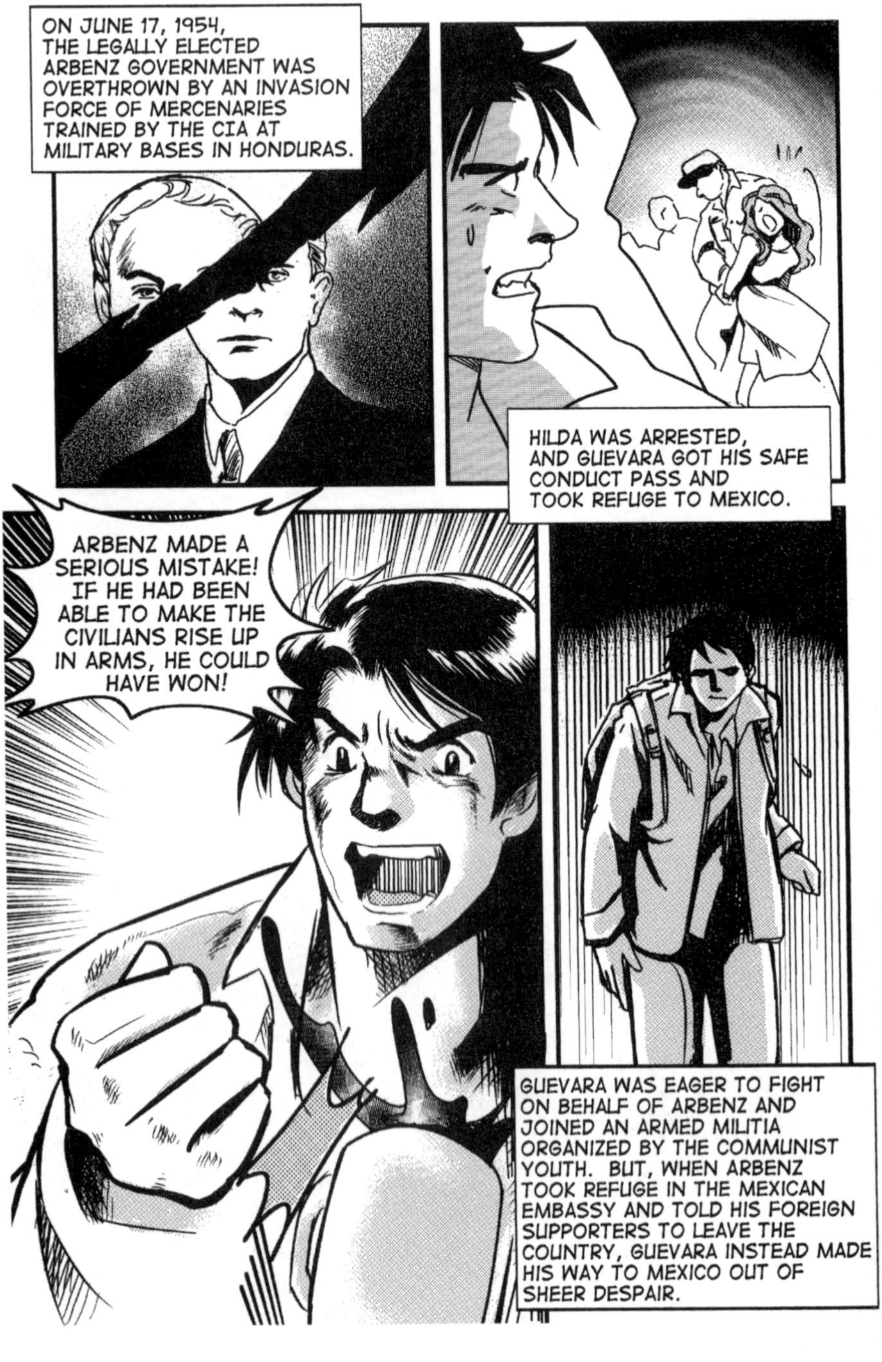
ON JUNE 17, 1954, THE LEGALLY ELECTED ARBENZ GOVERNMENT WAS OVERTHROWN BY AN INVASION FORCE OF MERCENARIES TRAINED BY THE CIA AT MILITARY BASES IN HONDURAS.
HILDA WAS ARRESTED, AND GUEVARA GOT HIS SAFE CONDUCT PASS AND TOOK REFUGE TO MEXICO.
ARBENZ MADE A SERIOUS MISTAKE! IF HE HAD BEEN ABLE TO MAKE THE CIVILIANS RISE UP IN ARMS, HE COULD HAVE WON!
GUEVARA WAS EAGER TO FIGHT ON BEHALF OF ARBENZ AND JOINED AN ARMED MILITIA ORGANIZED BY THE COMMUNIST YOUTH. BUT, WHEN ARBENZ TOOK REFUGE IN THE MEXICAN EMBASSY AND TOLD HIS FOREIGN SUPPORTERS TO LEAVE THE COUNTRY, GUEVARA INSTEAD MADE HIS WAY TO MEXICO OUT OF SHEER DESPAIR.

MEXICO HAS NO INTEREST IN WHO I AM AND WHAT I DID. I MANAGED TO ENTER THE COUNTRY WITH NO PARTICULAR INTERFERENCE.

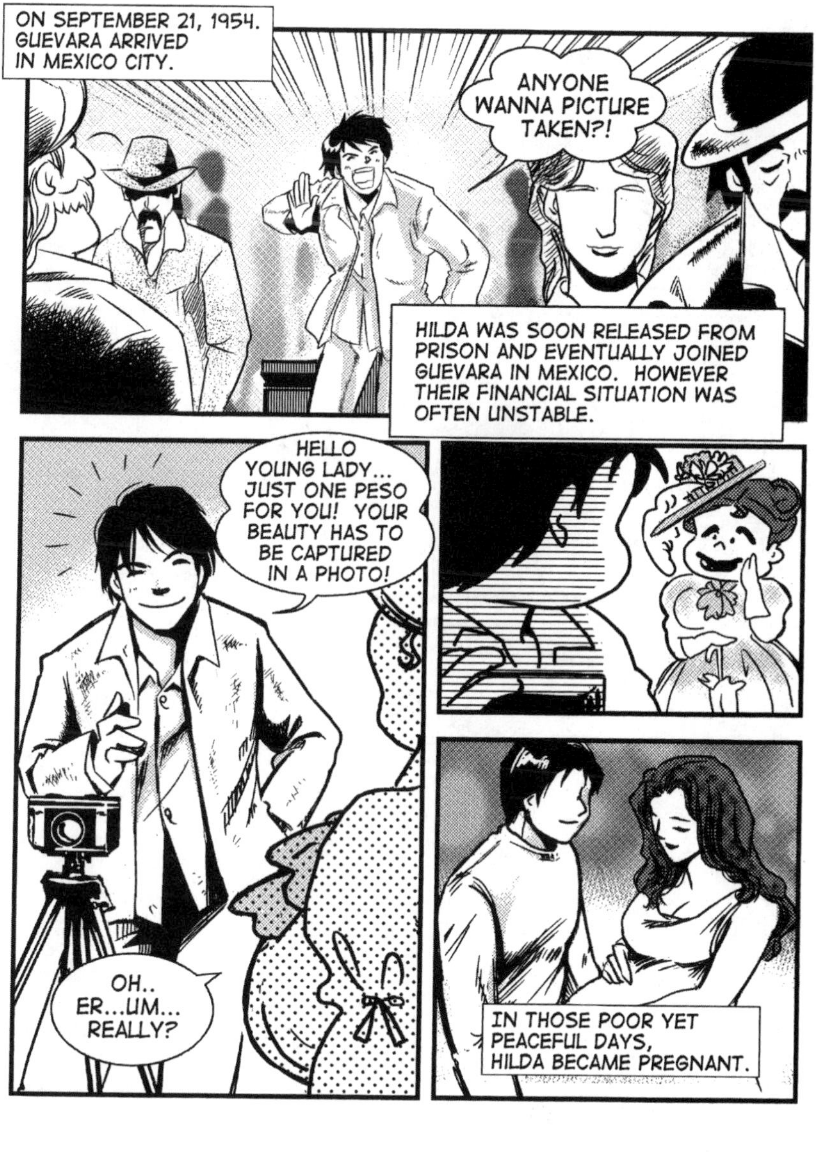
ON SEPTEMBER 21, 1954. GUEVARA ARRIVED IN MEXICO CITY.
ANYONE WANNA PICTURE TAKEN?!
HILDA WAS SOON RELEASED FROM PRISON AND EVENTUALLY JOINED GUEVARA IN MEXICO. HOWEVER THEIR FINANCIAL SITUATION WAS OFTEN UNSTABLE.
HELLO YOUNG LADY... JUST ONE PESO FOR YOU! YOUR BEAUTY HAS TO BE CAPTURED IN A PHOTO!
OH.. ER...UM... REALLY?
IN THOSE POOR YET PEACEFUL DAYS, HILDA BECAME PREGNANT.

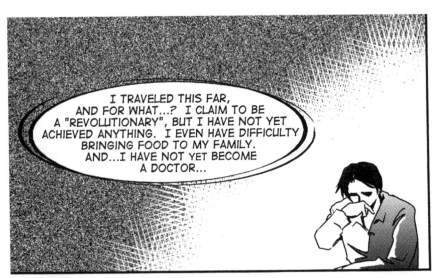

I TRAVELED THIS FAR, AND FOR WHAT...? I CLAIM TO BE A "REVOLUTIONARY", BUT I HAVE NOT YET ACHIEVED ANYTHING. I EVEN HAVE DIFFICULTY BRINGING FOOD TO MY FAMILY. AND...I HAVE NOT YET BECOME A DOCTOR...

SIGH...

OI!

IS THAT YOU, CHE? HOW ARE YOU DOING?

NOT WELL, I GUESS.

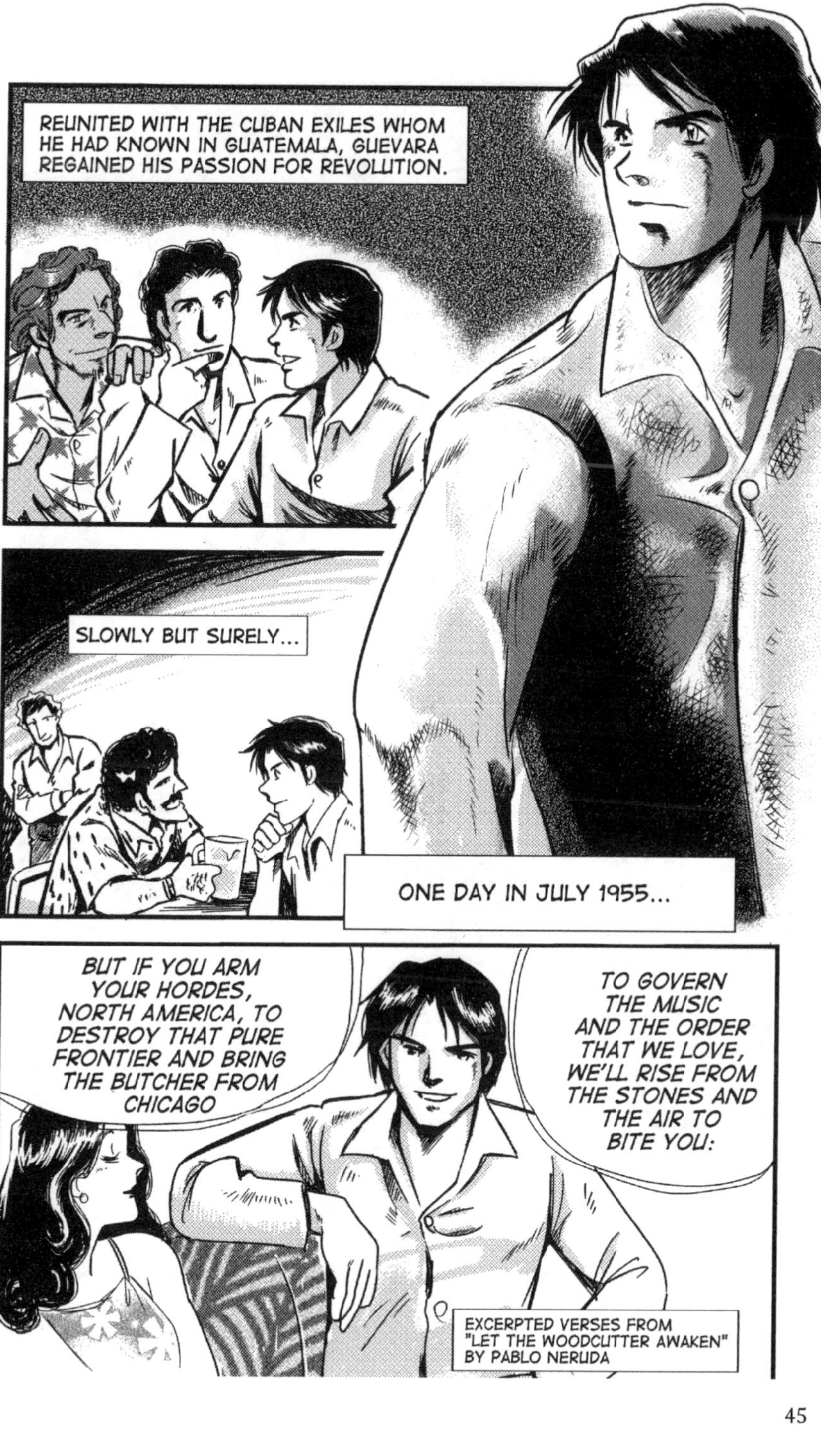
REUNITED WITH THE CUBAN EXILES WHOM HE HAD KNOWN IN GUATEMALA, GUEVARA REGAINED HIS PASSION FOR REVOLUTION.
SLOWLY BUT SURELY...
ONE DAY IN JULY 1955...
BUT IF YOU ARM YOUR HORDES, NORTH AMERICA, TO DESTROY THAT PURE FRONTIER AND BRING THE BUTCHER FROM CHICAGO
TO GOVERN THE MUSIC AND THE ORDER THAT WE LOVE, WE'LL RISE FROM THE STONES AND THE AIR TO BITE YOU:
EXCERPTED VERSES FROM "LET THE WOODCUTTER AWAKEN" BY PABLO NERUDA

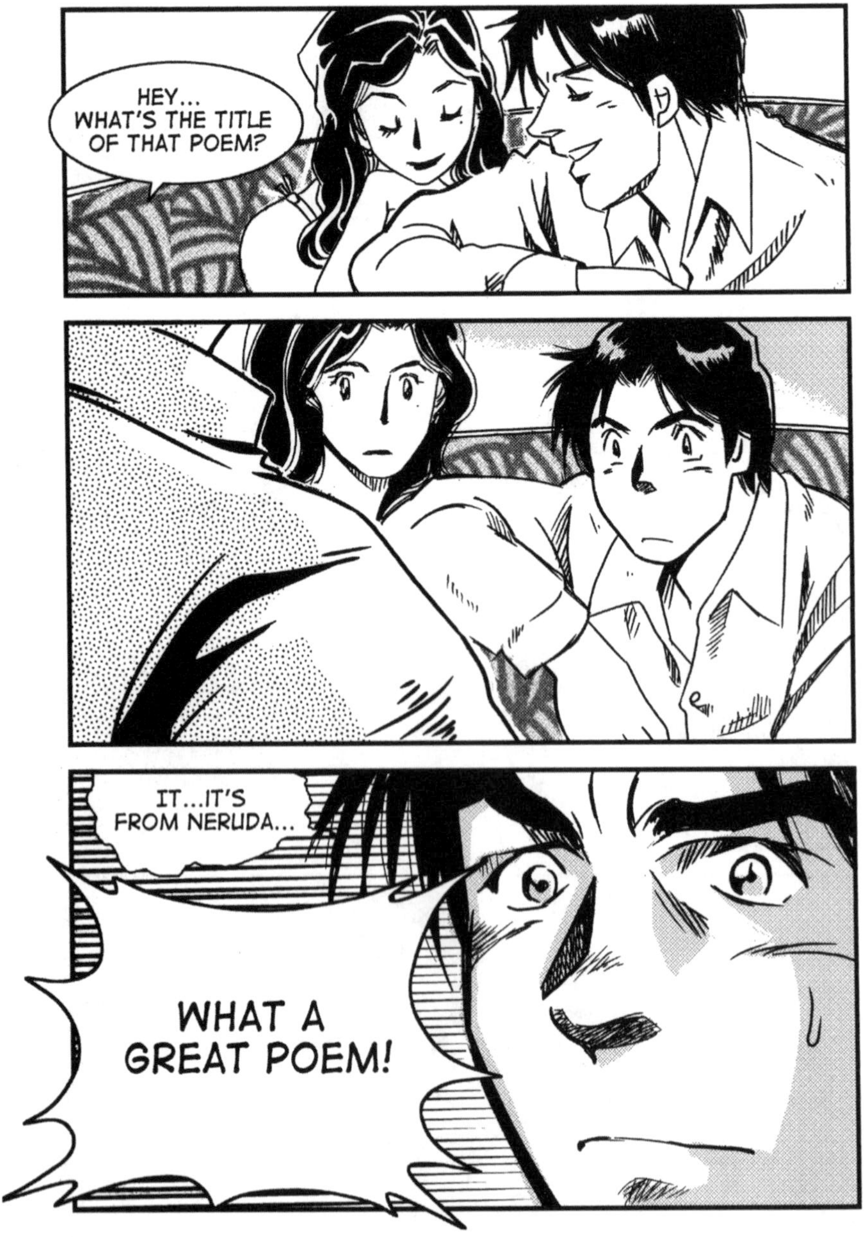
HEY...
WHAT'S THE TITLE
OF THAT POEM?
IT...IT'S
FROM NERUDA...
WHAT A
GREAT POEM!

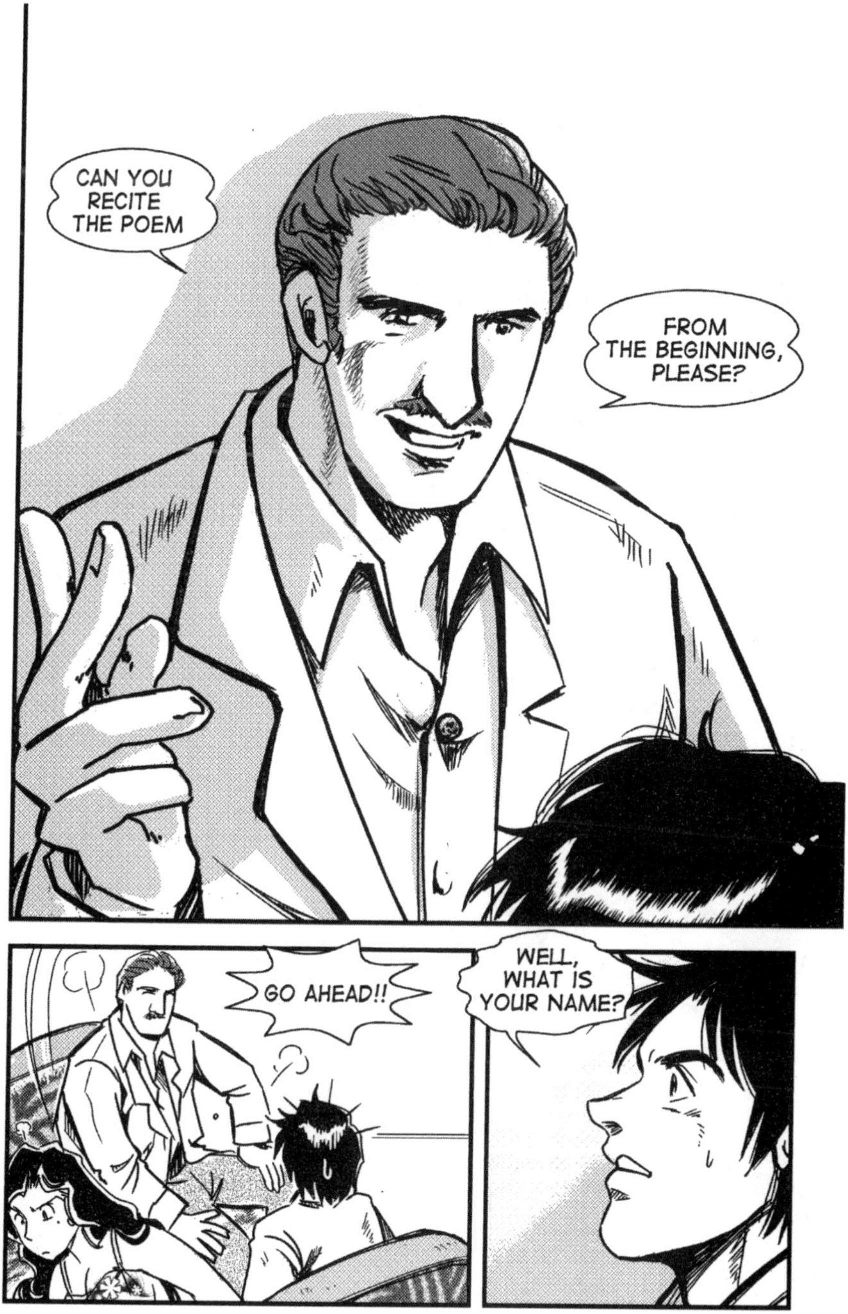
CAN YOU RECITE THE POEM
FROM THE BEGINNING, PLEASE?
GO AHEAD!!
WELL, WHAT IS YOUR NAME?

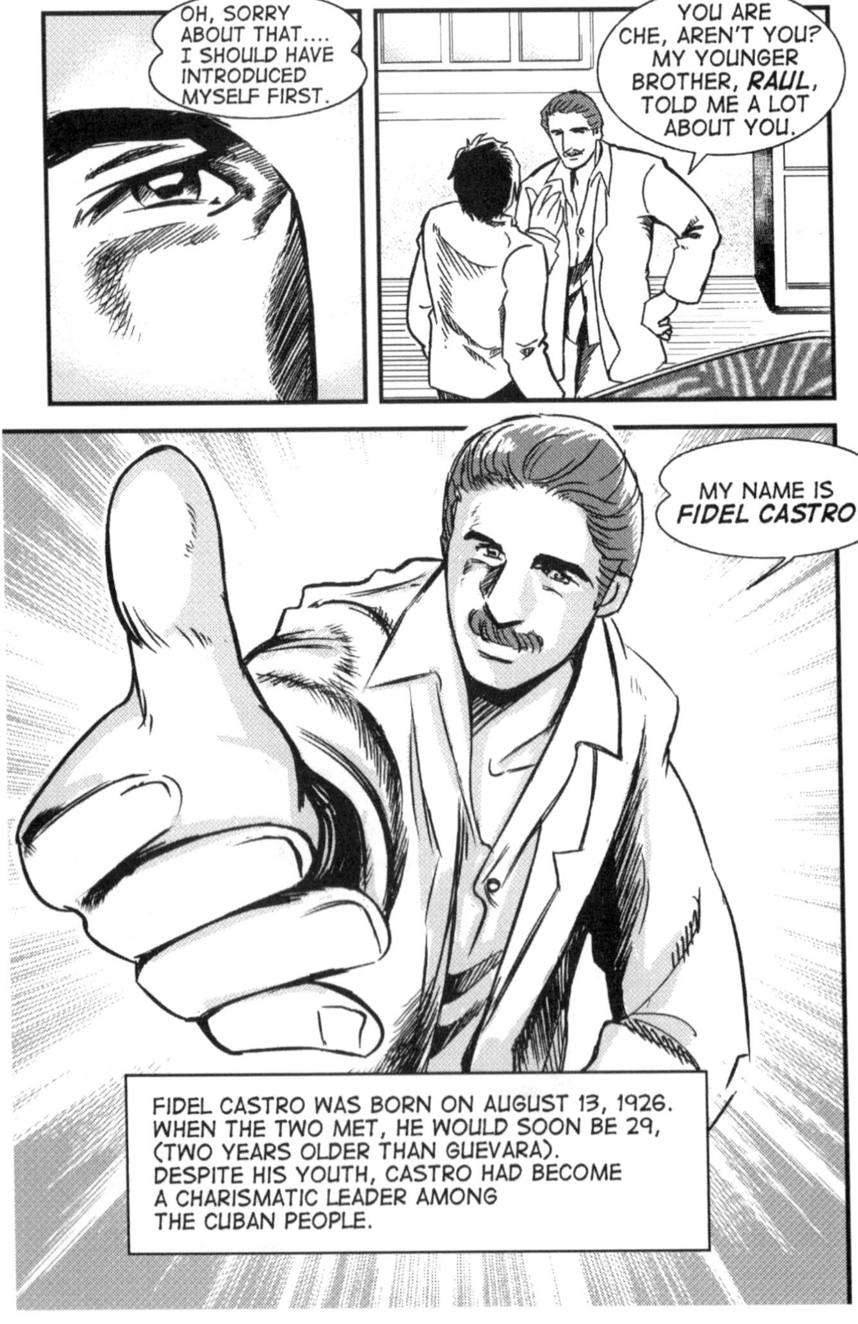
YOU ARE CHE, AREN'T YOU? MY YOUNGER BROTHER, RAUL, TOLD ME A LOT ABOUT YOU.
OH, SORRY ABOUT THAT.... I SHOULD HAVE INTRODUCED MYSELF FIRST.
MY NAME IS FIDEL CASTRO.
FIDEL CASTRO WAS BORN ON AUGUST 13, 1926. WHEN THE TWO MET, HE WOULD SOON BE 29, (TWO YEARS OLDER THAN GUEVARA). DESPITE HIS YOUTH, CASTRO HAD BECOME A CHARISMATIC LEADER AMONG THE CUBAN PEOPLE.

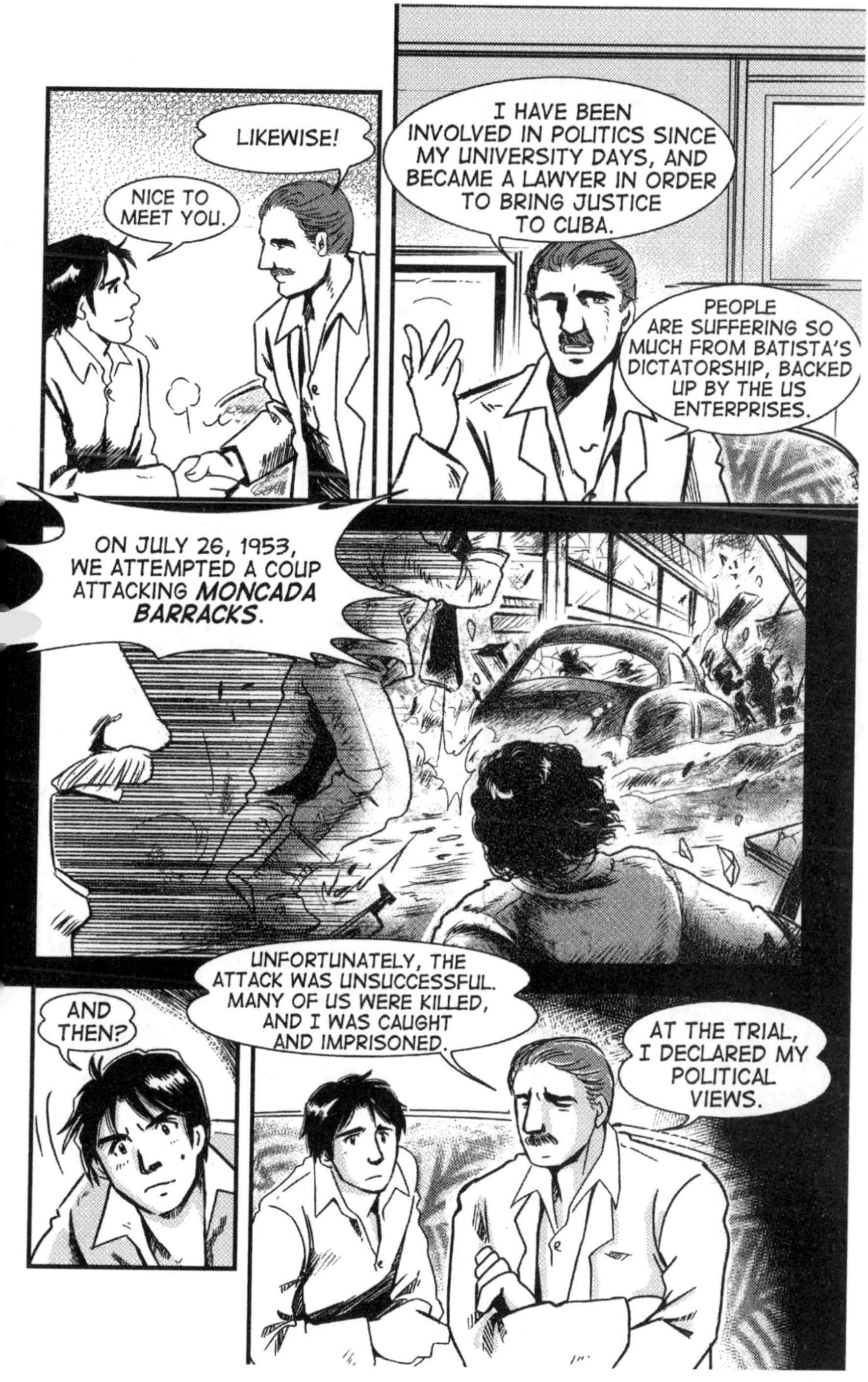
NICE TO MEET YOU.
LIKEWISE!
I HAVE BEEN INVOLVED IN POLITICS SINCE MY UNIVERSITY DAYS, AND BECAME A LAWYER IN ORDER TO BRING JUSTICE TO CUBA.
PEOPLE ARE SUFFERING SO MUCH FROM BATISTA'S DICTATORSHIP, BACKED UP BY THE US ENTERPRISES.
ON JULY 26, 1953, WE ATTEMPTED A COUP ATTACKING *MONCADA BARRACKS*.
AND THEN?
UNFORTUNATELY, THE ATTACK WAS UNSUCCESSFUL. MANY OF US WERE KILLED, AND I WAS CAUGHT AND IMPRISONED.
AT THE TRIAL, I DECLARED MY POLITICAL VIEWS.

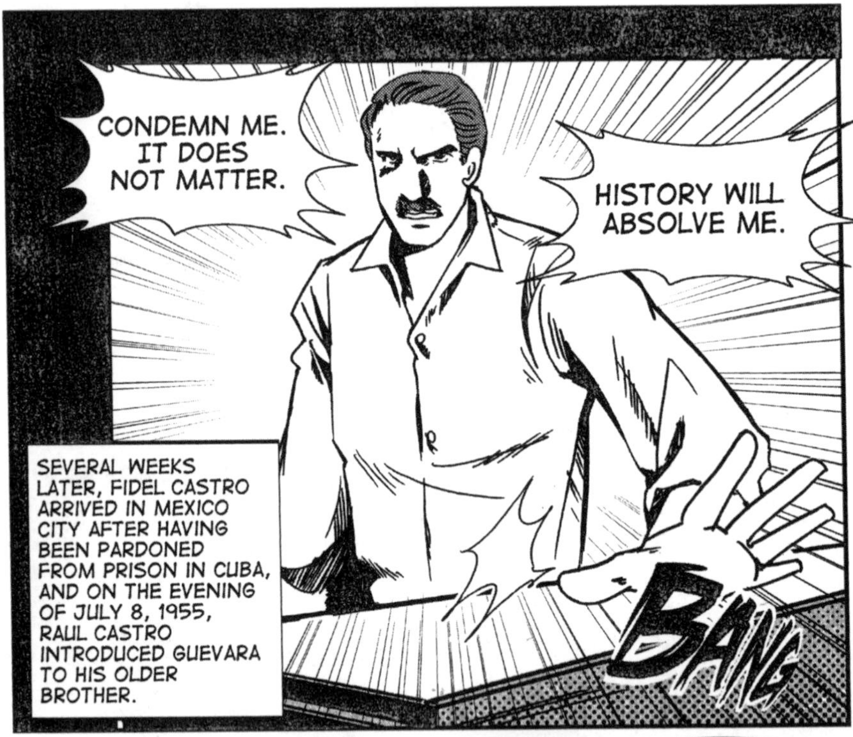
CONDEMN ME. IT DOES NOT MATTER.
HISTORY WILL ABSOLVE ME.
SEVERAL WEEKS LATER, FIDEL CASTRO ARRIVED IN MEXICO CITY AFTER HAVING BEEN PARDONED FROM PRISON IN CUBA, AND ON THE EVENING OF JULY 8, 1955, RAUL CASTRO INTRODUCED GUEVARA TO HIS OLDER BROTHER.
BANG

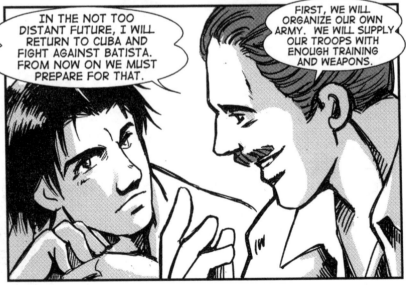

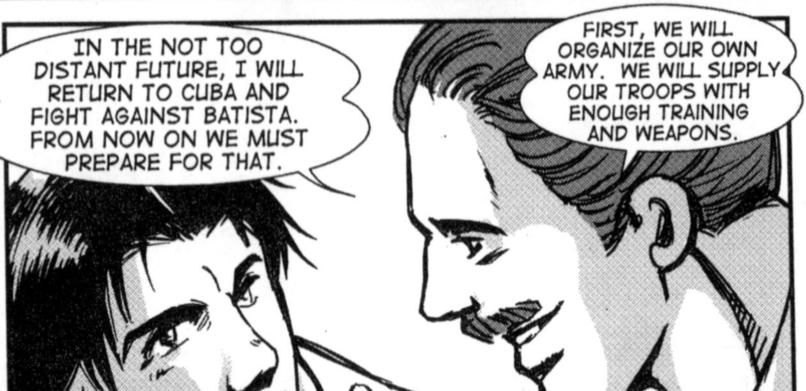
IN THE NOT TOO DISTANT FUTURE, I WILL RETURN TO CUBA AND FIGHT AGAINST BATISTA. FROM NOW ON WE MUST PREPARE FOR THAT.
FIRST, WE WILL ORGANIZE OUR OWN ARMY. WE WILL SUPPLY OUR TROOPS WITH ENOUGH TRAINING AND WEAPONS.

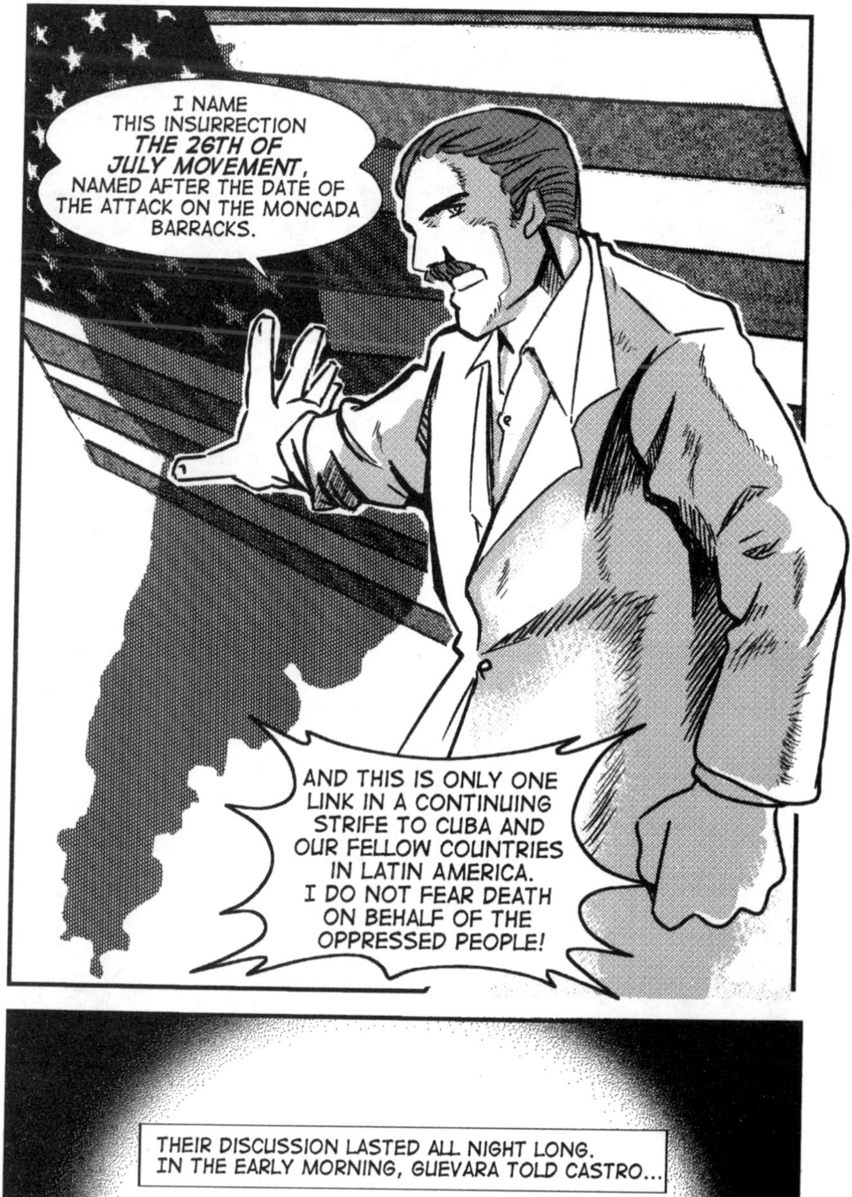
I NAME THIS INSURRECTION THE 26TH OF JULY MOVEMENT, NAMED AFTER THE DATE OF THE ATTACK ON THE MONCADA BARRACKS.
AND THIS IS ONLY ONE LINK IN A CONTINUING STRIFE TO CUBA AND OUR FELLOW COUNTRIES IN LATIN AMERICA. I DO NOT FEAR DEATH ON BEHALF OF THE OPPRESSED PEOPLE!
THEIR DISCUSSION LASTED ALL NIGHT LONG. IN THE EARLY MORNING, GUEVARA TOLD CASTRO...

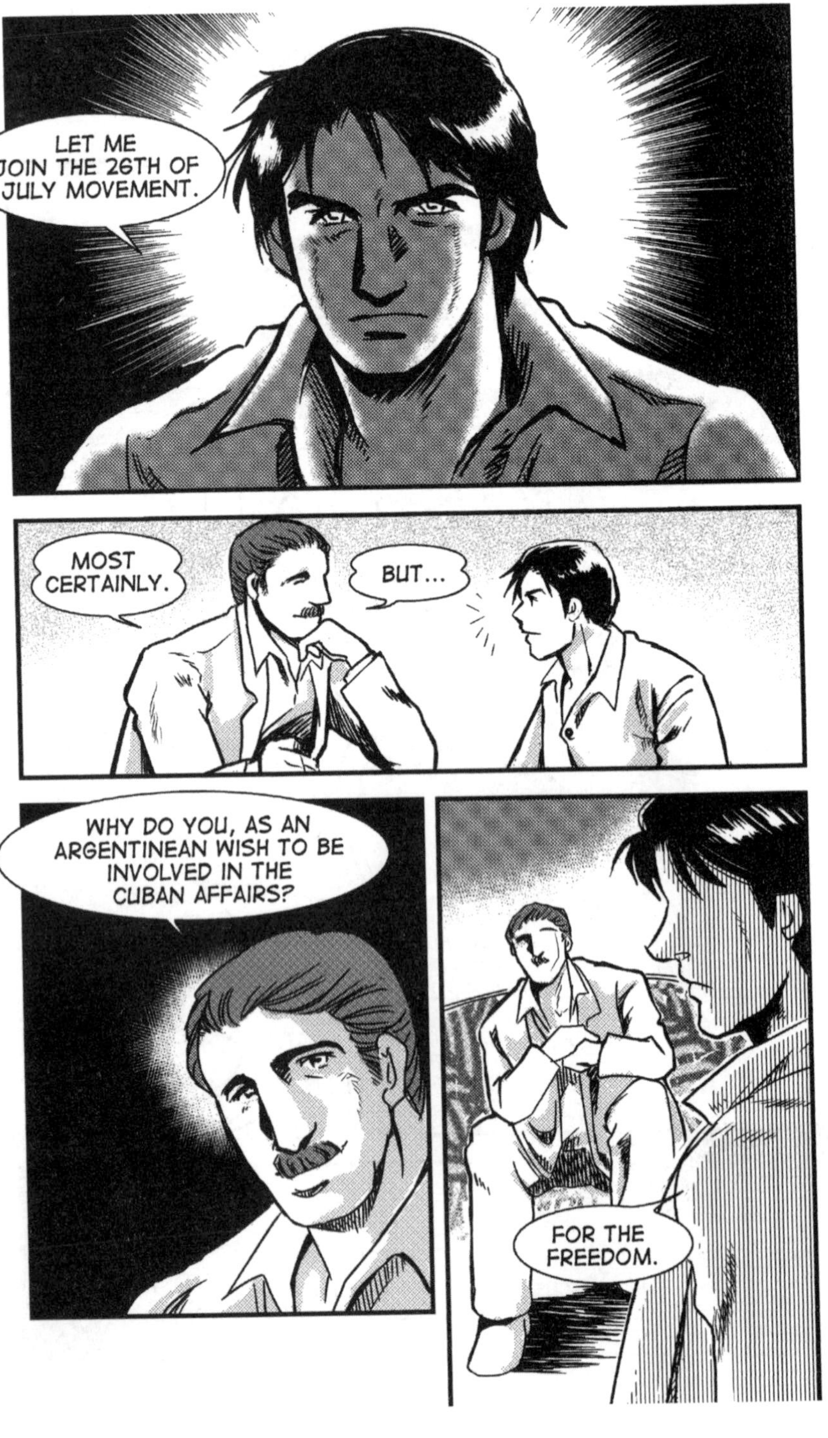
LET ME JOIN THE 26TH OF JULY MOVEMENT.
MOST CERTAINLY.
BUT...
WHY DO YOU, AS AN ARGENTINEAN WISH TO BE INVOLVED IN THE CUBAN AFFAIRS?
FOR THE FREEDOM.

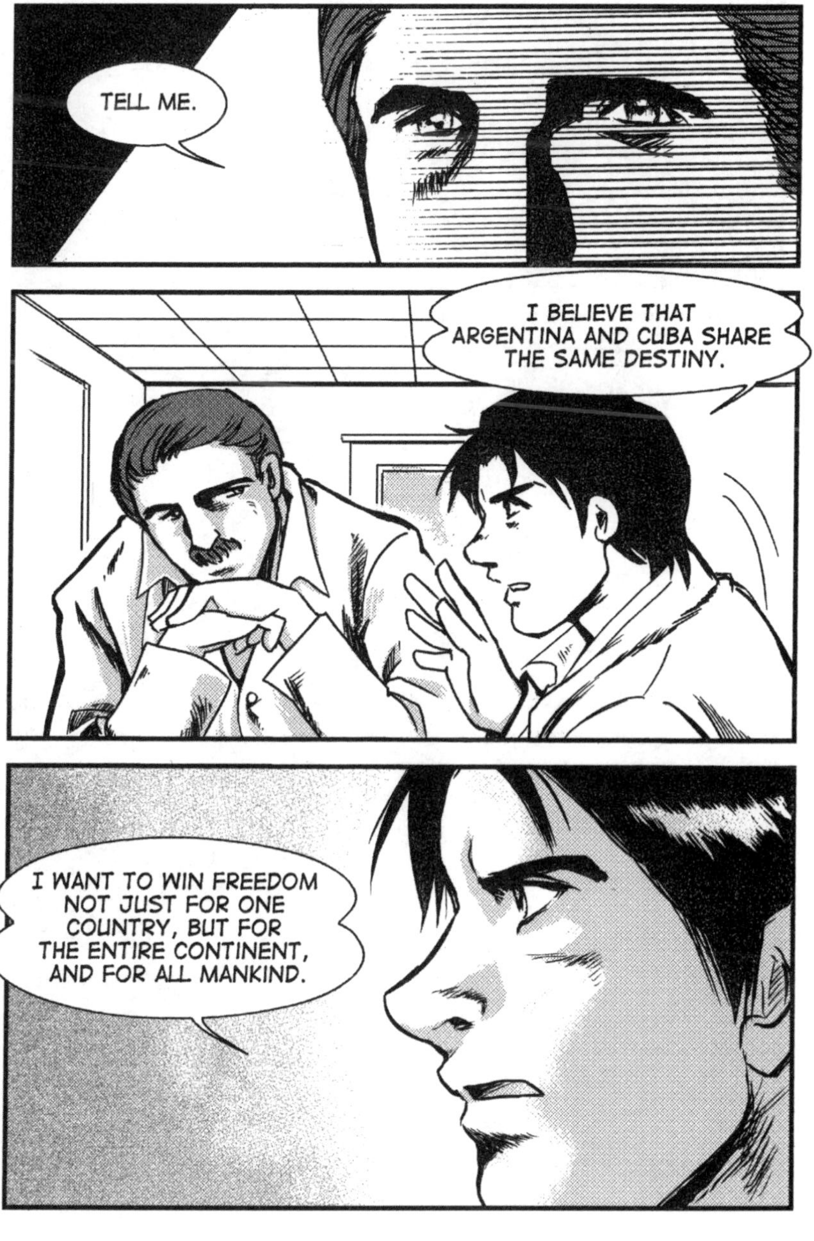
TELL ME.
I BELIEVE THAT ARGENTINA AND CUBA SHARE THE SAME DESTINY.
I WANT TO WIN FREEDOM NOT JUST FOR ONE COUNTRY, BUT FOR THE ENTIRE CONTINENT, AND FOR ALL MANKIND.

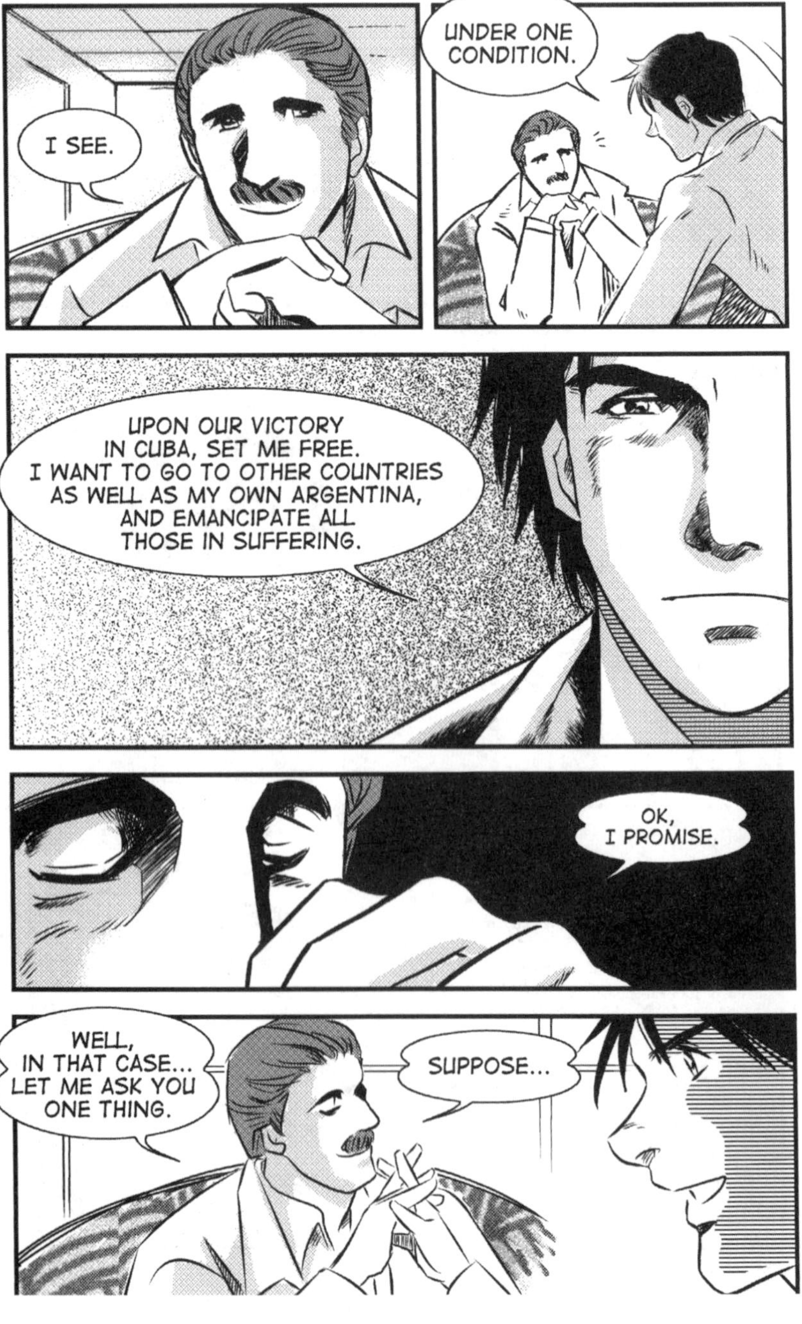
I SEE.
UNDER ONE CONDITION.
UPON OUR VICTORY IN CUBA, SET ME FREE. I WANT TO GO TO OTHER COUNTRIES AS WELL AS MY OWN ARGENTINA, AND EMANCIPATE ALL THOSE IN SUFFERING.
OK, I PROMISE.
WELL, IN THAT CASE... LET ME ASK YOU ONE THING.
SUPPOSE...

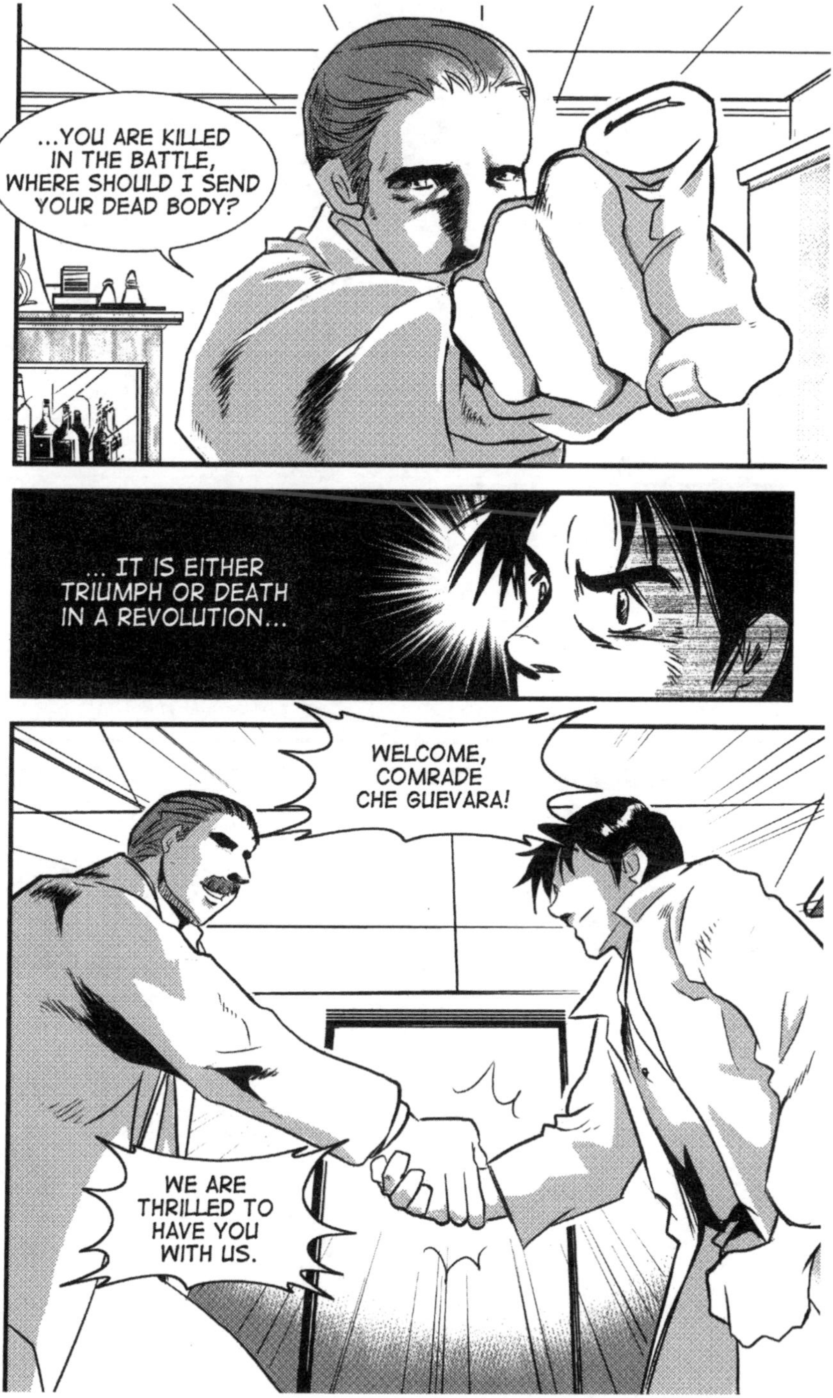
...YOU ARE KILLED IN THE BATTLE, WHERE SHOULD I SEND YOUR DEAD BODY?
... IT IS EITHER TRIUMPH OR DEATH IN A REVOLUTION...
WELCOME, COMRADE CHE GUEVARA!
WE ARE THRILLED TO HAVE YOU WITH US.

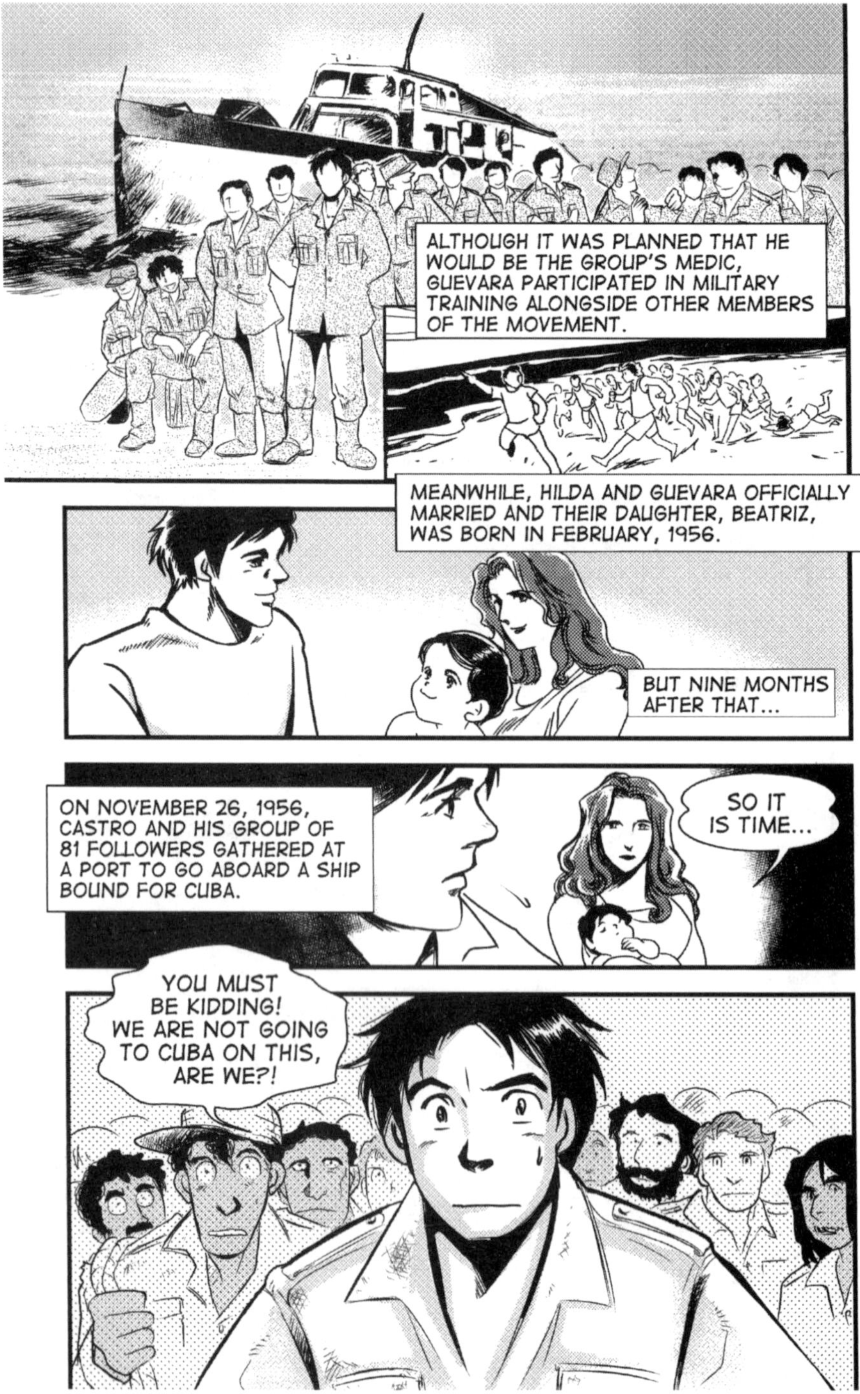
ALTHOUGH IT WAS PLANNED THAT HE WOULD BE THE GROUP'S MEDIC, GUEVARA PARTICIPATED IN MILITARY TRAINING ALONGSIDE OTHER MEMBERS OF THE MOVEMENT.
MEANWHILE, HILDA AND GUEVARA OFFICIALLY MARRIED AND THEIR DAUGHTER, BEATRIZ, WAS BORN IN FEBRUARY, 1956.
BUT NINE MONTHS AFTER THAT...
ON NOVEMBER 26, 1956, CASTRO AND HIS GROUP OF 81 FOLLOWERS GATHERED AT A PORT TO GO ABOARD A SHIP BOUND FOR CUBA.
SO IT IS TIME...
YOU MUST BE KIDDING! WE ARE NOT GOING TO CUBA ON THIS, ARE WE?!

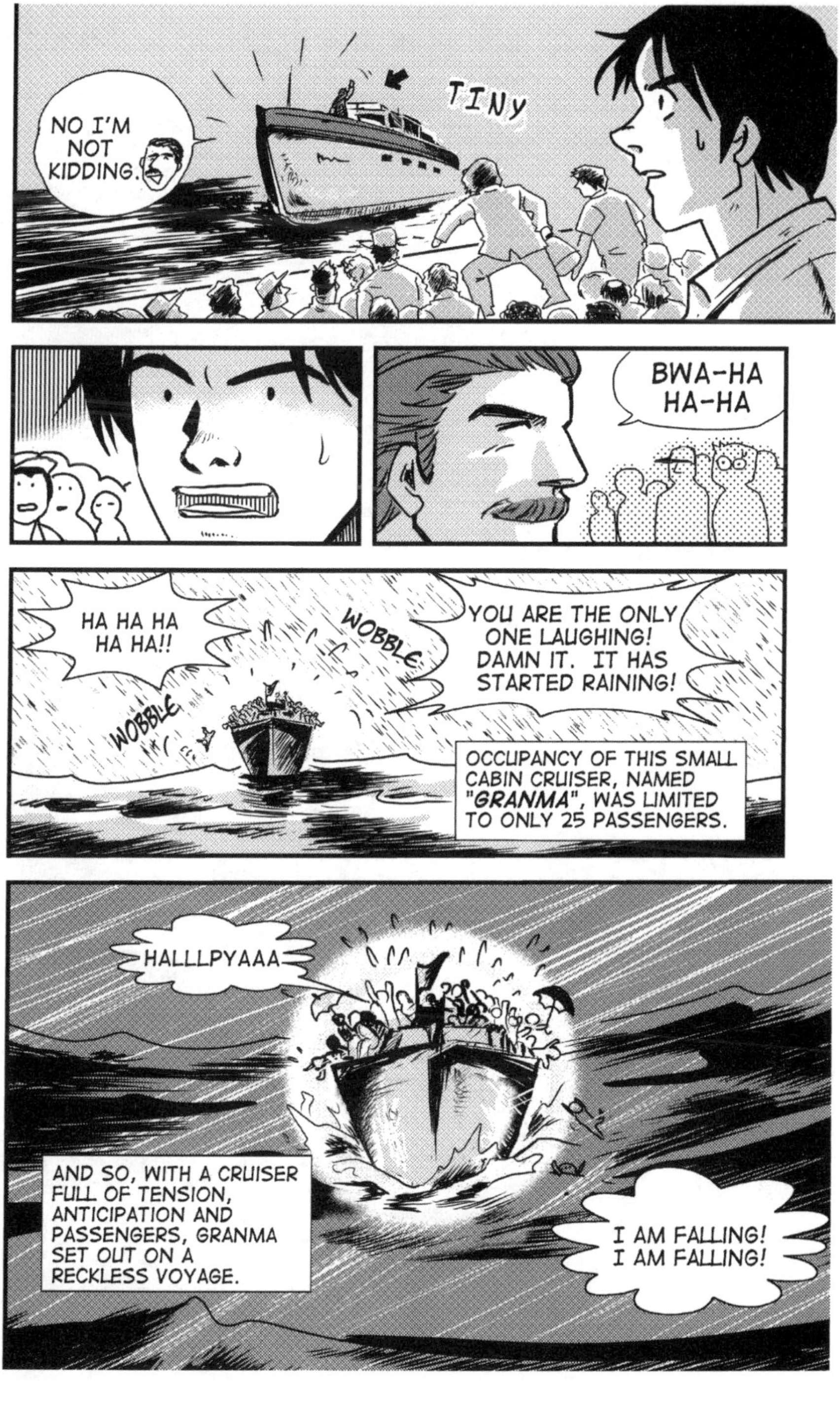
NO I'M NOT KIDDING.
TINY
BWA-HA HA-HA
HA HA HA HA HA!!
WOBBLE
YOU ARE THE ONLY ONE LAUGHING! DAMN IT. IT HAS STARTED RAINING!
WOBBLE
OCCUPANCY OF THIS SMALL CABIN CRUISER, NAMED "GRANMA", WAS LIMITED TO ONLY 25 PASSENGERS.
HALLLPYAAA
AND SO, WITH A CRUISER FULL OF TENSION, ANTICIPATION AND PASSENGERS, GRANMA SET OUT ON A RECKLESS VOYAGE.
I AM FALLING! I AM FALLING!

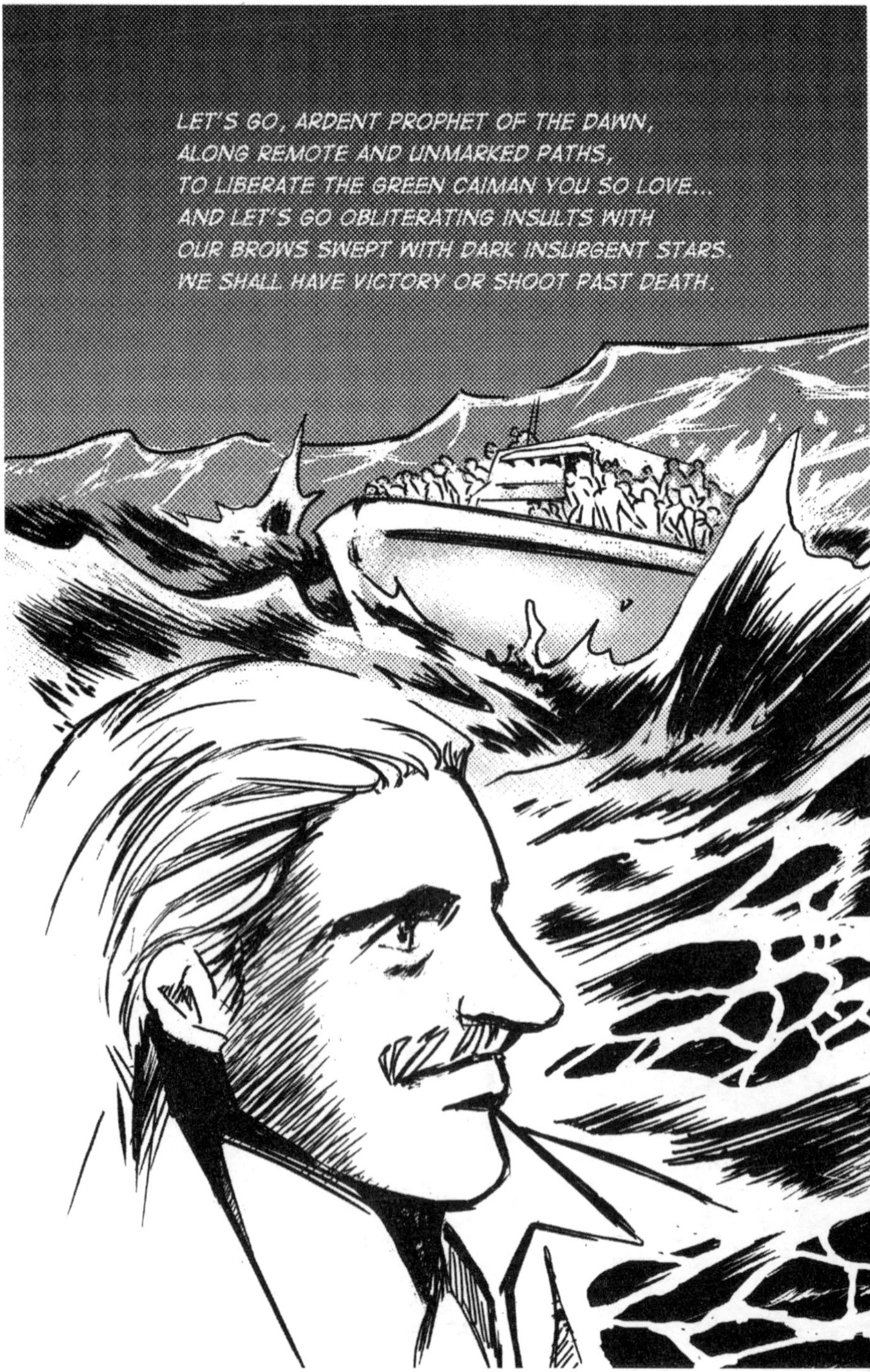
LET'S GO, ARDENT PROPHET OF THE DAWN,
ALONG REMOTE AND UNMARKED PATHS,
TO LIBERATE THE GREEN CAIMAN YOU SO LOVE...
AND LET'S GO OBLITERATING INSULTS WITH
OUR BROWS SWEPT WITH DARK INSURGENT STARS.
WE SHALL HAVE VICTORY OR SHOOT PAST DEATH.

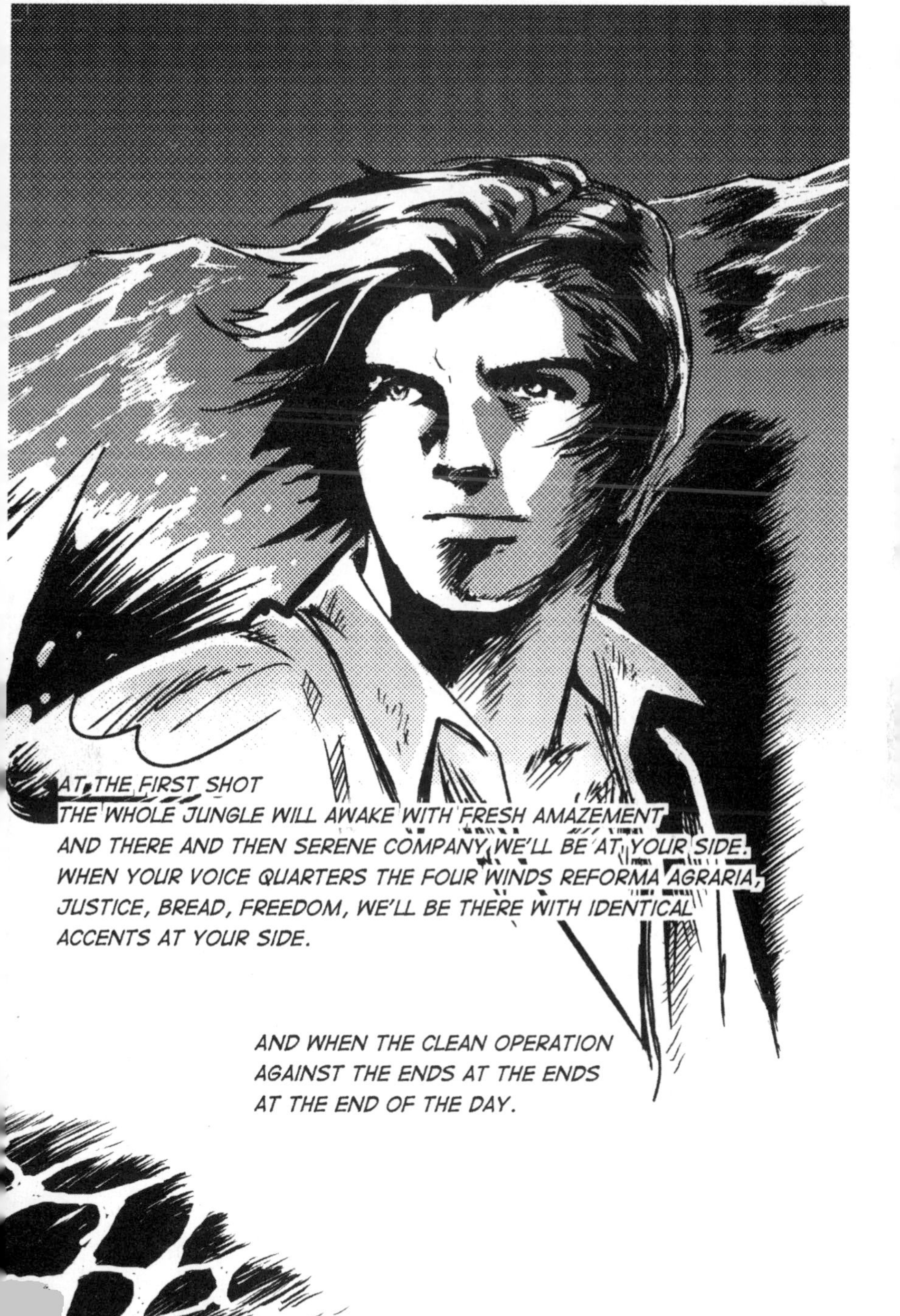
AT THE FIRST SHOT
THE WHOLE JUNGLE WILL AWAKE WITH FRESH AMAZEMENT
AND THERE AND THEN SERENE COMPANY WE'LL BE AT YOUR SIDE.
WHEN YOUR VOICE QUARTERS THE FOUR WINDS REFORMA AGRARIA,
JUSTICE, BREAD, FREEDOM, WE'LL BE THERE WITH IDENTICAL
ACCENTS AT YOUR SIDE.
AND WHEN THE CLEAN OPERATION
AGAINST THE ENDS AT THE ENDS
AT THE END OF THE DAY.

CHAPTER 3   GUERRILLA

1956 - 1959

I am not a liberator.
Liberators do not exist.
The people liberate themselves.

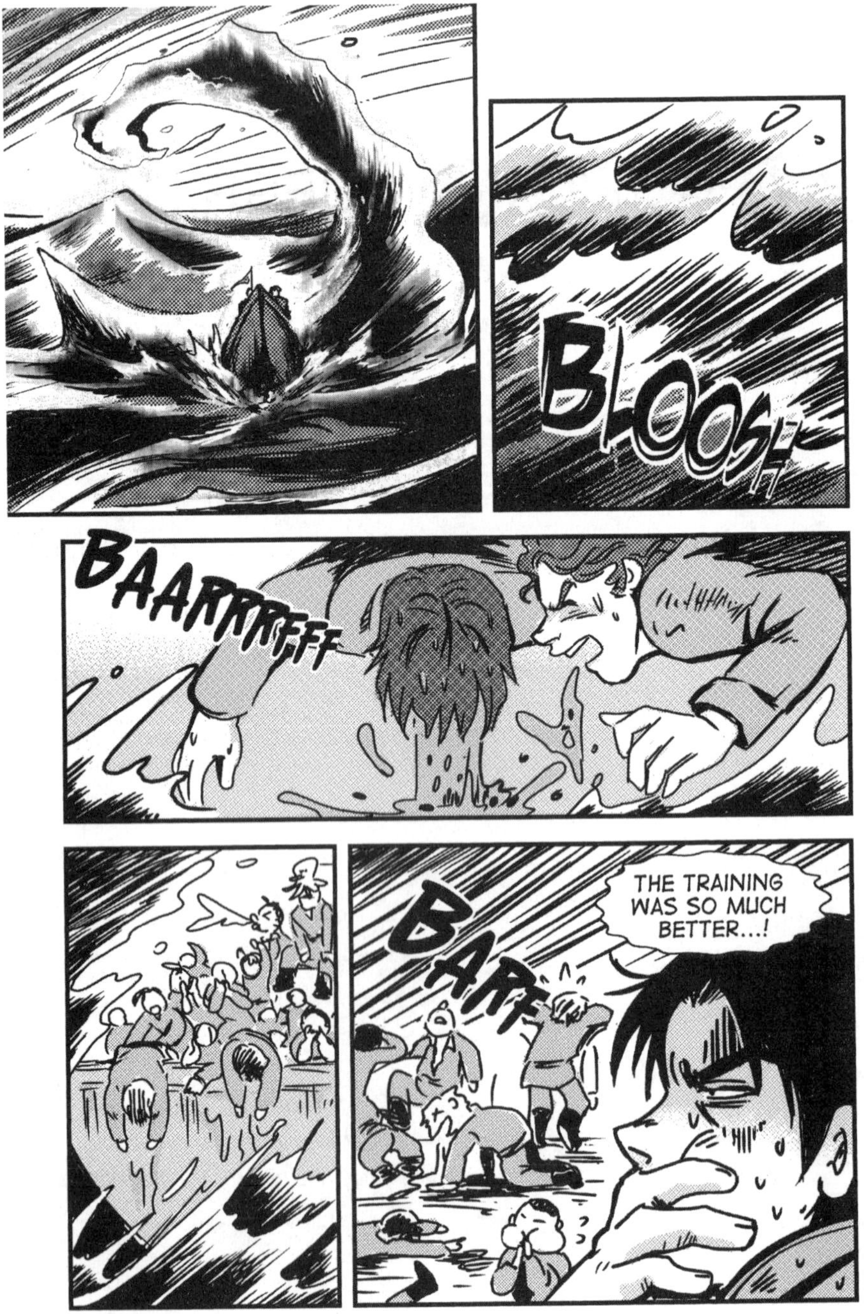
BLOOSH
BAARRRRFFF
BARF
THE TRAINING WAS SO MUCH BETTER...!

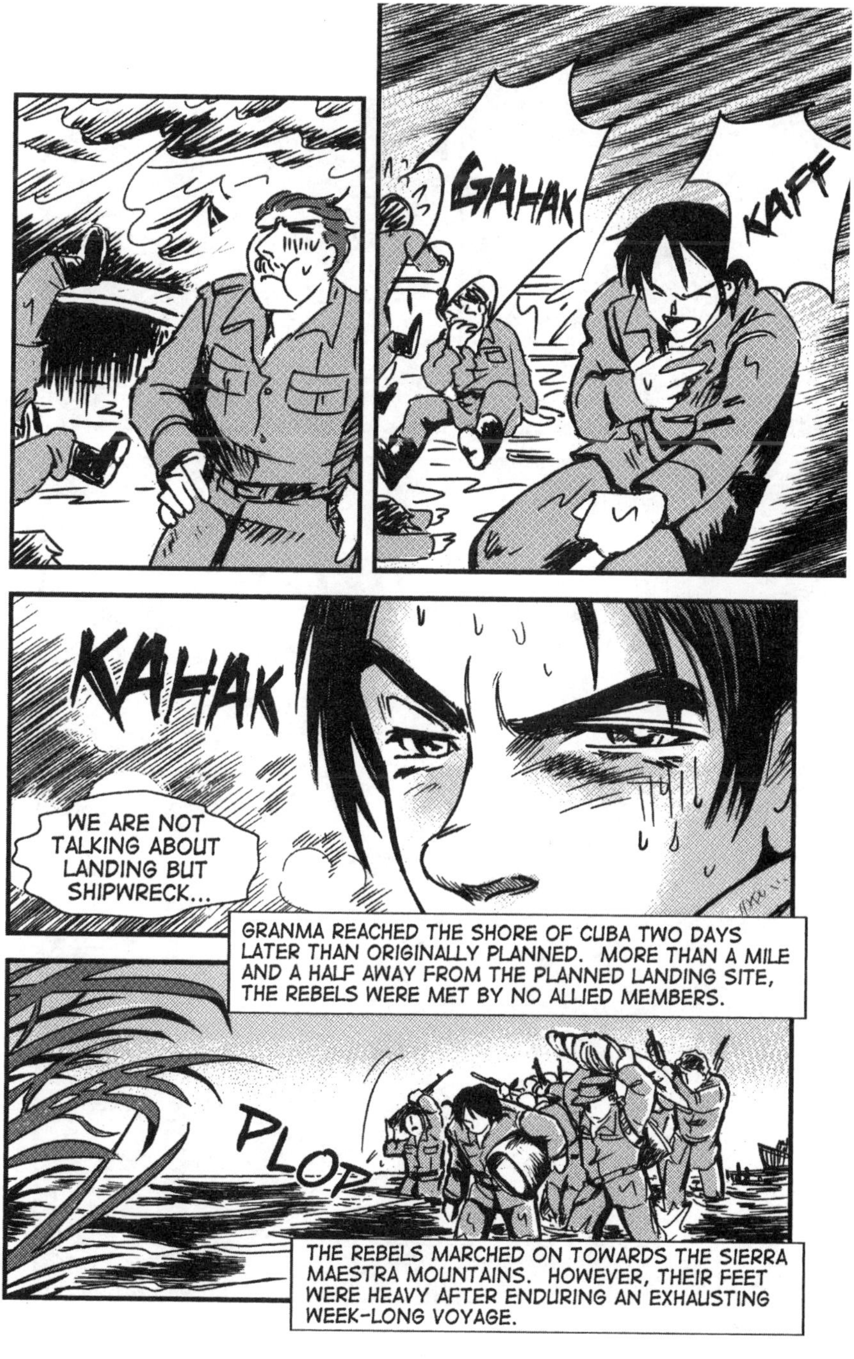
GAHAK
KAFF
KAHAK
WE ARE NOT TALKING ABOUT LANDING BUT SHIPWRECK...
GRANMA REACHED THE SHORE OF CUBA TWO DAYS LATER THAN ORIGINALLY PLANNED. MORE THAN A MILE AND A HALF AWAY FROM THE PLANNED LANDING SITE, THE REBELS WERE MET BY NO ALLIED MEMBERS.
PLOP
THE REBELS MARCHED ON TOWARDS THE SIERRA MAESTRA MOUNTAINS. HOWEVER, THEIR FEET WERE HEAVY AFTER ENDURING AN EXHAUSTING WEEK-LONG VOYAGE.

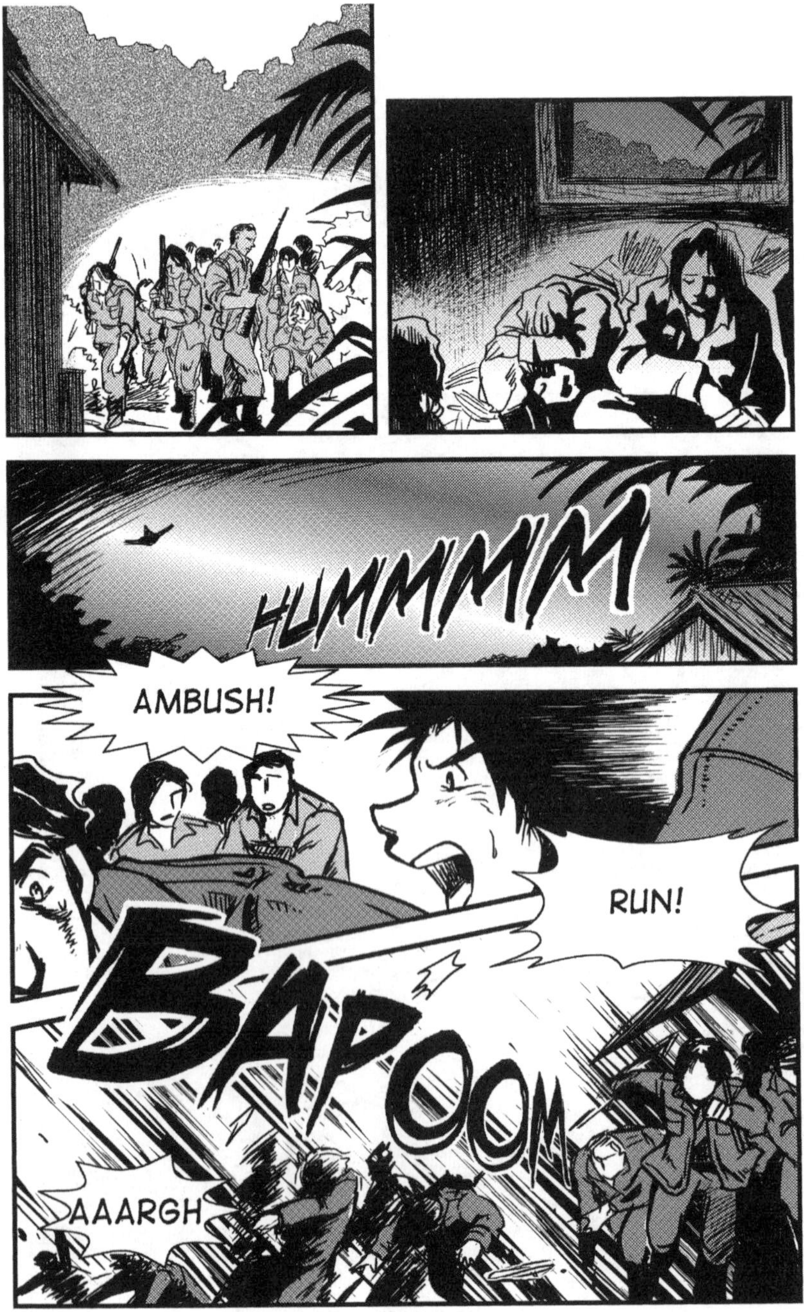
HUMMMMM
AMBUSH!
RUN!
BAPOOM
AAARGH

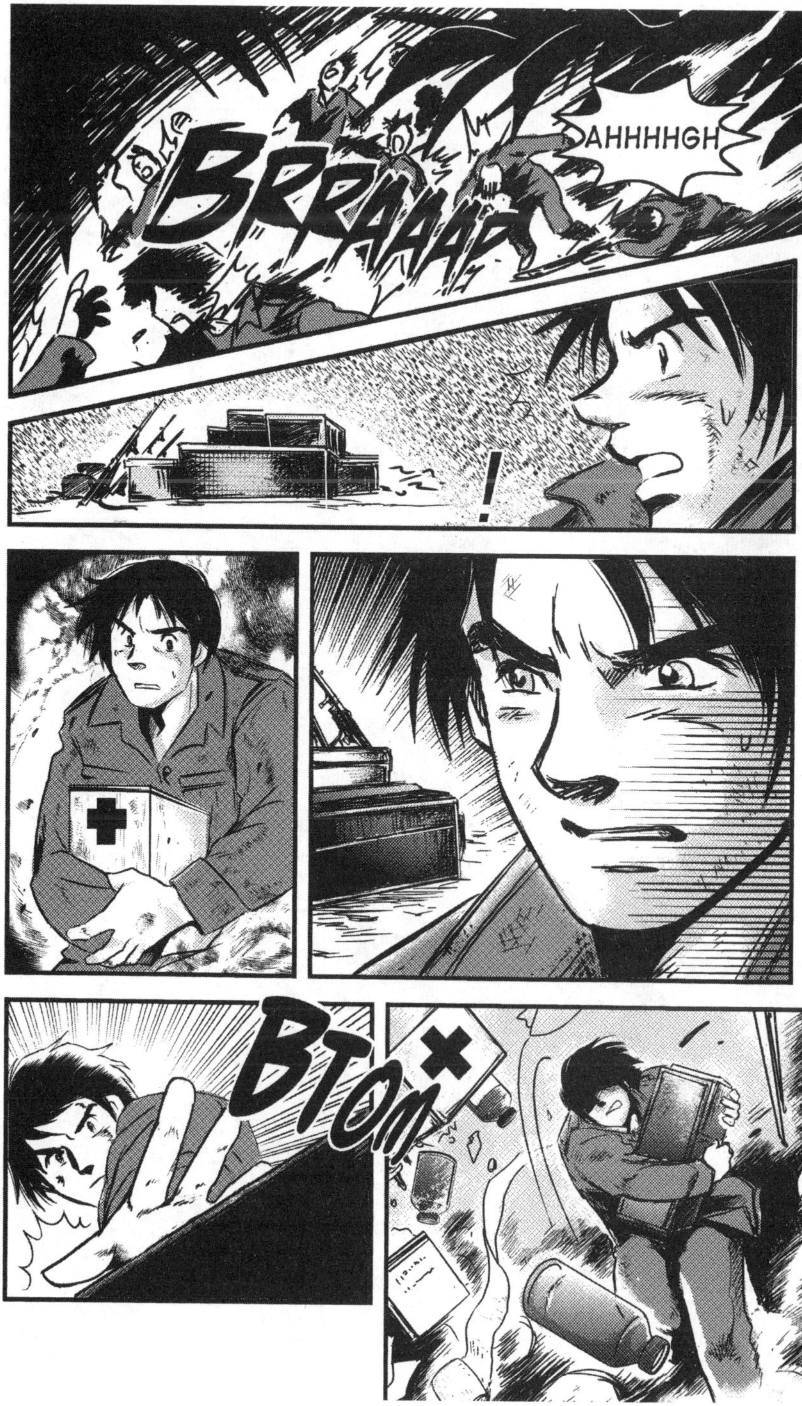
AHHHHGH
BRRAAAAP
BTOM

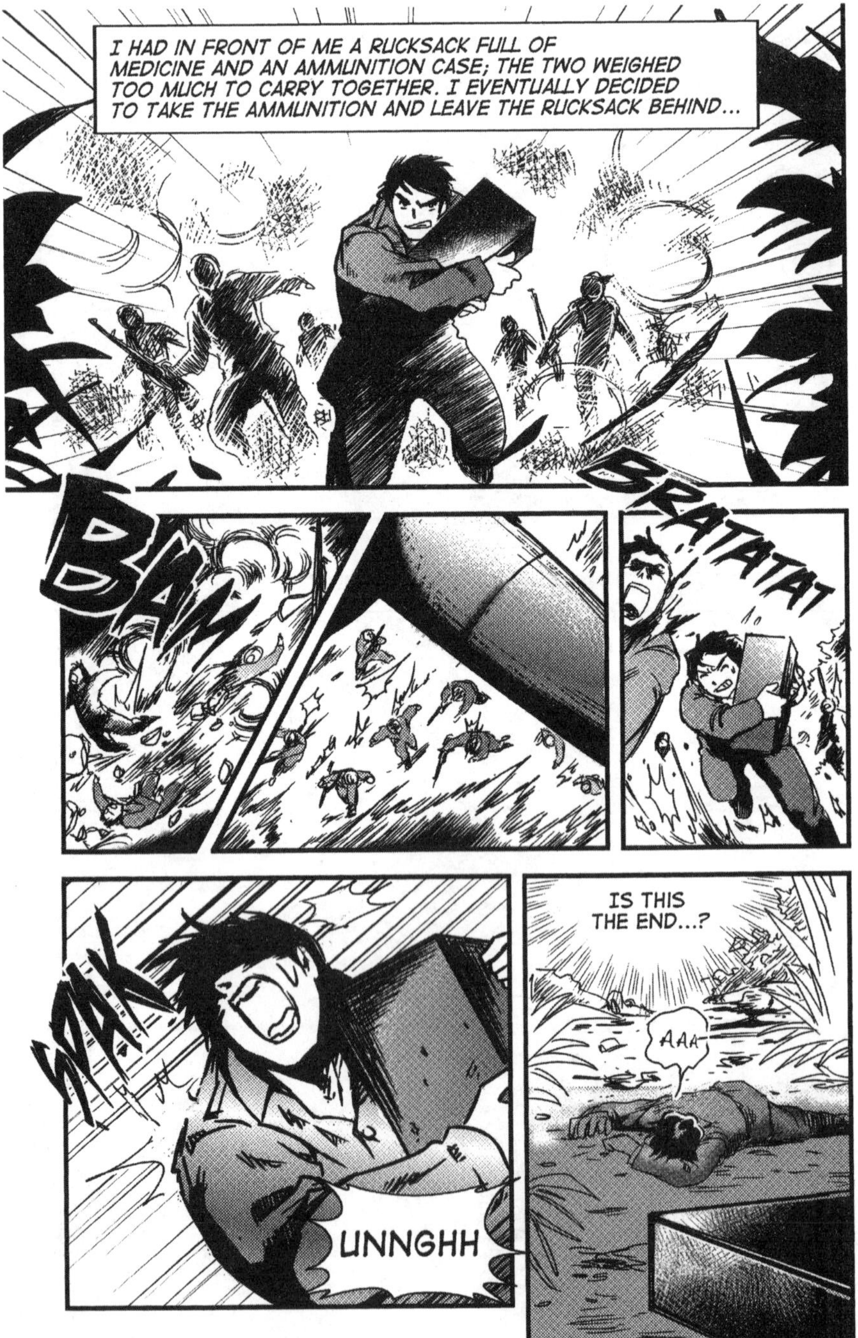
I HAD IN FRONT OF ME A RUCKSACK FULL OF MEDICINE AND AN AMMUNITION CASE; THE TWO WEIGHED TOO MUCH TO CARRY TOGETHER. I EVENTUALLY DECIDED TO TAKE THE AMMUNITION AND LEAVE THE RUCKSACK BEHIND...
BAM
BRATATAT
SPAK
UNNGHH
IS THIS THE END...?
AAA

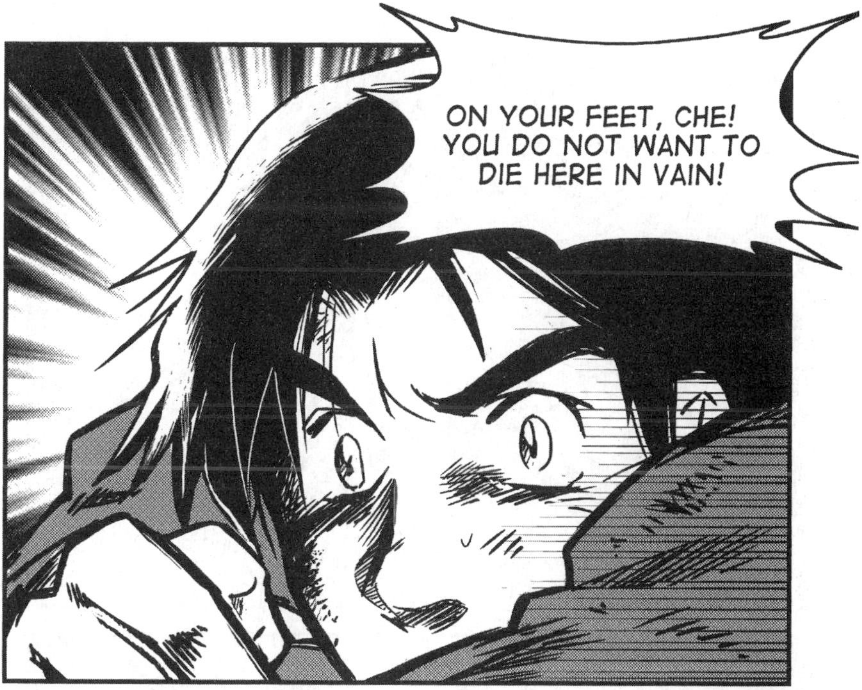
ON YOUR FEET, CHE! YOU DO NOT WANT TO DIE HERE IN VAIN!

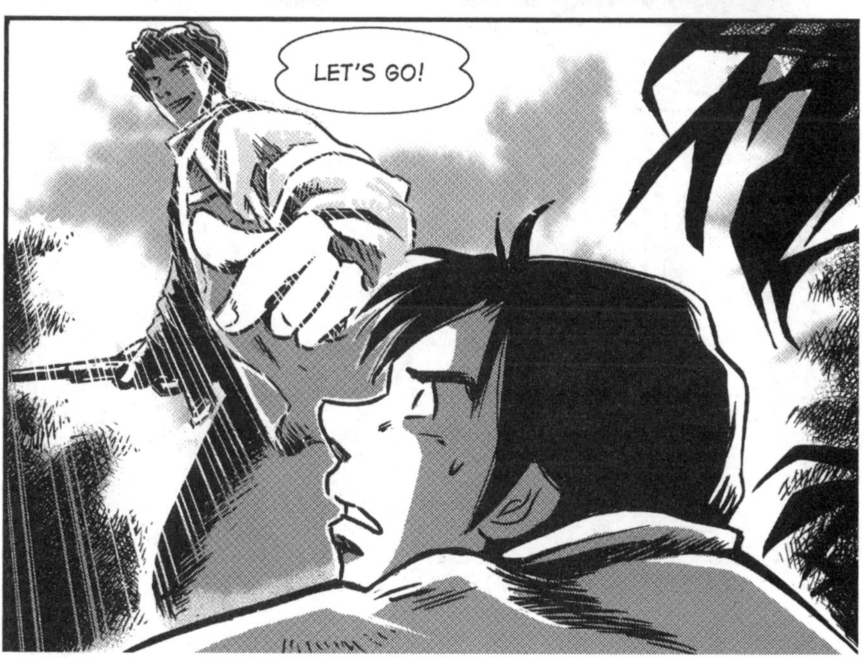
LET'S GO!

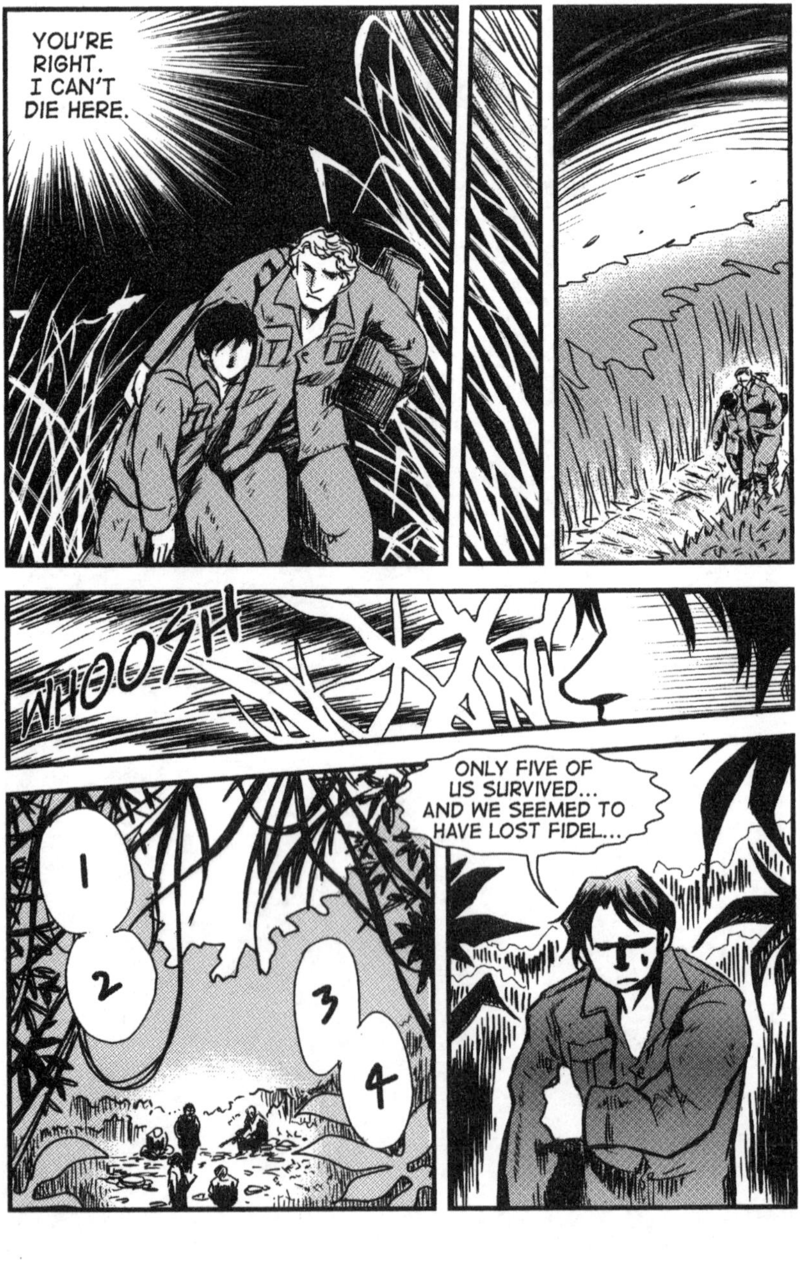
YOU'RE RIGHT. I CAN'T DIE HERE.
WHOOSH
1
2
3
4
ONLY FIVE OF US SURVIVED... AND WE SEEMED TO HAVE LOST FIDEL...

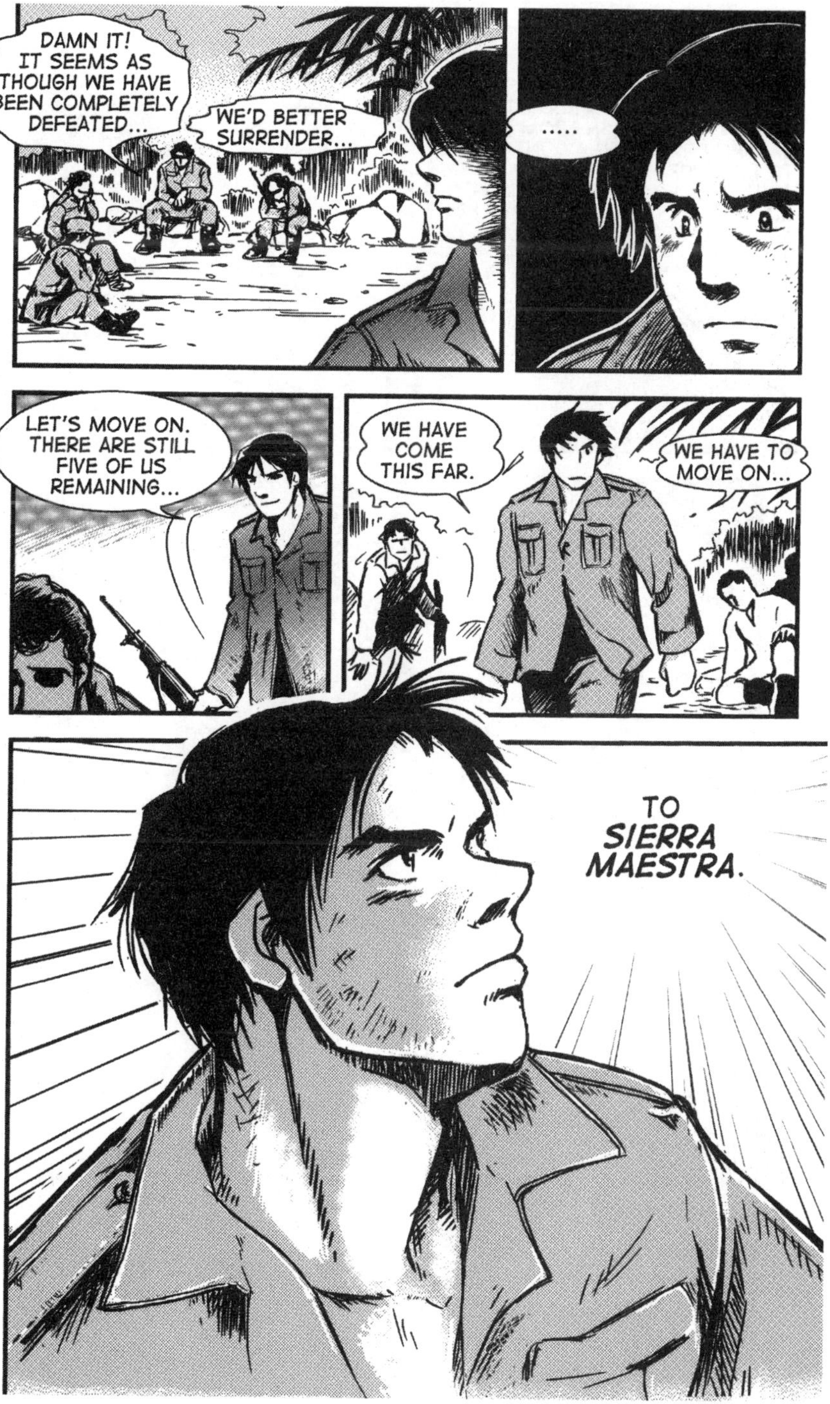
DAMN IT! IT SEEMS AS THOUGH WE HAVE BEEN COMPLETELY DEFEATED...
WE'D BETTER SURRENDER...
.....
LET'S MOVE ON. THERE ARE STILL FIVE OF US REMAINING...
WE HAVE COME THIS FAR.
WE HAVE TO MOVE ON...
TO SIERRA MAESTRA.

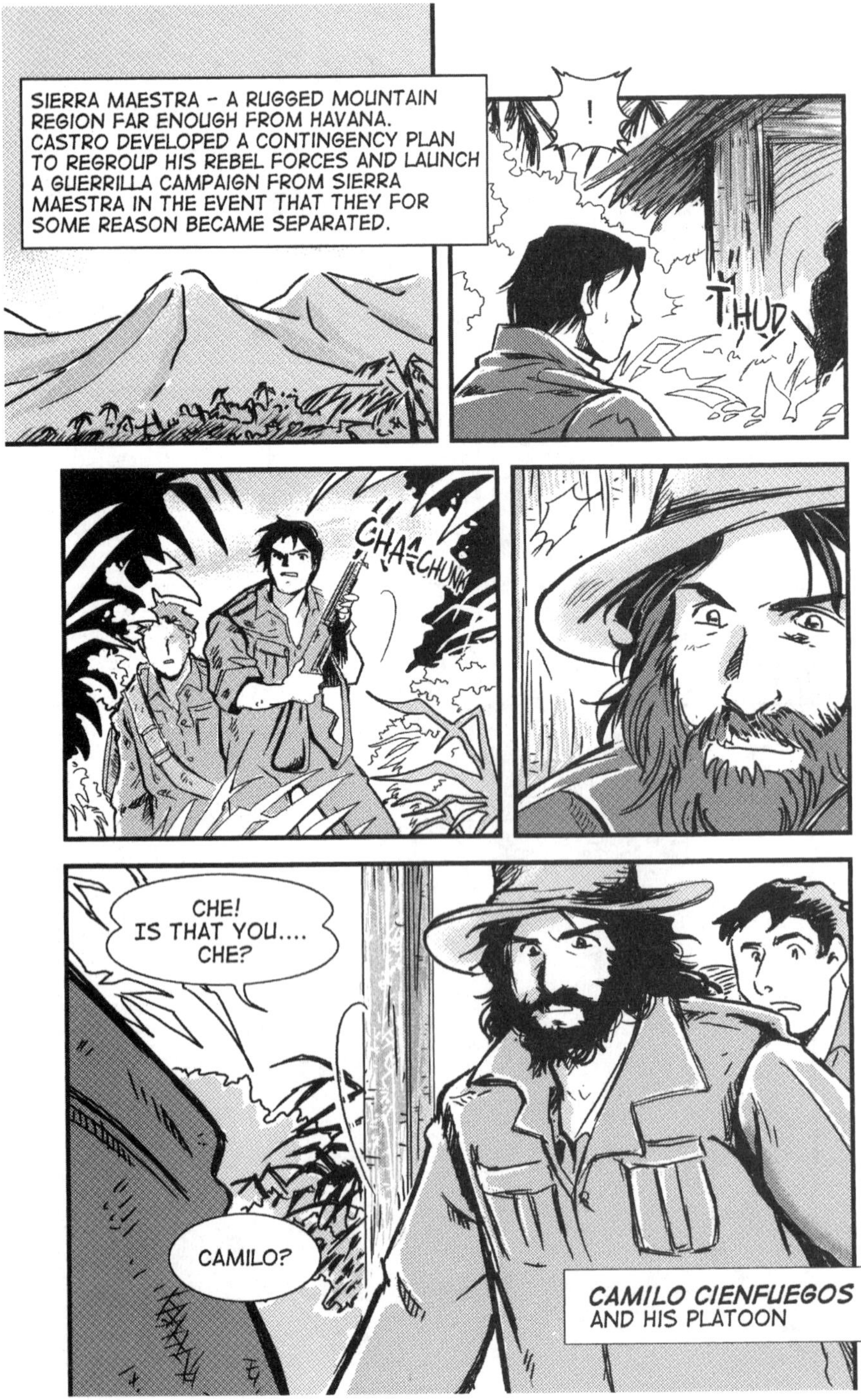
SIERRA MAESTRA - A RUGGED MOUNTAIN REGION FAR ENOUGH FROM HAVANA. CASTRO DEVELOPED A CONTINGENCY PLAN TO REGROUP HIS REBEL FORCES AND LAUNCH A GUERRILLA CAMPAIGN FROM SIERRA MAESTRA IN THE EVENT THAT THEY FOR SOME REASON BECAME SEPARATED.
!
THUD
CHA-CHUNK
CHE! IS THAT YOU.... CHE?
CAMILO?
CAMILO CIENFUEGOS AND HIS PLATOON

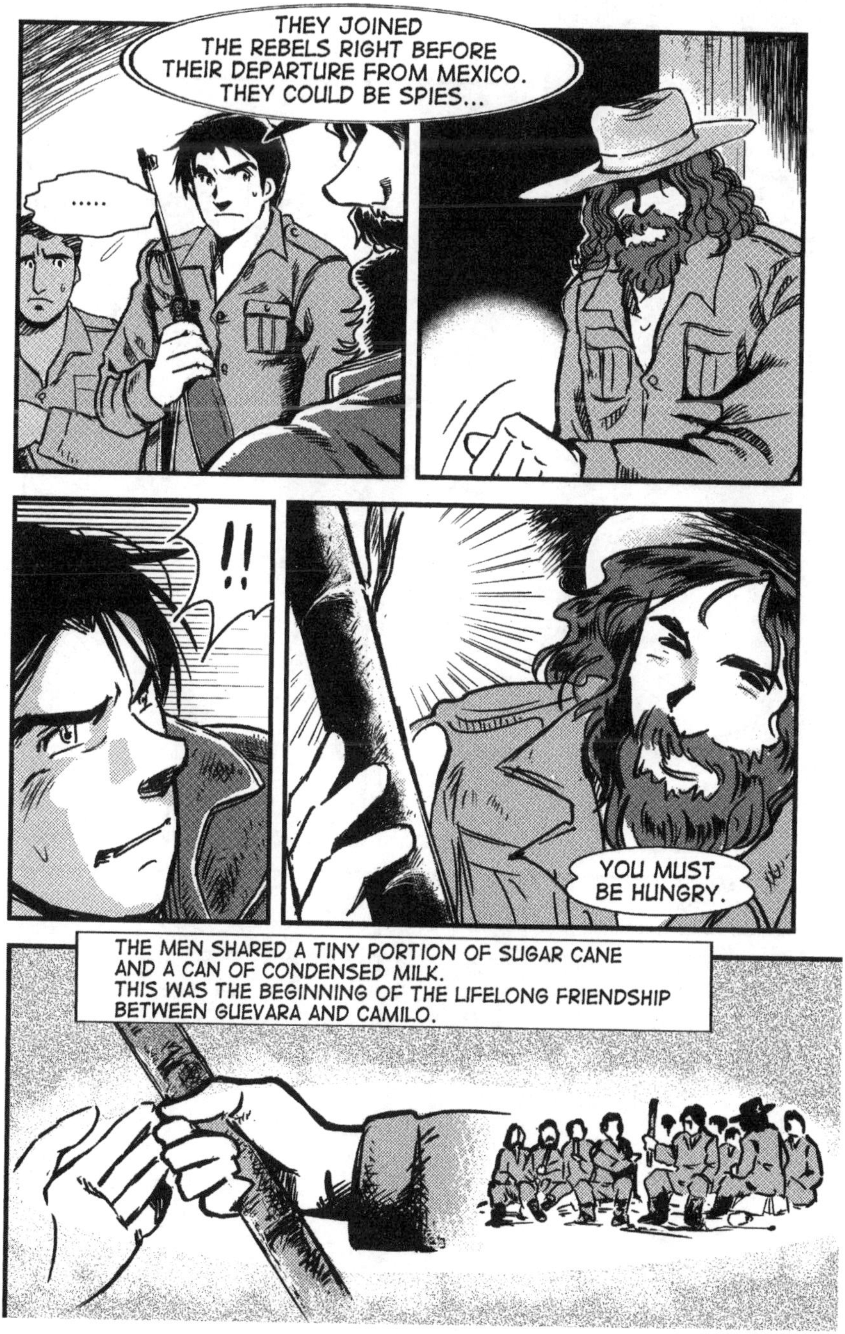
THEY JOINED THE REBELS RIGHT BEFORE THEIR DEPARTURE FROM MEXICO. THEY COULD BE SPIES...
.....
!!
YOU MUST BE HUNGRY.
THE MEN SHARED A TINY PORTION OF SUGAR CANE AND A CAN OF CONDENSED MILK. THIS WAS THE BEGINNING OF THE LIFELONG FRIENDSHIP BETWEEN GUEVARA AND CAMILO.

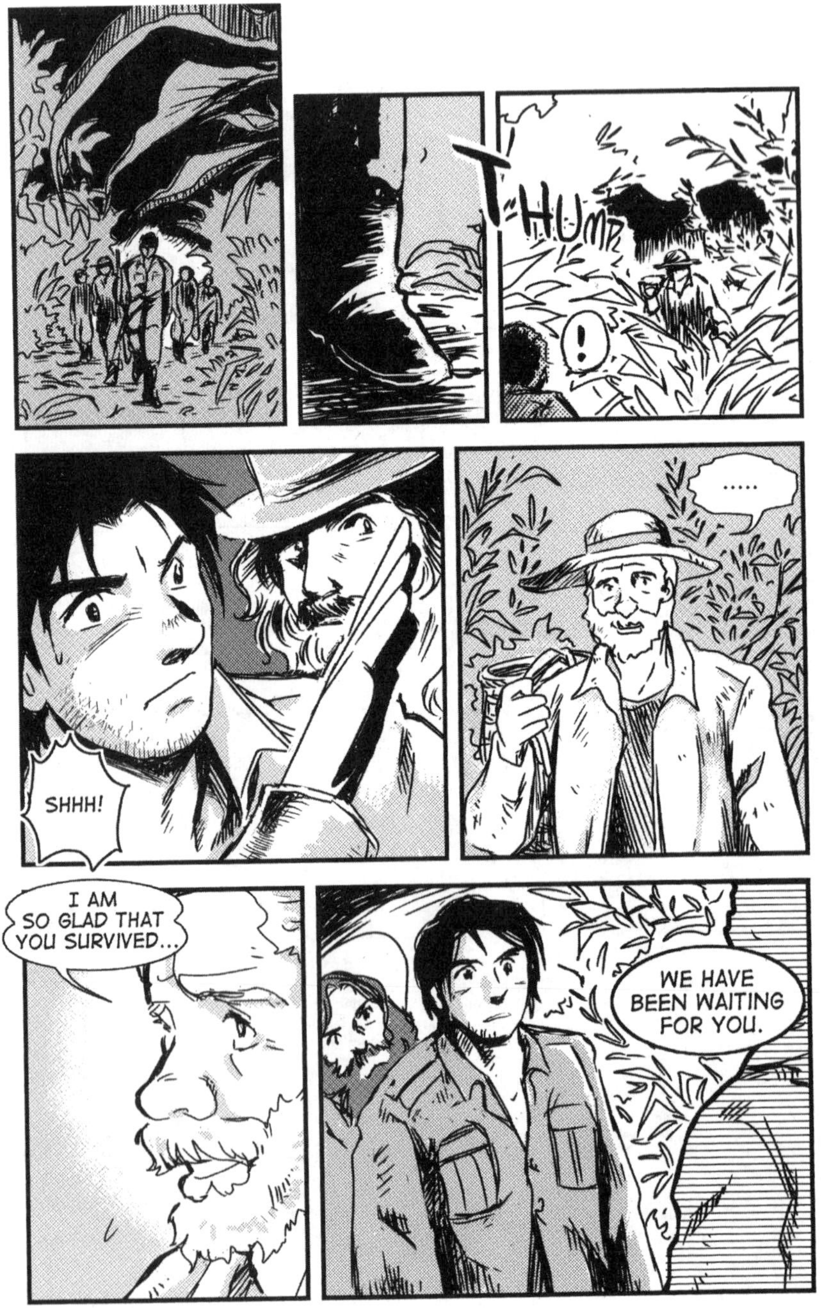
THUMP
!
SHHH!
.....
I AM SO GLAD THAT YOU SURVIVED...
WE HAVE BEEN WAITING FOR YOU.

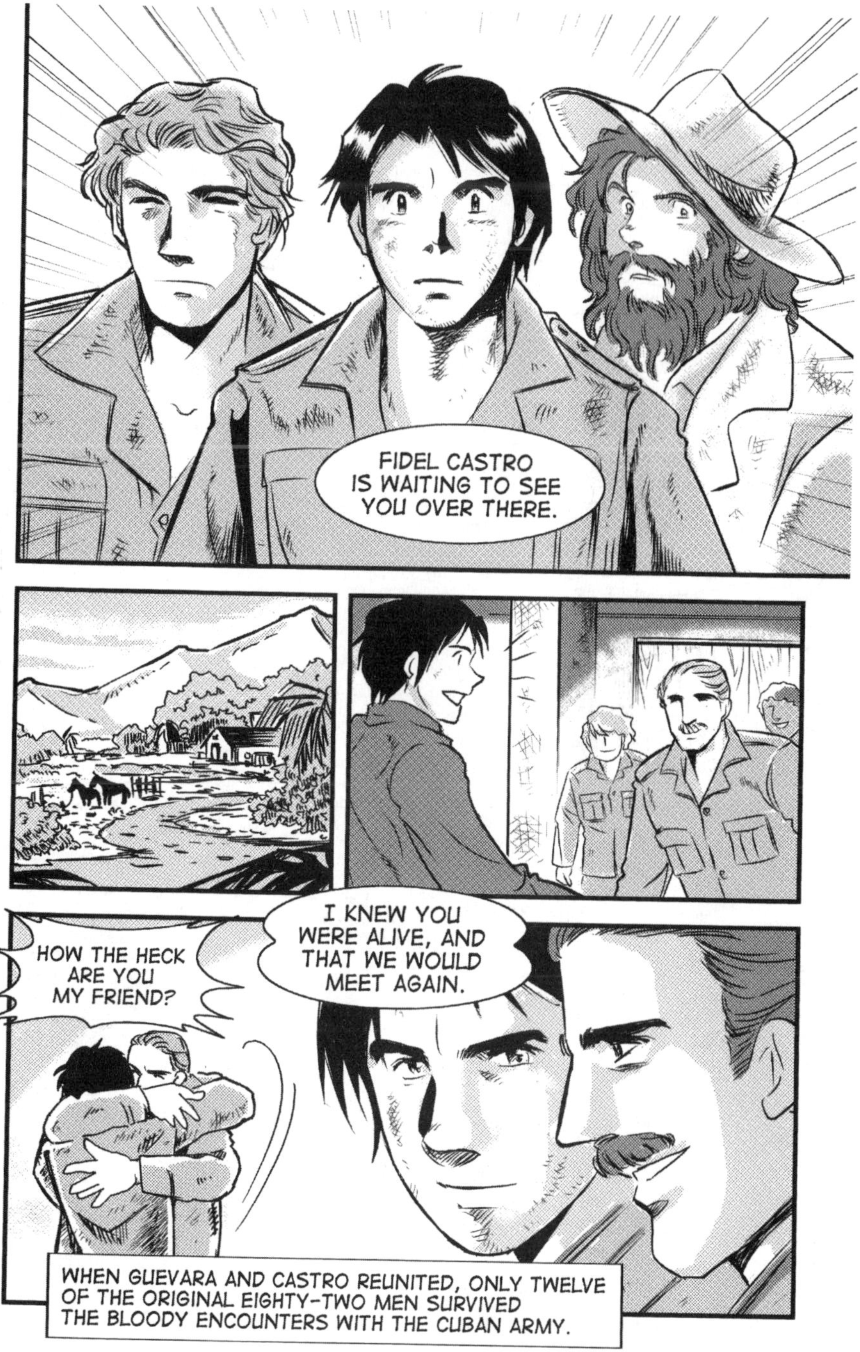
FIDEL CASTRO IS WAITING TO SEE YOU OVER THERE.
HOW THE HECK ARE YOU MY FRIEND?
I KNEW YOU WERE ALIVE, AND THAT WE WOULD MEET AGAIN.
WHEN GUEVARA AND CASTRO REUNITED, ONLY TWELVE OF THE ORIGINAL EIGHTY-TWO MEN SURVIVED THE BLOODY ENCOUNTERS WITH THE CUBAN ARMY.

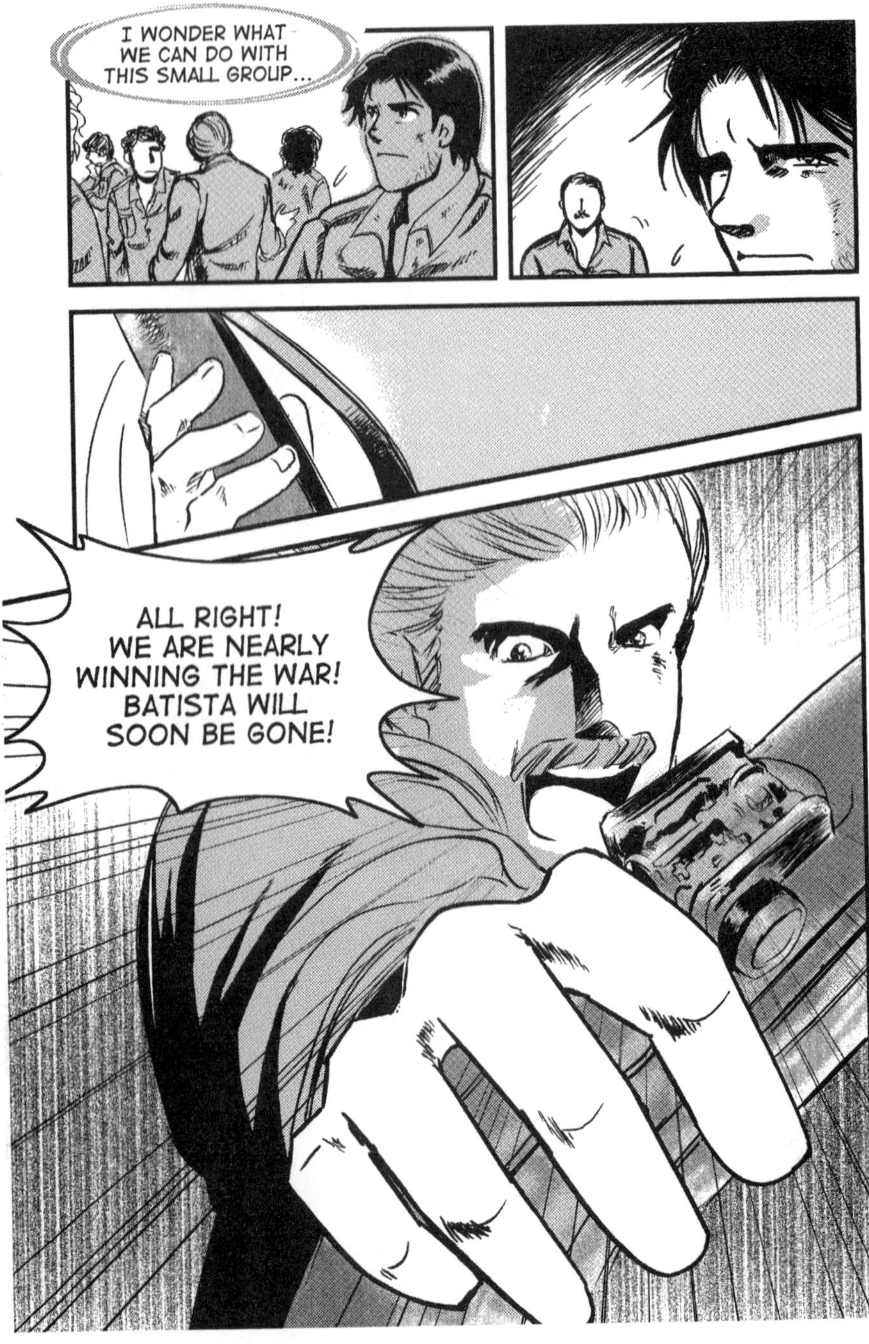
I WONDER WHAT WE CAN DO WITH THIS SMALL GROUP...
ALL RIGHT! WE ARE NEARLY WINNING THE WAR! BATISTA WILL SOON BE GONE!

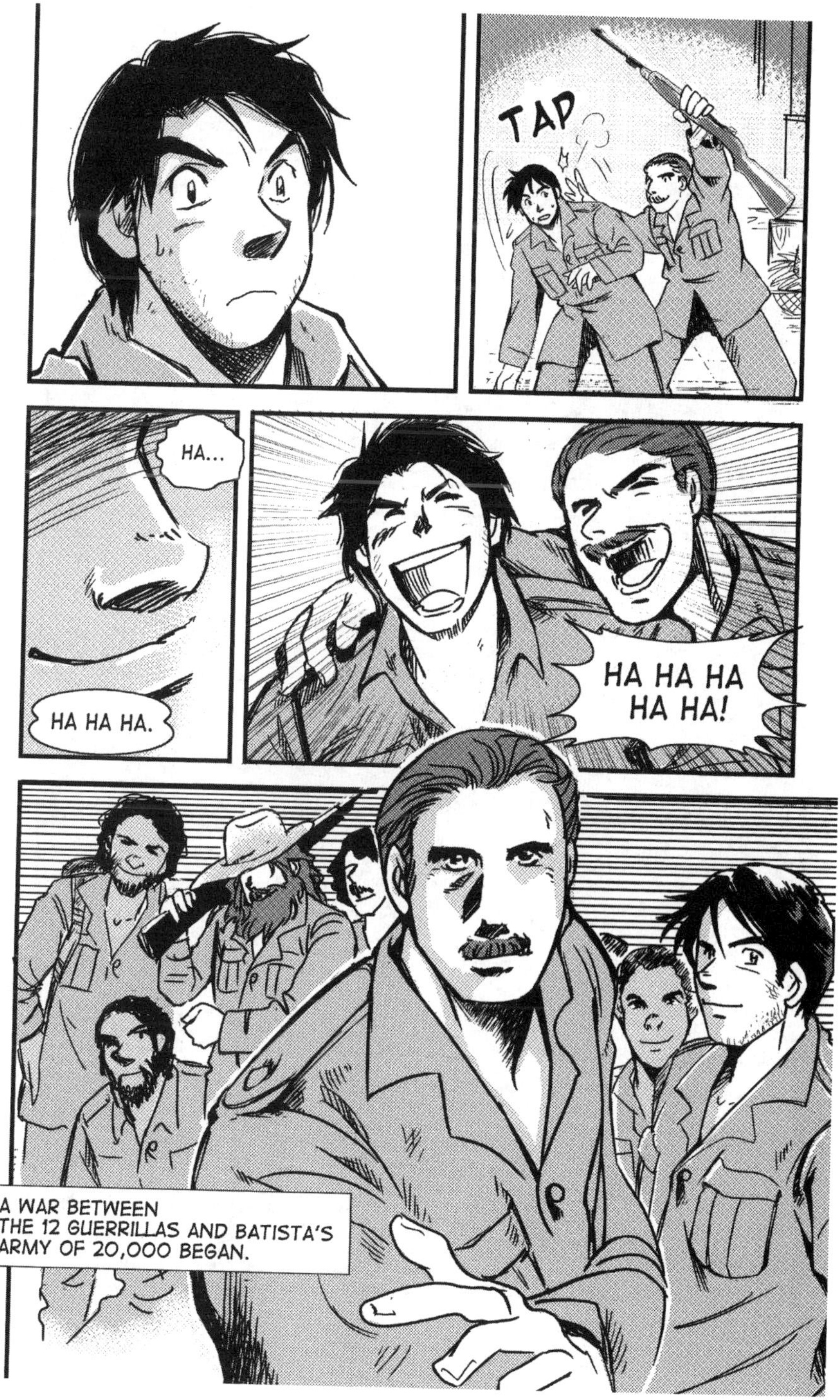
TAP
HA...
HA HA HA.
HA HA HA HA HA!
A WAR BETWEEN THE 12 GUERRILLAS AND BATISTA'S ARMY OF 20,000 BEGAN.

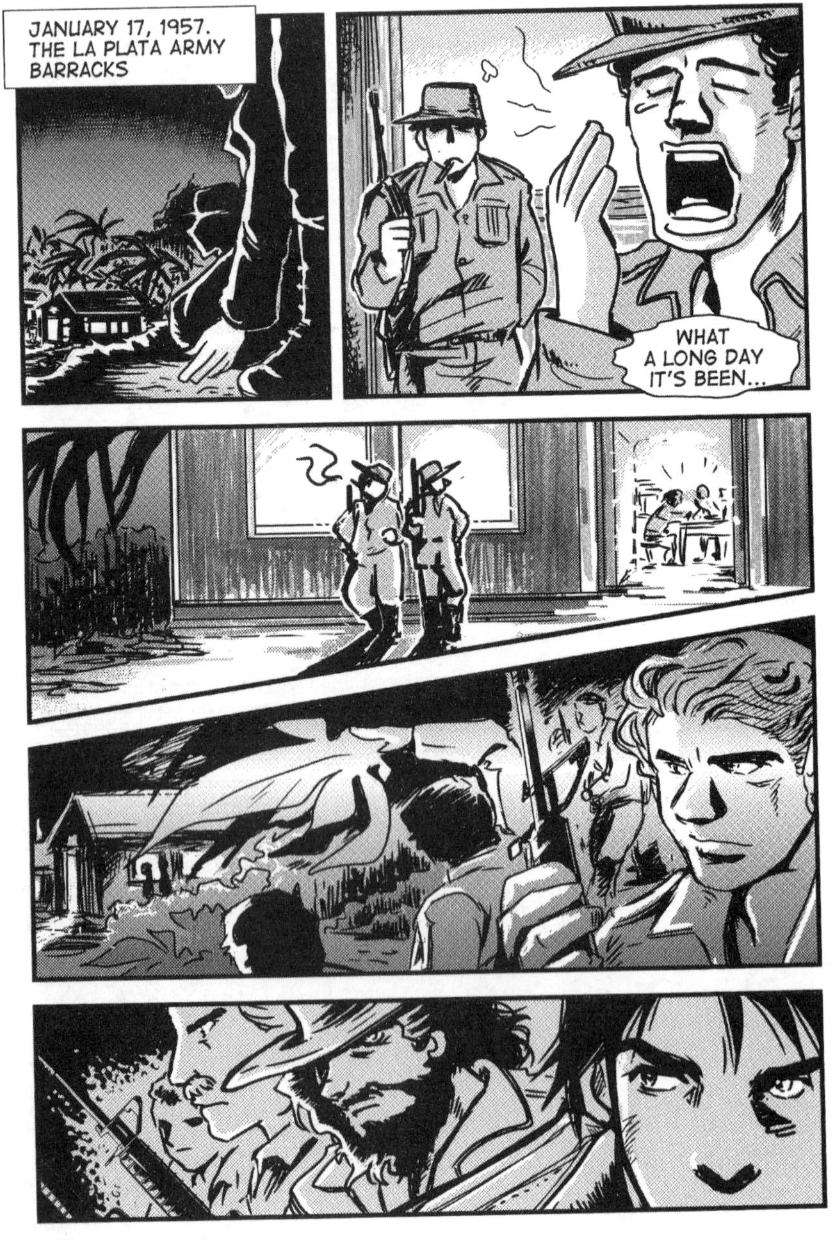
JANUARY 17, 1957. THE LA PLATA ARMY BARRACKS
WHAT A LONG DAY IT'S BEEN...

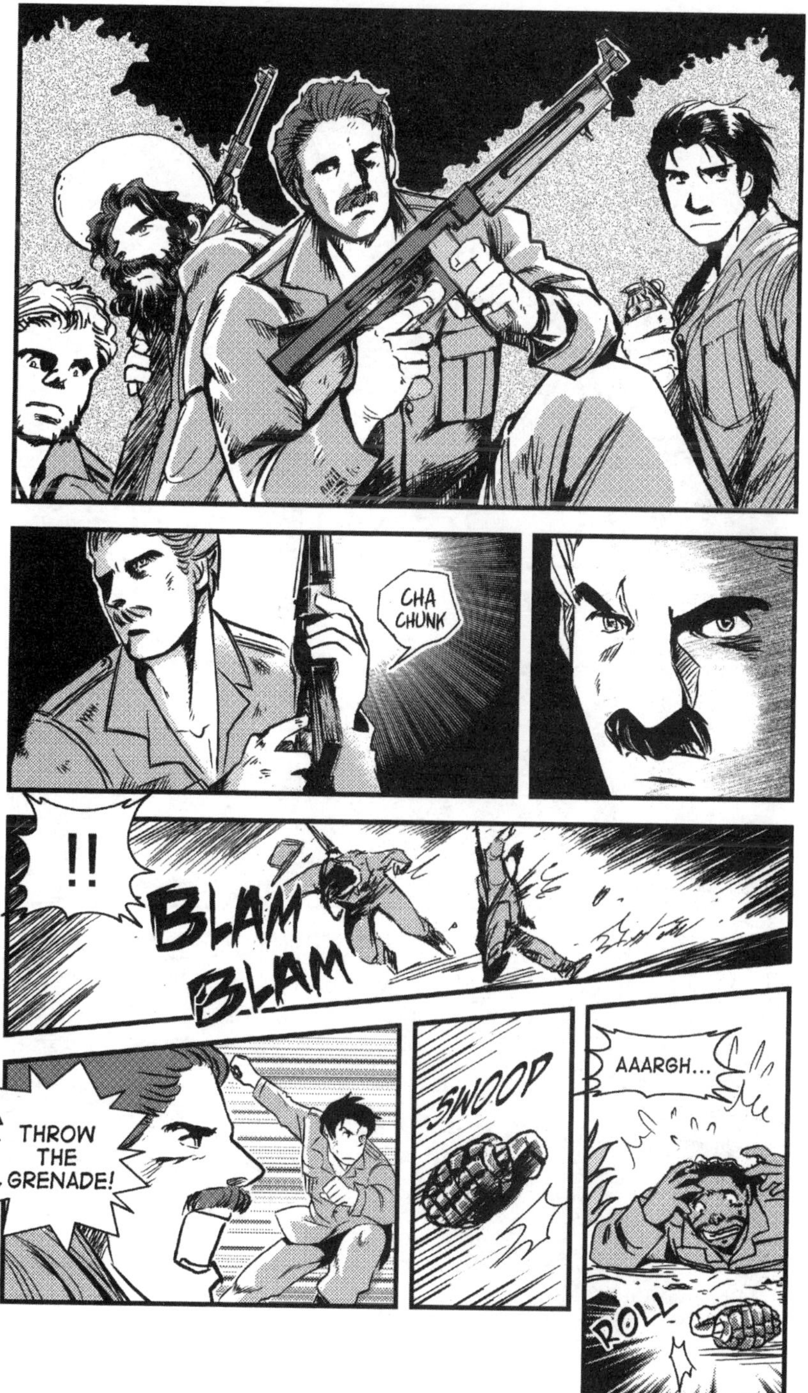
CHA CHUNK
!!
BLAM BLAM
THROW THE GRENADE!
SWOOP
AAARGH...
ROLL

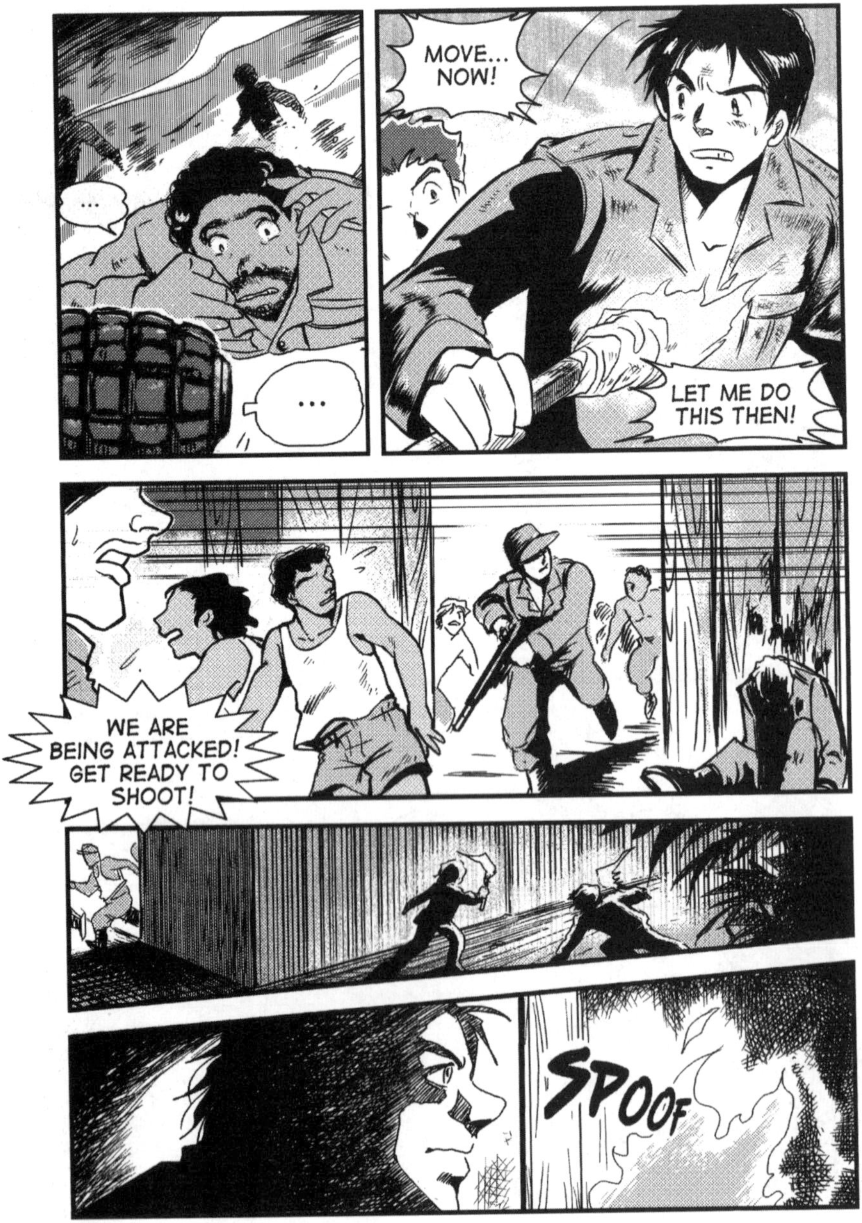
MOVE... NOW!
LET ME DO THIS THEN!
...
...
WE ARE BEING ATTACKED! GET READY TO SHOOT!
SPOOF

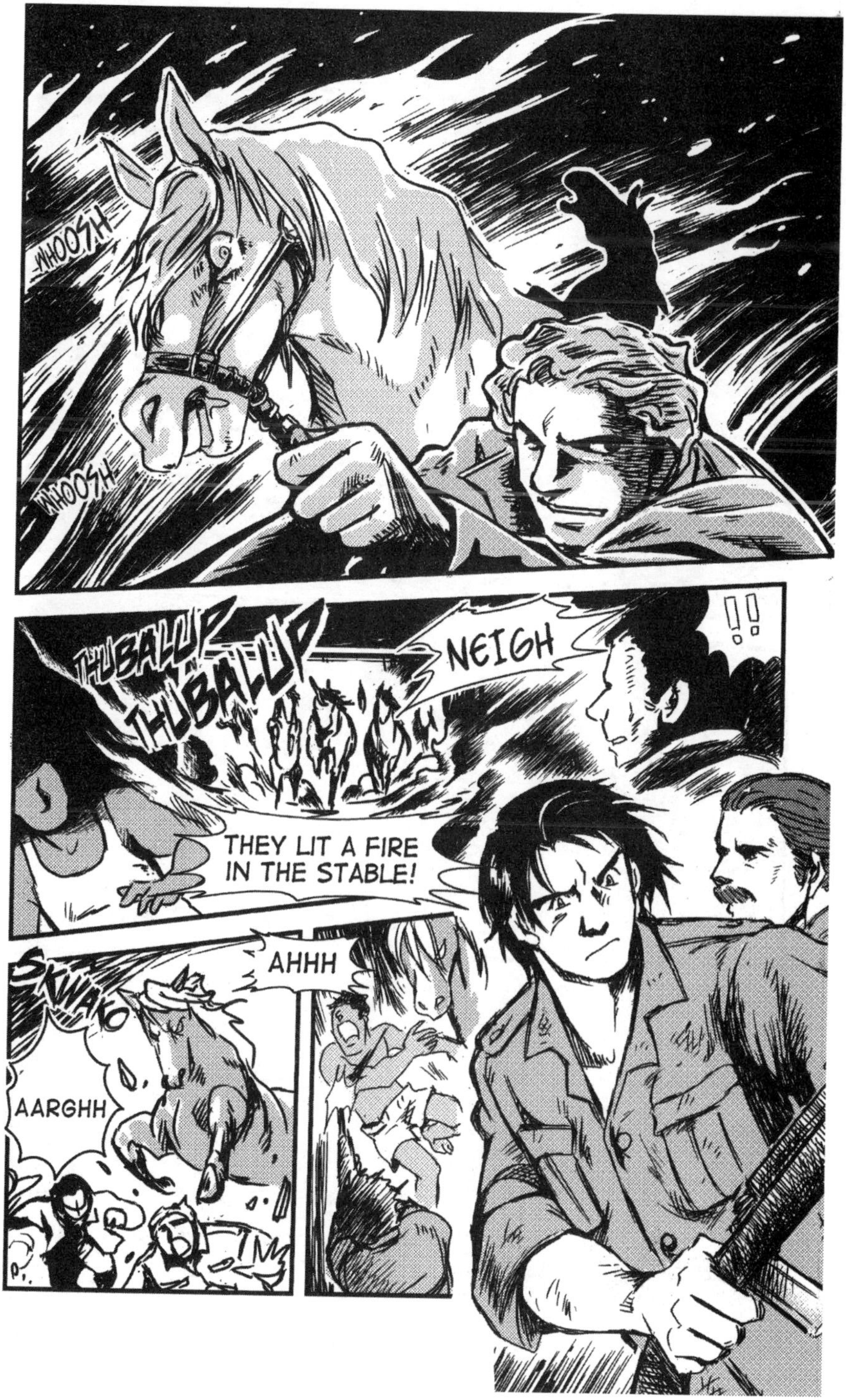
WHOOSH
WHOOSH
THUBALUP
THUBALUP
NEIGH
!!
THEY LIT A FIRE IN THE STABLE!
SKWAK
AARGHH
AHHH

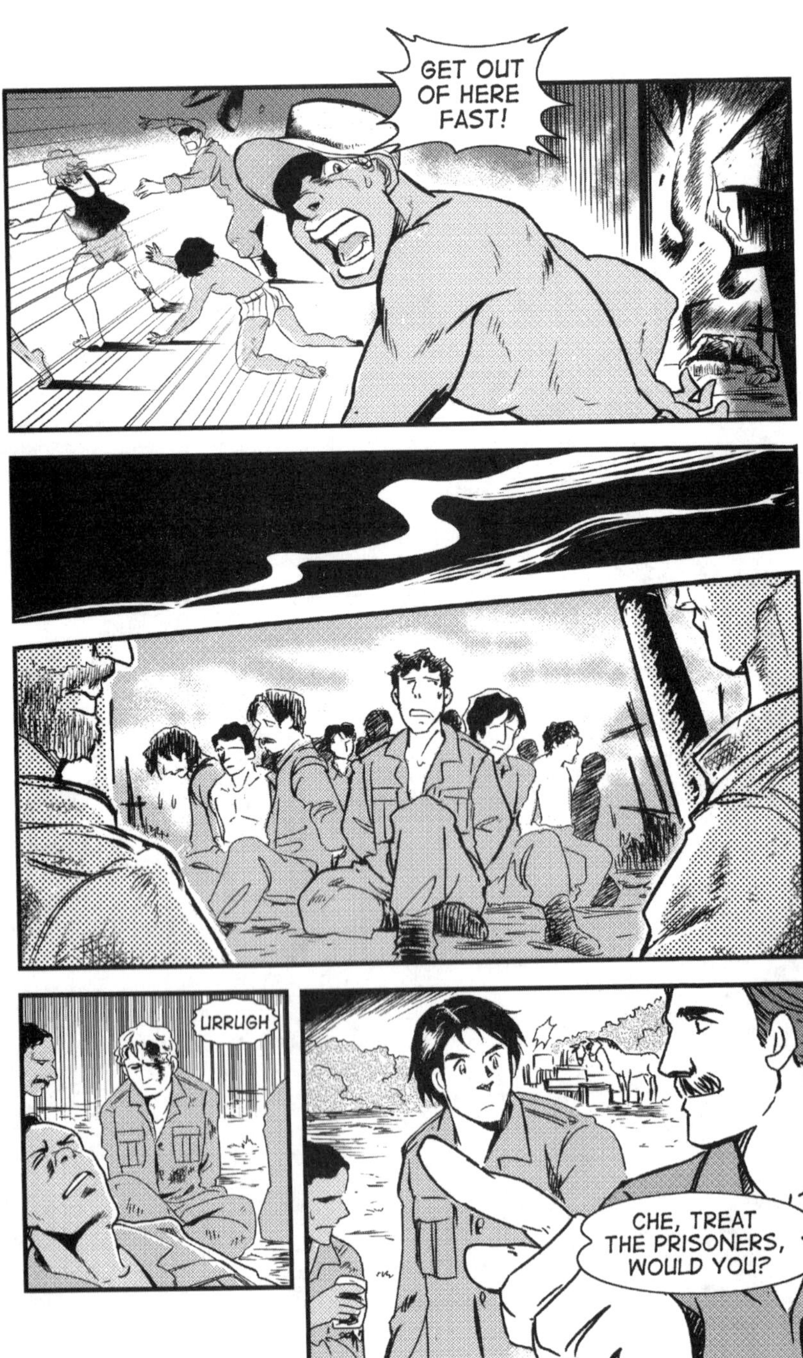
GET OUT OF HERE FAST!
CHE, TREAT THE PRISONERS, WOULD YOU?
URRUGH

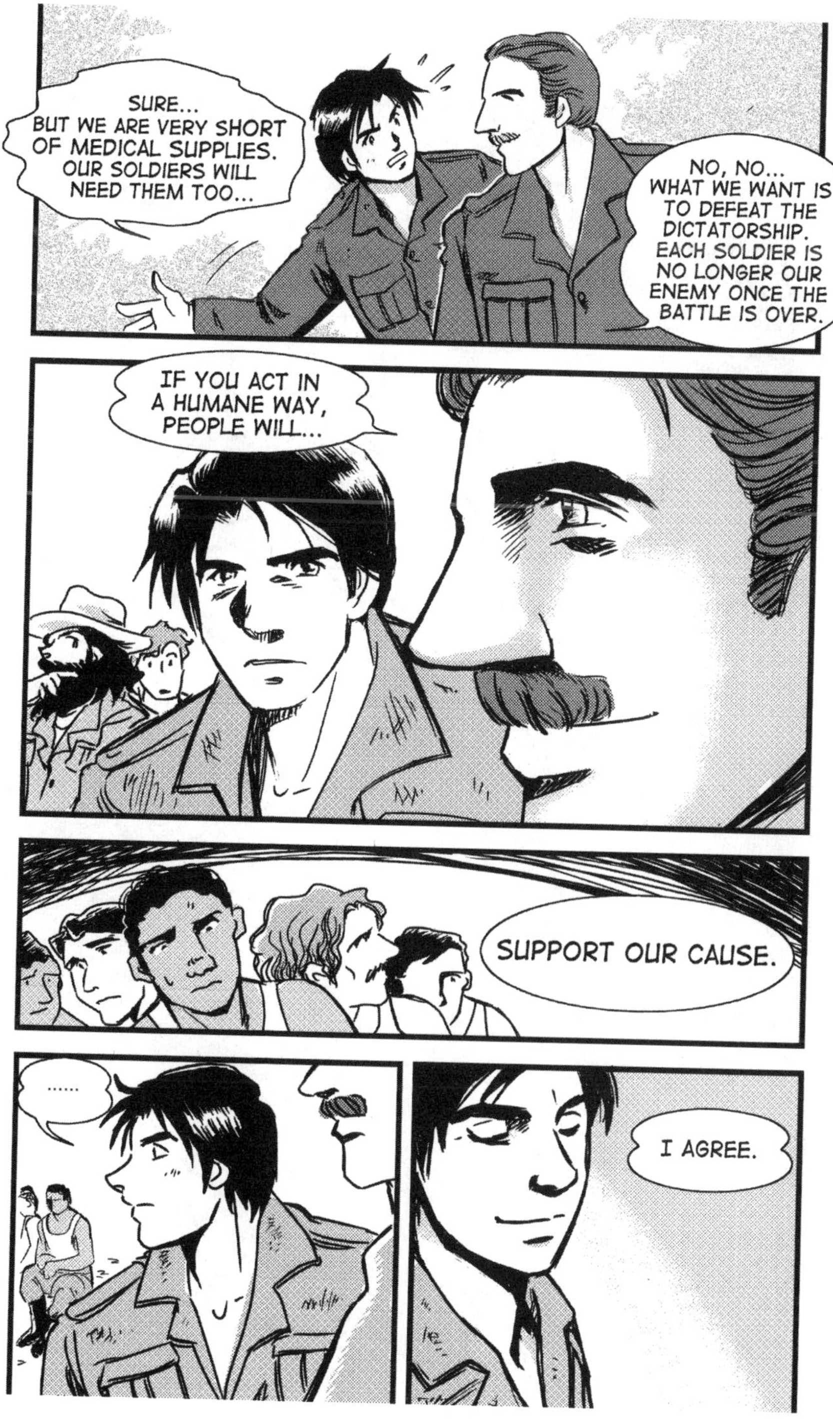
SURE... BUT WE ARE VERY SHORT OF MEDICAL SUPPLIES. OUR SOLDIERS WILL NEED THEM TOO...
NO, NO... WHAT WE WANT IS TO DEFEAT THE DICTATORSHIP. EACH SOLDIER IS NO LONGER OUR ENEMY ONCE THE BATTLE IS OVER.
IF YOU ACT IN A HUMANE WAY, PEOPLE WILL...
SUPPORT OUR CAUSE.
......
I AGREE.

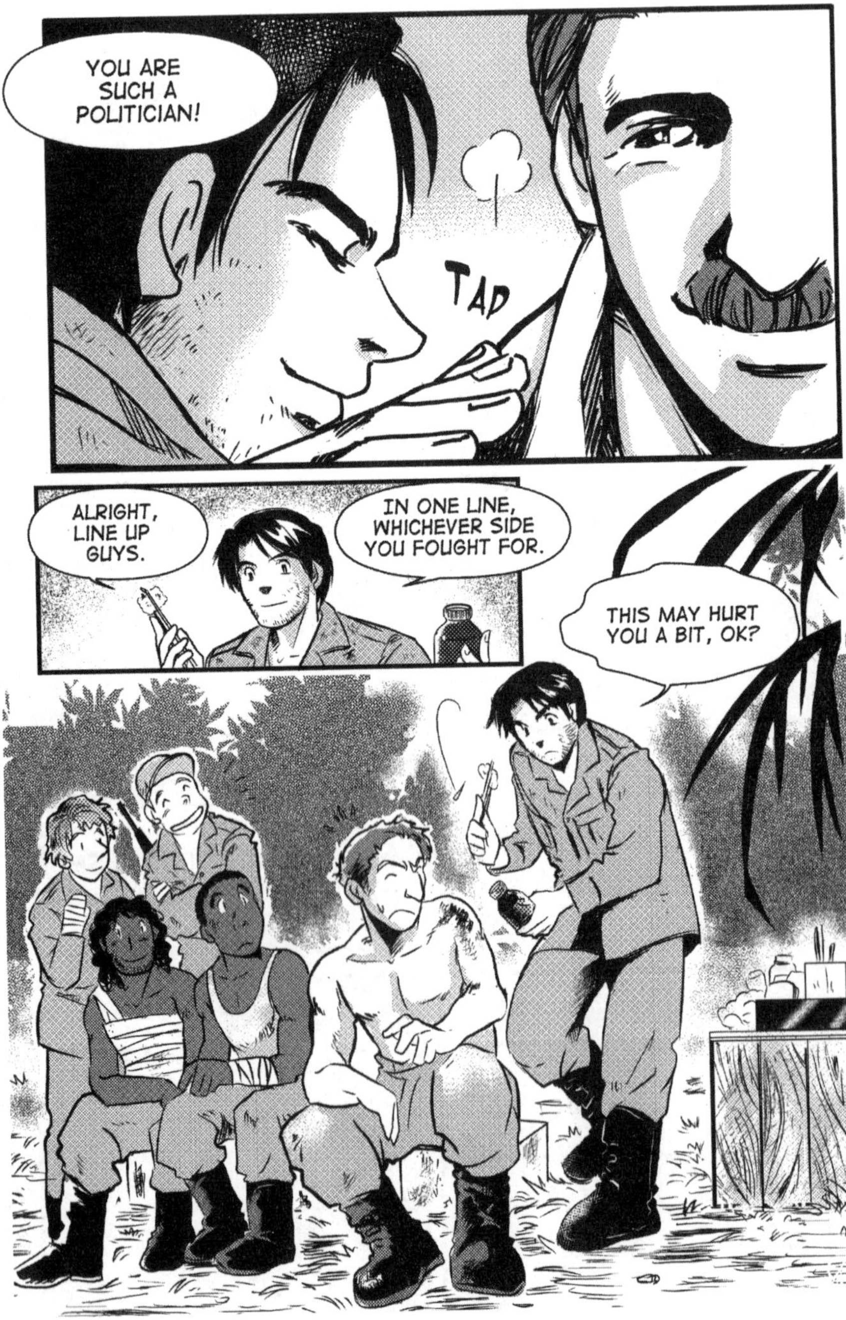
YOU ARE SUCH A POLITICIAN!
TAD
ALRIGHT, LINE UP GUYS.
IN ONE LINE, WHICHEVER SIDE YOU FOUGHT FOR.
THIS MAY HURT YOU A BIT, OK?

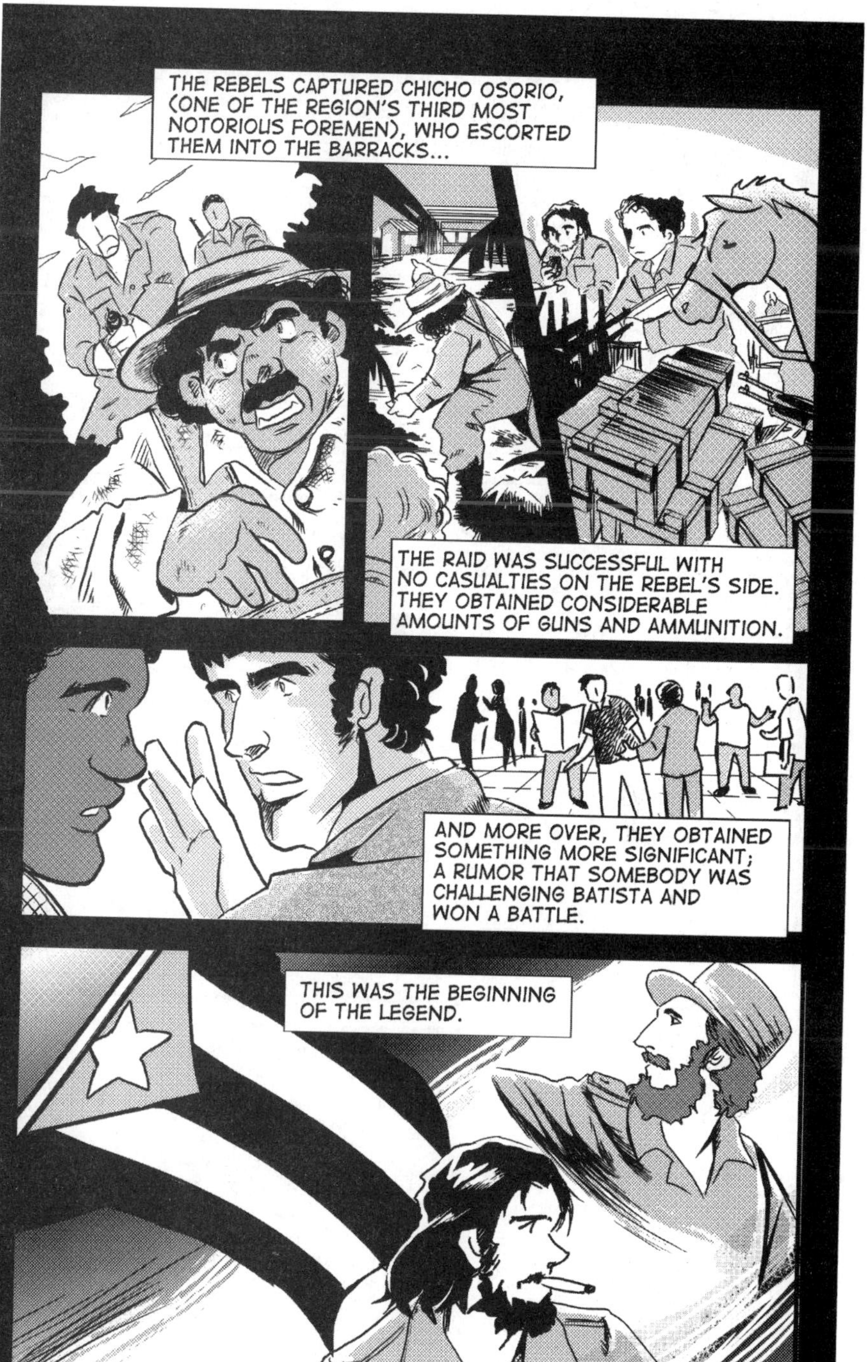
THE REBELS CAPTURED CHICHO OSORIO, (ONE OF THE REGION'S THIRD MOST NOTORIOUS FOREMEN), WHO ESCORTED THEM INTO THE BARRACKS...
THE RAID WAS SUCCESSFUL WITH NO CASUALTIES ON THE REBEL'S SIDE. THEY OBTAINED CONSIDERABLE AMOUNTS OF GUNS AND AMMUNITION.
AND MORE OVER, THEY OBTAINED SOMETHING MORE SIGNIFICANT; A RUMOR THAT SOMEBODY WAS CHALLENGING BATISTA AND WON A BATTLE.
THIS WAS THE BEGINNING OF THE LEGEND.

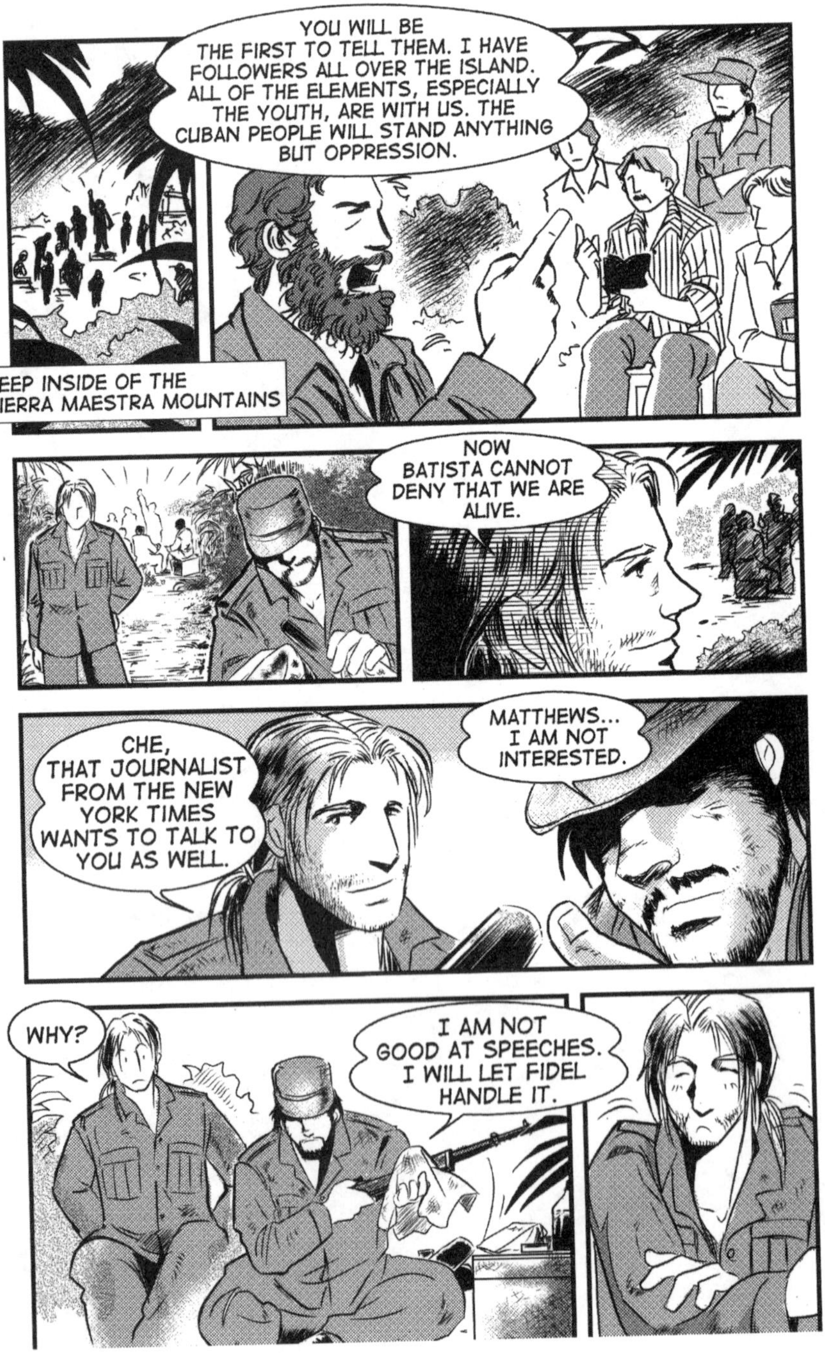
DEEP INSIDE OF THE SIERRA MAESTRA MOUNTAINS
YOU WILL BE THE FIRST TO TELL THEM. I HAVE FOLLOWERS ALL OVER THE ISLAND. ALL OF THE ELEMENTS, ESPECIALLY THE YOUTH, ARE WITH US. THE CUBAN PEOPLE WILL STAND ANYTHING BUT OPPRESSION.
NOW BATISTA CANNOT DENY THAT WE ARE ALIVE.
CHE, THAT JOURNALIST FROM THE NEW YORK TIMES WANTS TO TALK TO YOU AS WELL.
MATTHEWS... I AM NOT INTERESTED.
WHY?
I AM NOT GOOD AT SPEECHES. I WILL LET FIDEL HANDLE IT.

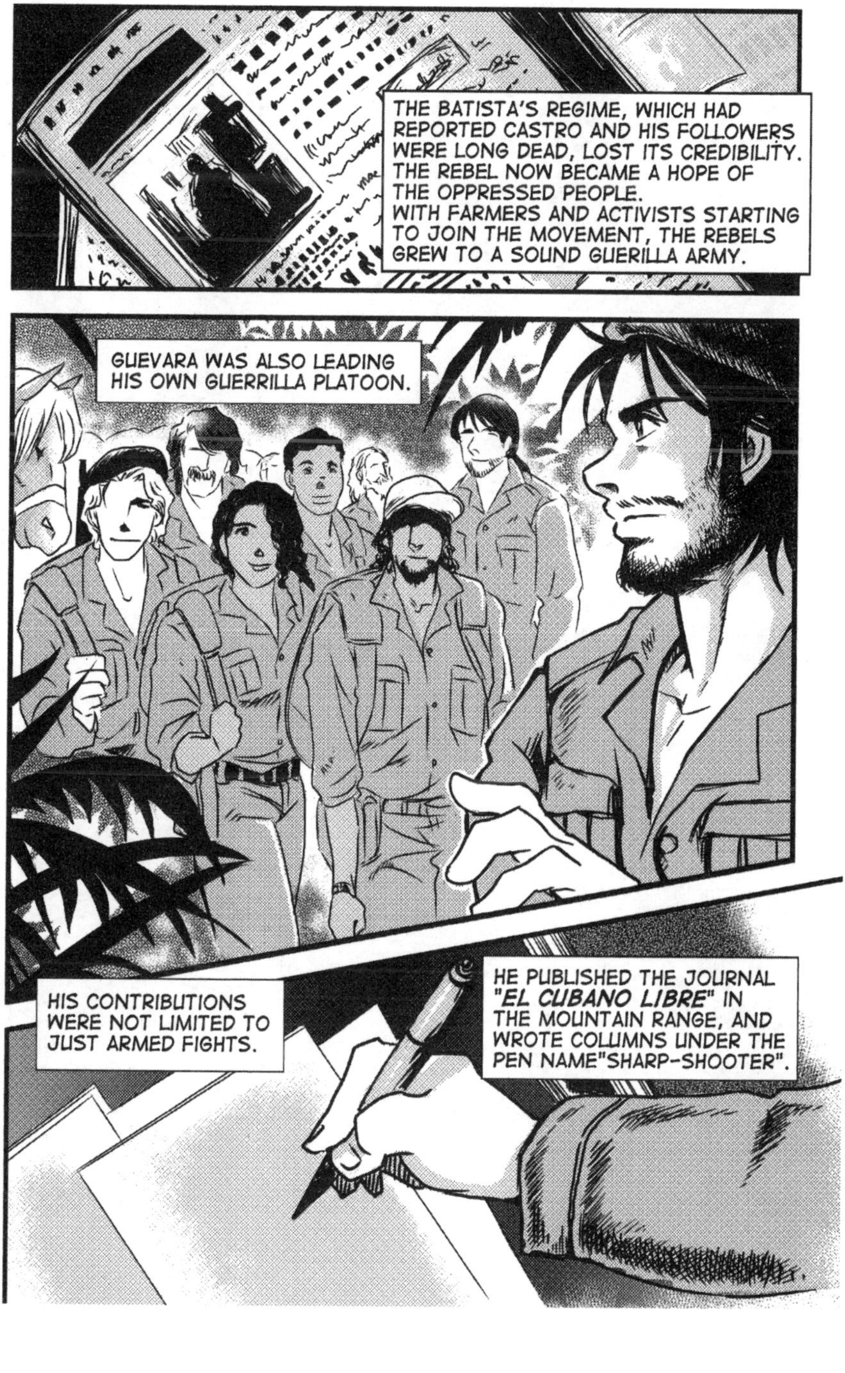
THE BATISTA'S REGIME, WHICH HAD REPORTED CASTRO AND HIS FOLLOWERS WERE LONG DEAD, LOST ITS CREDIBILITY. THE REBEL NOW BECAME A HOPE OF THE OPPRESSED PEOPLE.
WITH FARMERS AND ACTIVISTS STARTING TO JOIN THE MOVEMENT, THE REBELS GREW TO A SOUND GUERILLA ARMY.
GUEVARA WAS ALSO LEADING HIS OWN GUERRILLA PLATOON.
HIS CONTRIBUTIONS WERE NOT LIMITED TO JUST ARMED FIGHTS.
HE PUBLISHED THE JOURNAL "*EL CUBANO LIBRE*" IN THE MOUNTAIN RANGE, AND WROTE COLUMNS UNDER THE PEN NAME"SHARP-SHOOTER".

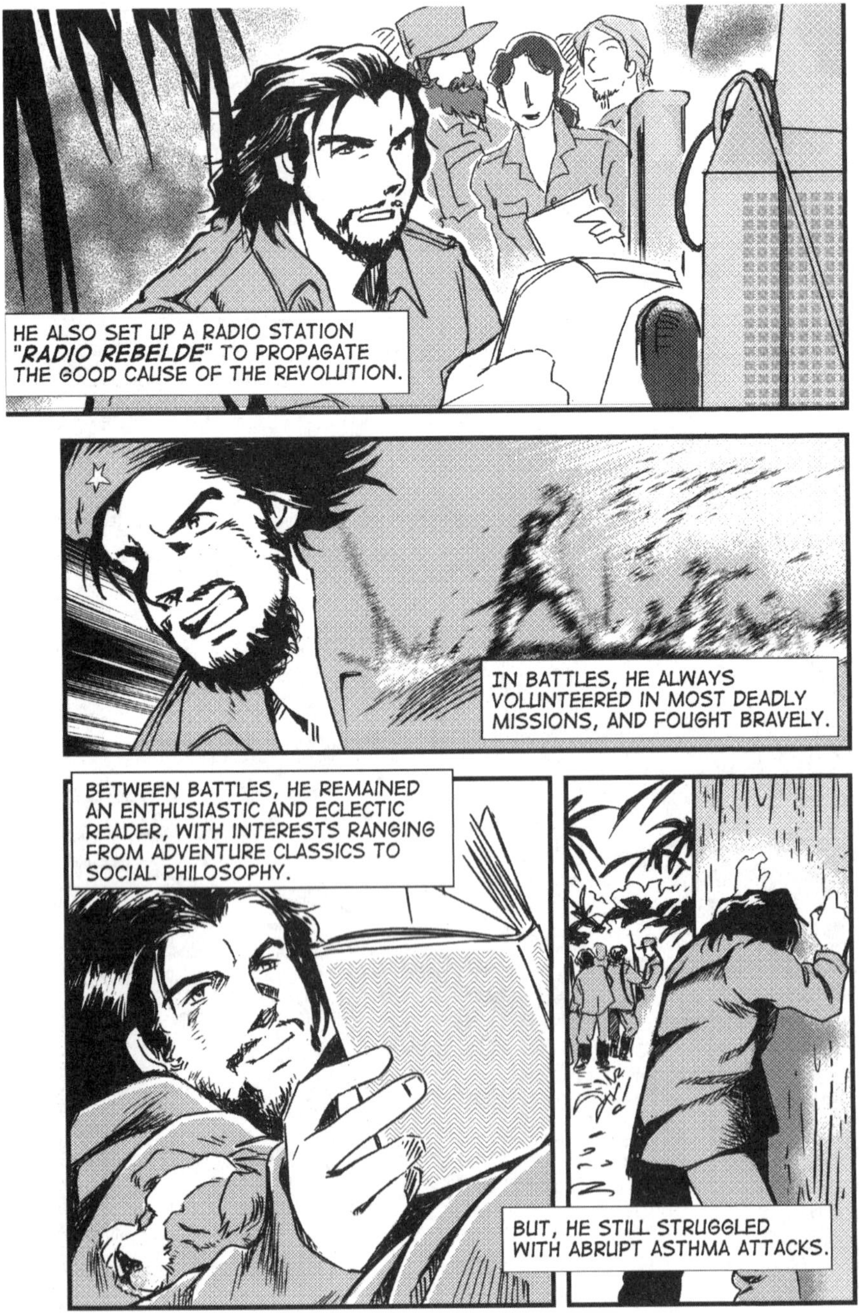
HE ALSO SET UP A RADIO STATION "RADIO REBELDE" TO PROPAGATE THE GOOD CAUSE OF THE REVOLUTION.
IN BATTLES, HE ALWAYS VOLUNTEERED IN MOST DEADLY MISSIONS, AND FOUGHT BRAVELY.
BETWEEN BATTLES, HE REMAINED AN ENTHUSIASTIC AND ECLECTIC READER, WITH INTERESTS RANGING FROM ADVENTURE CLASSICS TO SOCIAL PHILOSOPHY.
BUT, HE STILL STRUGGLED WITH ABRUPT ASTHMA ATTACKS.

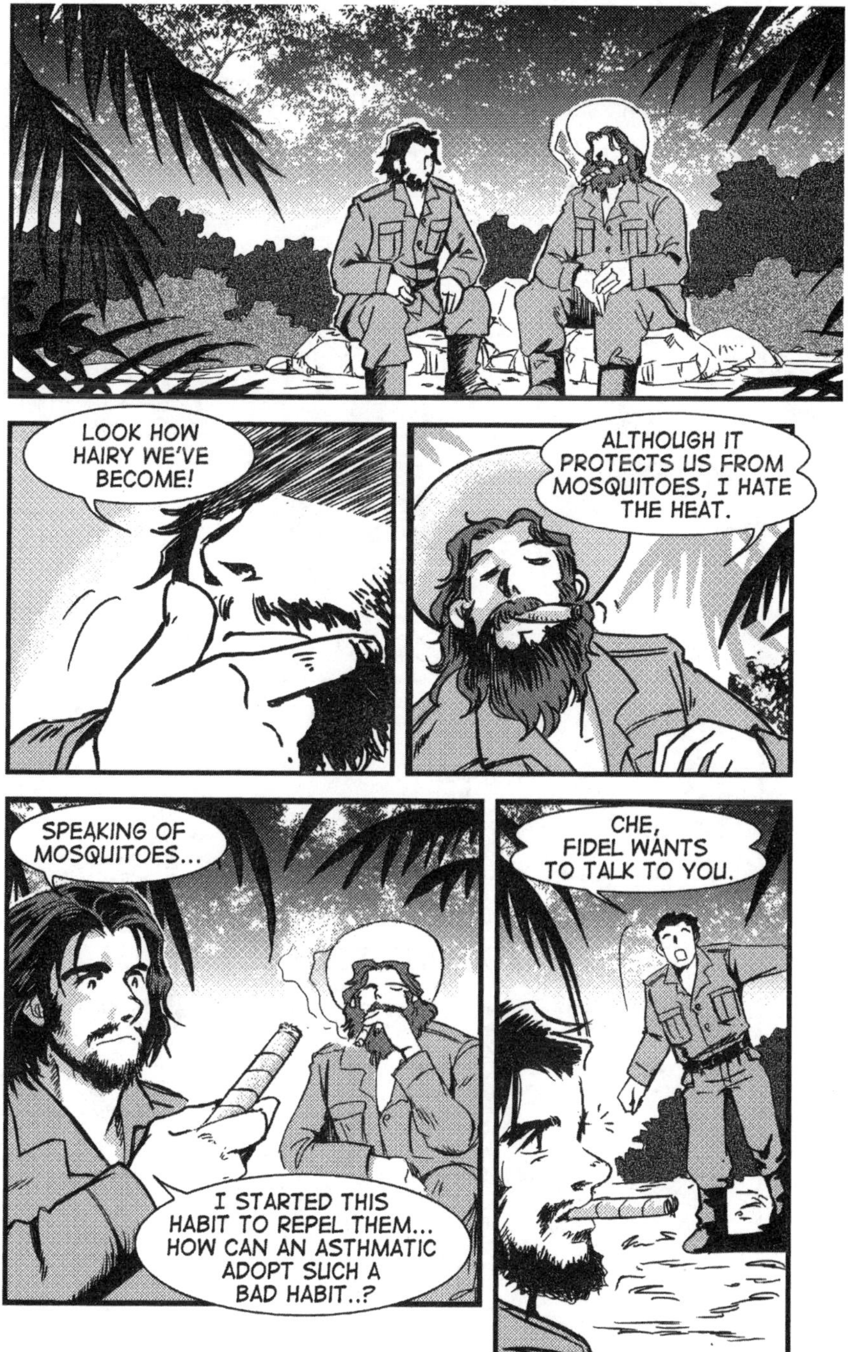
LOOK HOW HAIRY WE'VE BECOME!
ALTHOUGH IT PROTECTS US FROM MOSQUITOES, I HATE THE HEAT.
SPEAKING OF MOSQUITOES...
I STARTED THIS HABIT TO REPEL THEM... HOW CAN AN ASTHMATIC ADOPT SUCH A BAD HABIT..?
CHE, FIDEL WANTS TO TALK TO YOU.

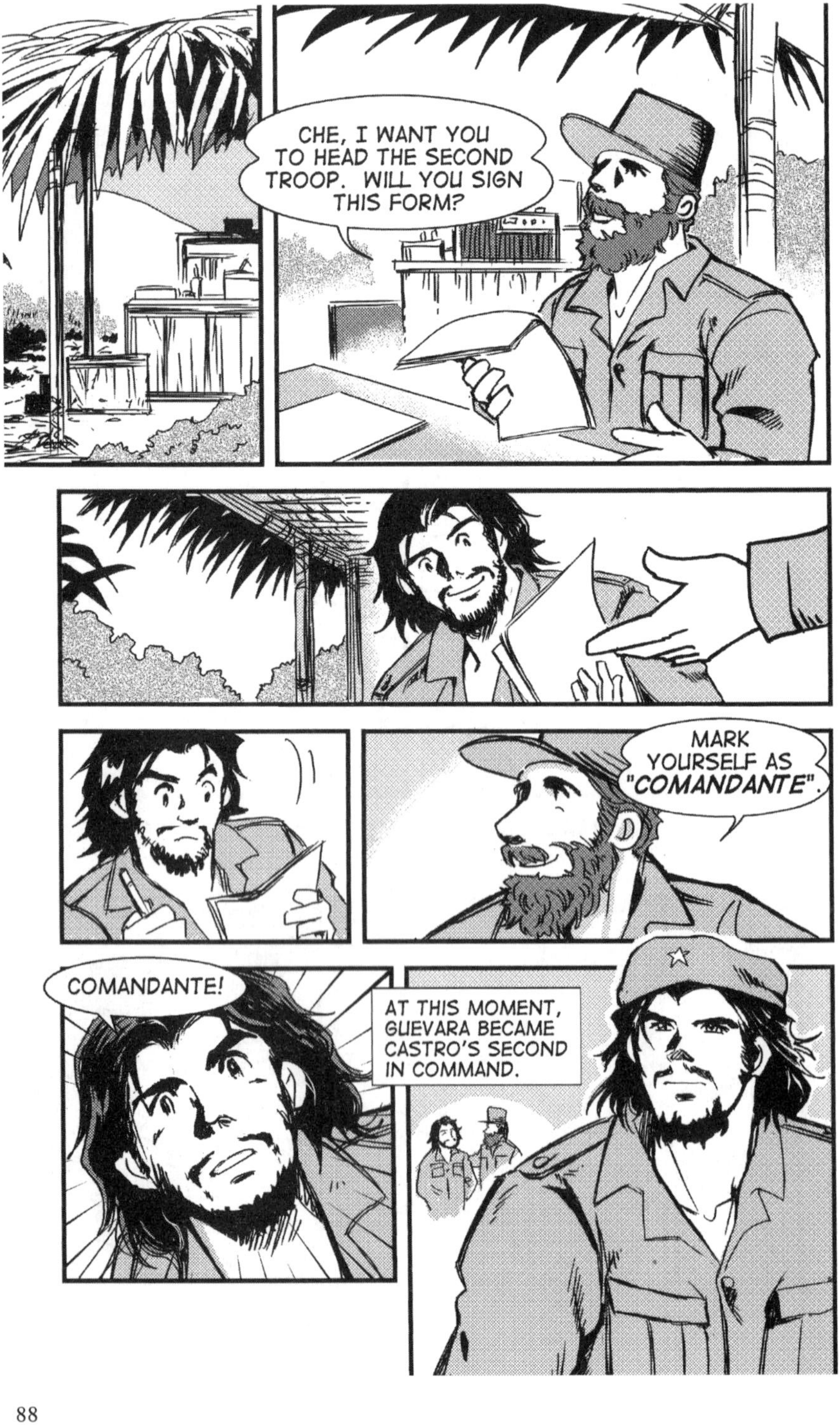
CHE, I WANT YOU TO HEAD THE SECOND TROOP. WILL YOU SIGN THIS FORM?
MARK YOURSELF AS "COMANDANTE".
COMANDANTE!
AT THIS MOMENT, GUEVARA BECAME CASTRO'S SECOND IN COMMAND.

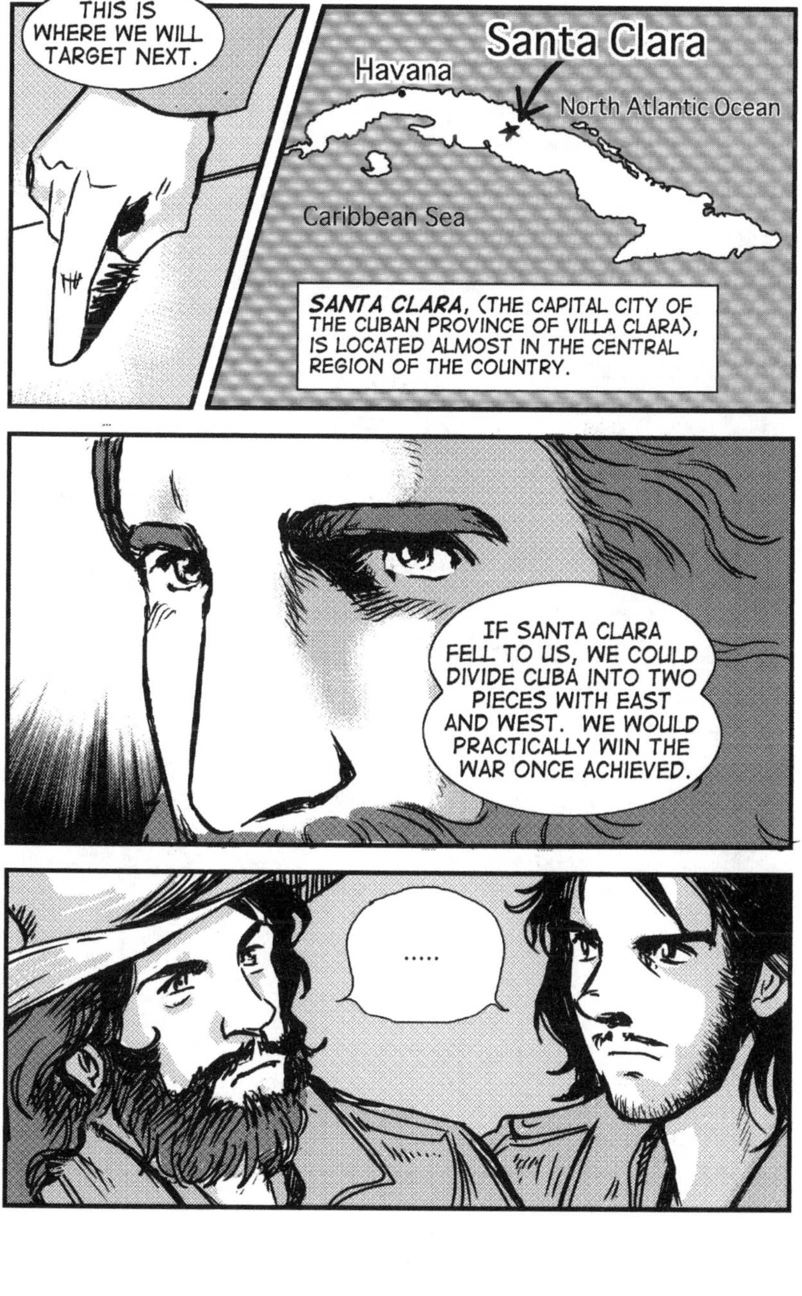
THIS IS WHERE WE WILL TARGET NEXT.
Santa Clara
Havana
North Atlantic Ocean
Caribbean Sea
SANTA CLARA, (THE CAPITAL CITY OF THE CUBAN PROVINCE OF VILLA CLARA), IS LOCATED ALMOST IN THE CENTRAL REGION OF THE COUNTRY.
IF SANTA CLARA FELL TO US, WE COULD DIVIDE CUBA INTO TWO PIECES WITH EAST AND WEST. WE WOULD PRACTICALLY WIN THE WAR ONCE ACHIEVED.
.....

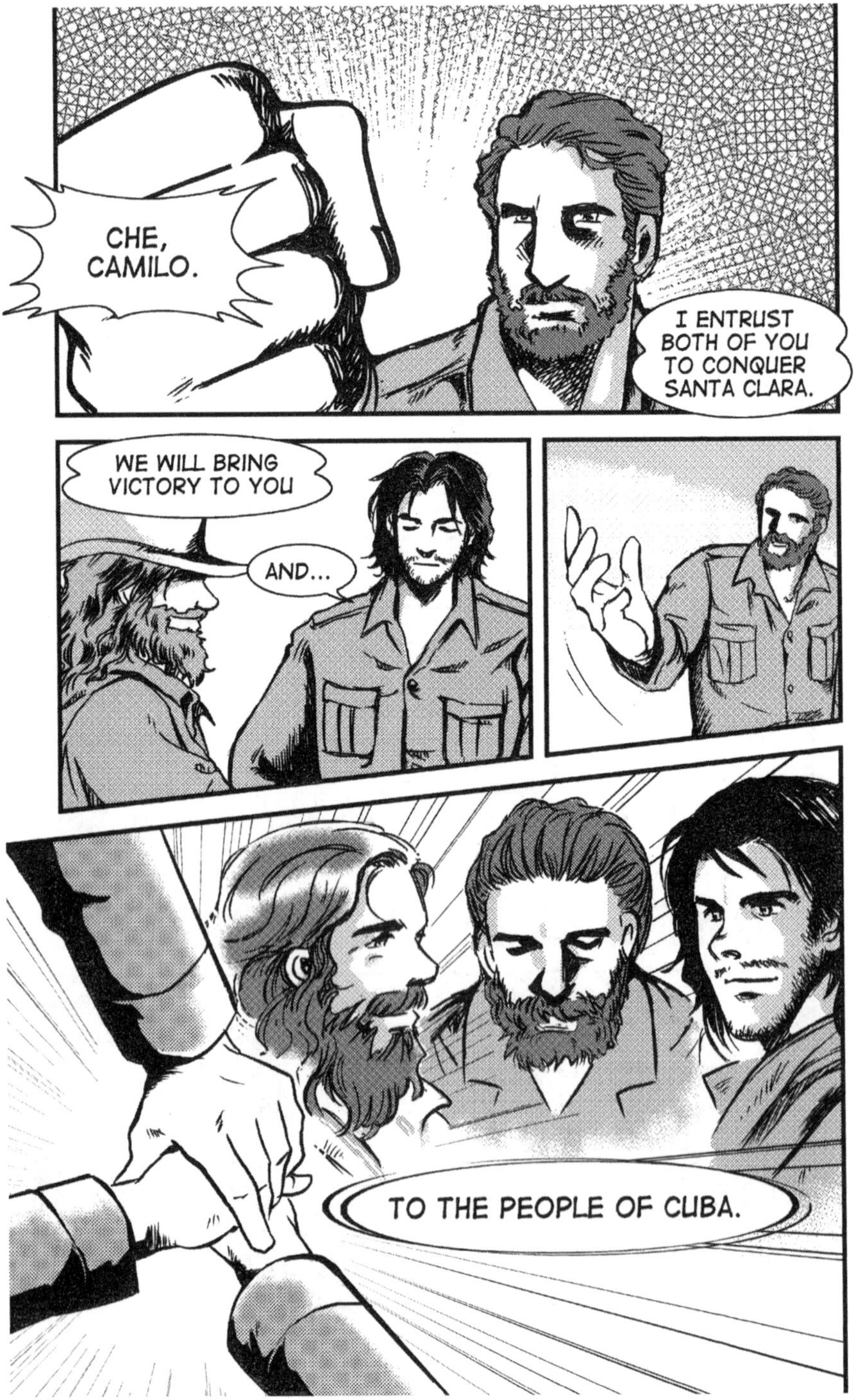
CHE, CAMILO.
I ENTRUST BOTH OF YOU TO CONQUER SANTA CLARA.
WE WILL BRING VICTORY TO YOU
AND...
TO THE PEOPLE OF CUBA.

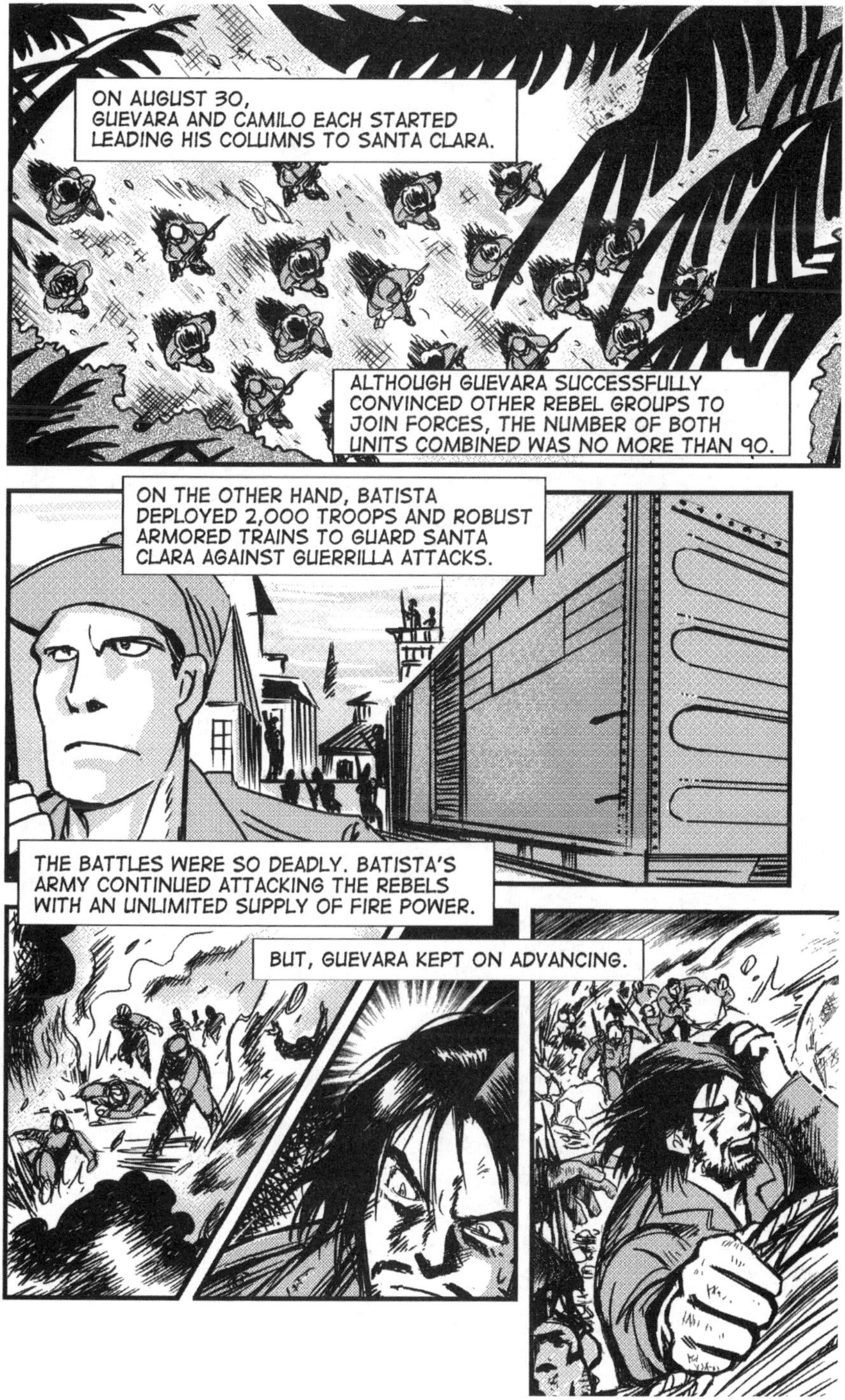
ON AUGUST 30, GUEVARA AND CAMILO EACH STARTED LEADING HIS COLUMNS TO SANTA CLARA.
ALTHOUGH GUEVARA SUCCESSFULLY CONVINCED OTHER REBEL GROUPS TO JOIN FORCES, THE NUMBER OF BOTH UNITS COMBINED WAS NO MORE THAN 90.
ON THE OTHER HAND, BATISTA DEPLOYED 2,000 TROOPS AND ROBUST ARMORED TRAINS TO GUARD SANTA CLARA AGAINST GUERRILLA ATTACKS.
THE BATTLES WERE SO DEADLY. BATISTA'S ARMY CONTINUED ATTACKING THE REBELS WITH AN UNLIMITED SUPPLY OF FIRE POWER.
BUT, GUEVARA KEPT ON ADVANCING.

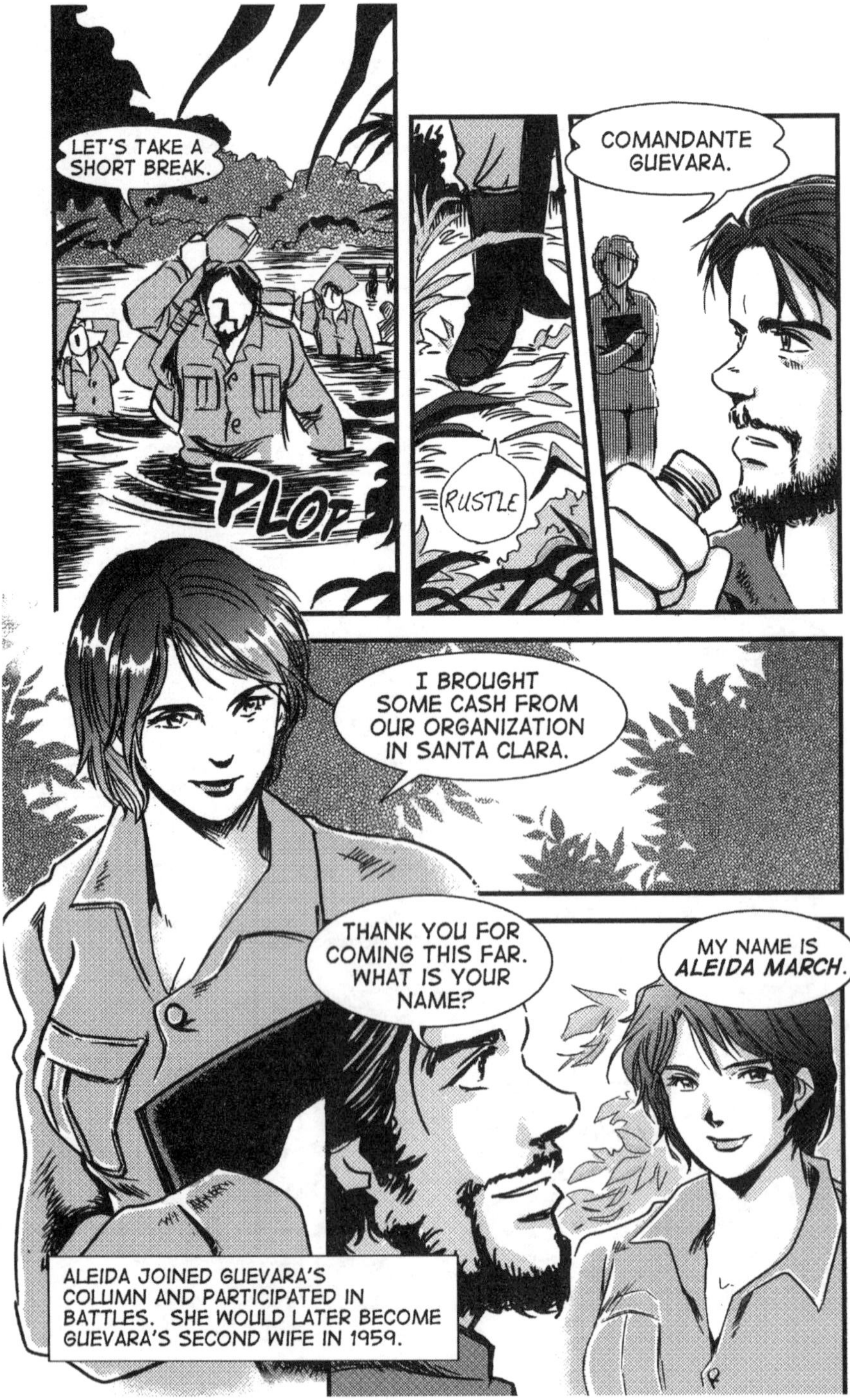
LET'S TAKE A SHORT BREAK.
PLOP
RUSTLE
COMANDANTE GUEVARA.
I BROUGHT SOME CASH FROM OUR ORGANIZATION IN SANTA CLARA.
THANK YOU FOR COMING THIS FAR. WHAT IS YOUR NAME?
MY NAME IS ALEIDA MARCH.
ALEIDA JOINED GUEVARA'S COLUMN AND PARTICIPATED IN BATTLES. SHE WOULD LATER BECOME GUEVARA'S SECOND WIFE IN 1959.

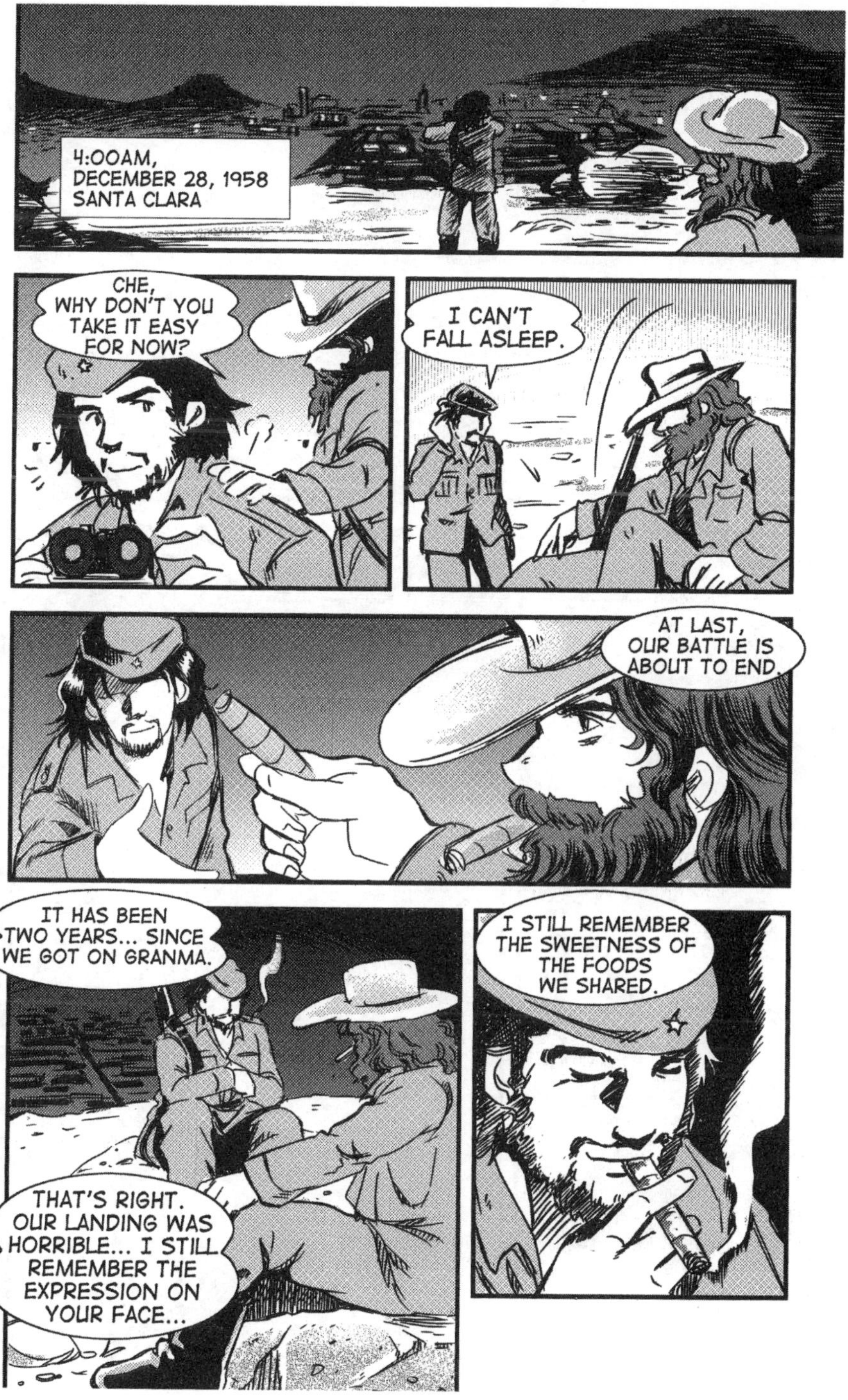
4:00AM,
DECEMBER 28, 1958
SANTA CLARA
CHE, WHY DON'T YOU TAKE IT EASY FOR NOW?
I CAN'T FALL ASLEEP.
AT LAST, OUR BATTLE IS ABOUT TO END.
IT HAS BEEN TWO YEARS... SINCE WE GOT ON GRANMA.
THAT'S RIGHT. OUR LANDING WAS HORRIBLE... I STILL REMEMBER THE EXPRESSION ON YOUR FACE...
I STILL REMEMBER THE SWEETNESS OF THE FOODS WE SHARED.

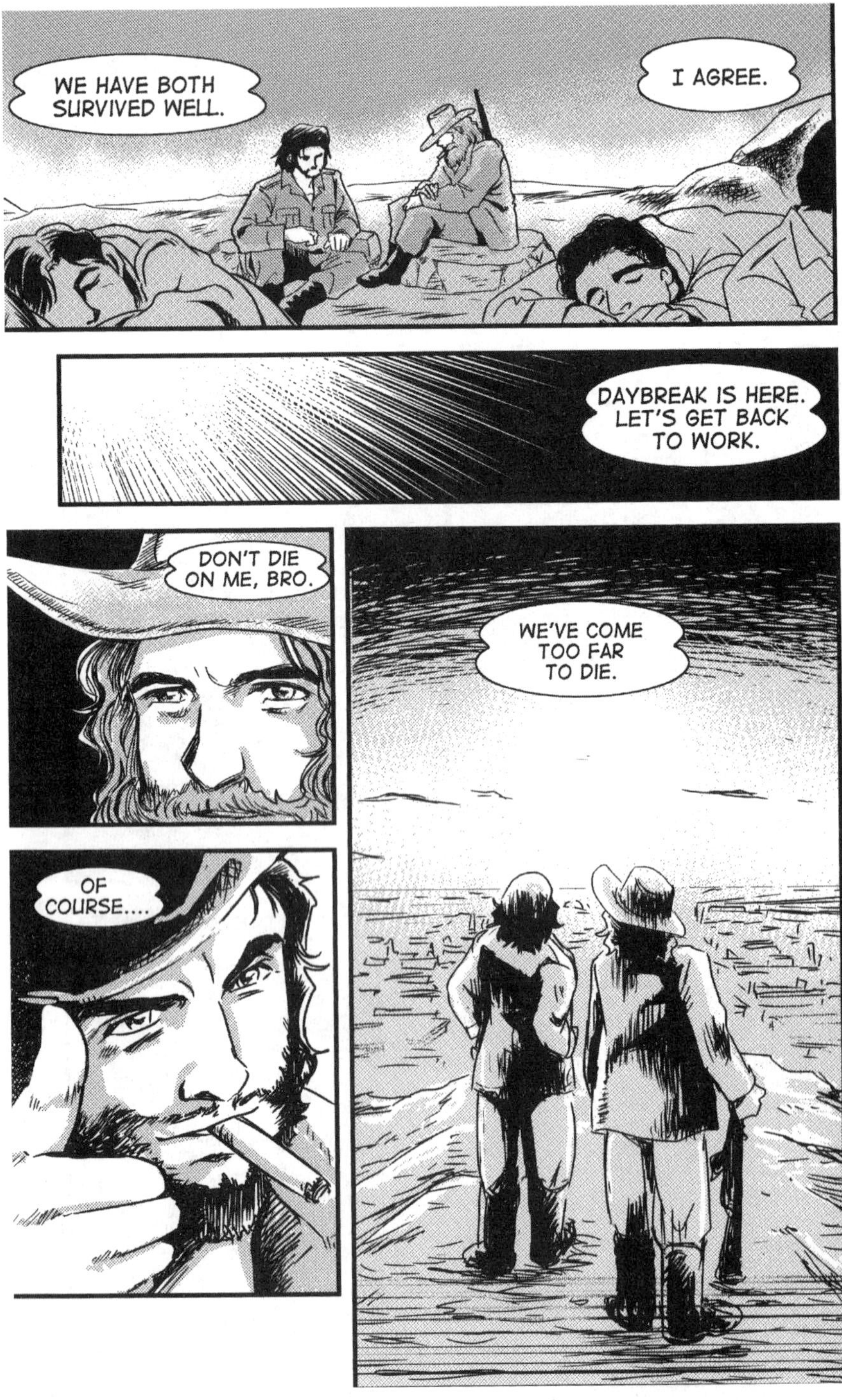
WE HAVE BOTH SURVIVED WELL.
I AGREE.
DAYBREAK IS HERE. LET'S GET BACK TO WORK.
DON'T DIE ON ME, BRO.
OF COURSE....
WE'VE COME TOO FAR TO DIE.

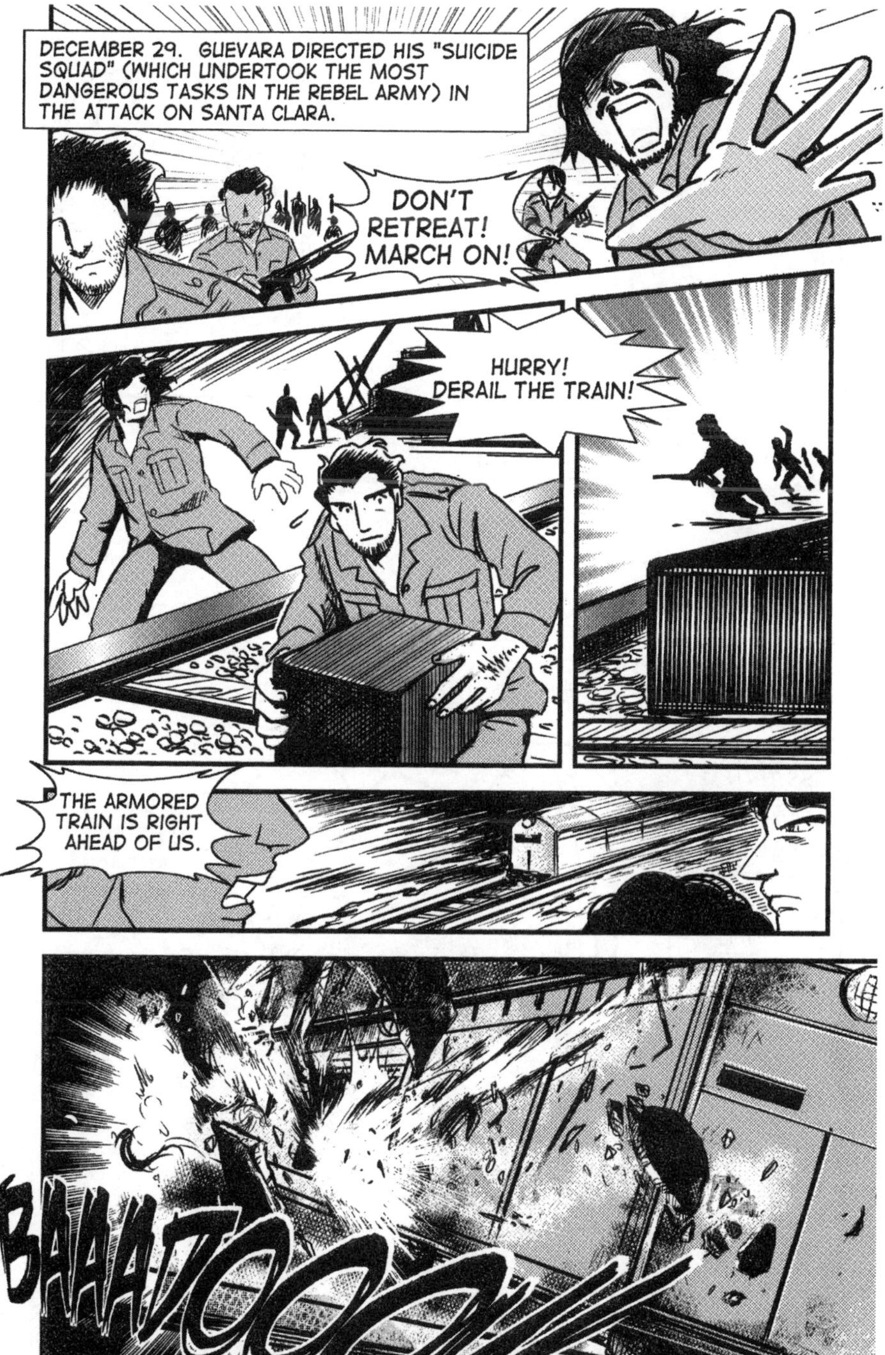
DECEMBER 29. GUEVARA DIRECTED HIS "SUICIDE SQUAD" (WHICH UNDERTOOK THE MOST DANGEROUS TASKS IN THE REBEL ARMY) IN THE ATTACK ON SANTA CLARA.
DON'T RETREAT! MARCH ON!
HURRY! DERAIL THE TRAIN!
THE ARMORED TRAIN IS RIGHT AHEAD OF US.

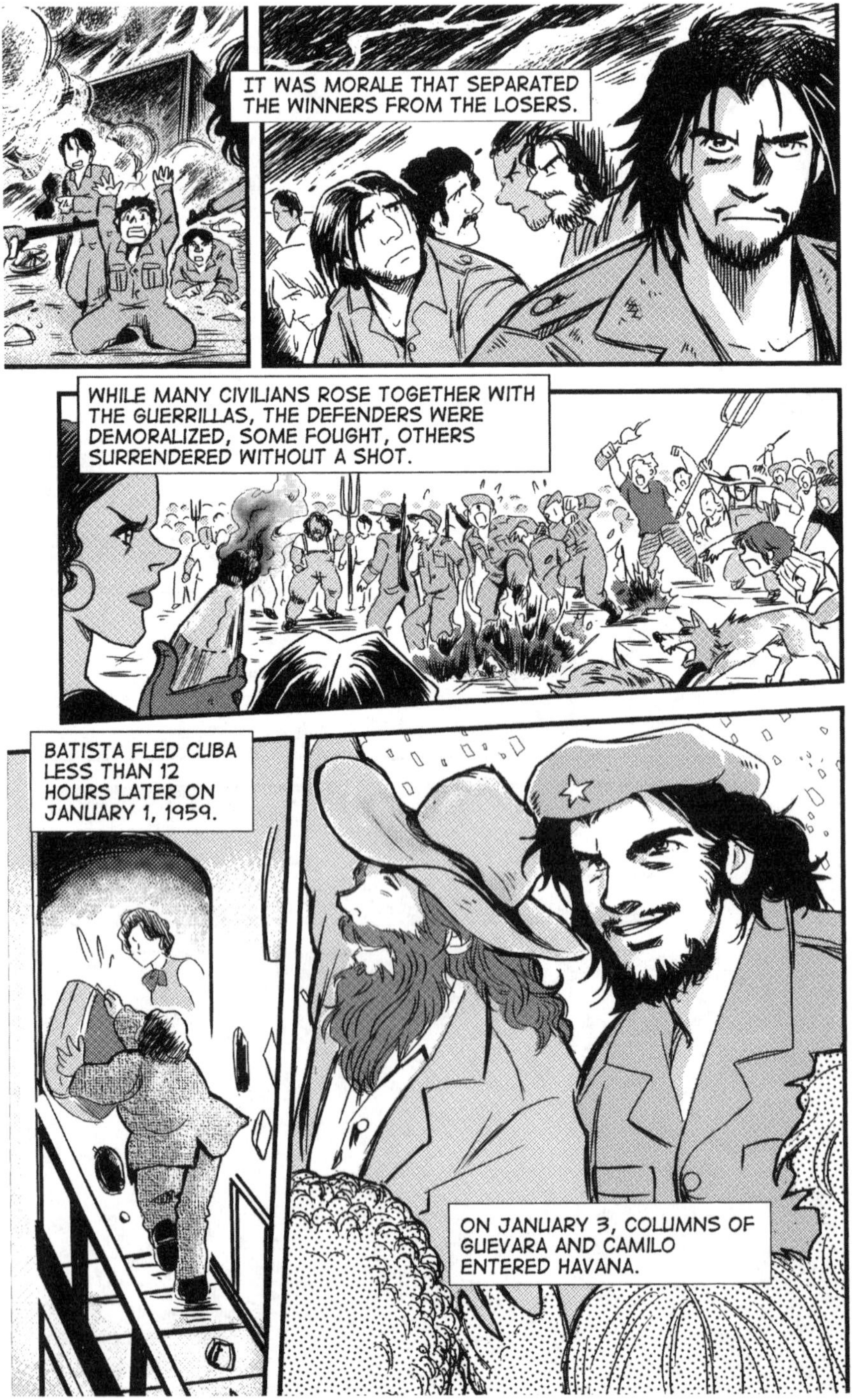
IT WAS MORALE THAT SEPARATED THE WINNERS FROM THE LOSERS.
WHILE MANY CIVILIANS ROSE TOGETHER WITH THE GUERRILLAS, THE DEFENDERS WERE DEMORALIZED, SOME FOUGHT, OTHERS SURRENDERED WITHOUT A SHOT.
BATISTA FLED CUBA LESS THAN 12 HOURS LATER ON JANUARY 1, 1959.
ON JANUARY 3, COLUMNS OF GUEVARA AND CAMILO ENTERED HAVANA.

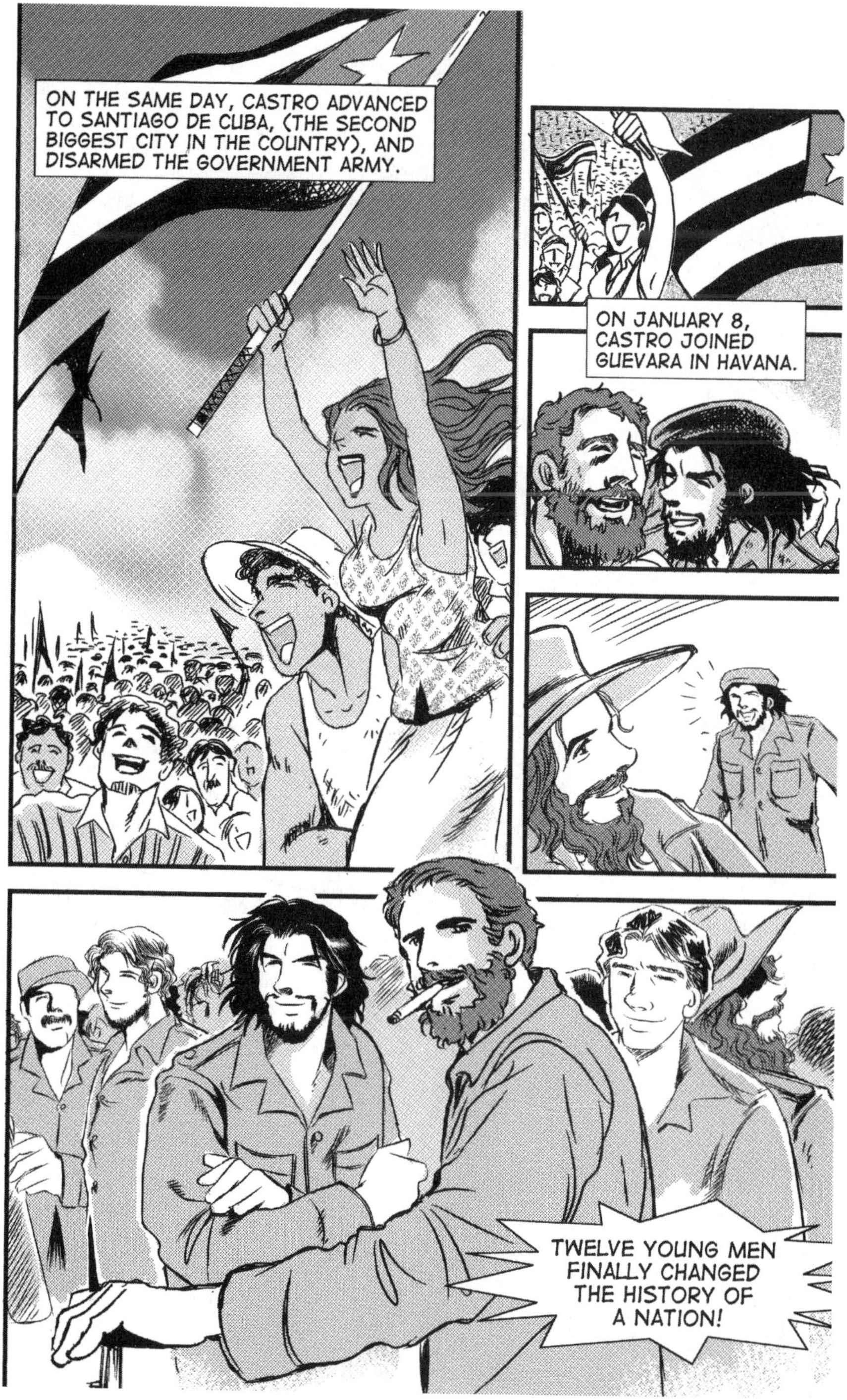
ON THE SAME DAY, CASTRO ADVANCED TO SANTIAGO DE CUBA, (THE SECOND BIGGEST CITY IN THE COUNTRY), AND DISARMED THE GOVERNMENT ARMY.
ON JANUARY 8, CASTRO JOINED GUEVARA IN HAVANA.
TWELVE YOUNG MEN FINALLY CHANGED THE HISTORY OF A NATION!

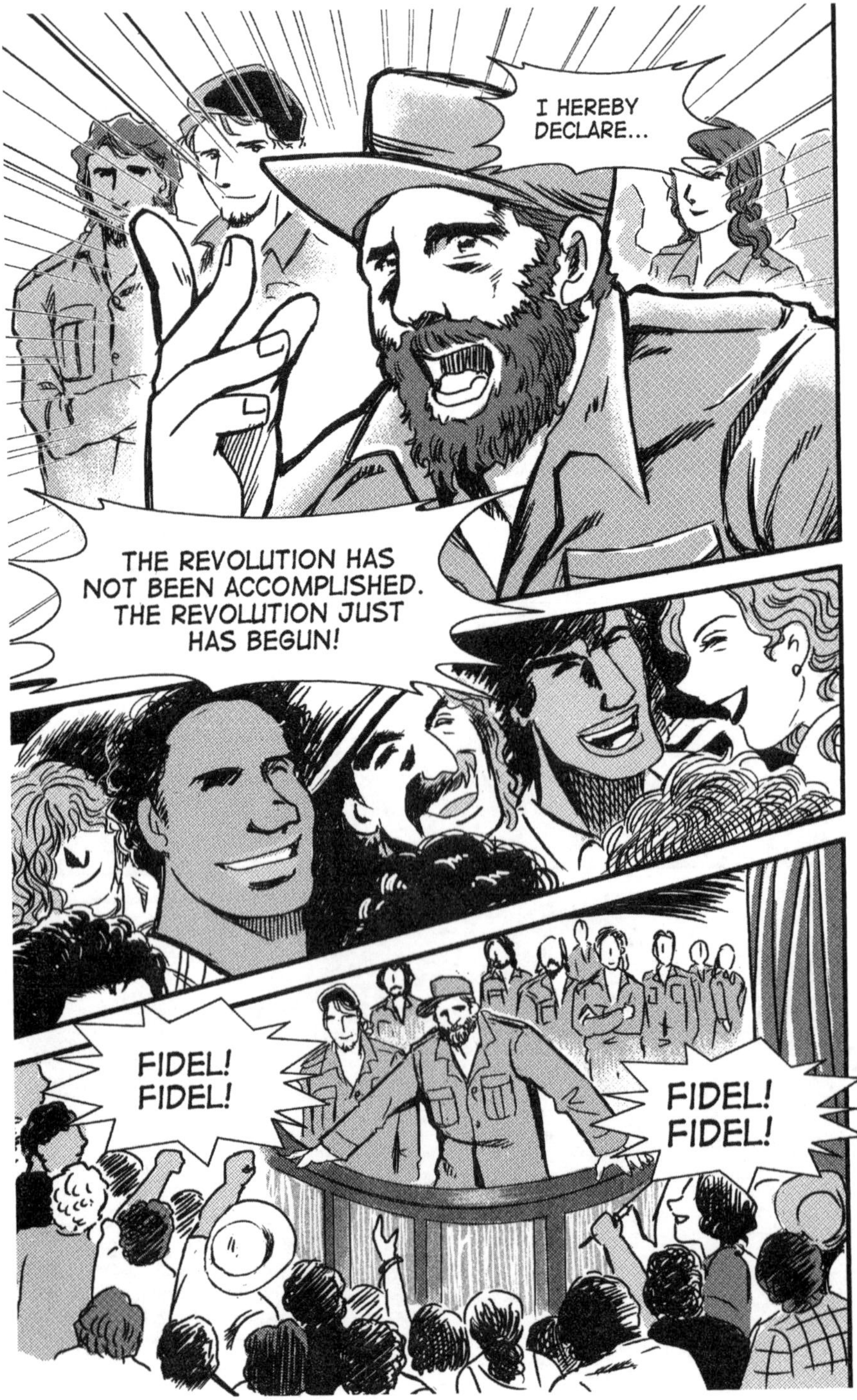
I HEREBY DECLARE...
THE REVOLUTION HAS NOT BEEN ACCOMPLISHED. THE REVOLUTION JUST HAS BEGUN!
FIDEL! FIDEL!
FIDEL! FIDEL!

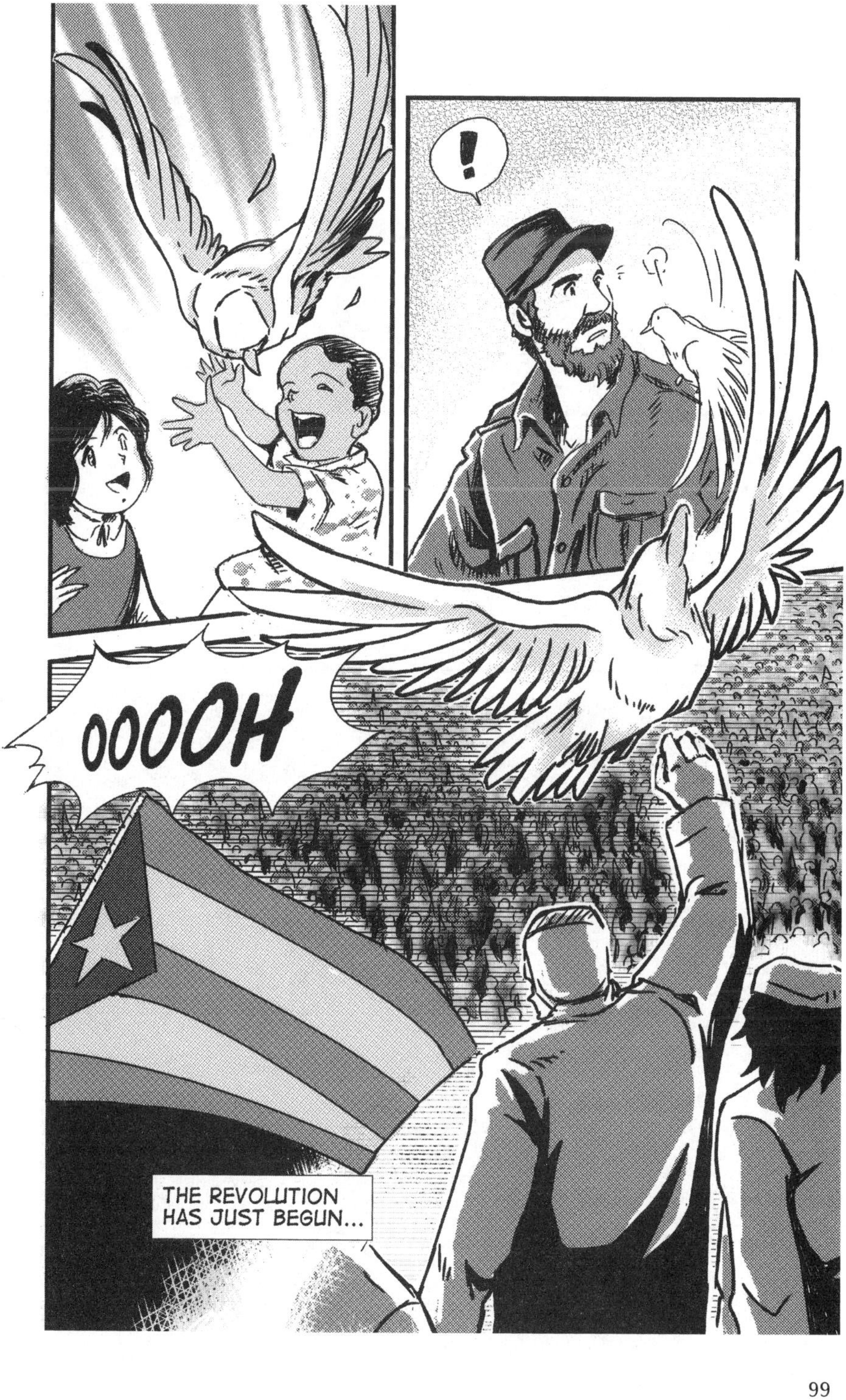
!
OOOOH
THE REVOLUTION HAS JUST BEGUN...

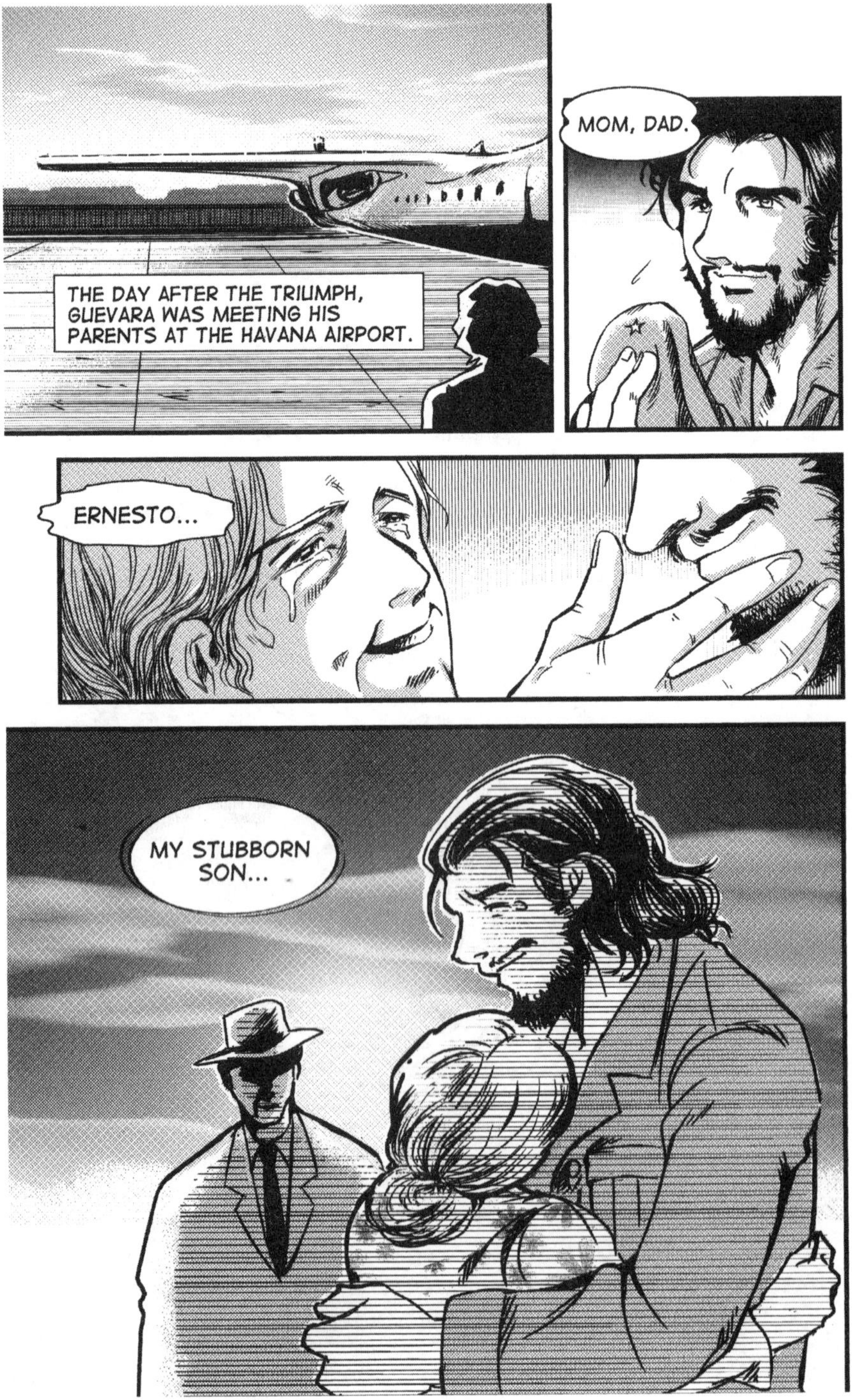
THE DAY AFTER THE TRIUMPH, GUEVARA WAS MEETING HIS PARENTS AT THE HAVANA AIRPORT.
MOM, DAD.
ERNESTO...
MY STUBBORN SON...

CHAPTER 4

REVOLUTIONARY

1959 - 1965

There is no other definition of socialism valid for us
than that of the abolition of the exploitation of man by man.

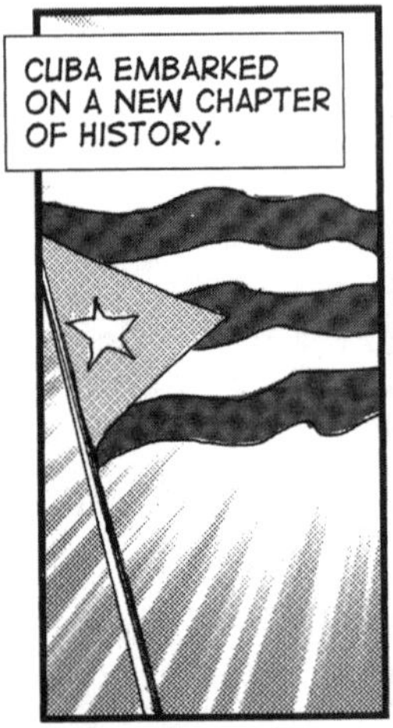
CUBA EMBARKED ON A NEW CHAPTER OF HISTORY.

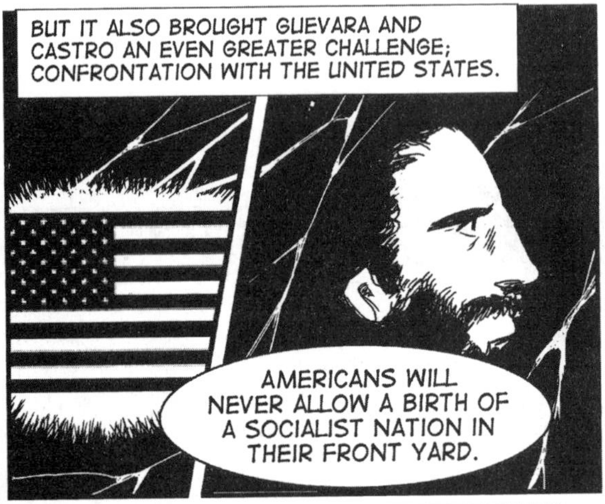
BUT IT ALSO BROUGHT GUEVARA AND CASTRO AN EVEN GREATER CHALLENGE; CONFRONTATION WITH THE UNITED STATES.
AMERICANS WILL NEVER ALLOW A BIRTH OF A SOCIALIST NATION IN THEIR FRONT YARD.

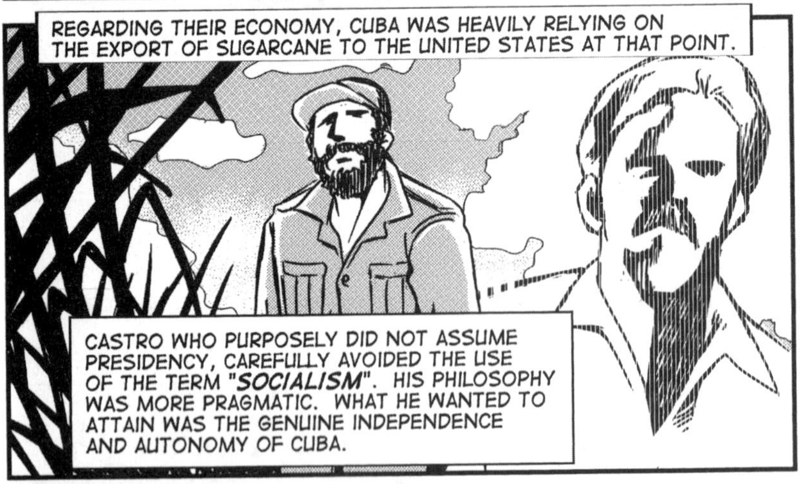
REGARDING THEIR ECONOMY, CUBA WAS HEAVILY RELYING ON THE EXPORT OF SUGARCANE TO THE UNITED STATES AT THAT POINT.
CASTRO WHO PURPOSELY DID NOT ASSUME PRESIDENCY, CAREFULLY AVOIDED THE USE OF THE TERM "*SOCIALISM*". HIS PHILOSOPHY WAS MORE PRAGMATIC. WHAT HE WANTED TO ATTAIN WAS THE GENUINE INDEPENDENCE AND AUTONOMY OF CUBA.

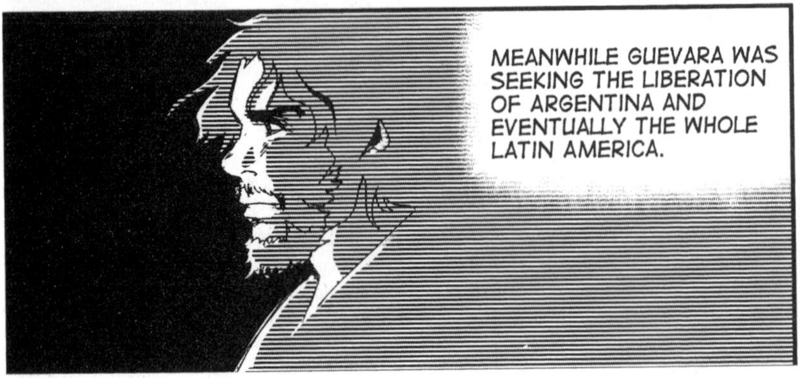
MEANWHILE GUEVARA WAS SEEKING THE LIBERATION OF ARGENTINA AND EVENTUALLY THE WHOLE LATIN AMERICA.

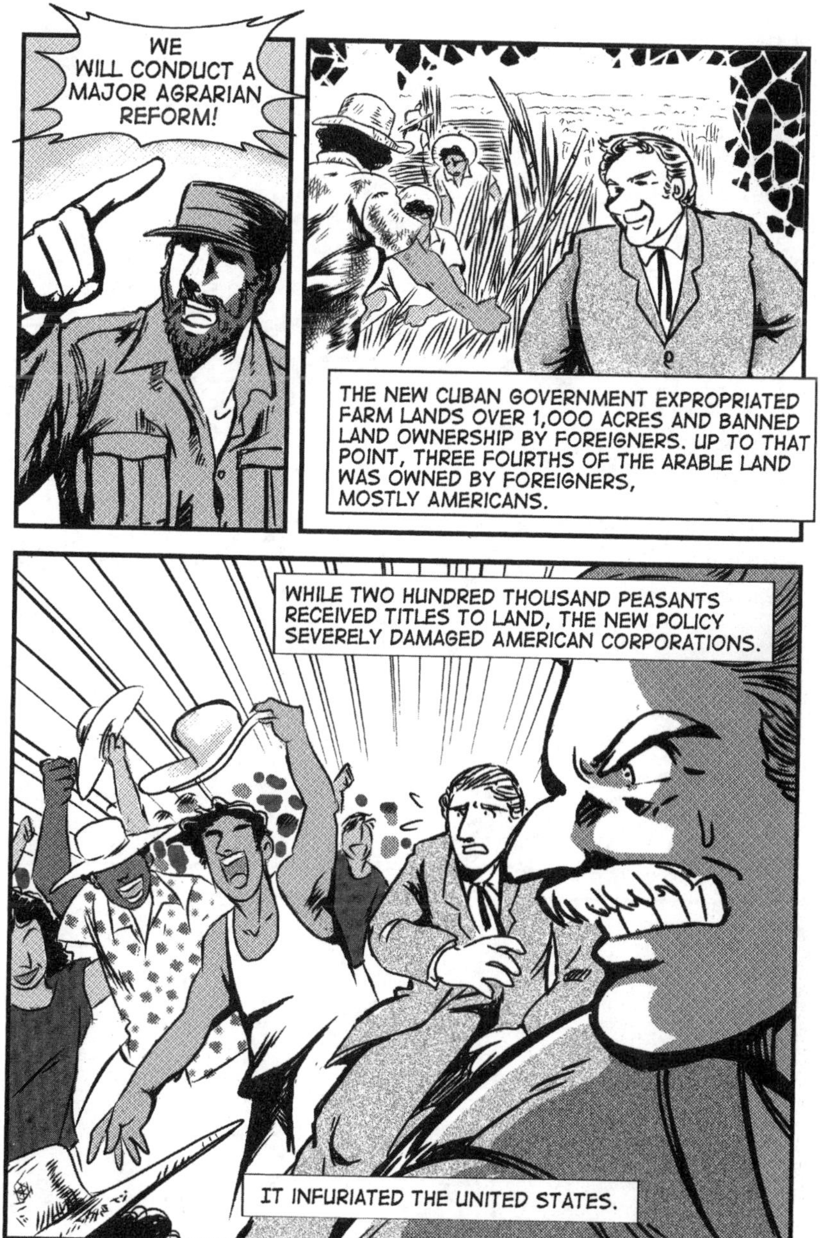
WE WILL CONDUCT A MAJOR AGRARIAN REFORM!
THE NEW CUBAN GOVERNMENT EXPROPRIATED FARM LANDS OVER 1,000 ACRES AND BANNED LAND OWNERSHIP BY FOREIGNERS. UP TO THAT POINT, THREE FOURTHS OF THE ARABLE LAND WAS OWNED BY FOREIGNERS, MOSTLY AMERICANS.
WHILE TWO HUNDRED THOUSAND PEASANTS RECEIVED TITLES TO LAND, THE NEW POLICY SEVERELY DAMAGED AMERICAN CORPORATIONS.
IT INFURIATED THE UNITED STATES.

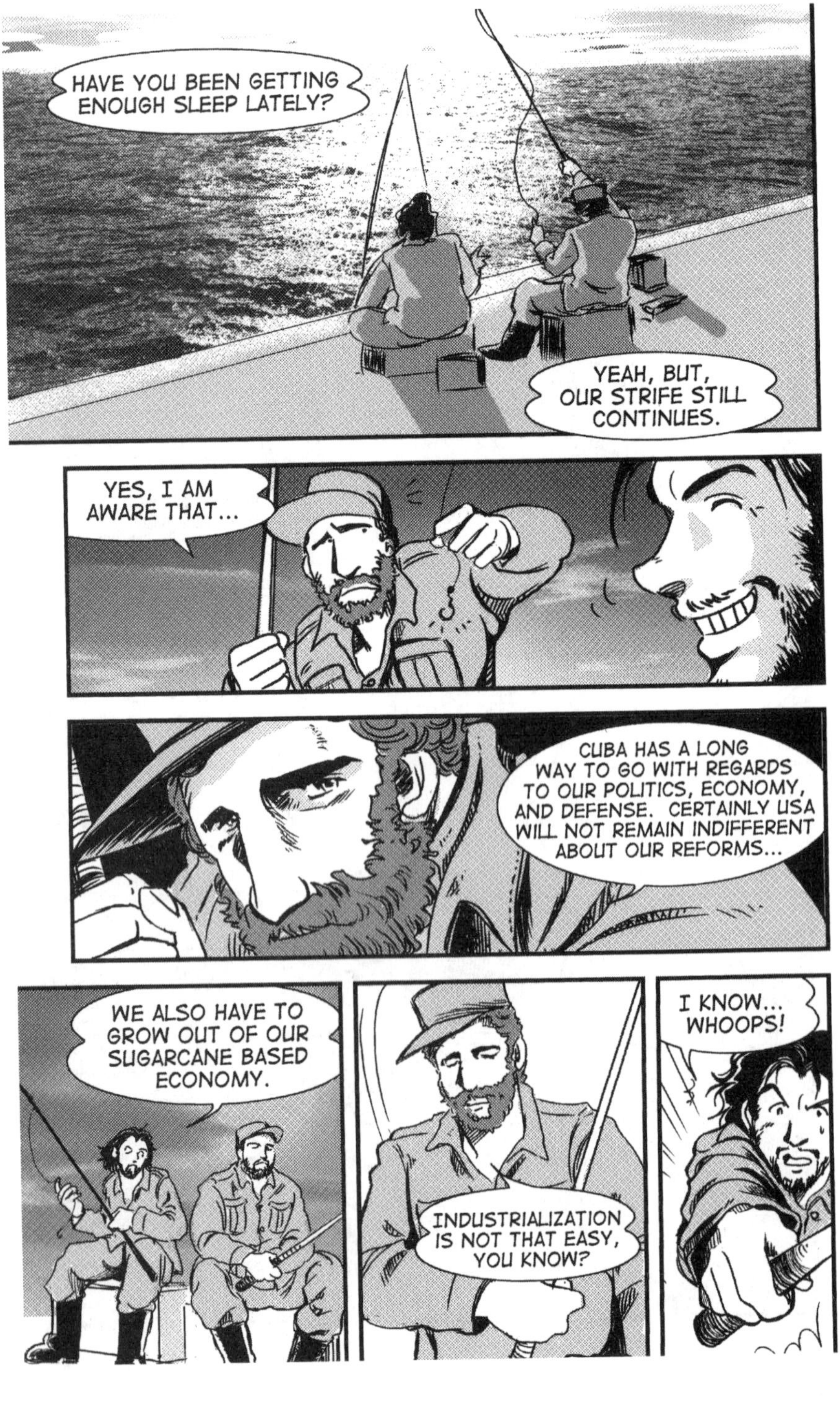
HAVE YOU BEEN GETTING ENOUGH SLEEP LATELY?
YEAH, BUT, OUR STRIFE STILL CONTINUES.
YES, I AM AWARE THAT...
CUBA HAS A LONG WAY TO GO WITH REGARDS TO OUR POLITICS, ECONOMY, AND DEFENSE. CERTAINLY USA WILL NOT REMAIN INDIFFERENT ABOUT OUR REFORMS...
WE ALSO HAVE TO GROW OUT OF OUR SUGARCANE BASED ECONOMY.
INDUSTRIALIZATION IS NOT THAT EASY, YOU KNOW?
I KNOW... WHOOPS!

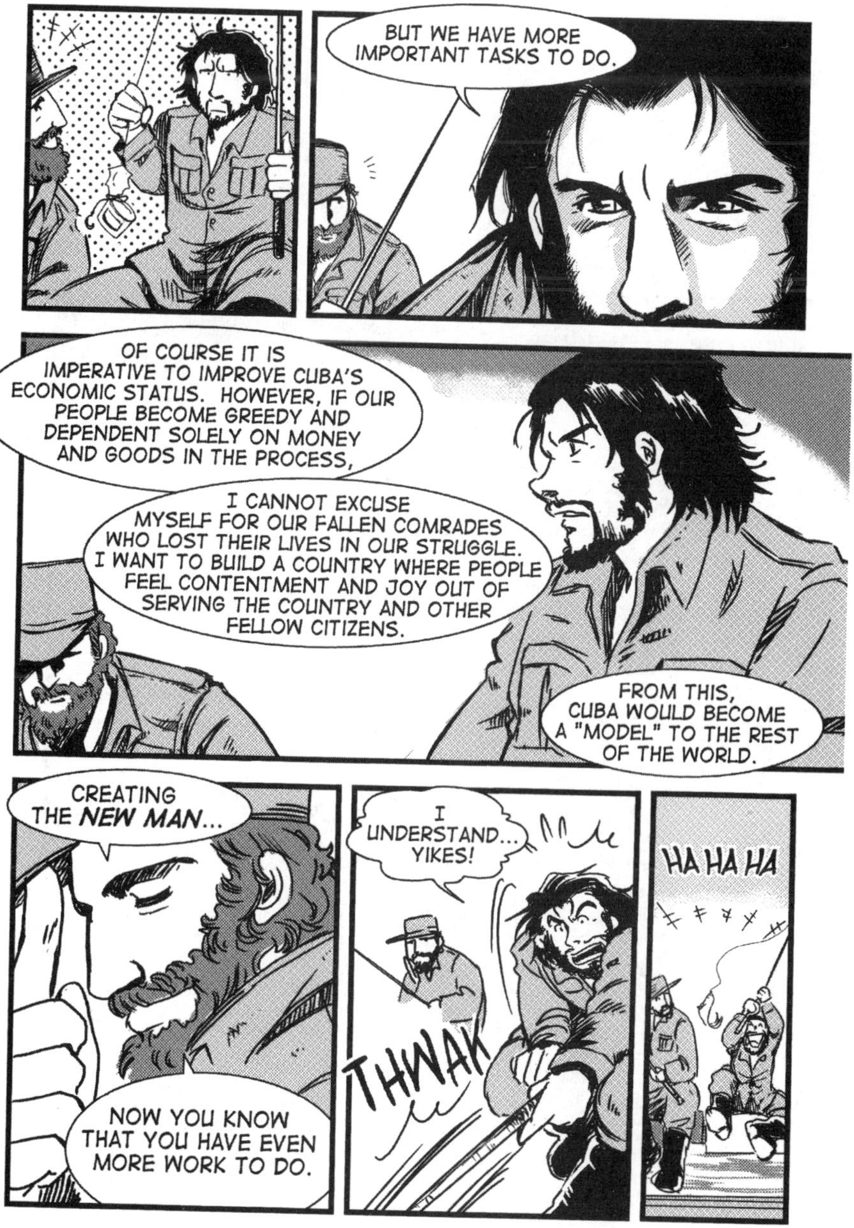
BUT WE HAVE MORE IMPORTANT TASKS TO DO.
OF COURSE IT IS IMPERATIVE TO IMPROVE CUBA'S ECONOMIC STATUS. HOWEVER, IF OUR PEOPLE BECOME GREEDY AND DEPENDENT SOLELY ON MONEY AND GOODS IN THE PROCESS,
I CANNOT EXCUSE MYSELF FOR OUR FALLEN COMRADES WHO LOST THEIR LIVES IN OUR STRUGGLE. I WANT TO BUILD A COUNTRY WHERE PEOPLE FEEL CONTENTMENT AND JOY OUT OF SERVING THE COUNTRY AND OTHER FELLOW CITIZENS.
FROM THIS, CUBA WOULD BECOME A "MODEL" TO THE REST OF THE WORLD.
CREATING THE ***NEW MAN***...
NOW YOU KNOW THAT YOU HAVE EVEN MORE WORK TO DO.
I UNDERSTAND... YIKES!
THWAK
HA HA HA

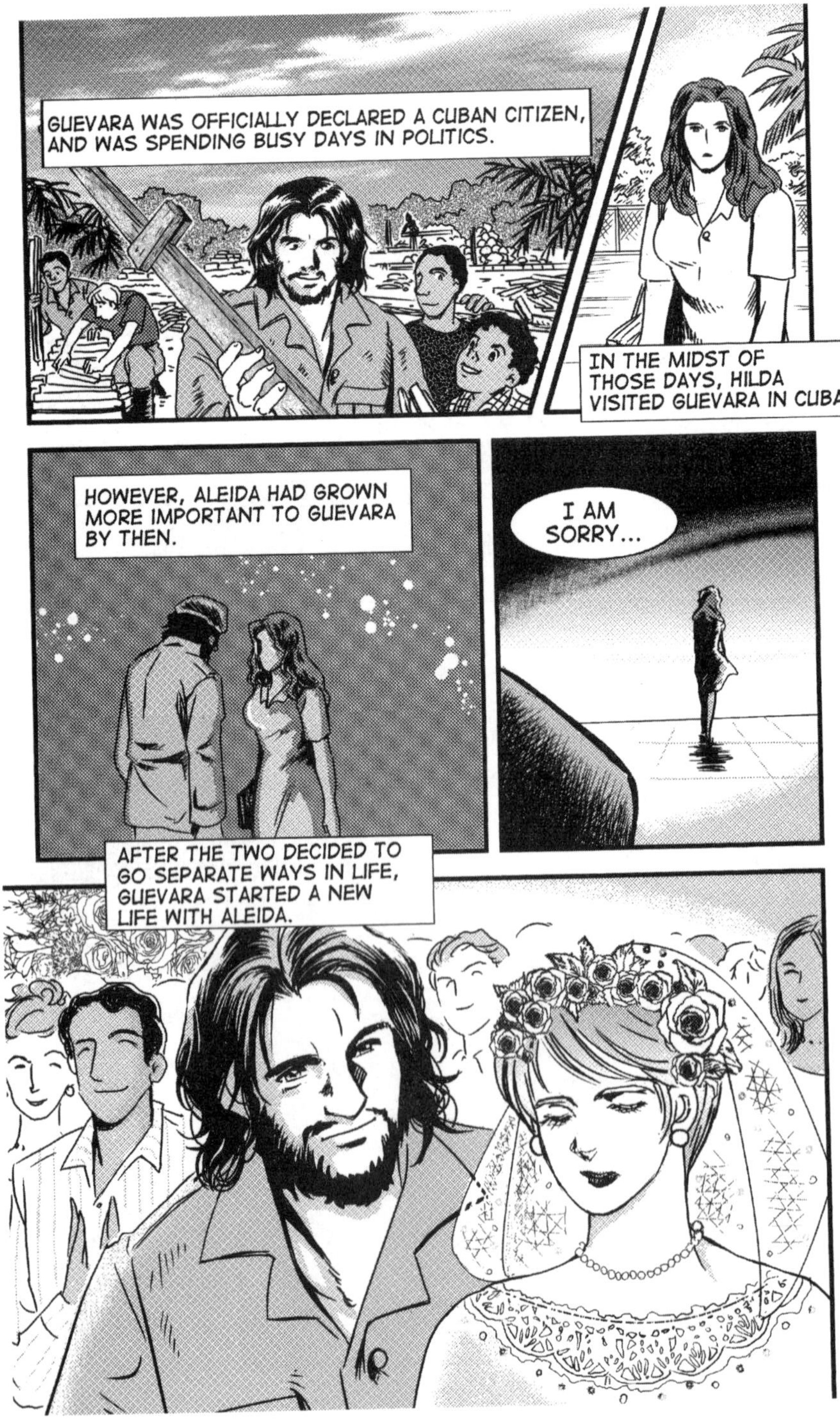
GUEVARA WAS OFFICIALLY DECLARED A CUBAN CITIZEN, AND WAS SPENDING BUSY DAYS IN POLITICS.
IN THE MIDST OF THOSE DAYS, HILDA VISITED GUEVARA IN CUBA.
HOWEVER, ALEIDA HAD GROWN MORE IMPORTANT TO GUEVARA BY THEN.
I AM SORRY...
AFTER THE TWO DECIDED TO GO SEPARATE WAYS IN LIFE, GUEVARA STARTED A NEW LIFE WITH ALEIDA.

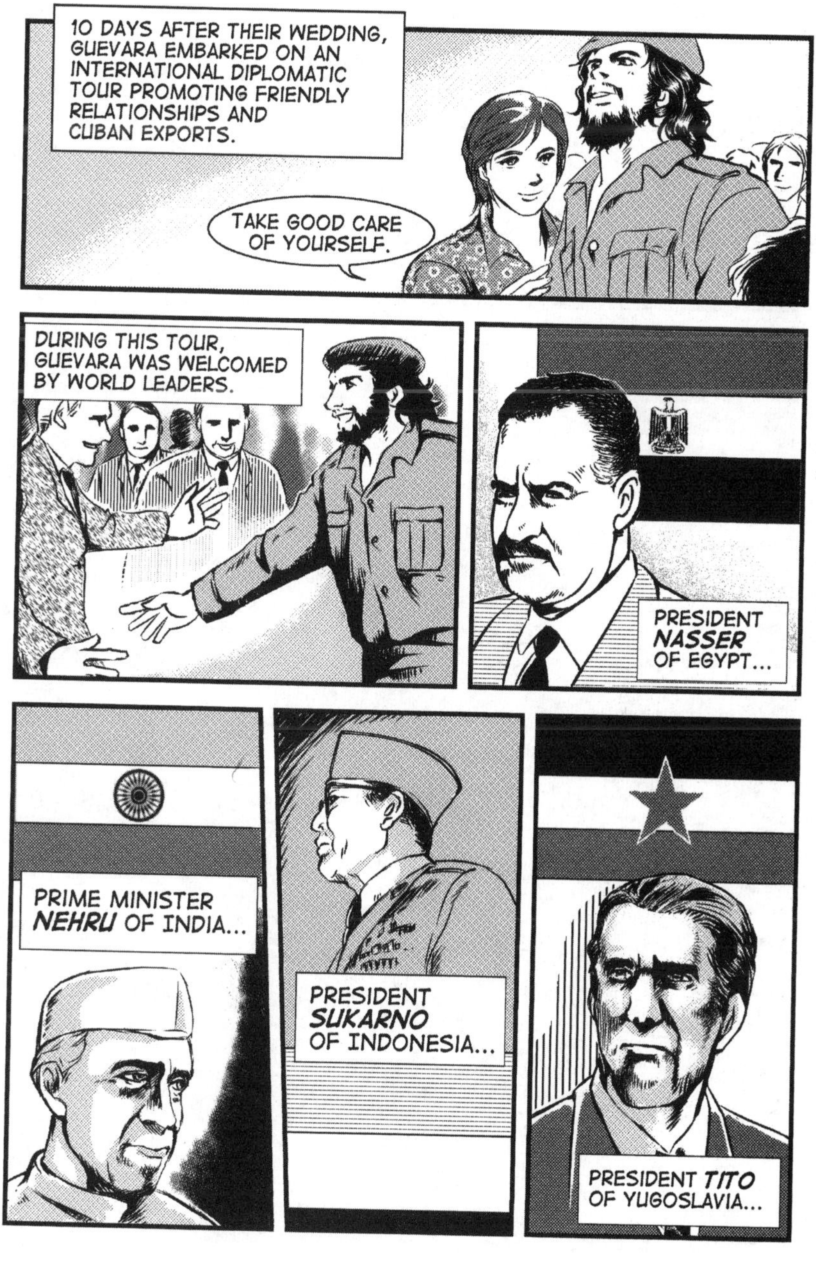
10 DAYS AFTER THEIR WEDDING, GUEVARA EMBARKED ON AN INTERNATIONAL DIPLOMATIC TOUR PROMOTING FRIENDLY RELATIONSHIPS AND CUBAN EXPORTS.
TAKE GOOD CARE OF YOURSELF.
DURING THIS TOUR, GUEVARA WAS WELCOMED BY WORLD LEADERS.
PRESIDENT *NASSER* OF EGYPT...
PRIME MINISTER *NEHRU* OF INDIA...
PRESIDENT *SUKARNO* OF INDONESIA...
PRESIDENT *TITO* OF YUGOSLAVIA...

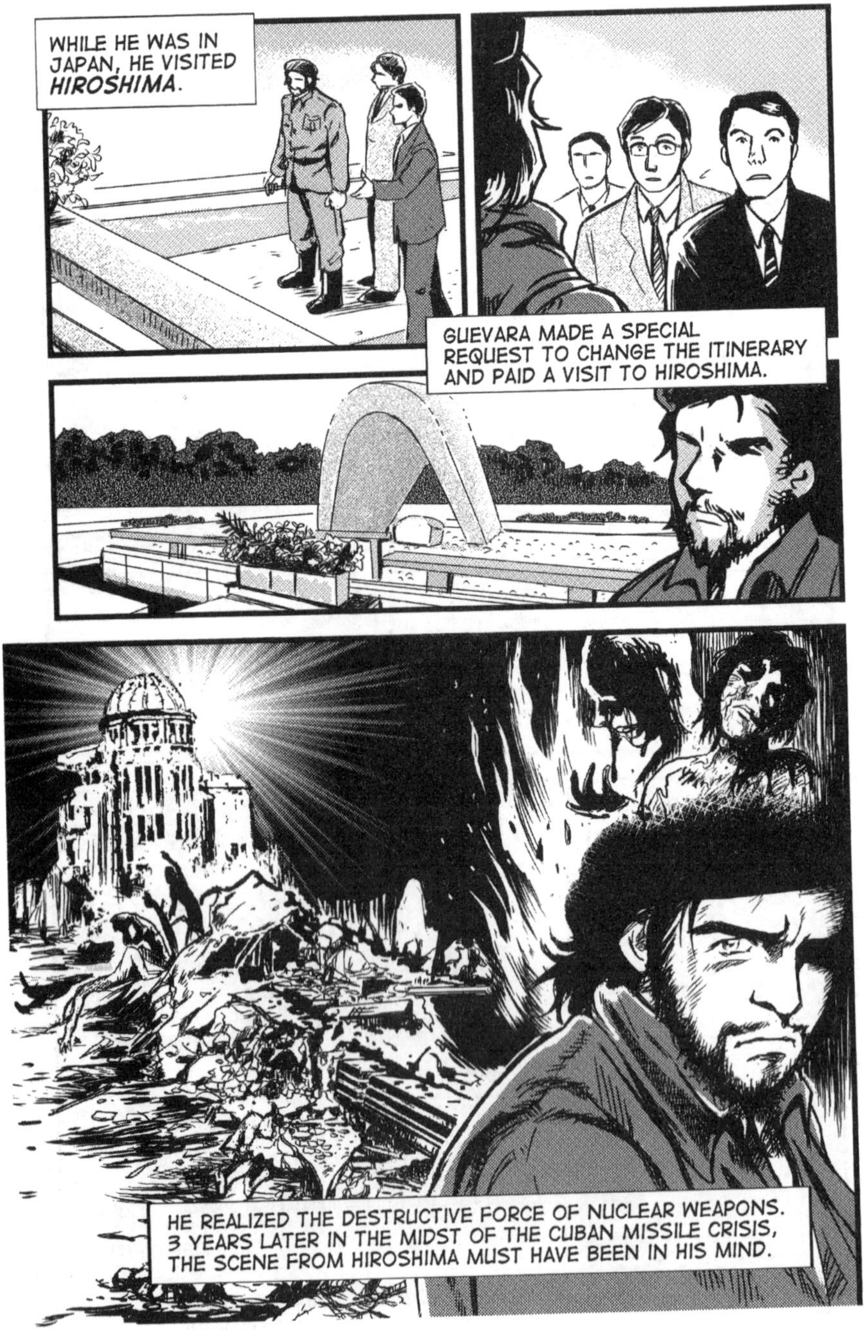
WHILE HE WAS IN JAPAN, HE VISITED *HIROSHIMA*.
GUEVARA MADE A SPECIAL REQUEST TO CHANGE THE ITINERARY AND PAID A VISIT TO HIROSHIMA.
HE REALIZED THE DESTRUCTIVE FORCE OF NUCLEAR WEAPONS. 3 YEARS LATER IN THE MIDST OF THE CUBAN MISSILE CRISIS, THE SCENE FROM HIROSHIMA MUST HAVE BEEN IN HIS MIND.

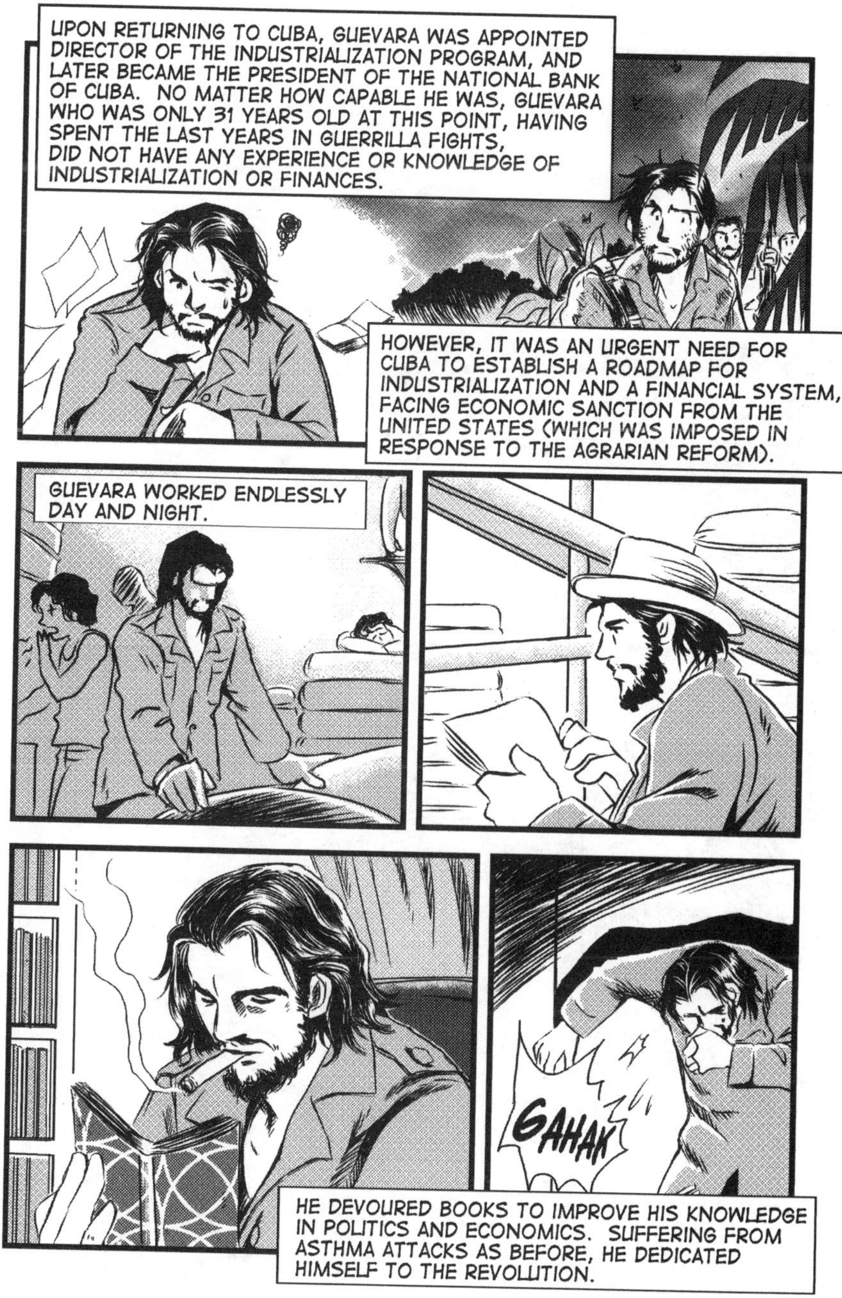
UPON RETURNING TO CUBA, GUEVARA WAS APPOINTED DIRECTOR OF THE INDUSTRIALIZATION PROGRAM, AND LATER BECAME THE PRESIDENT OF THE NATIONAL BANK OF CUBA. NO MATTER HOW CAPABLE HE WAS, GUEVARA WHO WAS ONLY 31 YEARS OLD AT THIS POINT, HAVING SPENT THE LAST YEARS IN GUERRILLA FIGHTS, DID NOT HAVE ANY EXPERIENCE OR KNOWLEDGE OF INDUSTRIALIZATION OR FINANCES.
HOWEVER, IT WAS AN URGENT NEED FOR CUBA TO ESTABLISH A ROADMAP FOR INDUSTRIALIZATION AND A FINANCIAL SYSTEM, FACING ECONOMIC SANCTION FROM THE UNITED STATES (WHICH WAS IMPOSED IN RESPONSE TO THE AGRARIAN REFORM).
GUEVARA WORKED ENDLESSLY DAY AND NIGHT.
GAHAK
HE DEVOURED BOOKS TO IMPROVE HIS KNOWLEDGE IN POLITICS AND ECONOMICS. SUFFERING FROM ASTHMA ATTACKS AS BEFORE, HE DEDICATED HIMSELF TO THE REVOLUTION.

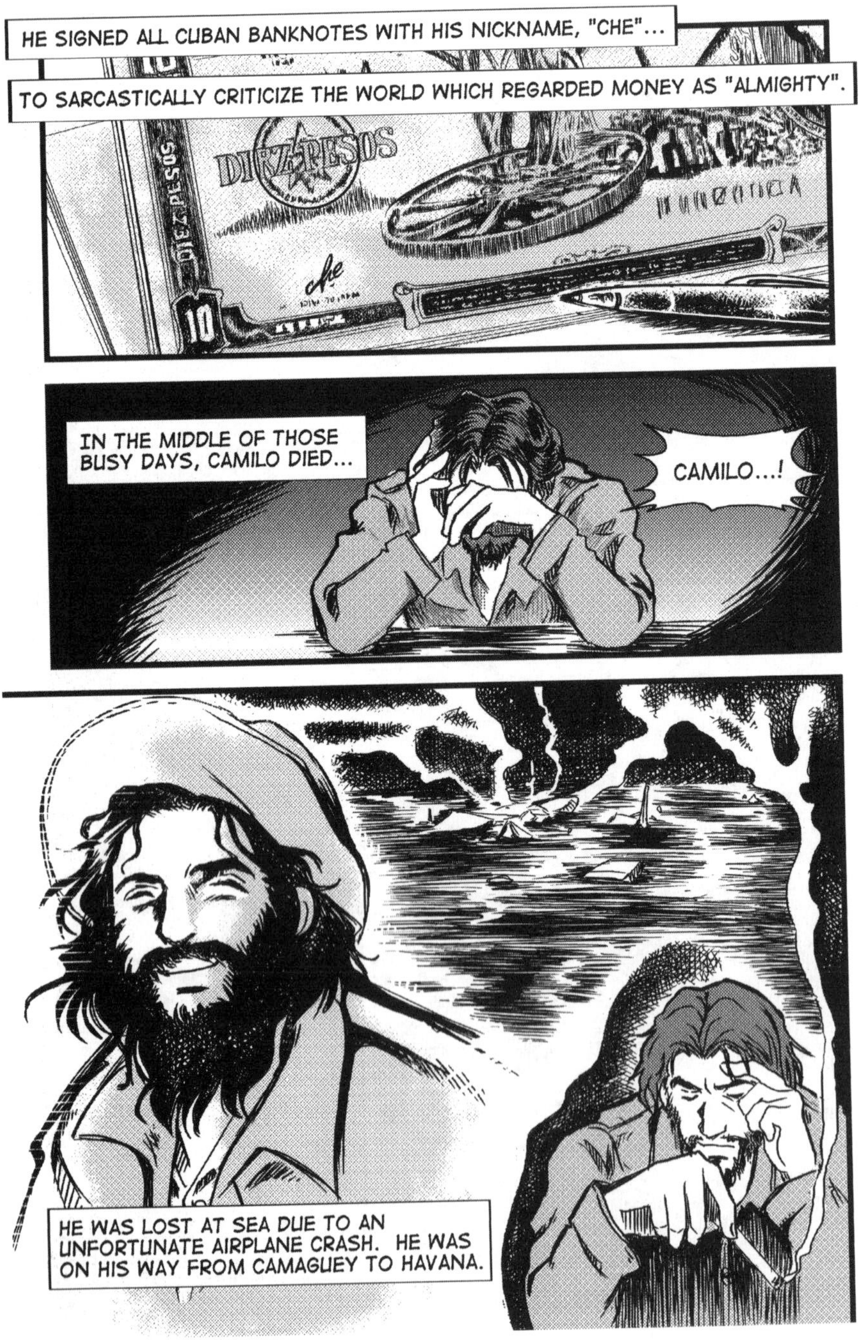
HE SIGNED ALL CUBAN BANKNOTES WITH HIS NICKNAME, "CHE"...
TO SARCASTICALLY CRITICIZE THE WORLD WHICH REGARDED MONEY AS "ALMIGHTY".
DIEZ PESOS
IN THE MIDDLE OF THOSE BUSY DAYS, CAMILO DIED...
CAMILO...!
HE WAS LOST AT SEA DUE TO AN UNFORTUNATE AIRPLANE CRASH. HE WAS ON HIS WAY FROM CAMAGUEY TO HAVANA.

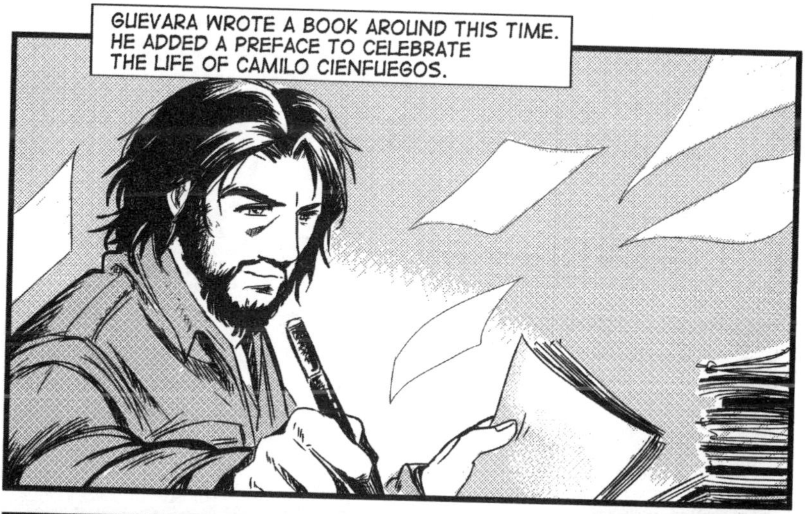
GUEVARA WROTE A BOOK AROUND THIS TIME. HE ADDED A PREFACE TO CELEBRATE THE LIFE OF CAMILO CIENFUEGOS.

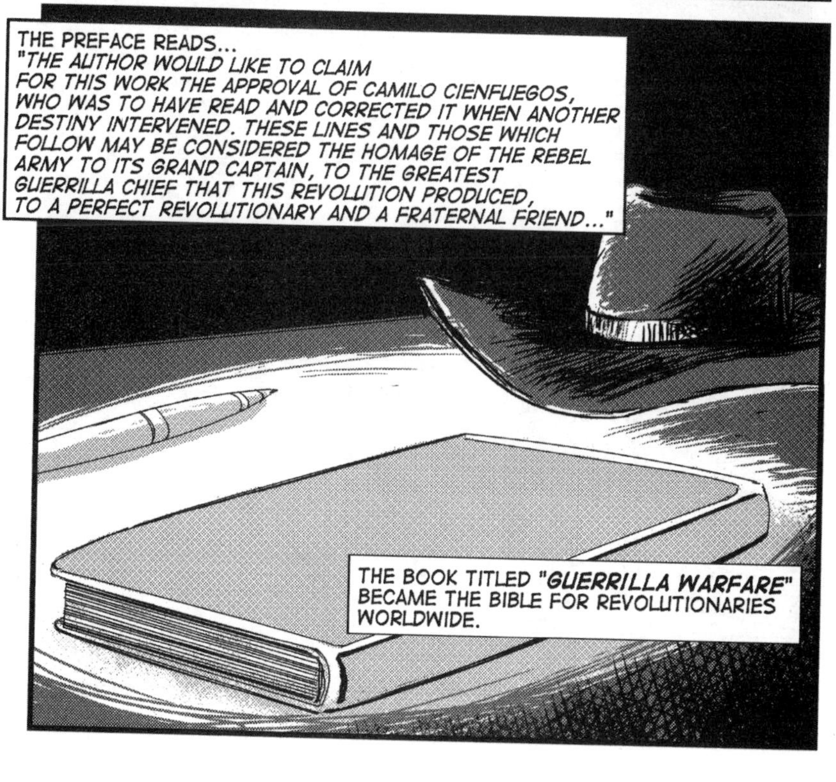
THE PREFACE READS... "THE AUTHOR WOULD LIKE TO CLAIM FOR THIS WORK THE APPROVAL OF CAMILO CIENFUEGOS, WHO WAS TO HAVE READ AND CORRECTED IT WHEN ANOTHER DESTINY INTERVENED. THESE LINES AND THOSE WHICH FOLLOW MAY BE CONSIDERED THE HOMAGE OF THE REBEL ARMY TO ITS GRAND CAPTAIN, TO THE GREATEST GUERRILLA CHIEF THAT THIS REVOLUTION PRODUCED, TO A PERFECT REVOLUTIONARY AND A FRATERNAL FRIEND..."
THE BOOK TITLED "GUERRILLA WARFARE" BECAME THE BIBLE FOR REVOLUTIONARIES WORLDWIDE.

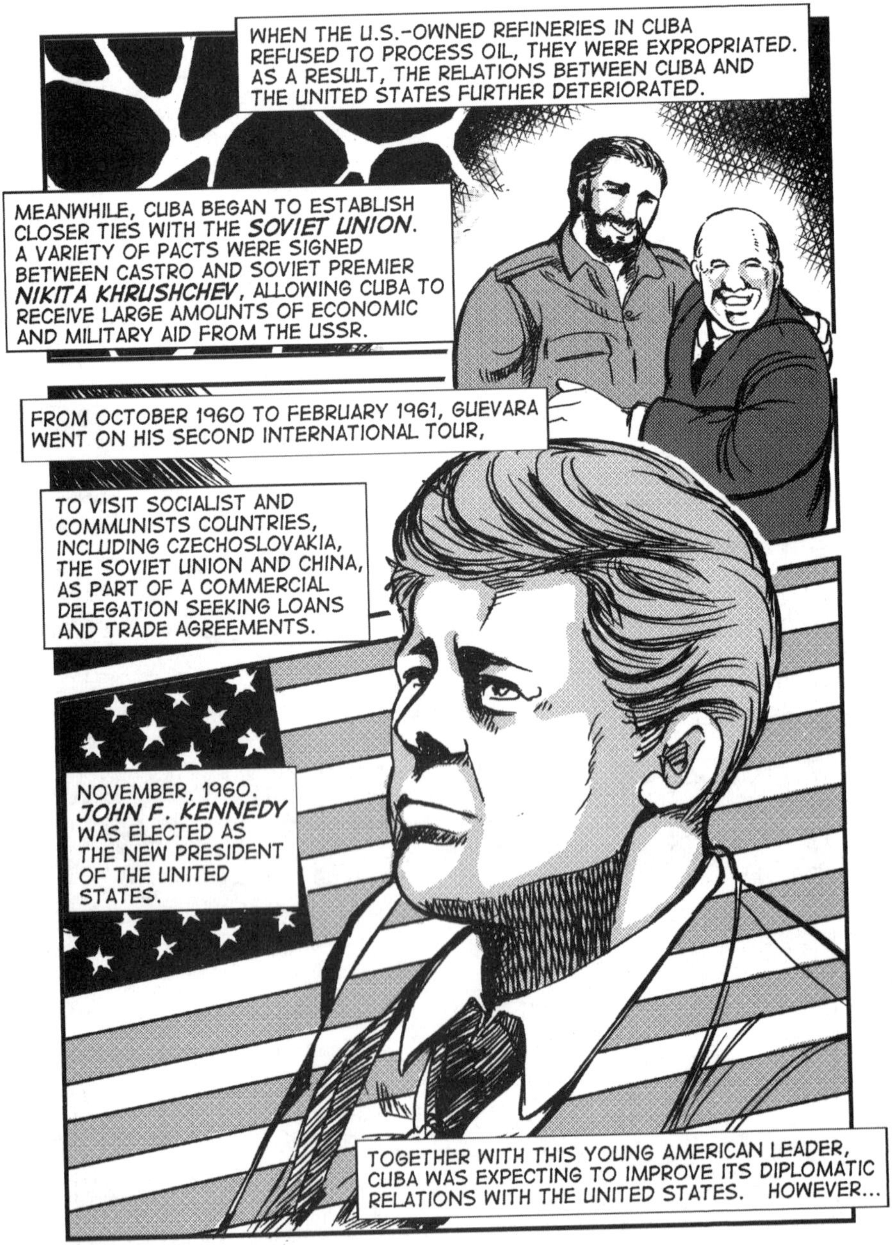
WHEN THE U.S.-OWNED REFINERIES IN CUBA REFUSED TO PROCESS OIL, THEY WERE EXPROPRIATED. AS A RESULT, THE RELATIONS BETWEEN CUBA AND THE UNITED STATES FURTHER DETERIORATED.
MEANWHILE, CUBA BEGAN TO ESTABLISH CLOSER TIES WITH THE ***SOVIET UNION***. A VARIETY OF PACTS WERE SIGNED BETWEEN CASTRO AND SOVIET PREMIER ***NIKITA KHRUSHCHEV***, ALLOWING CUBA TO RECEIVE LARGE AMOUNTS OF ECONOMIC AND MILITARY AID FROM THE USSR.
FROM OCTOBER 1960 TO FEBRUARY 1961, GUEVARA WENT ON HIS SECOND INTERNATIONAL TOUR,
TO VISIT SOCIALIST AND COMMUNISTS COUNTRIES, INCLUDING CZECHOSLOVAKIA, THE SOVIET UNION AND CHINA, AS PART OF A COMMERCIAL DELEGATION SEEKING LOANS AND TRADE AGREEMENTS.
NOVEMBER, 1960. ***JOHN F. KENNEDY*** WAS ELECTED AS THE NEW PRESIDENT OF THE UNITED STATES.
TOGETHER WITH THIS YOUNG AMERICAN LEADER, CUBA WAS EXPECTING TO IMPROVE ITS DIPLOMATIC RELATIONS WITH THE UNITED STATES. HOWEVER...

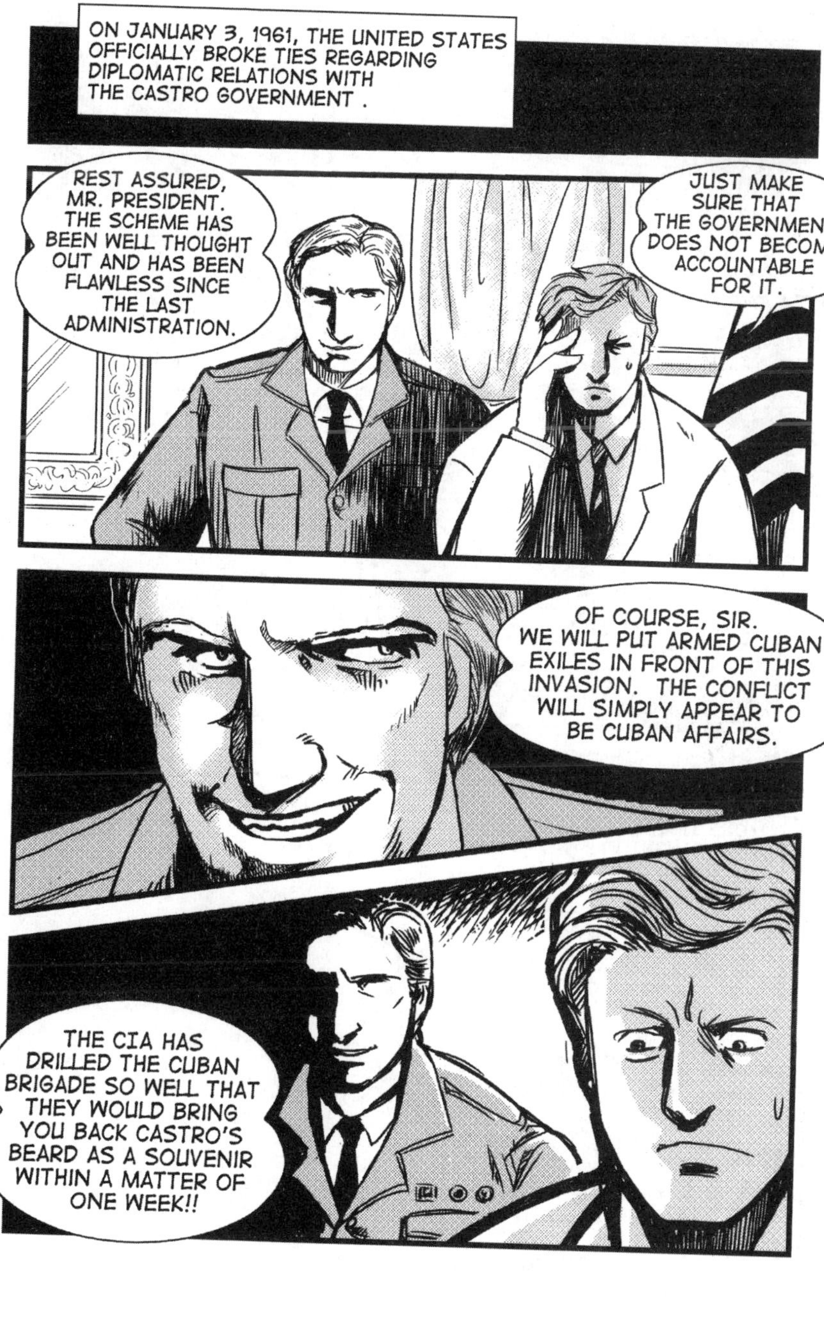
ON JANUARY 3, 1961, THE UNITED STATES OFFICIALLY BROKE TIES REGARDING DIPLOMATIC RELATIONS WITH THE CASTRO GOVERNMENT .
REST ASSURED, MR. PRESIDENT. THE SCHEME HAS BEEN WELL THOUGHT OUT AND HAS BEEN FLAWLESS SINCE THE LAST ADMINISTRATION.
JUST MAKE SURE THAT THE GOVERNMENT DOES NOT BECOME ACCOUNTABLE FOR IT.
OF COURSE, SIR. WE WILL PUT ARMED CUBAN EXILES IN FRONT OF THIS INVASION. THE CONFLICT WILL SIMPLY APPEAR TO BE CUBAN AFFAIRS.
THE CIA HAS DRILLED THE CUBAN BRIGADE SO WELL THAT THEY WOULD BRING YOU BACK CASTRO'S BEARD AS A SOUVENIR WITHIN A MATTER OF ONE WEEK!!

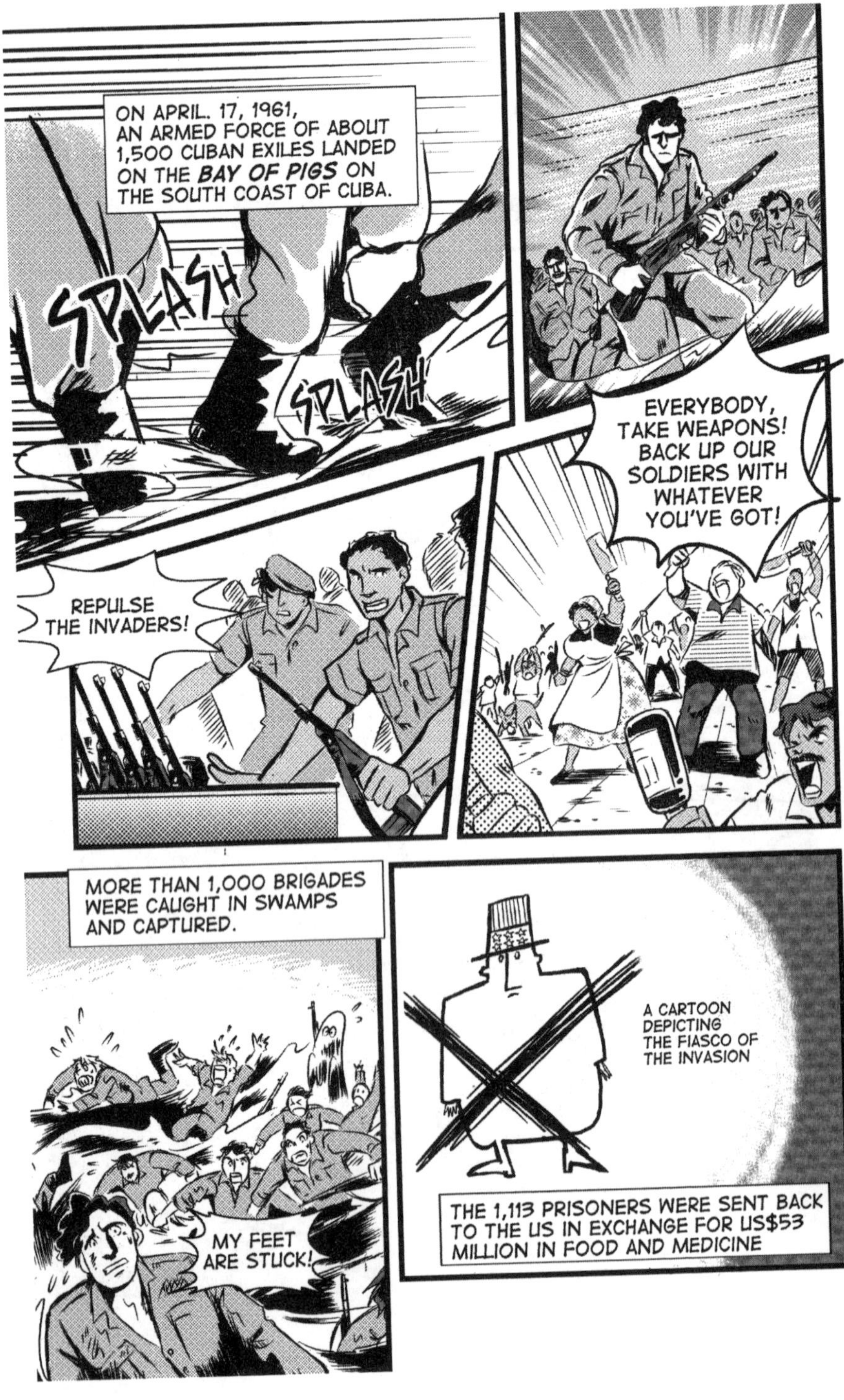
ON APRIL. 17, 1961, AN ARMED FORCE OF ABOUT 1,500 CUBAN EXILES LANDED ON THE *BAY OF PIGS* ON THE SOUTH COAST OF CUBA.
SPLASH
SPLASH
REPULSE THE INVADERS!
EVERYBODY, TAKE WEAPONS! BACK UP OUR SOLDIERS WITH WHATEVER YOU'VE GOT!
MORE THAN 1,000 BRIGADES WERE CAUGHT IN SWAMPS AND CAPTURED.
MY FEET ARE STUCK!
A CARTOON DEPICTING THE FIASCO OF THE INVASION
THE 1,113 PRISONERS WERE SENT BACK TO THE US IN EXCHANGE FOR US$53 MILLION IN FOOD AND MEDICINE

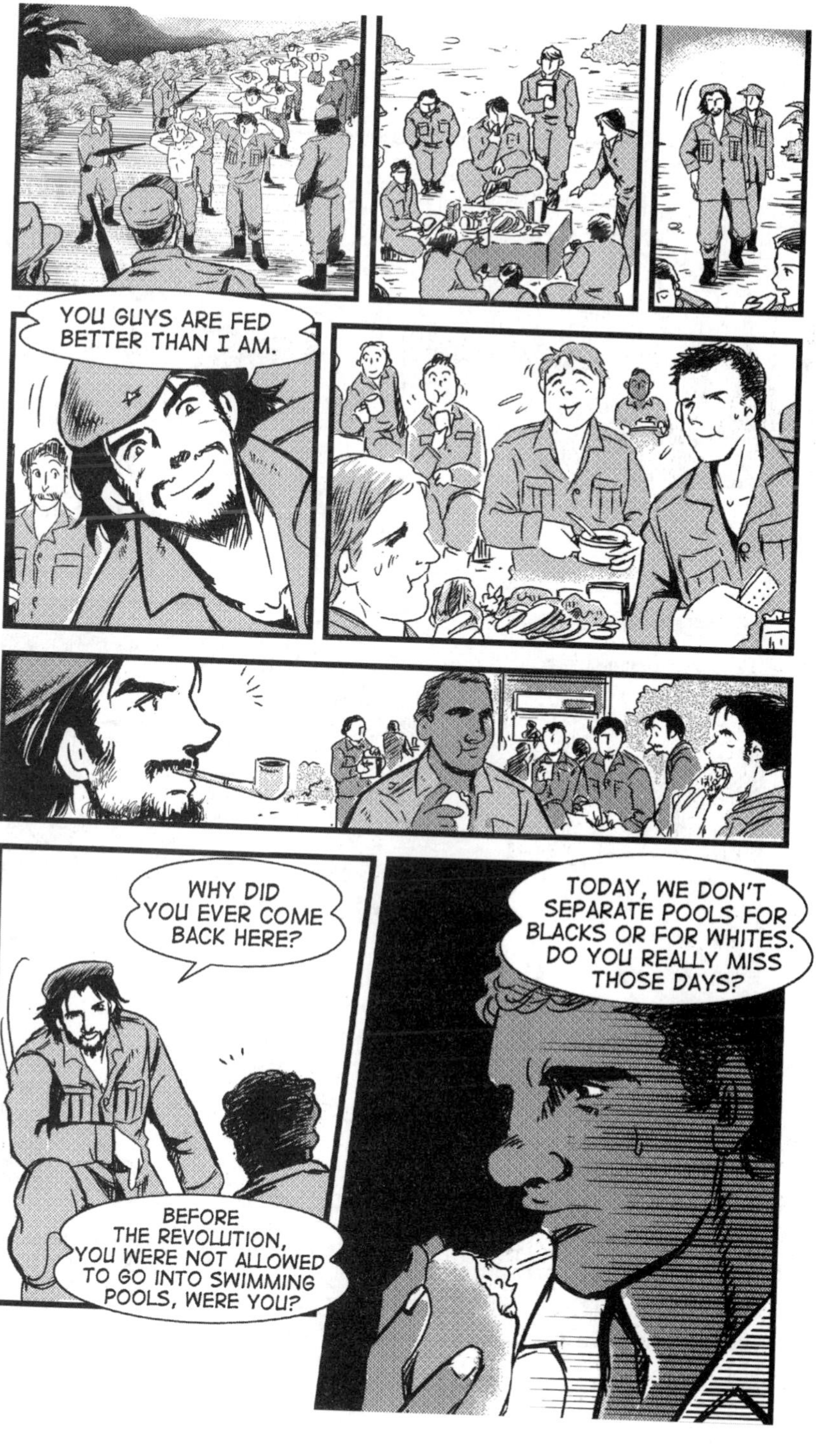
YOU GUYS ARE FED BETTER THAN I AM.
WHY DID YOU EVER COME BACK HERE?
BEFORE THE REVOLUTION, YOU WERE NOT ALLOWED TO GO INTO SWIMMING POOLS, WERE YOU?
TODAY, WE DON'T SEPARATE POOLS FOR BLACKS OR FOR WHITES. DO YOU REALLY MISS THOSE DAYS?

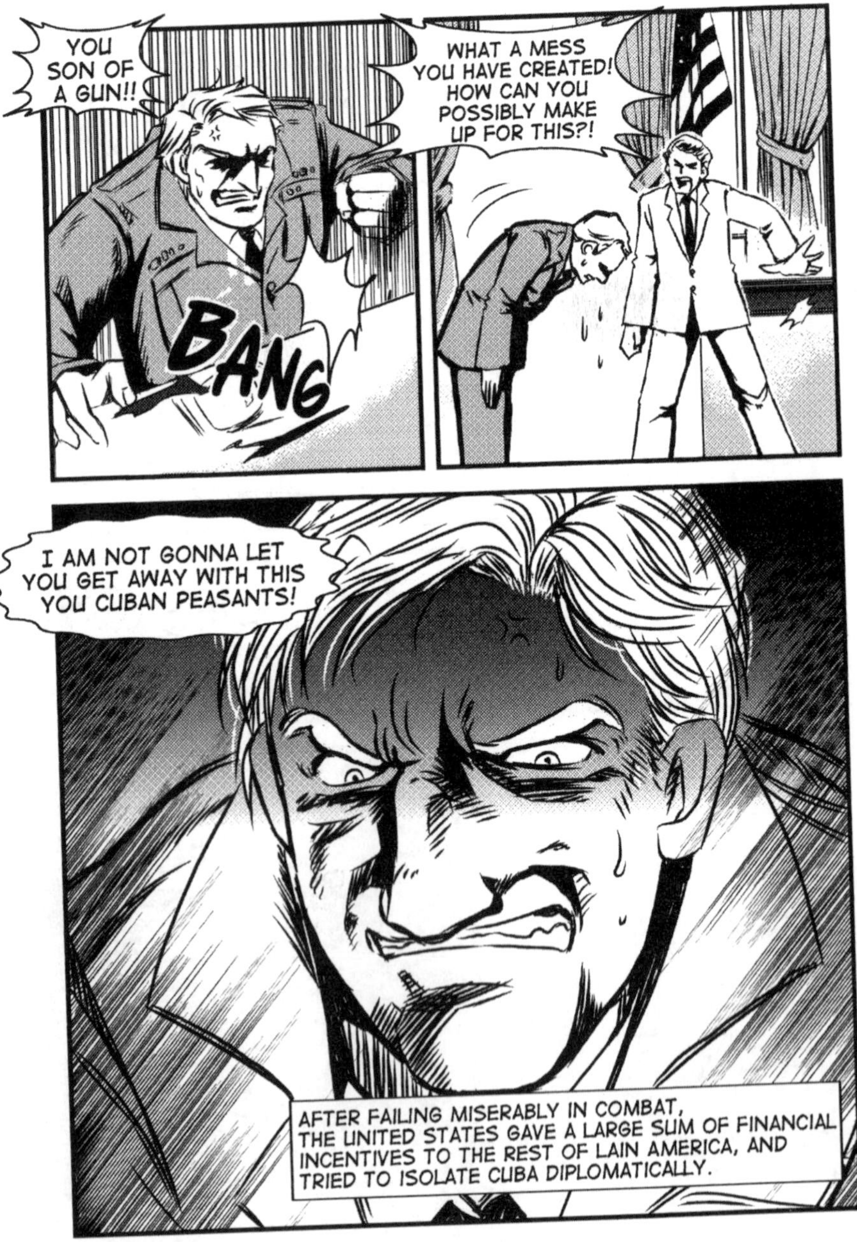
WHAT A MESS YOU HAVE CREATED! HOW CAN YOU POSSIBLY MAKE UP FOR THIS?!
YOU SON OF A GUN!!
BANG
I AM NOT GONNA LET YOU GET AWAY WITH THIS YOU CUBAN PEASANTS!
AFTER FAILING MISERABLY IN COMBAT, THE UNITED STATES GAVE A LARGE SUM OF FINANCIAL INCENTIVES TO THE REST OF LAIN AMERICA, AND TRIED TO ISOLATE CUBA DIPLOMATICALLY.

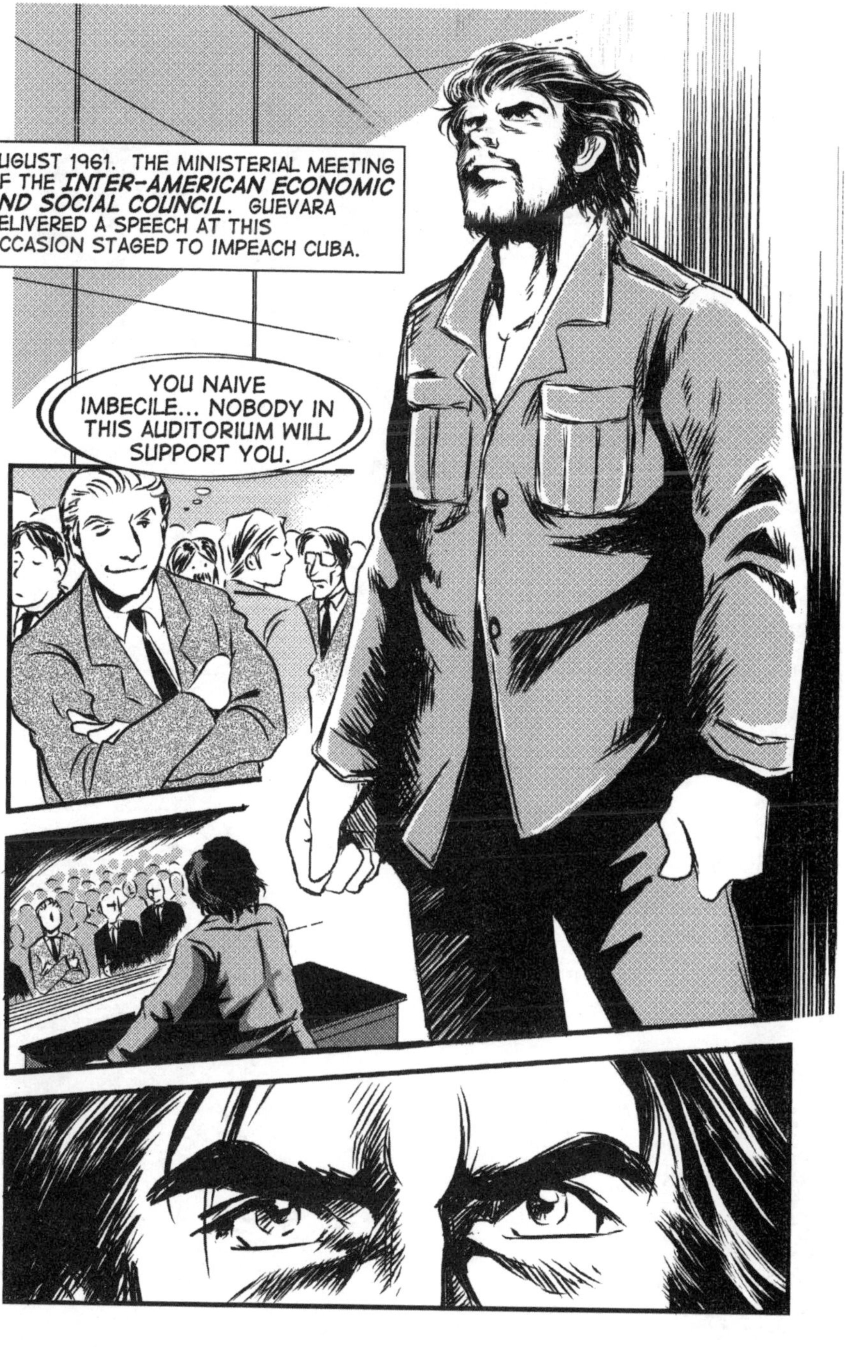
AUGUST 1961. THE MINISTERIAL MEETING OF THE *INTER-AMERICAN ECONOMIC AND SOCIAL COUNCIL*. GUEVARA DELIVERED A SPEECH AT THIS OCCASION STAGED TO IMPEACH CUBA.
YOU NAIVE IMBECILE... NOBODY IN THIS AUDITORIUM WILL SUPPORT YOU.

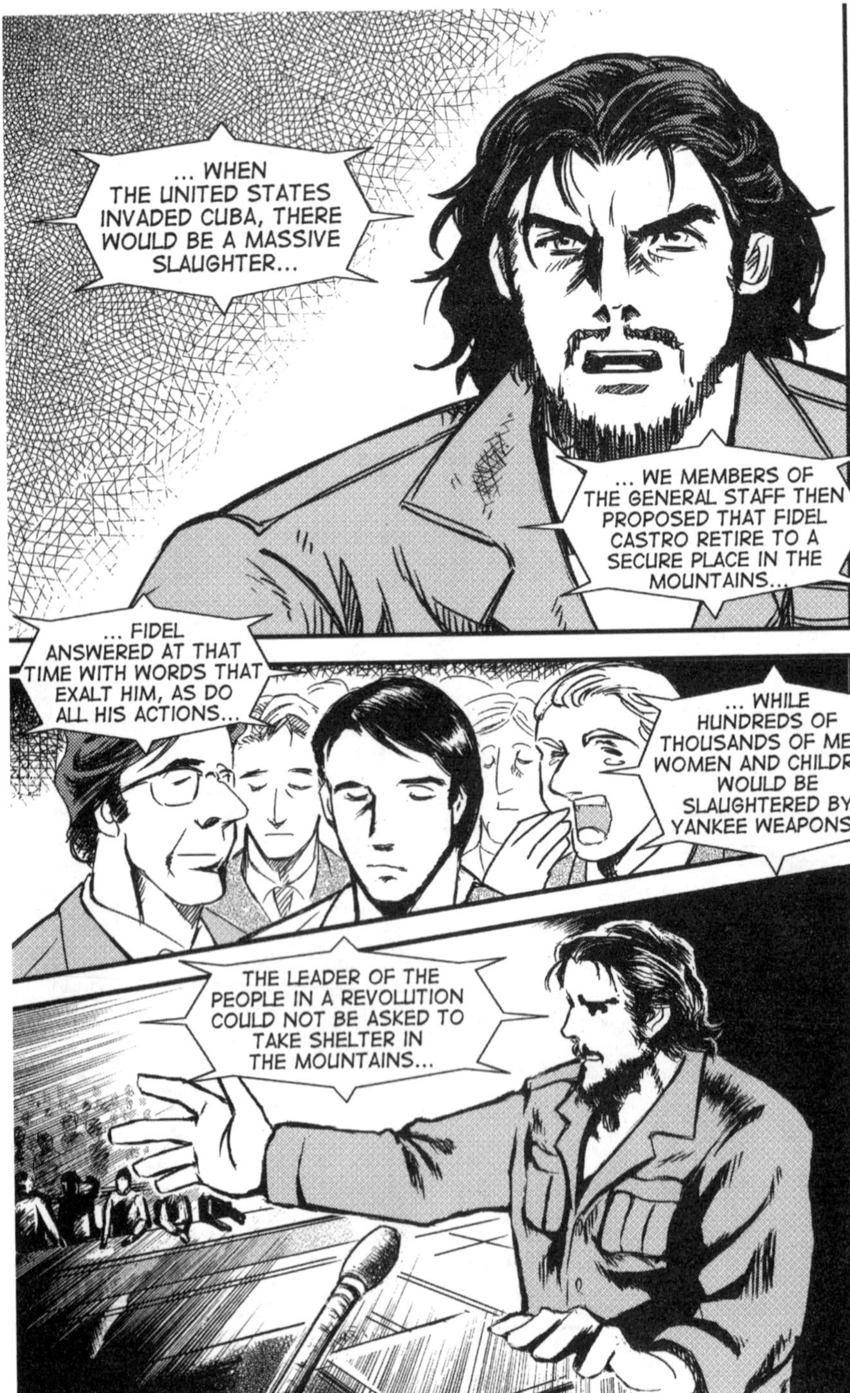
... WE MEMBERS OF THE GENERAL STAFF THEN PROPOSED THAT FIDEL CASTRO RETIRE TO A SECURE PLACE IN THE MOUNTAINS...
... WHEN THE UNITED STATES INVADED CUBA, THERE WOULD BE A MASSIVE SLAUGHTER...
... WHILE HUNDREDS OF THOUSANDS OF MEN, WOMEN AND CHILDREN WOULD BE SLAUGHTERED BY YANKEE WEAPONS...
... FIDEL ANSWERED AT THAT TIME WITH WORDS THAT EXALT HIM, AS DO ALL HIS ACTIONS...
THE LEADER OF THE PEOPLE IN A REVOLUTION COULD NOT BE ASKED TO TAKE SHELTER IN THE MOUNTAINS...

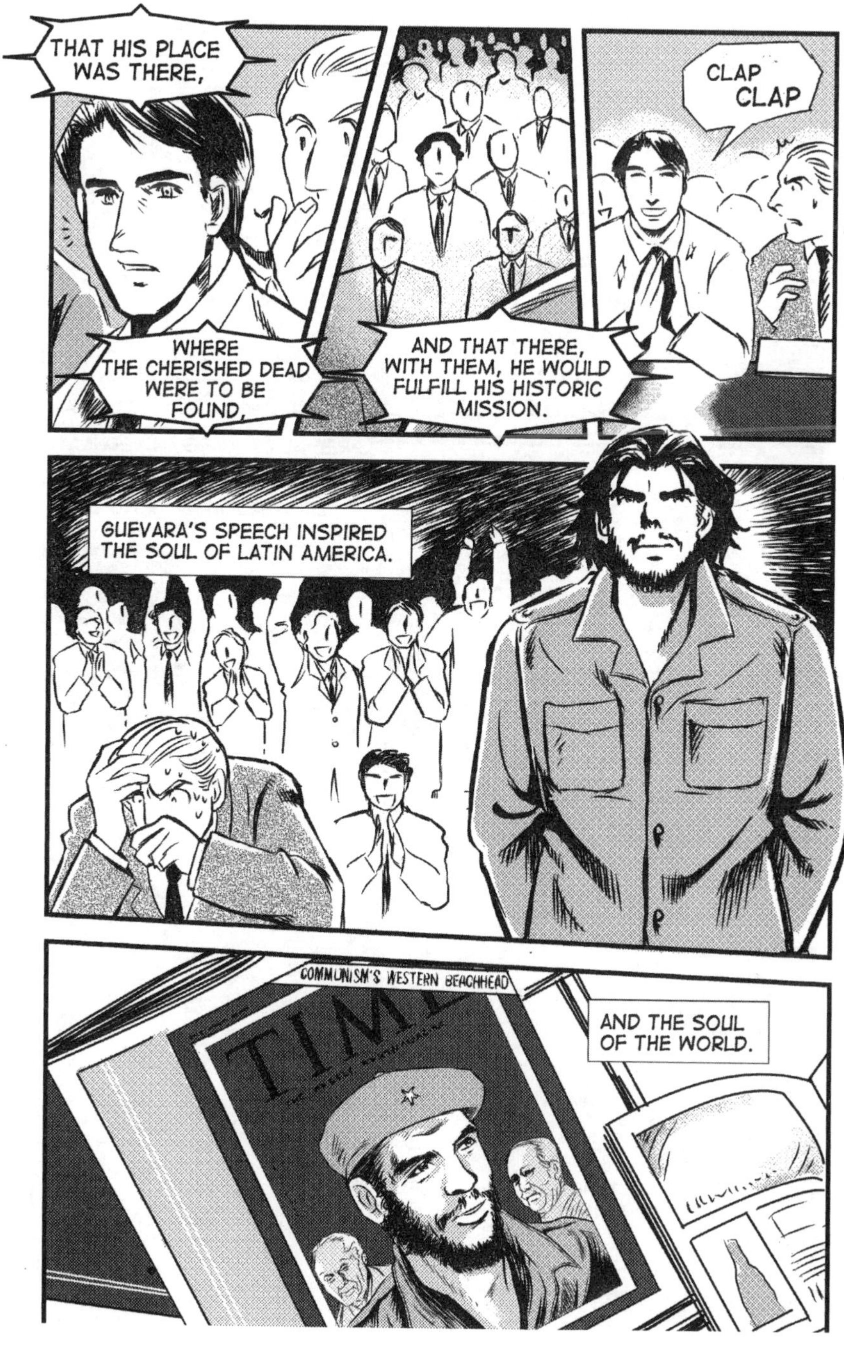
THAT HIS PLACE WAS THERE,
WHERE THE CHERISHED DEAD WERE TO BE FOUND,
AND THAT THERE, WITH THEM, HE WOULD FULFILL HIS HISTORIC MISSION.
CLAP CLAP
GUEVARA'S SPEECH INSPIRED THE SOUL OF LATIN AMERICA.
COMMUNISM'S WESTERN BEACHHEAD
TIME
AND THE SOUL OF THE WORLD.

AS RELATIONS WITH THE UNITED STATES REMAINED TENSE, CUBA UNDERTOOK A VARIETY OF REFORMS.

WE HAVE A GOOD HARVEST THIS YEAR...

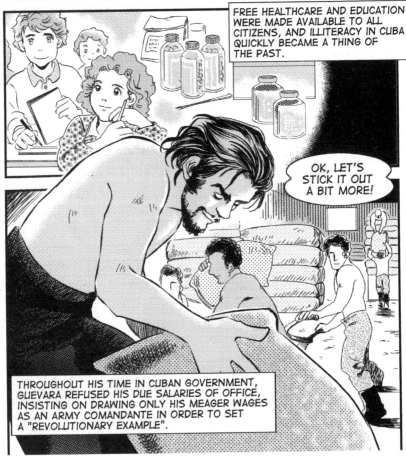

FREE HEALTHCARE AND EDUCATION WERE MADE AVAILABLE TO ALL CITIZENS, AND ILLITERACY IN CUBA QUICKLY BECAME A THING OF THE PAST.

OK, LET'S STICK IT OUT A BIT MORE!

THROUGHOUT HIS TIME IN CUBAN GOVERNMENT, GUEVARA REFUSED HIS DUE SALARIES OF OFFICE, INSISTING ON DRAWING ONLY HIS MEAGER WAGES AS AN ARMY COMANDANTE IN ORDER TO SET A "REVOLUTIONARY EXAMPLE".

120

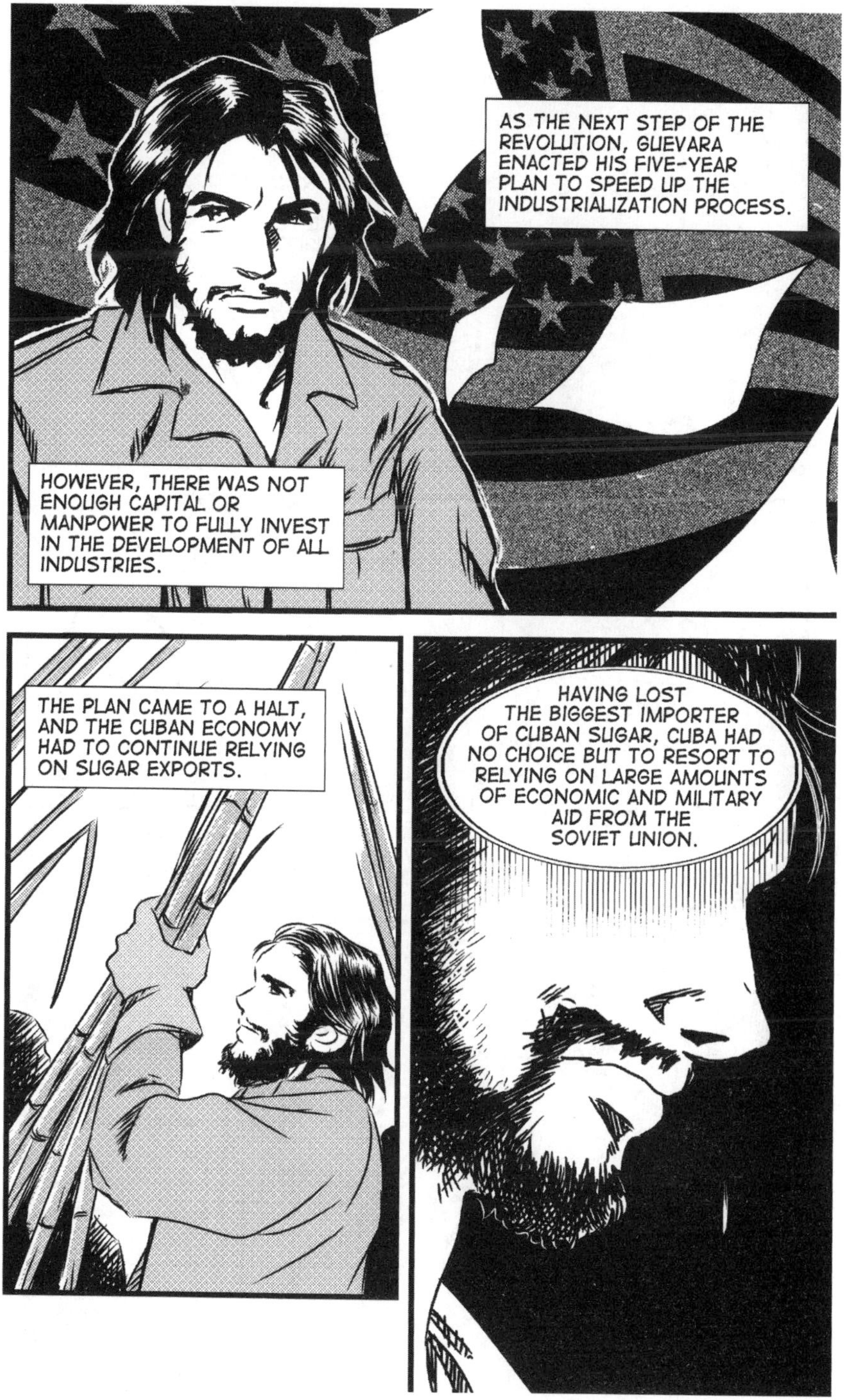
AS THE NEXT STEP OF THE REVOLUTION, GUEVARA ENACTED HIS FIVE-YEAR PLAN TO SPEED UP THE INDUSTRIALIZATION PROCESS.
HOWEVER, THERE WAS NOT ENOUGH CAPITAL OR MANPOWER TO FULLY INVEST IN THE DEVELOPMENT OF ALL INDUSTRIES.
THE PLAN CAME TO A HALT, AND THE CUBAN ECONOMY HAD TO CONTINUE RELYING ON SUGAR EXPORTS.
HAVING LOST THE BIGGEST IMPORTER OF CUBAN SUGAR, CUBA HAD NO CHOICE BUT TO RESORT TO RELYING ON LARGE AMOUNTS OF ECONOMIC AND MILITARY AID FROM THE SOVIET UNION.

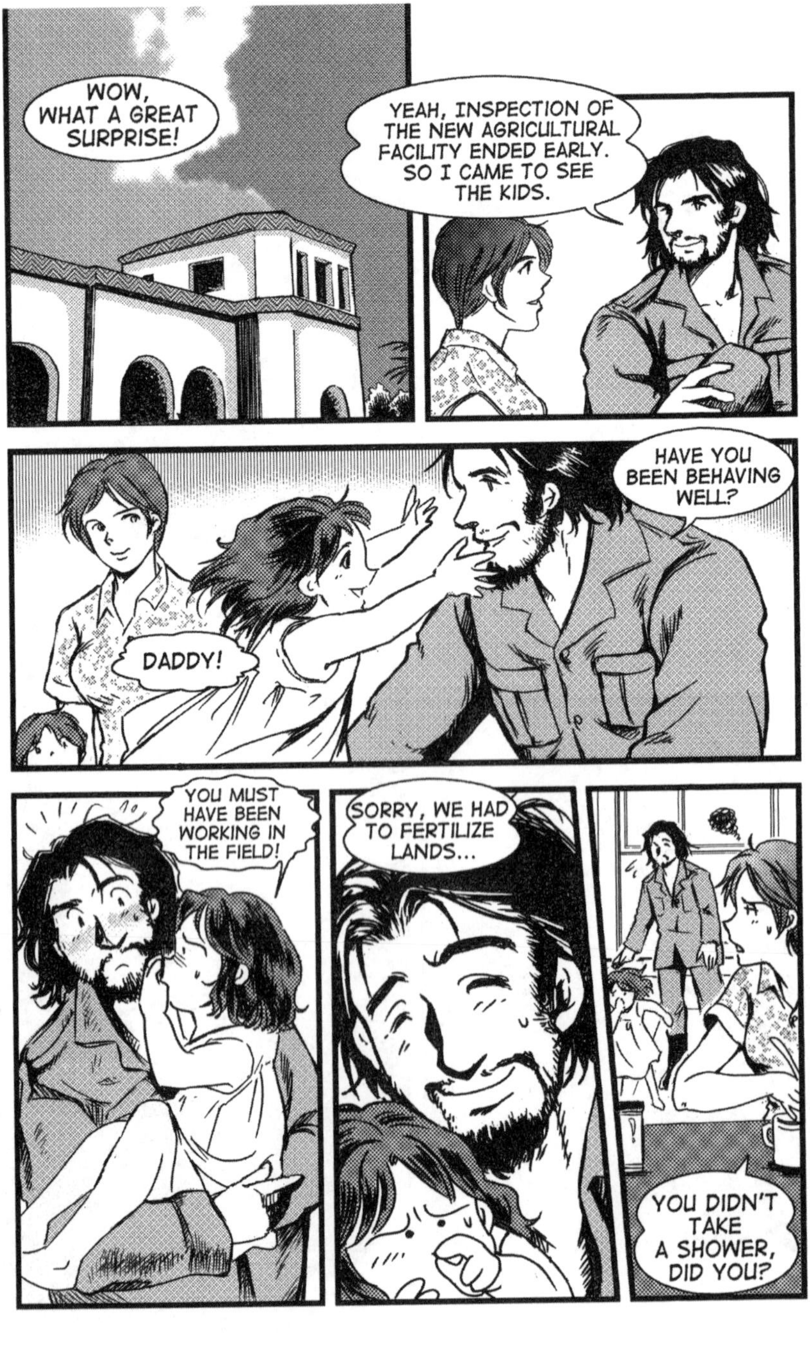
WOW, WHAT A GREAT SURPRISE!
YEAH, INSPECTION OF THE NEW AGRICULTURAL FACILITY ENDED EARLY. SO I CAME TO SEE THE KIDS.
HAVE YOU BEEN BEHAVING WELL?
DADDY!
YOU MUST HAVE BEEN WORKING IN THE FIELD!
SORRY, WE HAD TO FERTILIZE LANDS...
YOU DIDN'T TAKE A SHOWER, DID YOU?

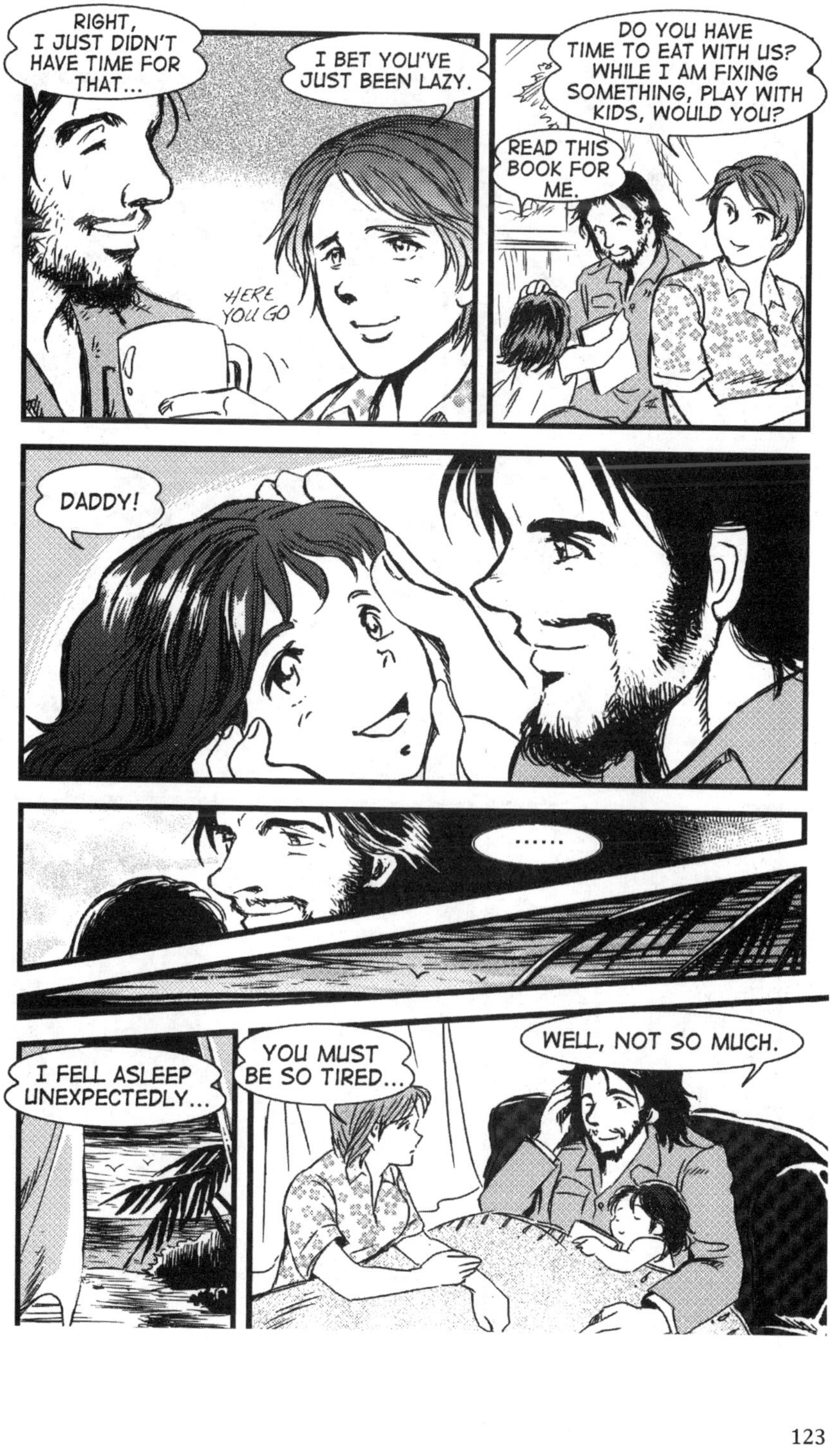
RIGHT, I JUST DIDN'T HAVE TIME FOR THAT...
I BET YOU'VE JUST BEEN LAZY.
HERE YOU GO
DO YOU HAVE TIME TO EAT WITH US? WHILE I AM FIXING SOMETHING, PLAY WITH KIDS, WOULD YOU?
READ THIS BOOK FOR ME.
DADDY!
......
I FELL ASLEEP UNEXPECTEDLY...
YOU MUST BE SO TIRED...
WELL, NOT SO MUCH.

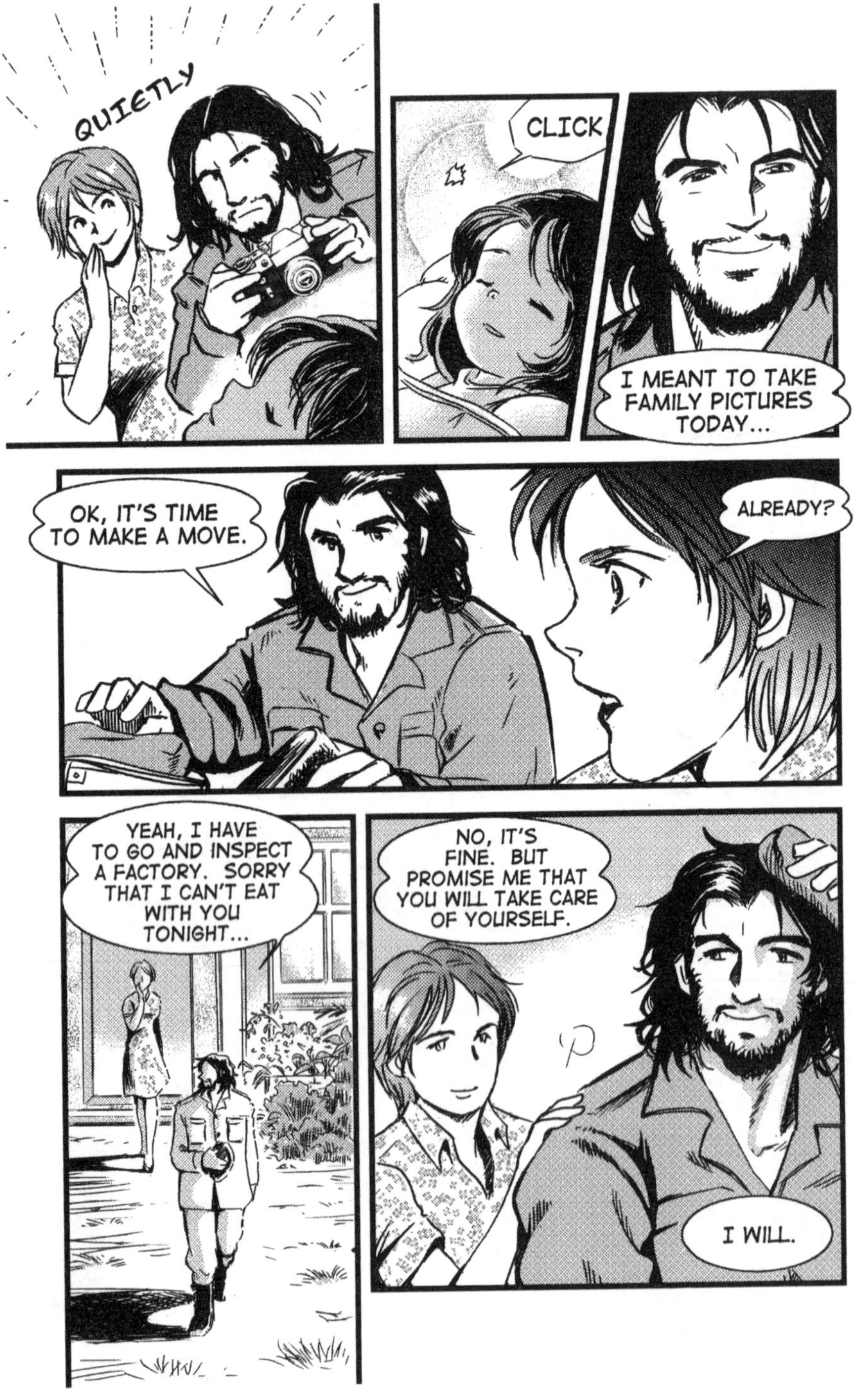
QUIETLY
CLICK
I MEANT TO TAKE FAMILY PICTURES TODAY...
OK, IT'S TIME TO MAKE A MOVE.
ALREADY?
YEAH, I HAVE TO GO AND INSPECT A FACTORY. SORRY THAT I CAN'T EAT WITH YOU TONIGHT...
NO, IT'S FINE. BUT PROMISE ME THAT YOU WILL TAKE CARE OF YOURSELF.
I WILL.

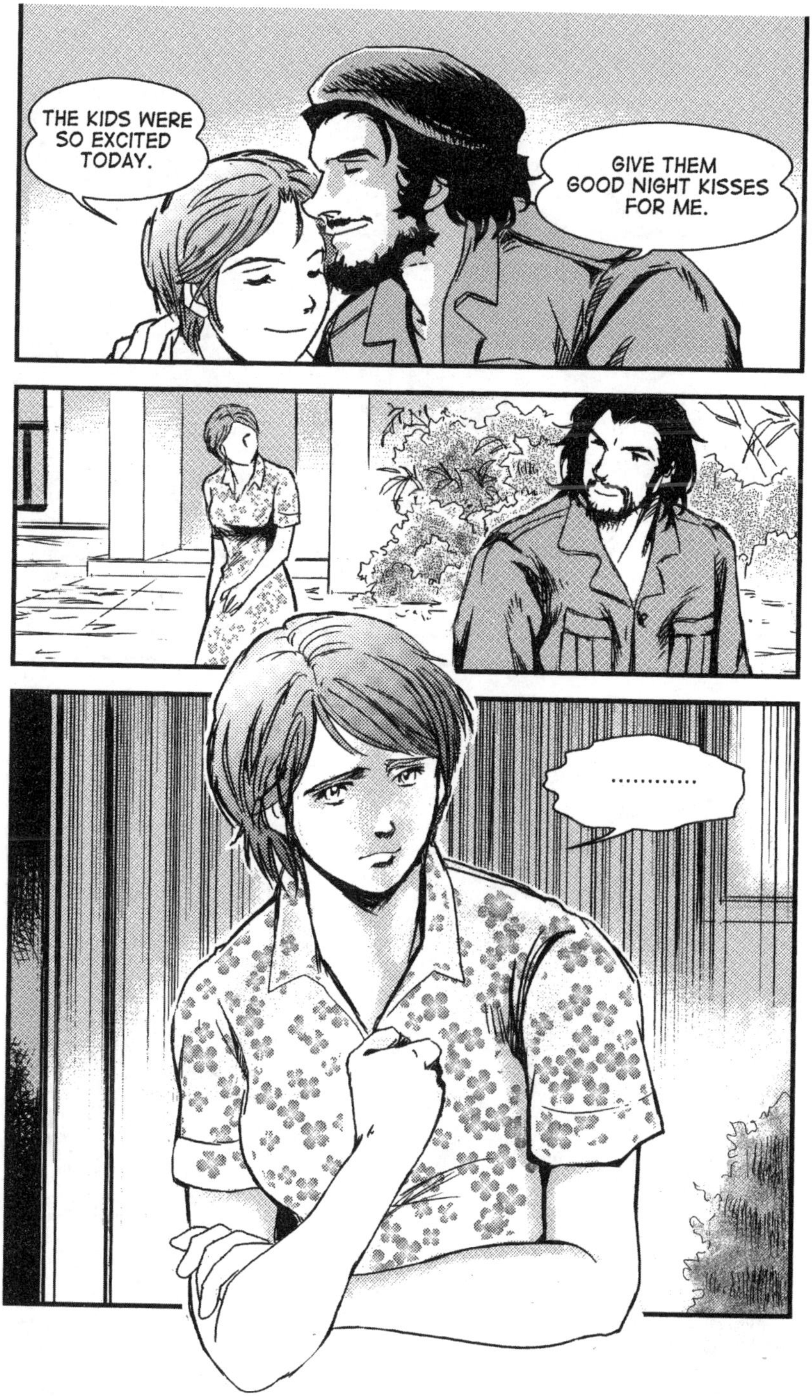
THE KIDS WERE SO EXCITED TODAY.
GIVE THEM GOOD NIGHT KISSES FOR ME.
....

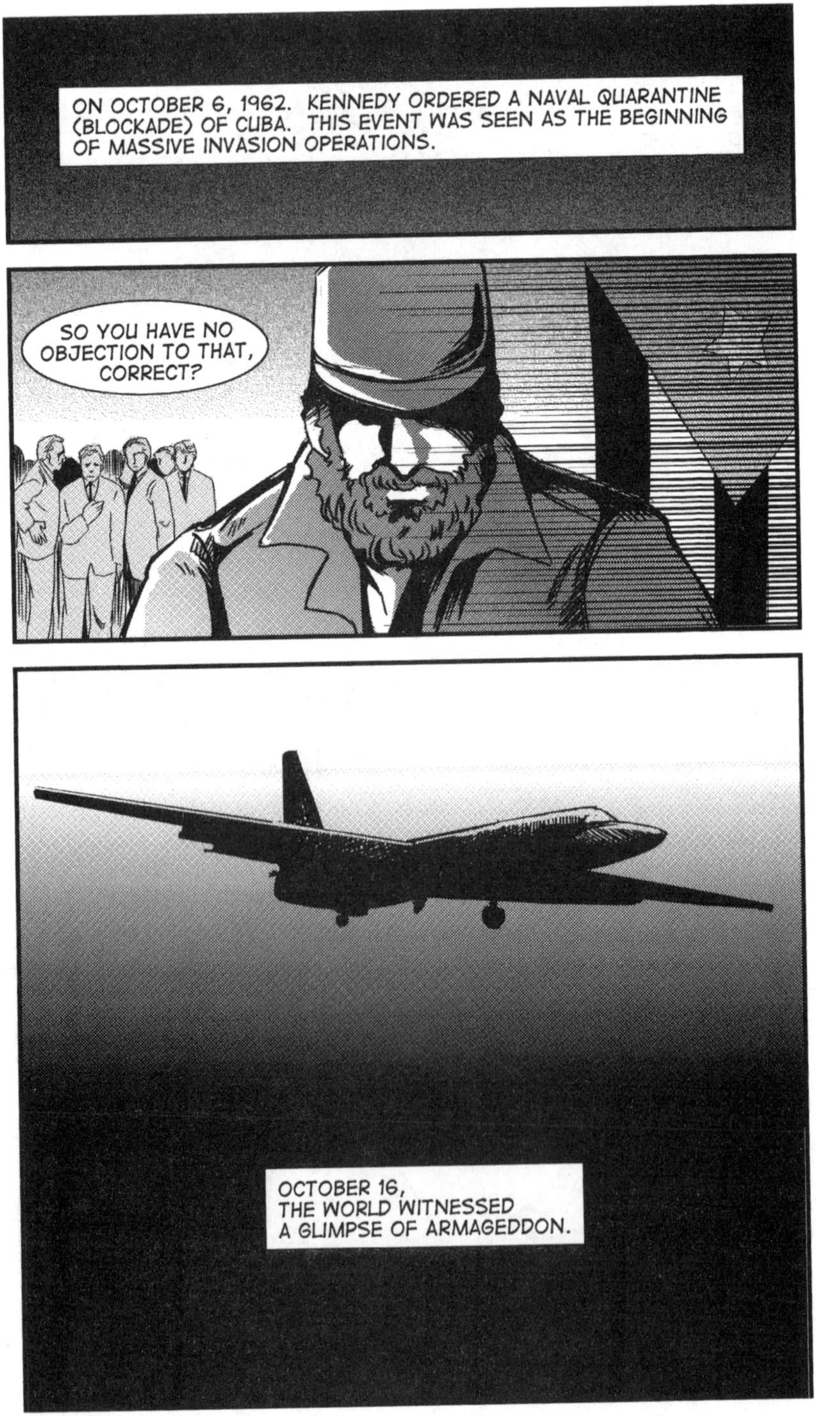
ON OCTOBER 6, 1962. KENNEDY ORDERED A NAVAL QUARANTINE (BLOCKADE) OF CUBA. THIS EVENT WAS SEEN AS THE BEGINNING OF MASSIVE INVASION OPERATIONS.
SO YOU HAVE NO OBJECTION TO THAT, CORRECT?
OCTOBER 16, THE WORLD WITNESSED A GLIMPSE OF ARMAGEDDON.

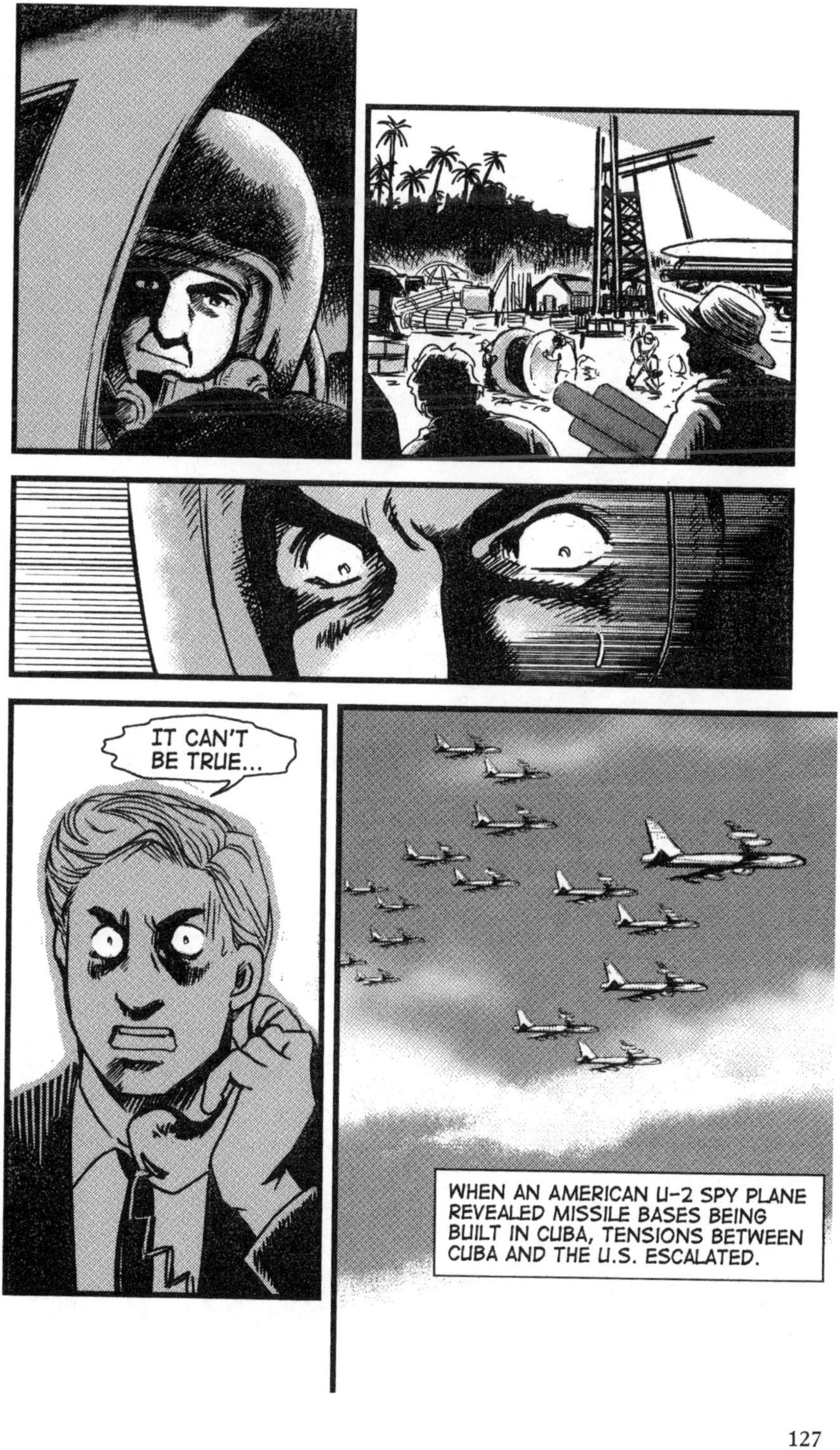
IT CAN'T BE TRUE...
WHEN AN AMERICAN U-2 SPY PLANE REVEALED MISSILE BASES BEING BUILT IN CUBA, TENSIONS BETWEEN CUBA AND THE U.S. ESCALATED.

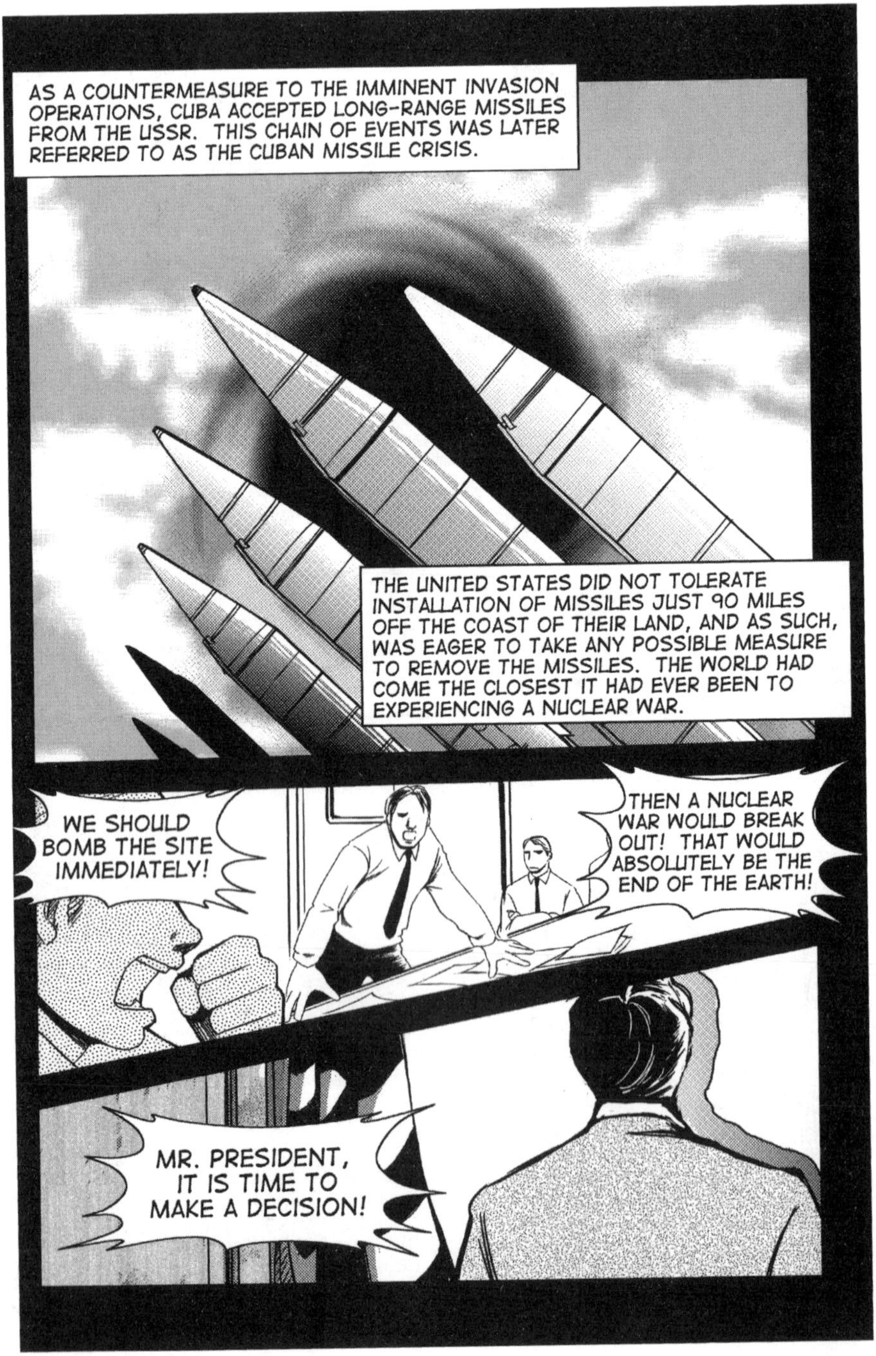

AS A COUNTERMEASURE TO THE IMMINENT INVASION OPERATIONS, CUBA ACCEPTED LONG-RANGE MISSILES FROM THE USSR. THIS CHAIN OF EVENTS WAS LATER REFERRED TO AS THE CUBAN MISSILE CRISIS.
THE UNITED STATES DID NOT TOLERATE INSTALLATION OF MISSILES JUST 90 MILES OFF THE COAST OF THEIR LAND, AND AS SUCH, WAS EAGER TO TAKE ANY POSSIBLE MEASURE TO REMOVE THE MISSILES. THE WORLD HAD COME THE CLOSEST IT HAD EVER BEEN TO EXPERIENCING A NUCLEAR WAR.
WE SHOULD BOMB THE SITE IMMEDIATELY!
THEN A NUCLEAR WAR WOULD BREAK OUT! THAT WOULD ABSOLUTELY BE THE END OF THE EARTH!
MR. PRESIDENT, IT IS TIME TO MAKE A DECISION!

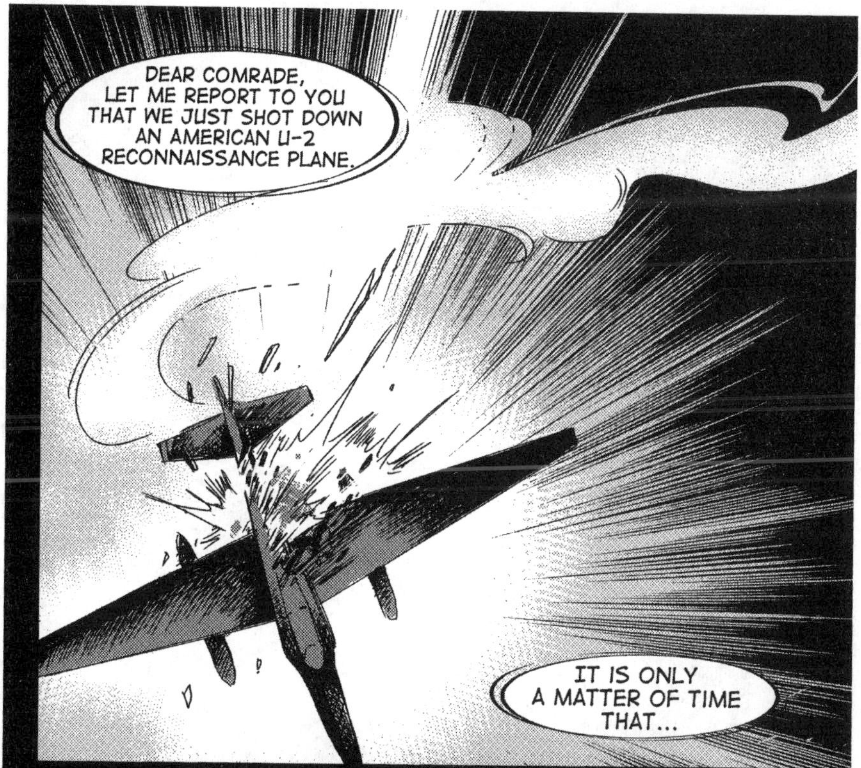
DEAR COMRADE, LET ME REPORT TO YOU THAT WE JUST SHOT DOWN AN AMERICAN U-2 RECONNAISSANCE PLANE.
IT IS ONLY A MATTER OF TIME THAT...
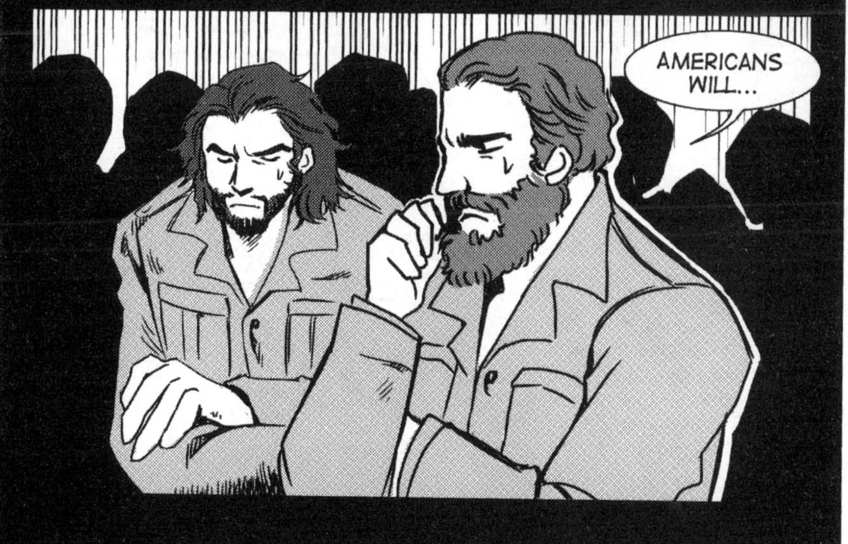
AMERICANS WILL...

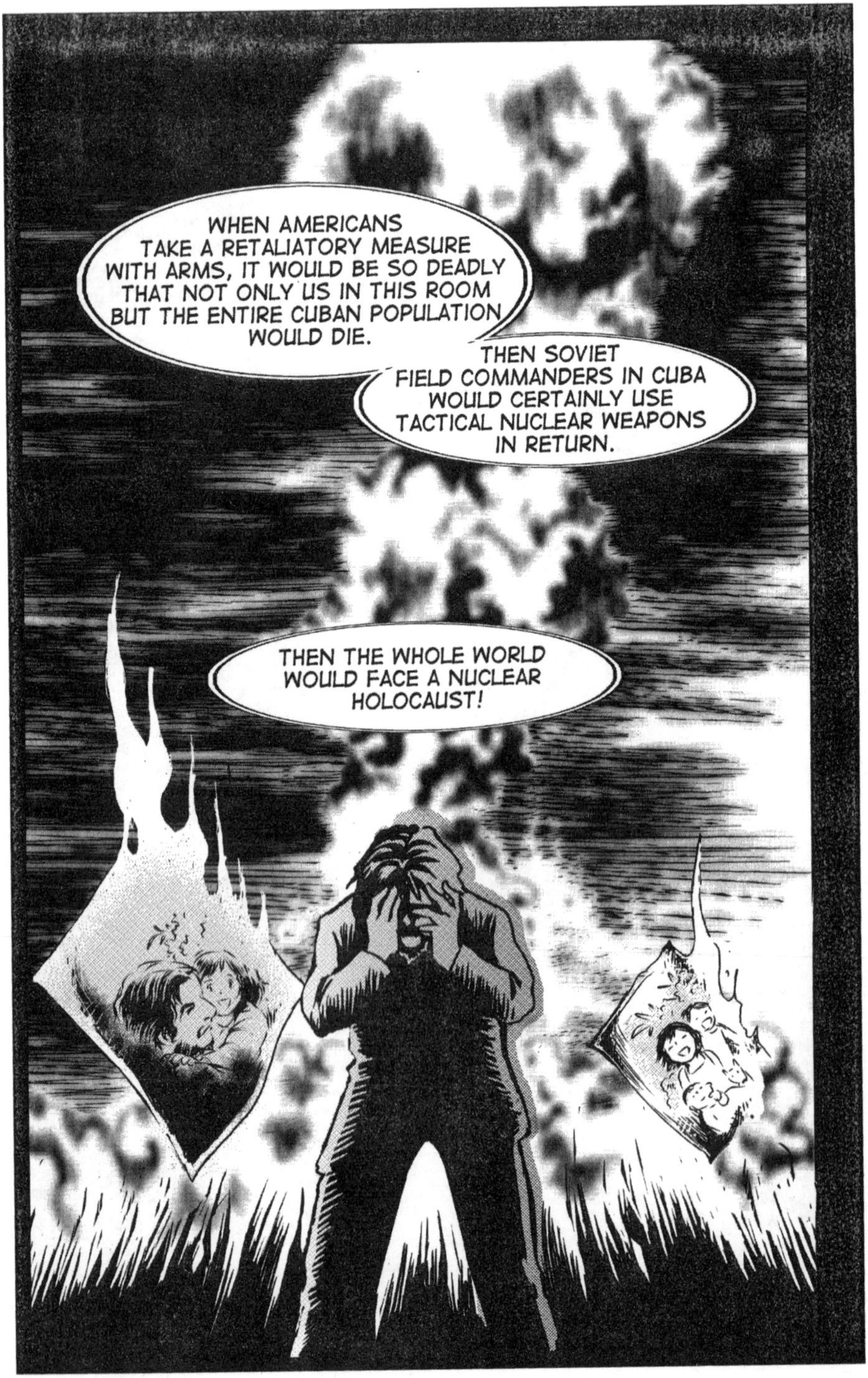
WHEN AMERICANS TAKE A RETALIATORY MEASURE WITH ARMS, IT WOULD BE SO DEADLY THAT NOT ONLY US IN THIS ROOM BUT THE ENTIRE CUBAN POPULATION WOULD DIE.
THEN SOVIET FIELD COMMANDERS IN CUBA WOULD CERTAINLY USE TACTICAL NUCLEAR WEAPONS IN RETURN.
THEN THE WHOLE WORLD WOULD FACE A NUCLEAR HOLOCAUST!

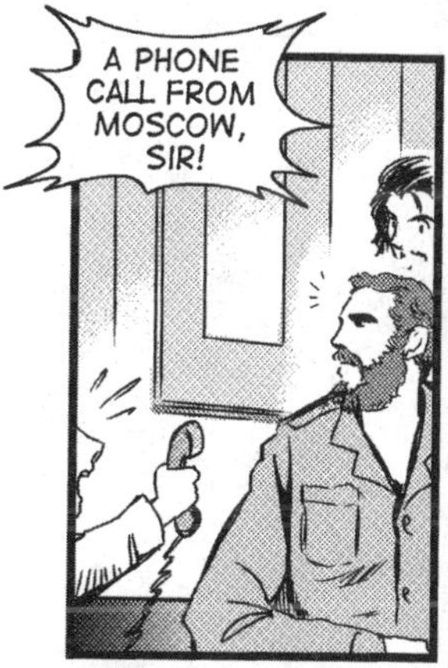
A PHONE CALL FROM MOSCOW, SIR!
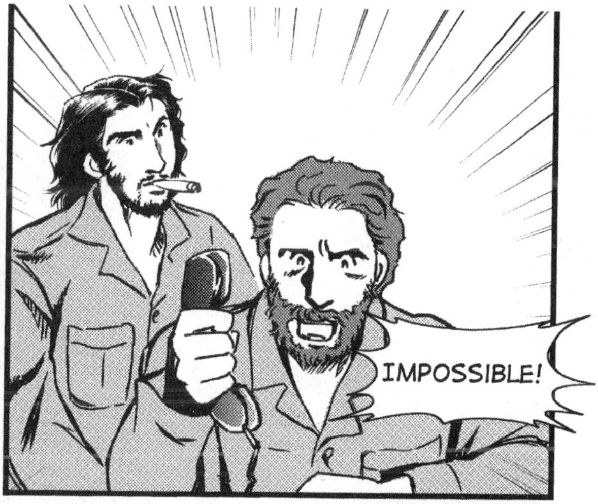
IMPOSSIBLE!
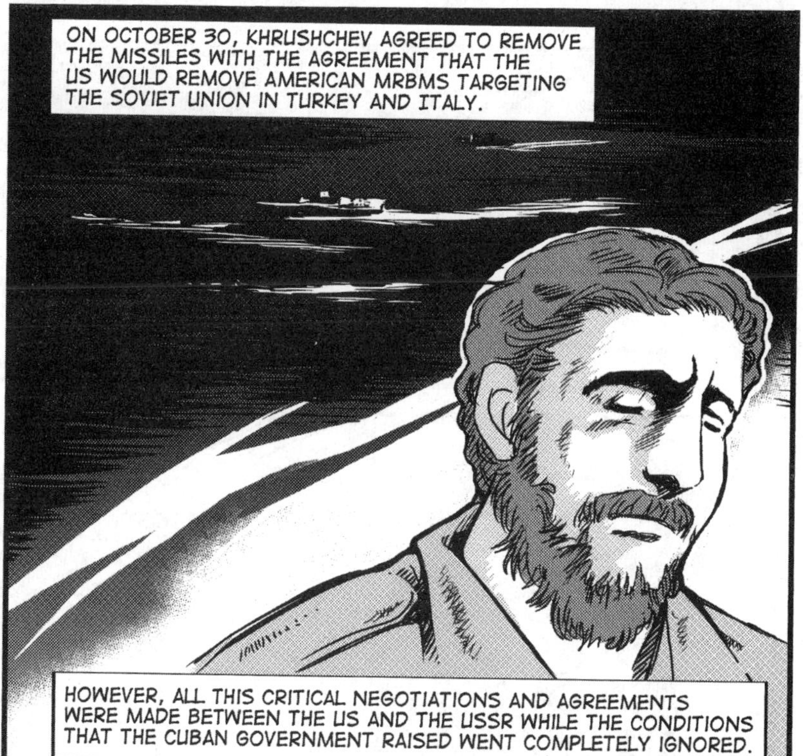
ON OCTOBER 30, KHRUSHCHEV AGREED TO REMOVE THE MISSILES WITH THE AGREEMENT THAT THE US WOULD REMOVE AMERICAN MRBMS TARGETING THE SOVIET UNION IN TURKEY AND ITALY.
HOWEVER, ALL THIS CRITICAL NEGOTIATIONS AND AGREEMENTS WERE MADE BETWEEN THE US AND THE USSR WHILE THE CONDITIONS THAT THE CUBAN GOVERNMENT RAISED WENT COMPLETELY IGNORED.

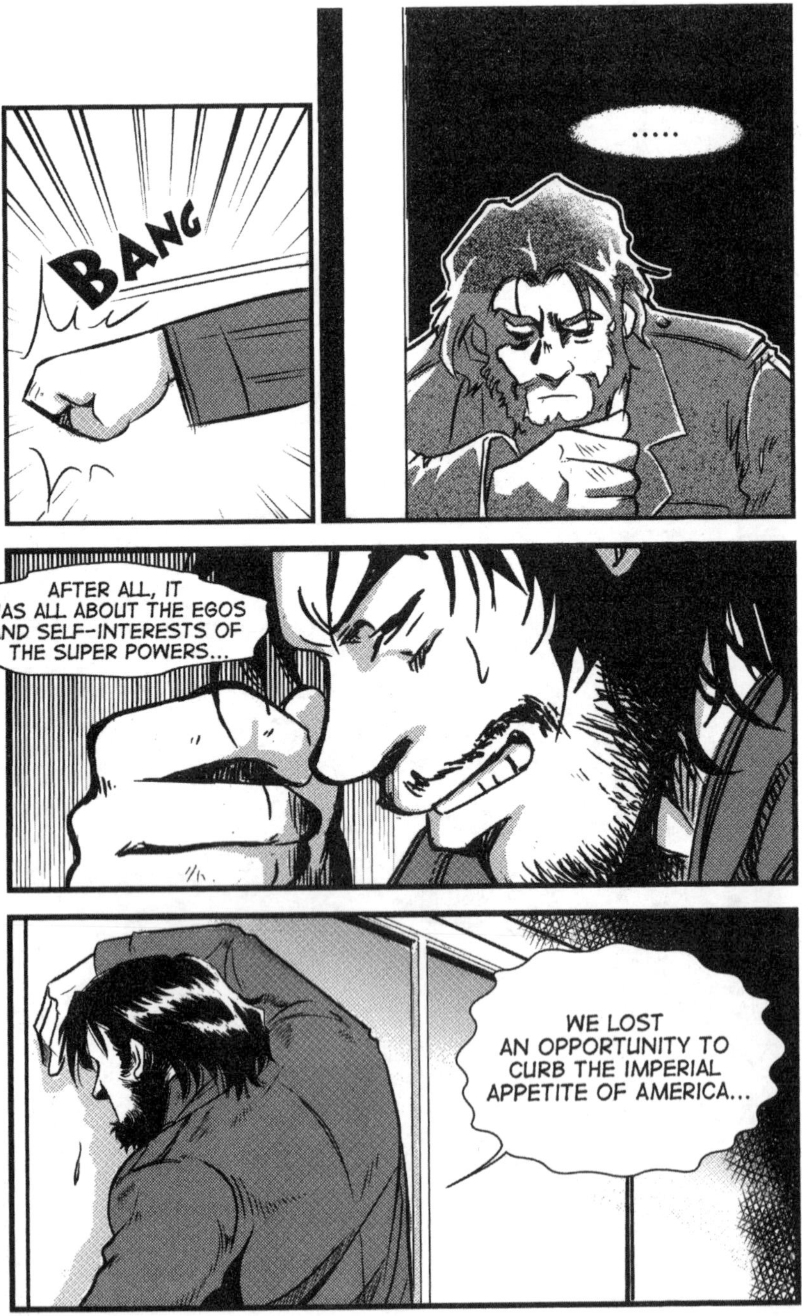
......
BANG
AFTER ALL, IT WAS ALL ABOUT THE EGOS AND SELF-INTERESTS OF THE SUPER POWERS...
WE LOST AN OPPORTUNITY TO CURB THE IMPERIAL APPETITE OF AMERICA...

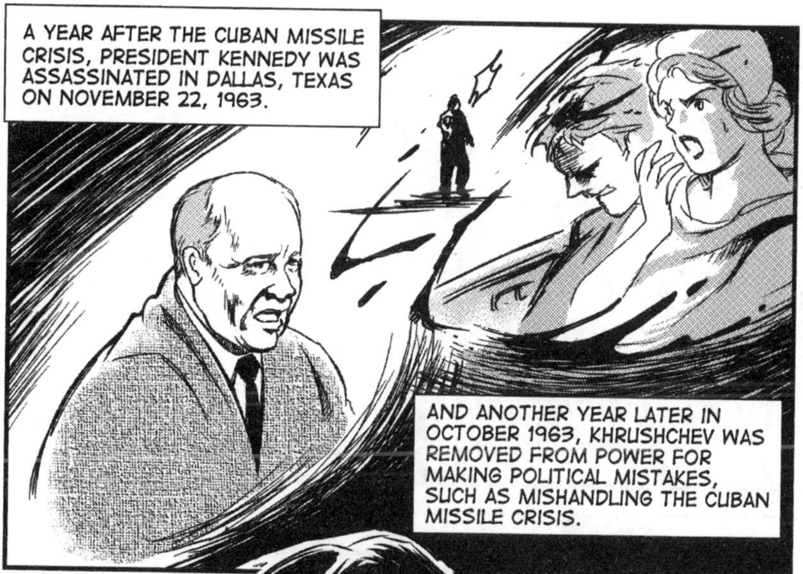
A YEAR AFTER THE CUBAN MISSILE CRISIS, PRESIDENT KENNEDY WAS ASSASSINATED IN DALLAS, TEXAS ON NOVEMBER 22, 1963.
AND ANOTHER YEAR LATER IN OCTOBER 1963, KHRUSHCHEV WAS REMOVED FROM POWER FOR MAKING POLITICAL MISTAKES, SUCH AS MISHANDLING THE CUBAN MISSILE CRISIS.

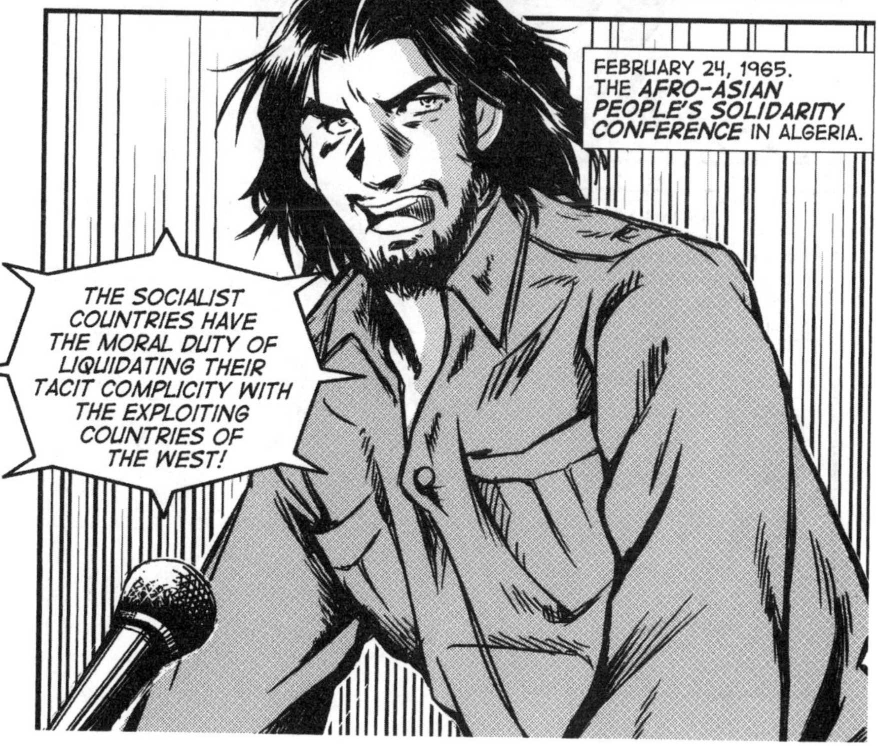
FEBRUARY 24, 1965. THE *AFRO-ASIAN PEOPLE'S SOLIDARITY CONFERENCE* IN ALGERIA.
THE SOCIALIST COUNTRIES HAVE THE MORAL DUTY OF LIQUIDATING THEIR TACIT COMPLICITY WITH THE EXPLOITING COUNTRIES OF THE WEST!

GUEVARA DETESTED ALL IMPERIALISTIC VIEWPOINTS WHETHER THEY WERE CARRIED OUT BY THE UNITED STATES OR THE SOVIET UNION. HOWEVER, HIS IDEALS INFURIATED THE KREMLIN.

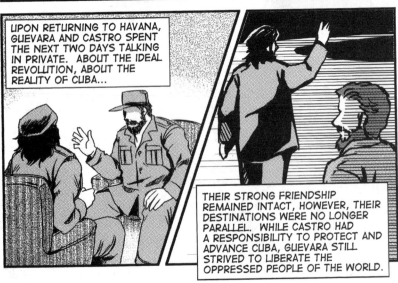

UPON RETURNING TO HAVANA, GUEVARA AND CASTRO SPENT THE NEXT TWO DAYS TALKING IN PRIVATE. ABOUT THE IDEAL REVOLUTION, ABOUT THE REALITY OF CUBA...

THEIR STRONG FRIENDSHIP REMAINED INTACT, HOWEVER, THEIR DESTINATIONS WERE NO LONGER PARALLEL. WHILE CASTRO HAD A RESPONSIBILITY TO PROTECT AND ADVANCE CUBA, GUEVARA STILL STRIVED TO LIBERATE THE OPPRESSED PEOPLE OF THE WORLD.

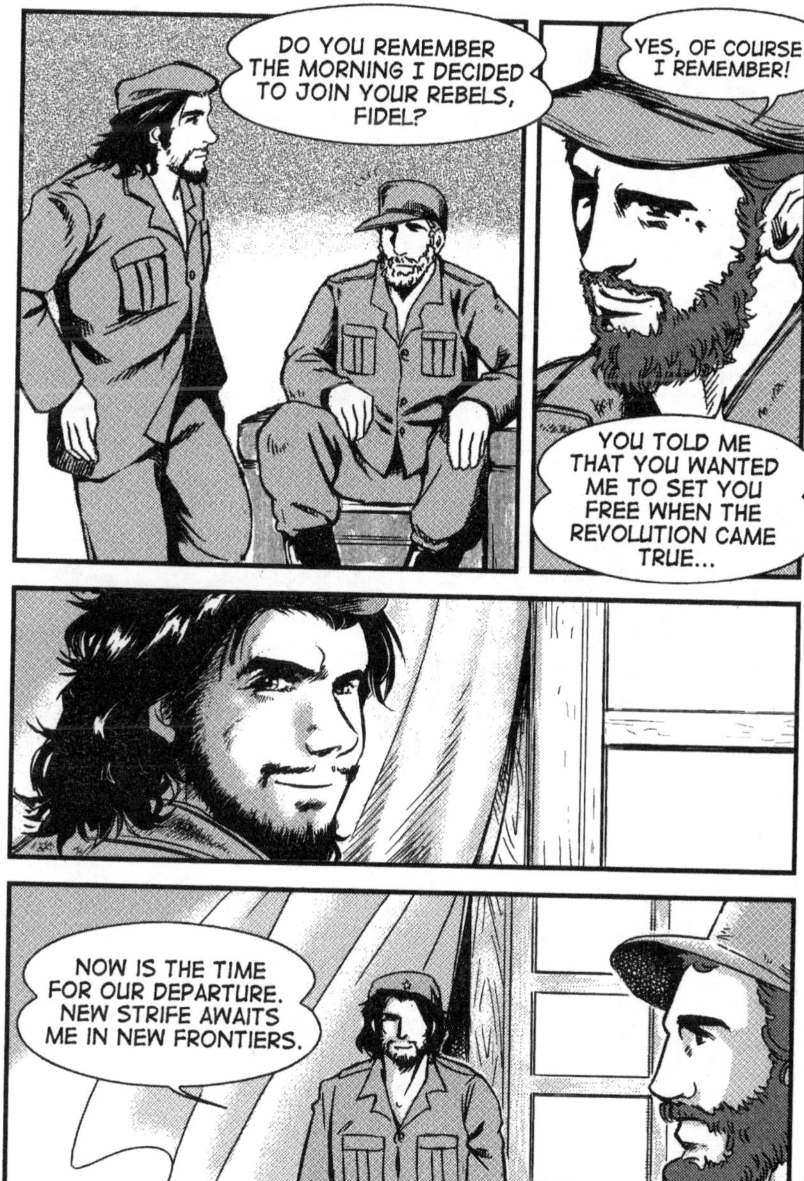
DO YOU REMEMBER THE MORNING I DECIDED TO JOIN YOUR REBELS, FIDEL?
YES, OF COURSE I REMEMBER!
YOU TOLD ME THAT YOU WANTED ME TO SET YOU FREE WHEN THE REVOLUTION CAME TRUE...
NOW IS THE TIME FOR OUR DEPARTURE. NEW STRIFE AWAITS ME IN NEW FRONTIERS.

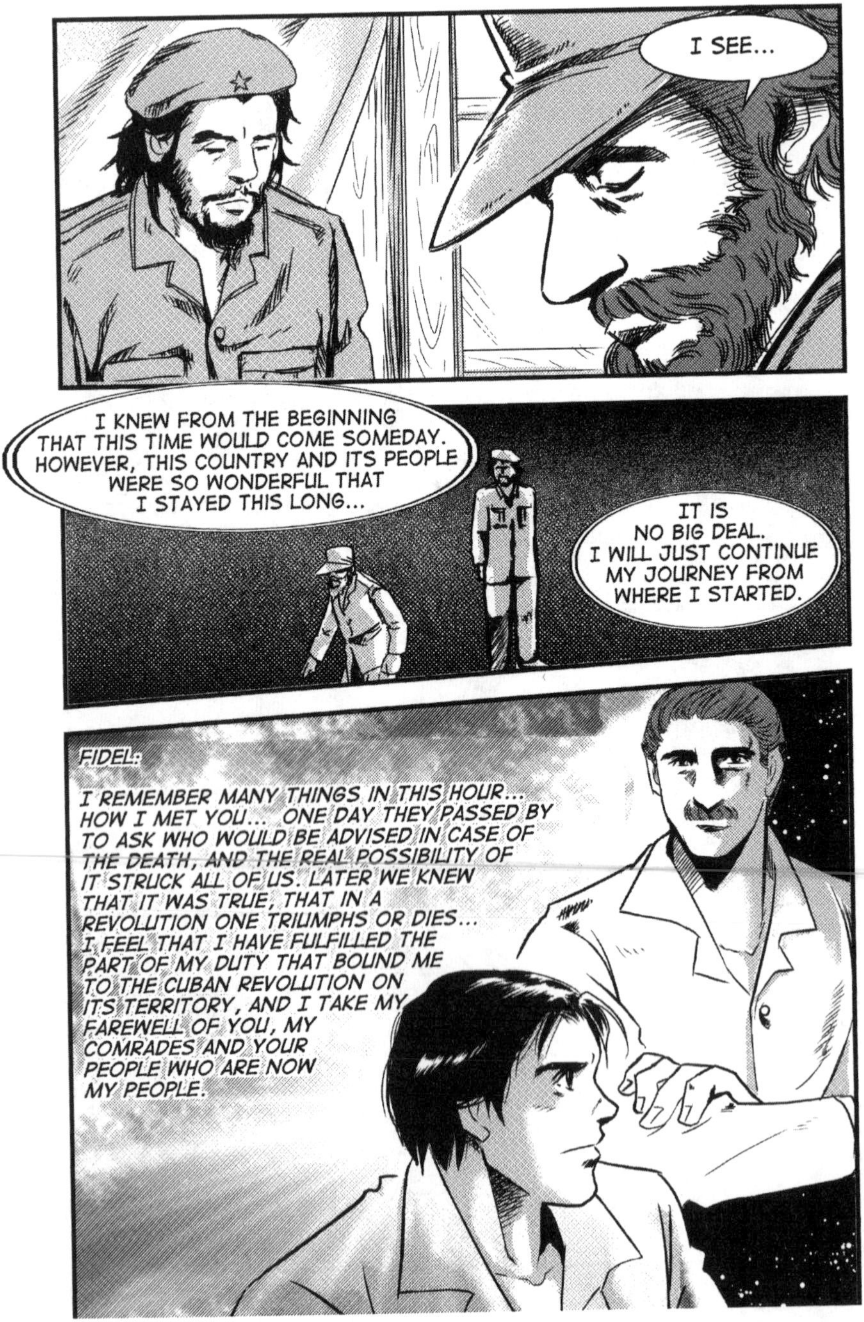
I SEE...
I KNEW FROM THE BEGINNING THAT THIS TIME WOULD COME SOMEDAY. HOWEVER, THIS COUNTRY AND ITS PEOPLE WERE SO WONDERFUL THAT I STAYED THIS LONG...
IT IS NO BIG DEAL. I WILL JUST CONTINUE MY JOURNEY FROM WHERE I STARTED.
FIDEL:
I REMEMBER MANY THINGS IN THIS HOUR... HOW I MET YOU... ONE DAY THEY PASSED BY TO ASK WHO WOULD BE ADVISED IN CASE OF THE DEATH, AND THE REAL POSSIBILITY OF IT STRUCK ALL OF US. LATER WE KNEW THAT IT WAS TRUE, THAT IN A REVOLUTION ONE TRIUMPHS OR DIES... I FEEL THAT I HAVE FULFILLED THE PART OF MY DUTY THAT BOUND ME TO THE CUBAN REVOLUTION ON ITS TERRITORY, AND I TAKE MY FAREWELL OF YOU, MY COMRADES AND YOUR PEOPLE WHO ARE NOW MY PEOPLE.

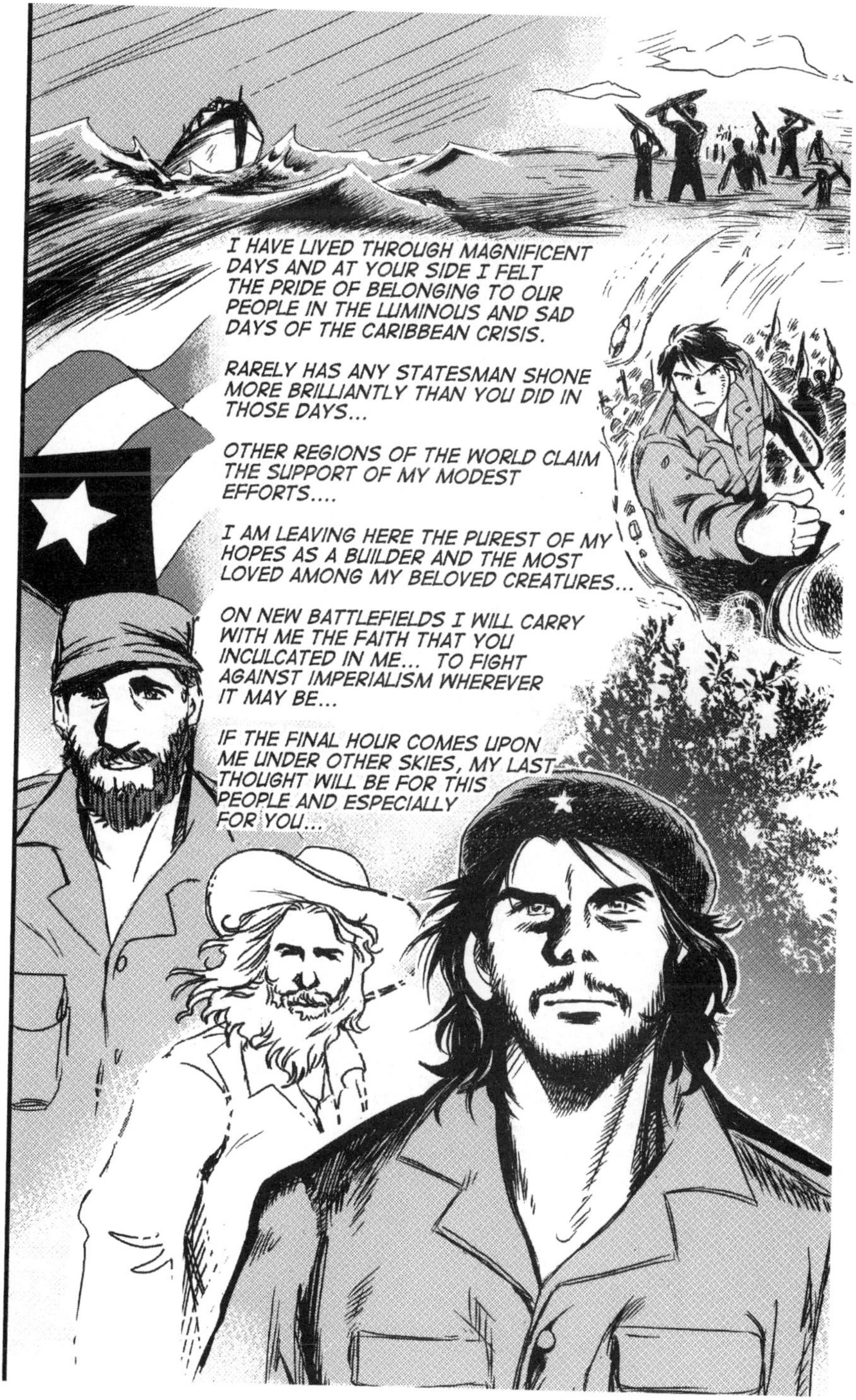
I HAVE LIVED THROUGH MAGNIFICENT DAYS AND AT YOUR SIDE I FELT THE PRIDE OF BELONGING TO OUR PEOPLE IN THE LUMINOUS AND SAD DAYS OF THE CARIBBEAN CRISIS.
RARELY HAS ANY STATESMAN SHONE MORE BRILLIANTLY THAN YOU DID IN THOSE DAYS...
OTHER REGIONS OF THE WORLD CLAIM THE SUPPORT OF MY MODEST EFFORTS....
I AM LEAVING HERE THE PUREST OF MY HOPES AS A BUILDER AND THE MOST LOVED AMONG MY BELOVED CREATURES...
ON NEW BATTLEFIELDS I WILL CARRY WITH ME THE FAITH THAT YOU INCULCATED IN ME... TO FIGHT AGAINST IMPERIALISM WHEREVER IT MAY BE...
IF THE FINAL HOUR COMES UPON ME UNDER OTHER SKIES, MY LAST THOUGHT WILL BE FOR THIS PEOPLE AND ESPECIALLY FOR YOU...

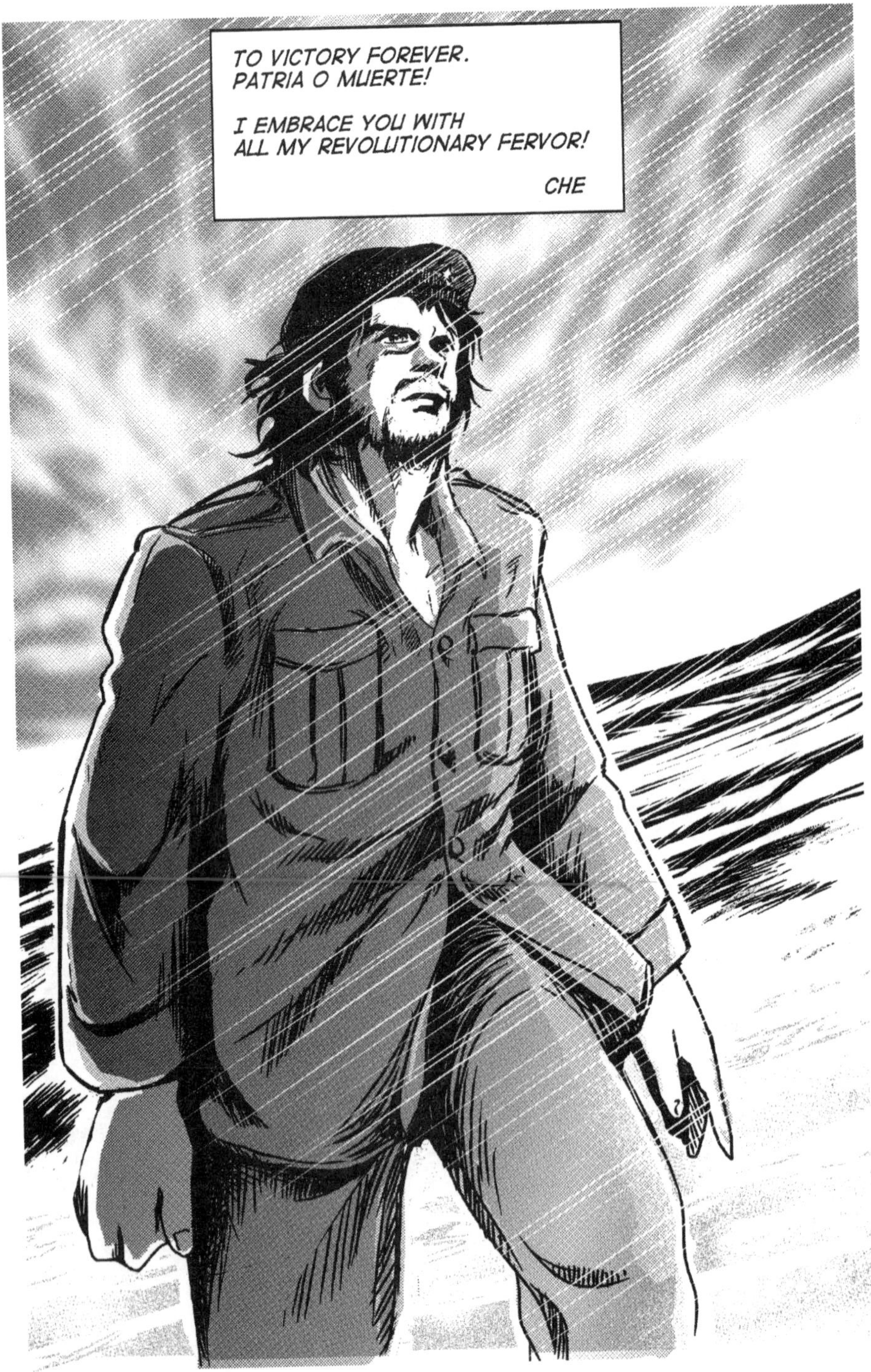
TO VICTORY FOREVER.
PATRIA O MUERTE!
I EMBRACE YOU WITH
ALL MY REVOLUTIONARY FERVOR!
CHE

CHAPTER 5

LEGEND

1956 - Present

Whenever death may surprise us, let it be welcome
if our battle cry has reached even one receptive ear
and another hand reaches out to take up our arms.

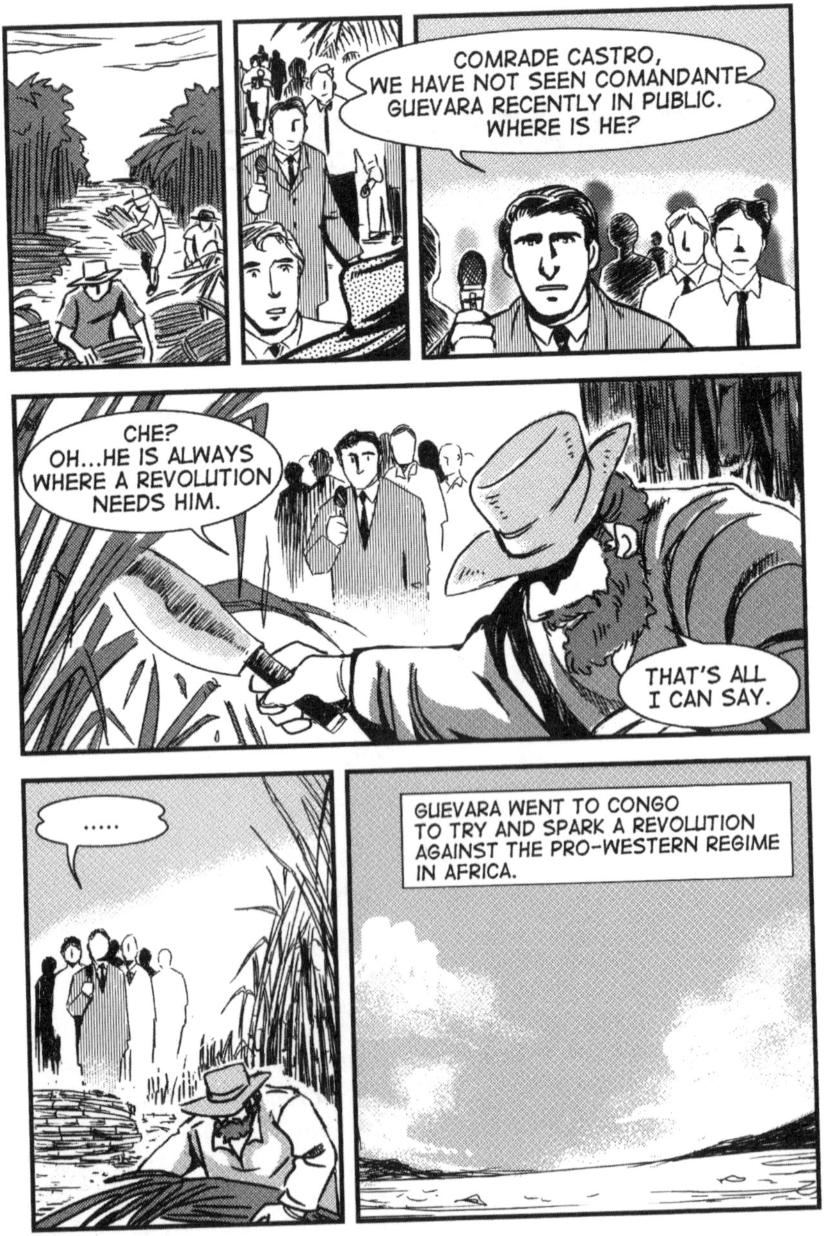
COMRADE CASTRO, WE HAVE NOT SEEN COMANDANTE GUEVARA RECENTLY IN PUBLIC. WHERE IS HE?
CHE? OH...HE IS ALWAYS WHERE A REVOLUTION NEEDS HIM.
THAT'S ALL I CAN SAY.
.....
GUEVARA WENT TO CONGO TO TRY AND SPARK A REVOLUTION AGAINST THE PRO-WESTERN REGIME IN AFRICA.

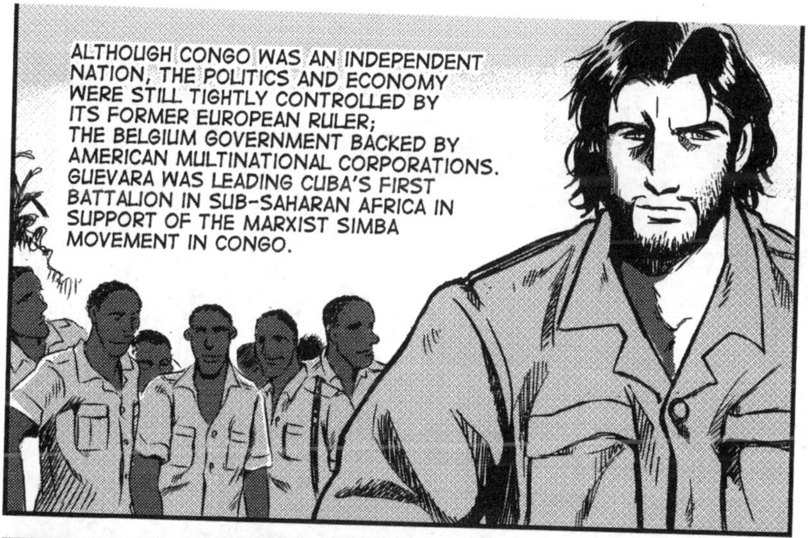
ALTHOUGH CONGO WAS AN INDEPENDENT NATION, THE POLITICS AND ECONOMY WERE STILL TIGHTLY CONTROLLED BY ITS FORMER EUROPEAN RULER; THE BELGIUM GOVERNMENT BACKED BY AMERICAN MULTINATIONAL CORPORATIONS. GUEVARA WAS LEADING CUBA'S FIRST BATTALION IN SUB-SAHARAN AFRICA IN SUPPORT OF THE MARXIST SIMBA MOVEMENT IN CONGO.

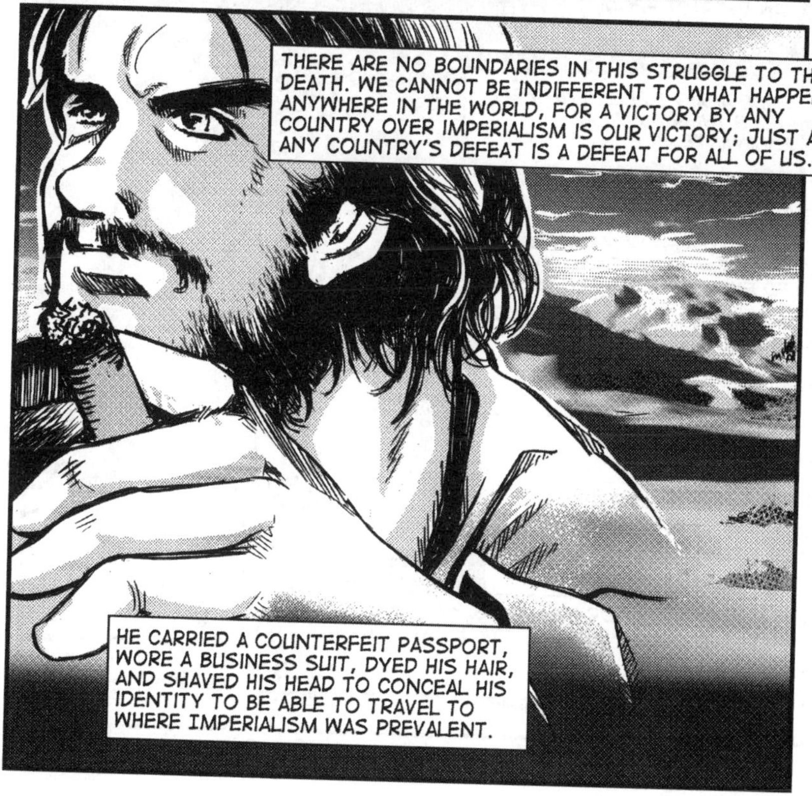
THERE ARE NO BOUNDARIES IN THIS STRUGGLE TO THE DEATH. WE CANNOT BE INDIFFERENT TO WHAT HAPPENS ANYWHERE IN THE WORLD, FOR A VICTORY BY ANY COUNTRY OVER IMPERIALISM IS OUR VICTORY; JUST AS ANY COUNTRY'S DEFEAT IS A DEFEAT FOR ALL OF US.
HE CARRIED A COUNTERFEIT PASSPORT, WORE A BUSINESS SUIT, DYED HIS HAIR, AND SHAVED HIS HEAD TO CONCEAL HIS IDENTITY TO BE ABLE TO TRAVEL TO WHERE IMPERIALISM WAS PREVALENT.

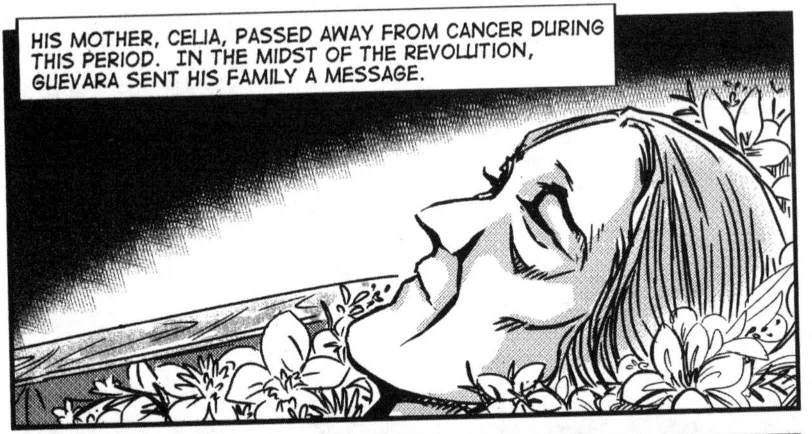
HIS MOTHER, CELIA, PASSED AWAY FROM CANCER DURING THIS PERIOD. IN THE MIDST OF THE REVOLUTION, GUEVARA SENT HIS FAMILY A MESSAGE.

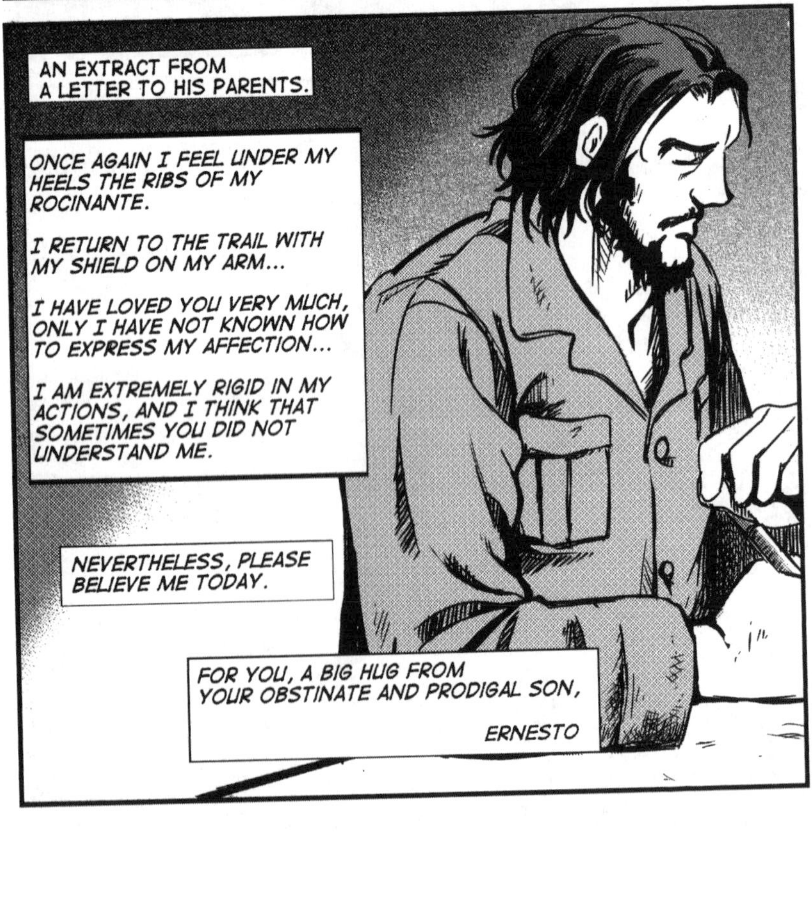
AN EXTRACT FROM A LETTER TO HIS PARENTS.
ONCE AGAIN I FEEL UNDER MY HEELS THE RIBS OF MY ROCINANTE.
I RETURN TO THE TRAIL WITH MY SHIELD ON MY ARM...
I HAVE LOVED YOU VERY MUCH, ONLY I HAVE NOT KNOWN HOW TO EXPRESS MY AFFECTION...
I AM EXTREMELY RIGID IN MY ACTIONS, AND I THINK THAT SOMETIMES YOU DID NOT UNDERSTAND ME.
NEVERTHELESS, PLEASE BELIEVE ME TODAY.
FOR YOU, A BIG HUG FROM YOUR OBSTINATE AND PRODIGAL SON,
ERNESTO

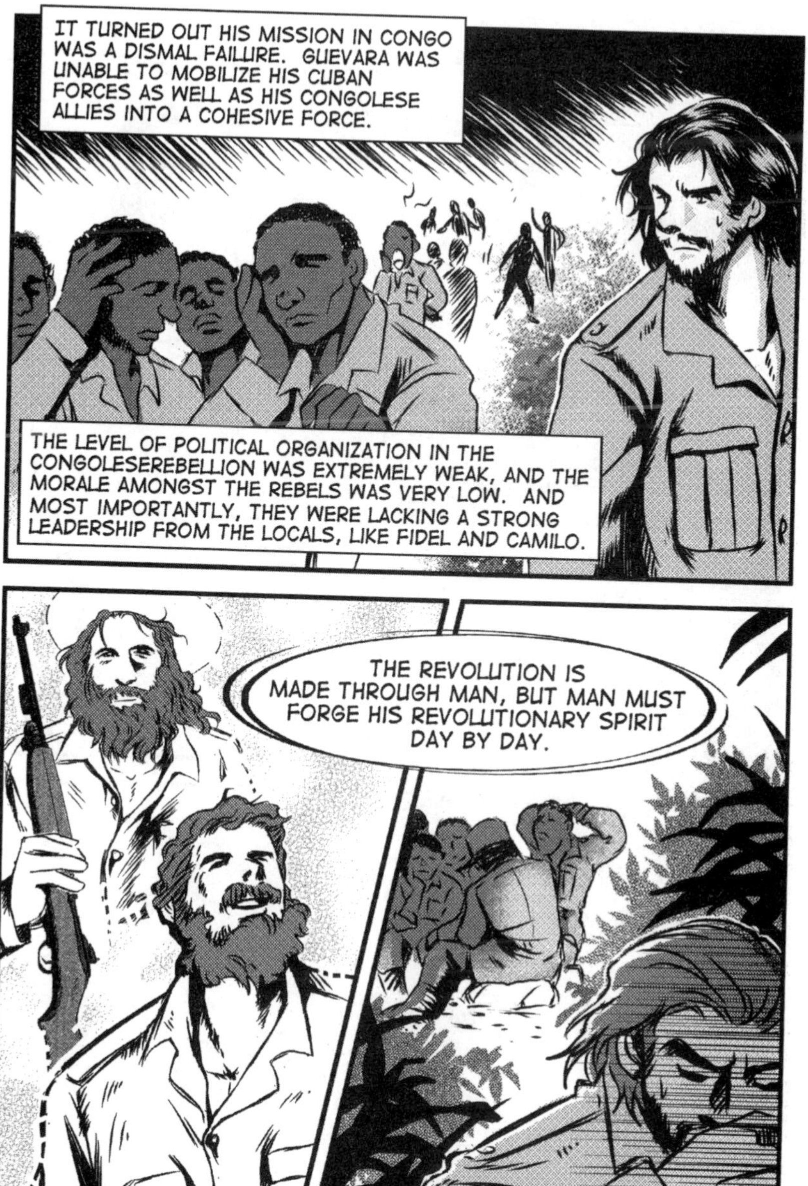
IT TURNED OUT HIS MISSION IN CONGO WAS A DISMAL FAILURE. GUEVARA WAS UNABLE TO MOBILIZE HIS CUBAN FORCES AS WELL AS HIS CONGOLESE ALLIES INTO A COHESIVE FORCE.
THE LEVEL OF POLITICAL ORGANIZATION IN THE CONGOLESEREBELLION WAS EXTREMELY WEAK, AND THE MORALE AMONGST THE REBELS WAS VERY LOW. AND MOST IMPORTANTLY, THEY WERE LACKING A STRONG LEADERSHIP FROM THE LOCALS, LIKE FIDEL AND CAMILO.
THE REVOLUTION IS MADE THROUGH MAN, BUT MAN MUST FORGE HIS REVOLUTIONARY SPIRIT DAY BY DAY.

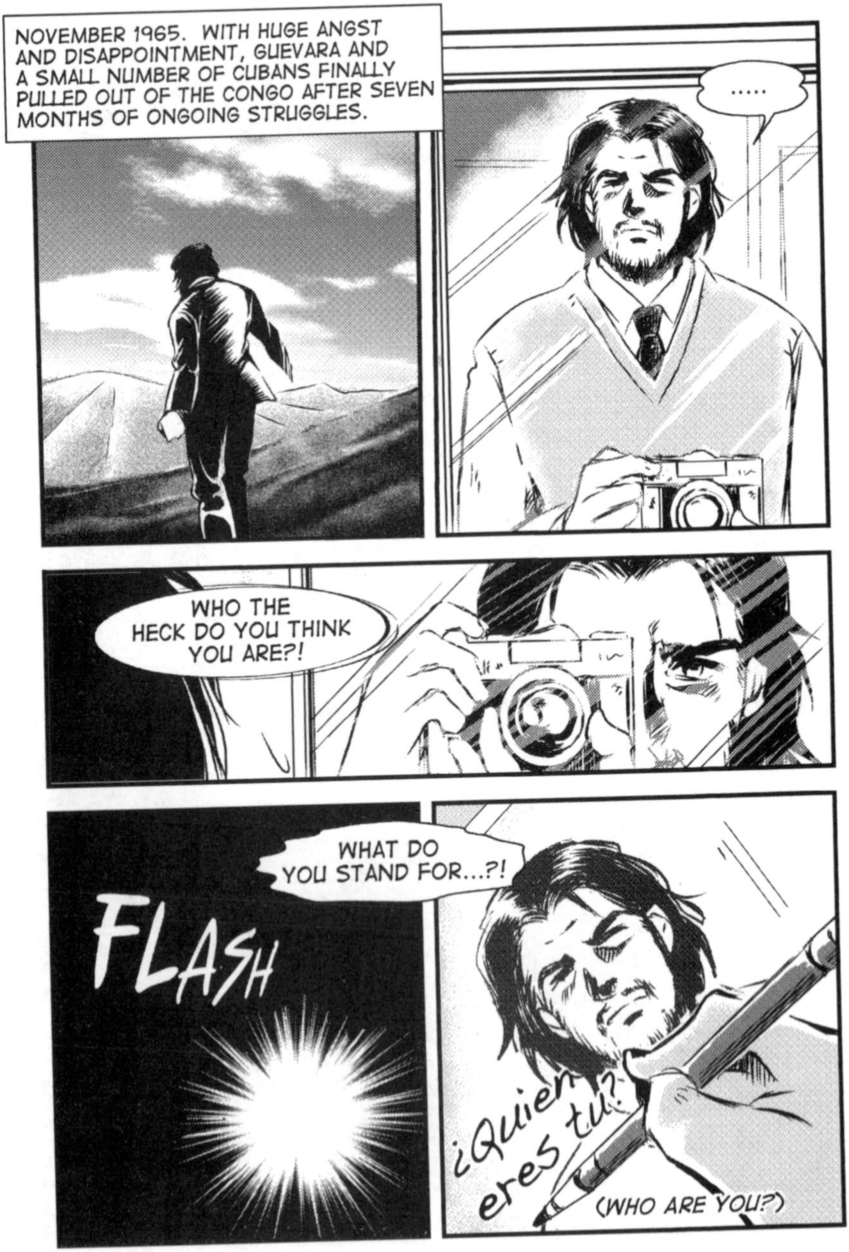
NOVEMBER 1965. WITH HUGE ANGST AND DISAPPOINTMENT, GUEVARA AND A SMALL NUMBER OF CUBANS FINALLY PULLED OUT OF THE CONGO AFTER SEVEN MONTHS OF ONGOING STRUGGLES.
.....
WHO THE HECK DO YOU THINK YOU ARE?!
FLASH
WHAT DO YOU STAND FOR...?!
¿Quien eres tu?
(WHO ARE YOU?)

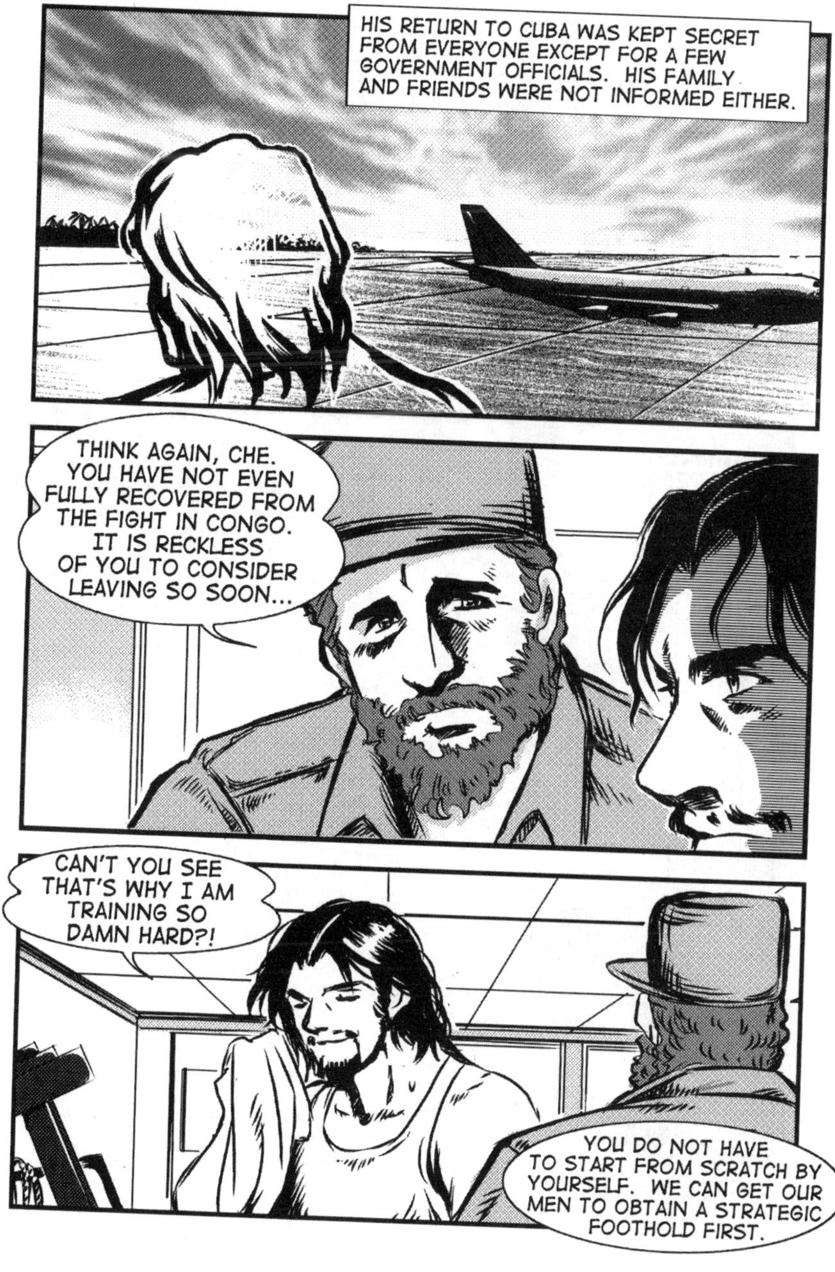
HIS RETURN TO CUBA WAS KEPT SECRET FROM EVERYONE EXCEPT FOR A FEW GOVERNMENT OFFICIALS. HIS FAMILY AND FRIENDS WERE NOT INFORMED EITHER.
THINK AGAIN, CHE. YOU HAVE NOT EVEN FULLY RECOVERED FROM THE FIGHT IN CONGO. IT IS RECKLESS OF YOU TO CONSIDER LEAVING SO SOON...
CAN'T YOU SEE THAT'S WHY I AM TRAINING SO DAMN HARD?!
YOU DO NOT HAVE TO START FROM SCRATCH BY YOURSELF. WE CAN GET OUR MEN TO OBTAIN A STRATEGIC FOOTHOLD FIRST.

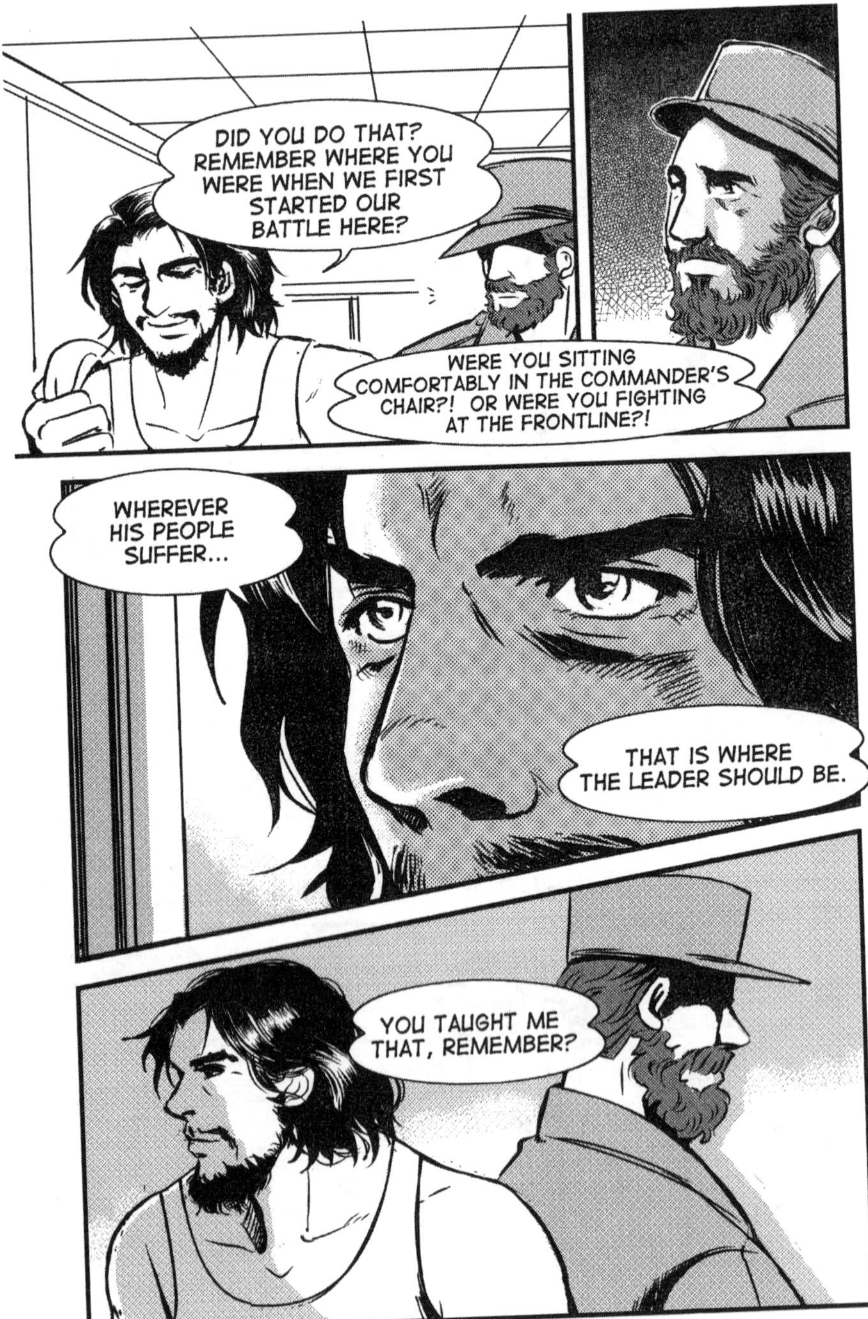
DID YOU DO THAT? REMEMBER WHERE YOU WERE WHEN WE FIRST STARTED OUR BATTLE HERE?
WERE YOU SITTING COMFORTABLY IN THE COMMANDER'S CHAIR?! OR WERE YOU FIGHTING AT THE FRONTLINE?!
WHEREVER HIS PEOPLE SUFFER...
THAT IS WHERE THE LEADER SHOULD BE.
YOU TAUGHT ME THAT, REMEMBER?

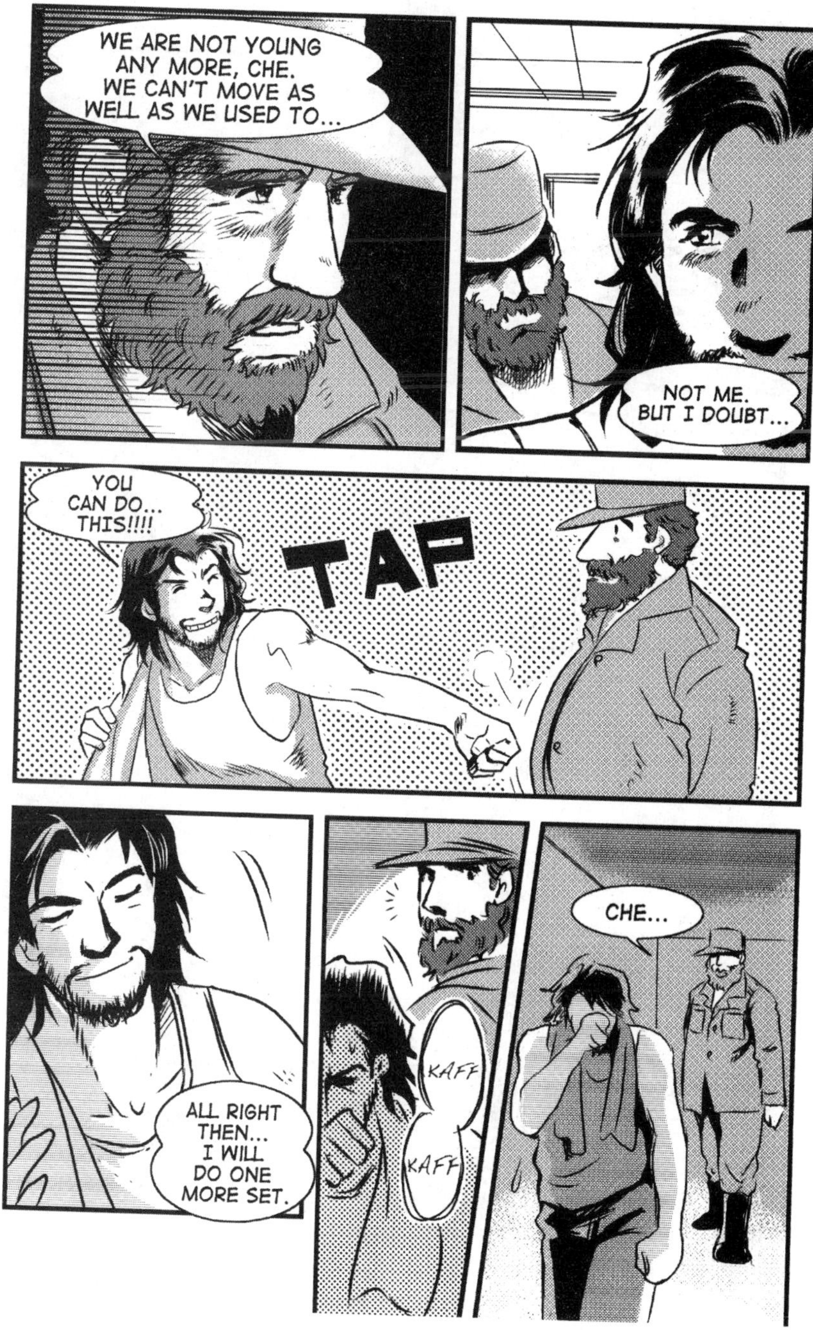
WE ARE NOT YOUNG ANY MORE, CHE. WE CAN'T MOVE AS WELL AS WE USED TO...
NOT ME. BUT I DOUBT...
YOU CAN DO... THIS!!!!
TAP
ALL RIGHT THEN... I WILL DO ONE MORE SET.
KAFF
KAFF
CHE...

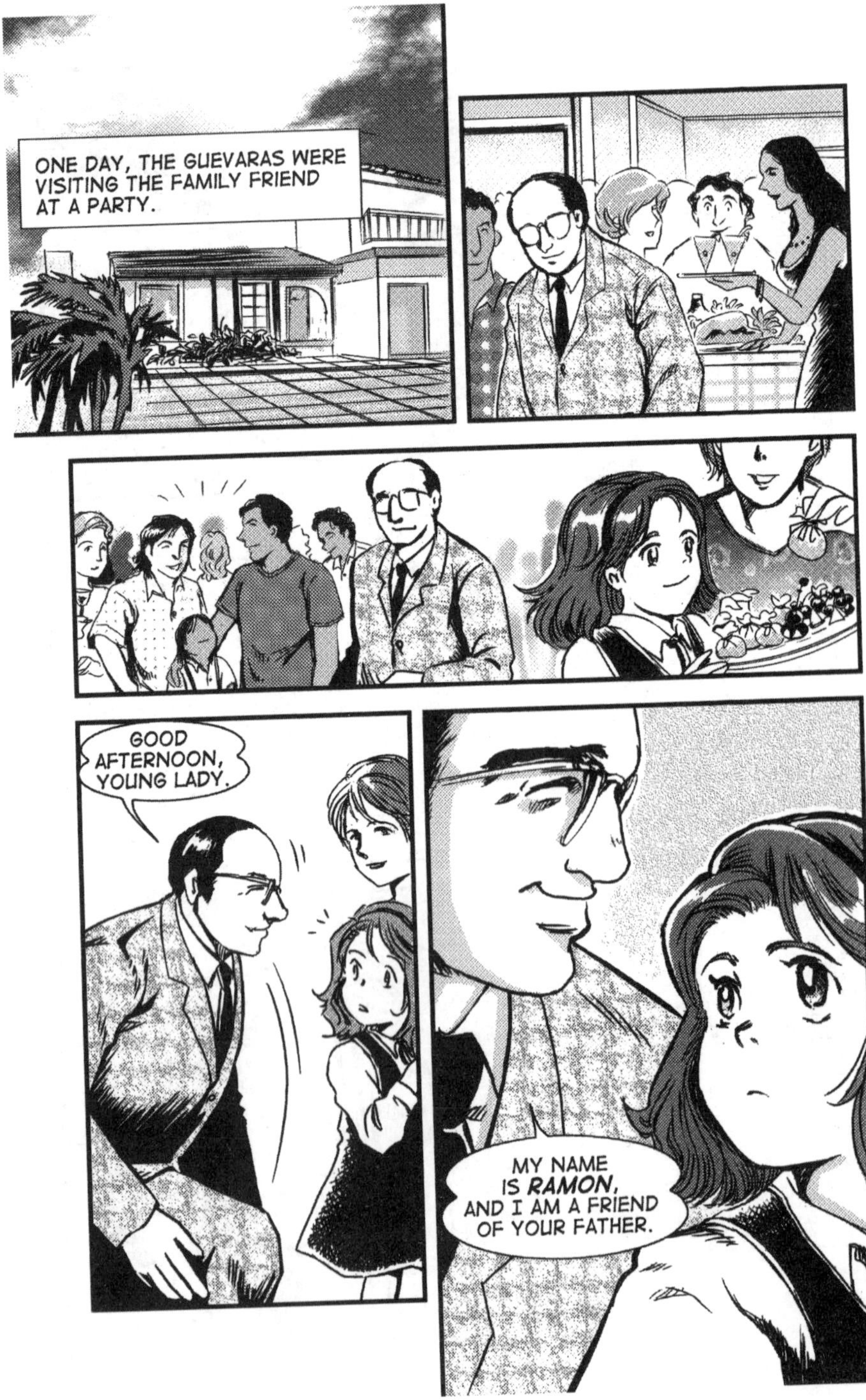
ONE DAY, THE GUEVARAS WERE VISITING THE FAMILY FRIEND AT A PARTY.
GOOD AFTERNOON, YOUNG LADY.
MY NAME IS ***RAMON***, AND I AM A FRIEND OF YOUR FATHER.

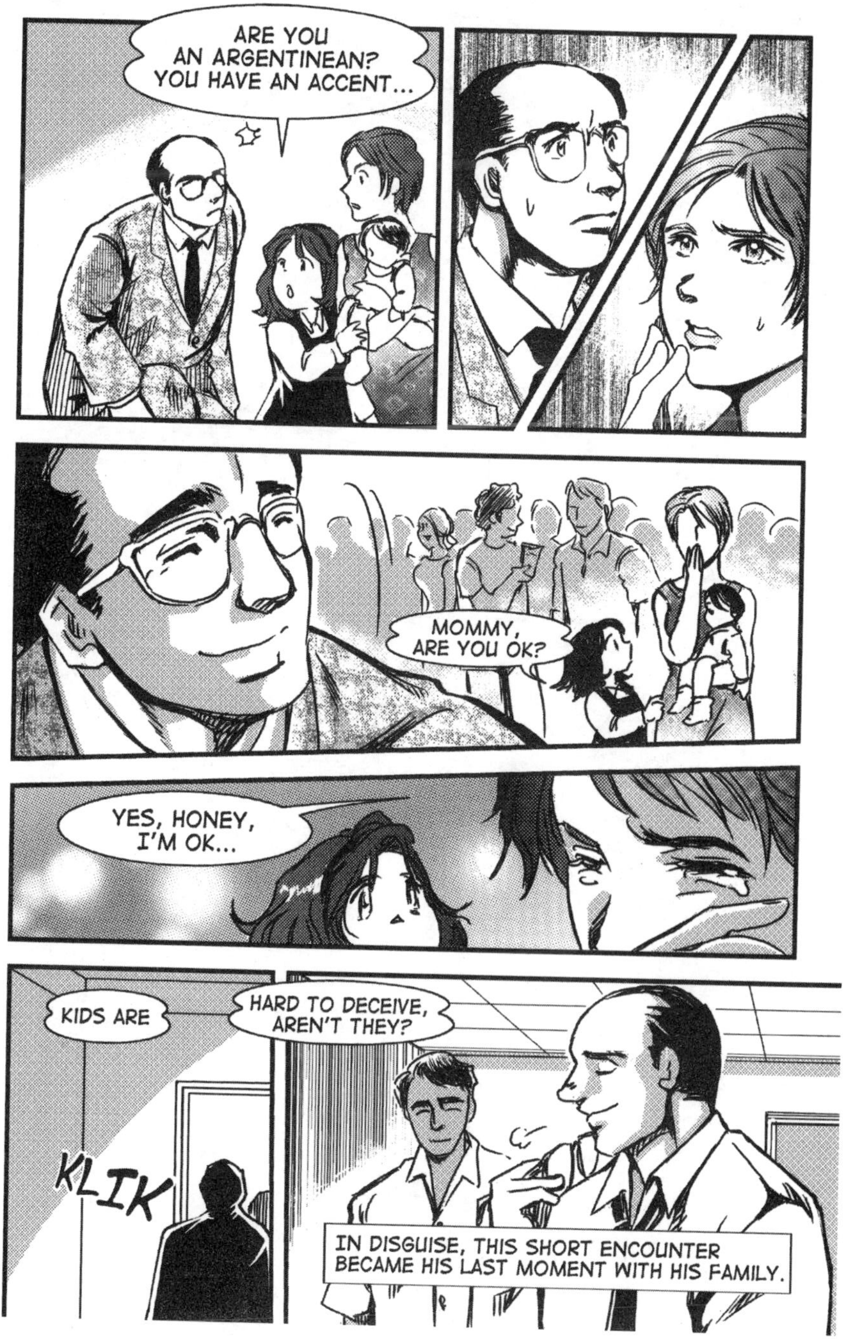
ARE YOU AN ARGENTINEAN? YOU HAVE AN ACCENT...
MOMMY, ARE YOU OK?
YES, HONEY, I'M OK...
KIDS ARE
HARD TO DECEIVE, AREN'T THEY?
KLIK
IN DISGUISE, THIS SHORT ENCOUNTER BECAME HIS LAST MOMENT WITH HIS FAMILY.

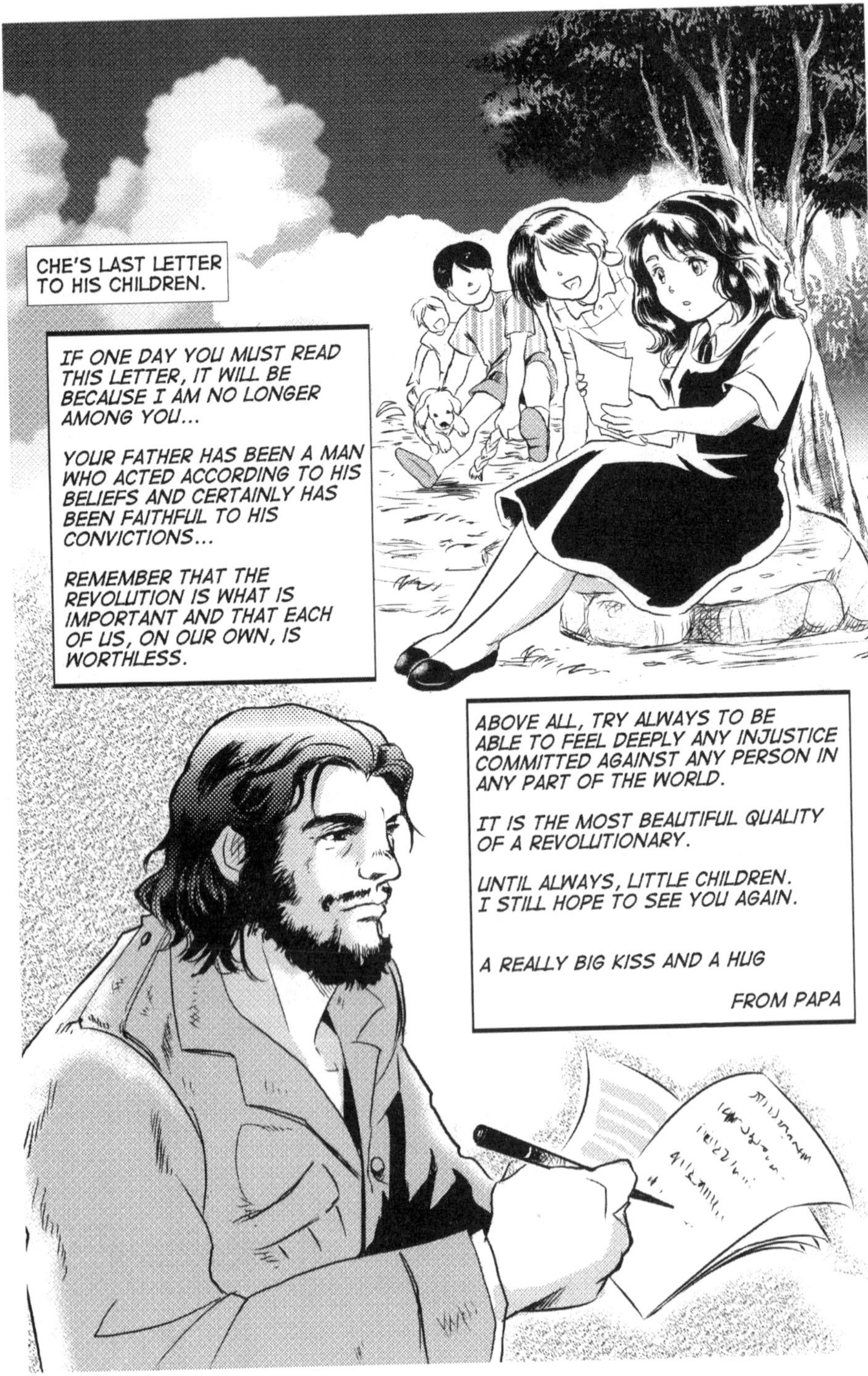
CHE'S LAST LETTER TO HIS CHILDREN.
IF ONE DAY YOU MUST READ THIS LETTER, IT WILL BE BECAUSE I AM NO LONGER AMONG YOU...
YOUR FATHER HAS BEEN A MAN WHO ACTED ACCORDING TO HIS BELIEFS AND CERTAINLY HAS BEEN FAITHFUL TO HIS CONVICTIONS...
REMEMBER THAT THE REVOLUTION IS WHAT IS IMPORTANT AND THAT EACH OF US, ON OUR OWN, IS WORTHLESS.
ABOVE ALL, TRY ALWAYS TO BE ABLE TO FEEL DEEPLY ANY INJUSTICE COMMITTED AGAINST ANY PERSON IN ANY PART OF THE WORLD.
IT IS THE MOST BEAUTIFUL QUALITY OF A REVOLUTIONARY.
UNTIL ALWAYS, LITTLE CHILDREN. I STILL HOPE TO SEE YOU AGAIN.
A REALLY BIG KISS AND A HUG
FROM PAPA

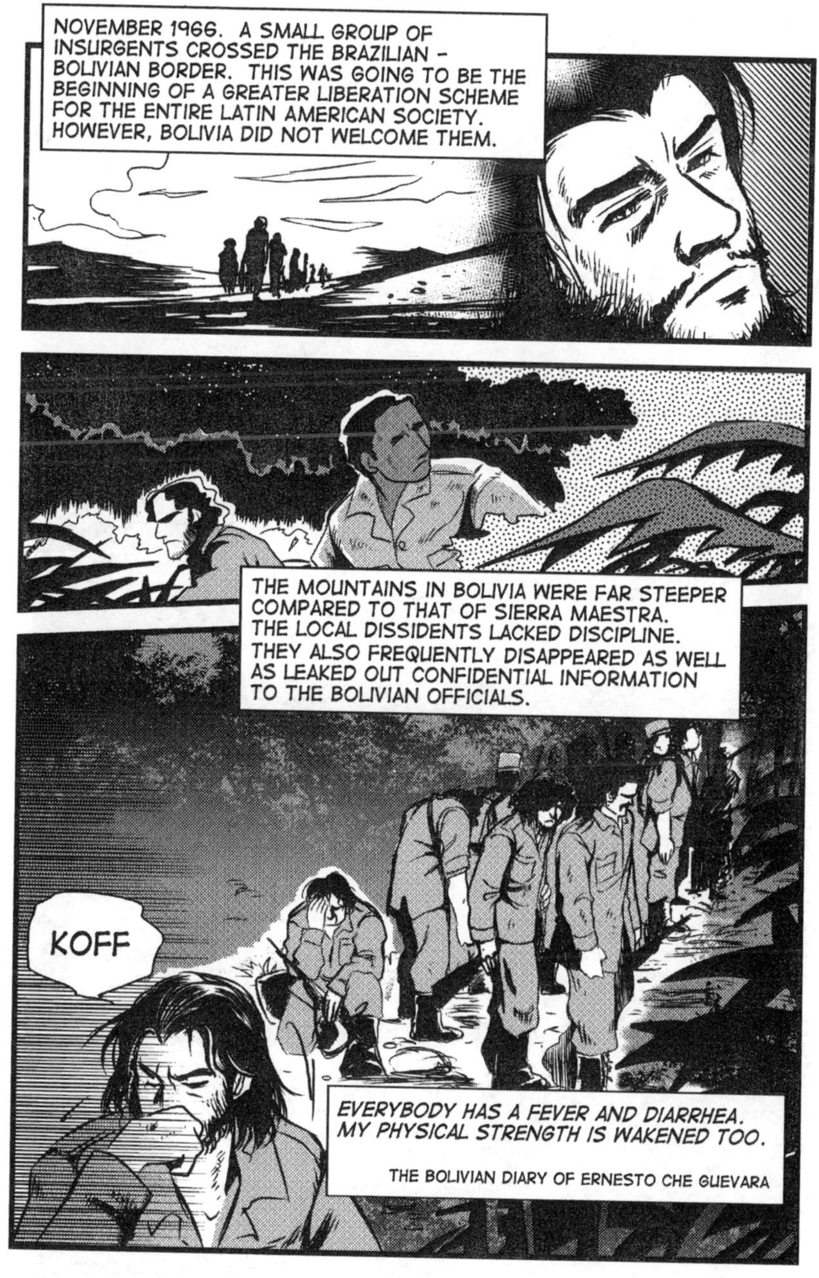
NOVEMBER 1966. A SMALL GROUP OF INSURGENTS CROSSED THE BRAZILIAN - BOLIVIAN BORDER. THIS WAS GOING TO BE THE BEGINNING OF A GREATER LIBERATION SCHEME FOR THE ENTIRE LATIN AMERICAN SOCIETY. HOWEVER, BOLIVIA DID NOT WELCOME THEM.
THE MOUNTAINS IN BOLIVIA WERE FAR STEEPER COMPARED TO THAT OF SIERRA MAESTRA. THE LOCAL DISSIDENTS LACKED DISCIPLINE. THEY ALSO FREQUENTLY DISAPPEARED AS WELL AS LEAKED OUT CONFIDENTIAL INFORMATION TO THE BOLIVIAN OFFICIALS.
KOFF
EVERYBODY HAS A FEVER AND DIARRHEA. MY PHYSICAL STRENGTH IS WAKENED TOO.
THE BOLIVIAN DIARY OF ERNESTO CHE GUEVARA

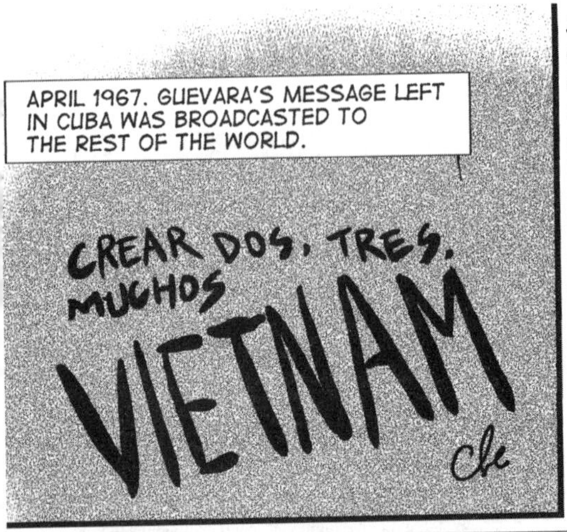
APRIL 1967. GUEVARA'S MESSAGE LEFT IN CUBA WAS BROADCASTED TO THE REST OF THE WORLD.
CREAR DOS, TRES. MUCHOS VIETNAM
Che

IT IS THE ROAD OF VIETNAM. (SOUTH) AMERICA, A FORGOTTEN CONTINENT IN THE LAST LIBERATION STRUGGLES, IS NOW BEGINNING TO MAKE ITSELF HEARD THROUGH THE TRI-CONTINENTAL AS, IN THE VOICE OF THE VANGUARD OF ITS PEOPLES, THE CUBAN REVOLUTION WILL TODAY HAVE A TASK OF MUCH GREATER RELEVANCE:

CREATING A SECOND OR A THIRD VIETNAM -

OR THE SECOND AND THE THIRD VIETNAM OF THE WORLD.

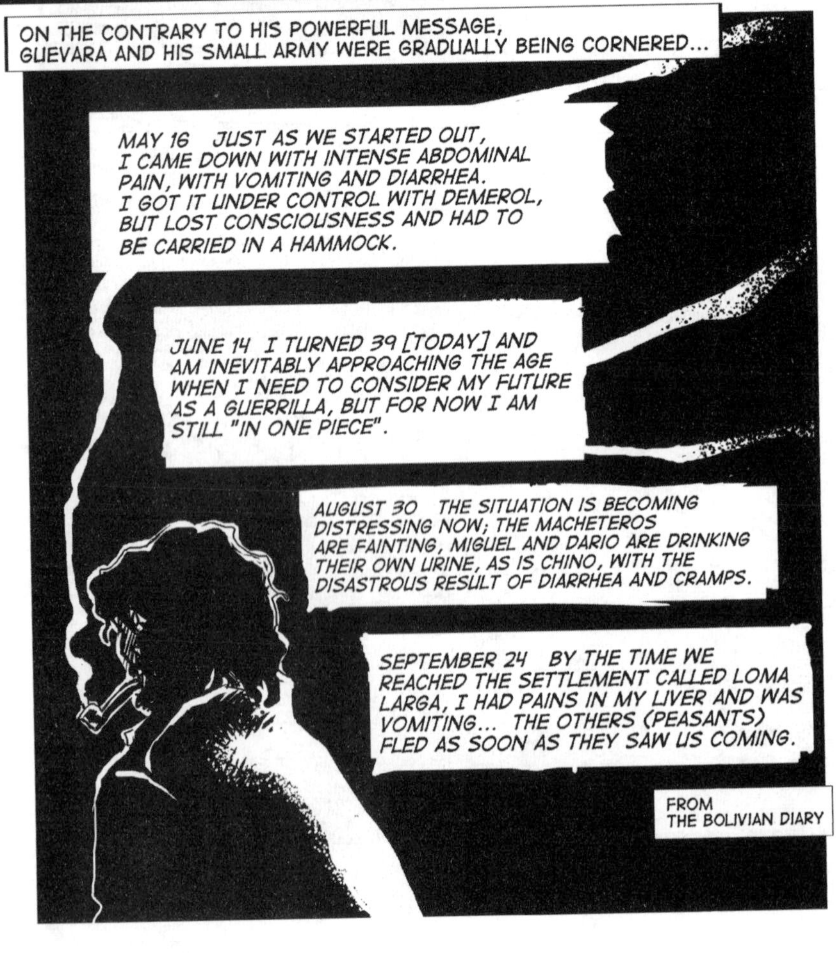
ON THE CONTRARY TO HIS POWERFUL MESSAGE, GUEVARA AND HIS SMALL ARMY WERE GRADUALLY BEING CORNERED...
MAY 16 JUST AS WE STARTED OUT, I CAME DOWN WITH INTENSE ABDOMINAL PAIN, WITH VOMITING AND DIARRHEA. I GOT IT UNDER CONTROL WITH DEMEROL, BUT LOST CONSCIOUSNESS AND HAD TO BE CARRIED IN A HAMMOCK.
JUNE 14 I TURNED 39 [TODAY] AND AM INEVITABLY APPROACHING THE AGE WHEN I NEED TO CONSIDER MY FUTURE AS A GUERRILLA, BUT FOR NOW I AM STILL "IN ONE PIECE".
AUGUST 30 THE SITUATION IS BECOMING DISTRESSING NOW; THE MACHETEROS ARE FAINTING, MIGUEL AND DARIO ARE DRINKING THEIR OWN URINE, AS IS CHINO, WITH THE DISASTROUS RESULT OF DIARRHEA AND CRAMPS.
SEPTEMBER 24 BY THE TIME WE REACHED THE SETTLEMENT CALLED LOMA LARGA, I HAD PAINS IN MY LIVER AND WAS VOMITING... THE OTHERS (PEASANTS) FLED AS SOON AS THEY SAW US COMING.
FROM THE BOLIVIAN DIARY

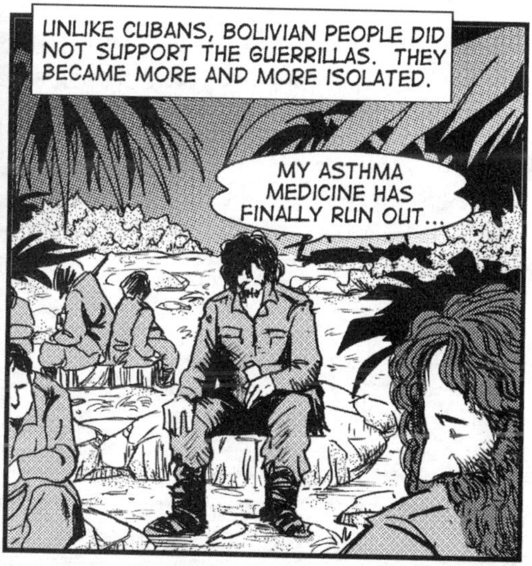
UNLIKE CUBANS, BOLIVIAN PEOPLE DID NOT SUPPORT THE GUERRILLAS. THEY BECAME MORE AND MORE ISOLATED.
MY ASTHMA MEDICINE HAS FINALLY RUN OUT...
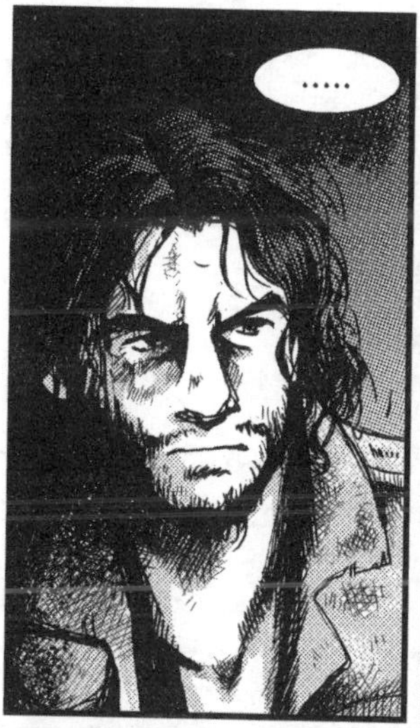
.....
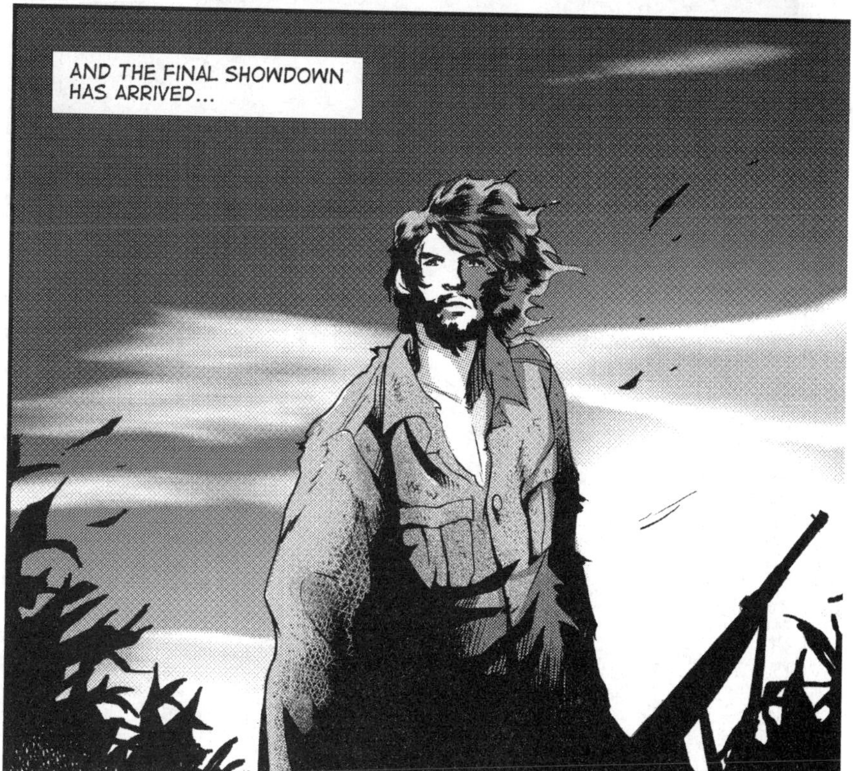
AND THE FINAL SHOWDOWN HAS ARRIVED...

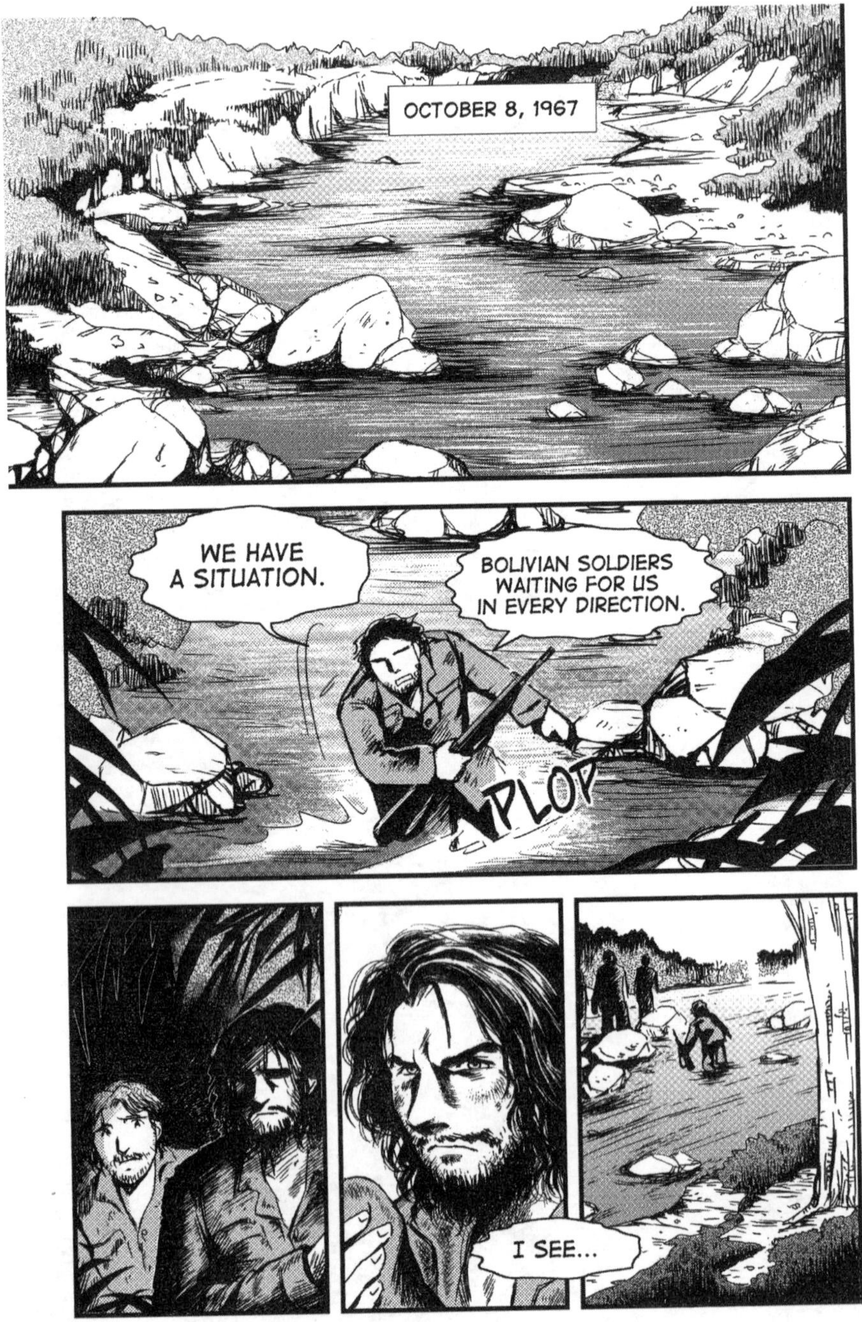
OCTOBER 8, 1967
WE HAVE A SITUATION.
BOLIVIAN SOLDIERS WAITING FOR US IN EVERY DIRECTION.
PLOP
I SEE...

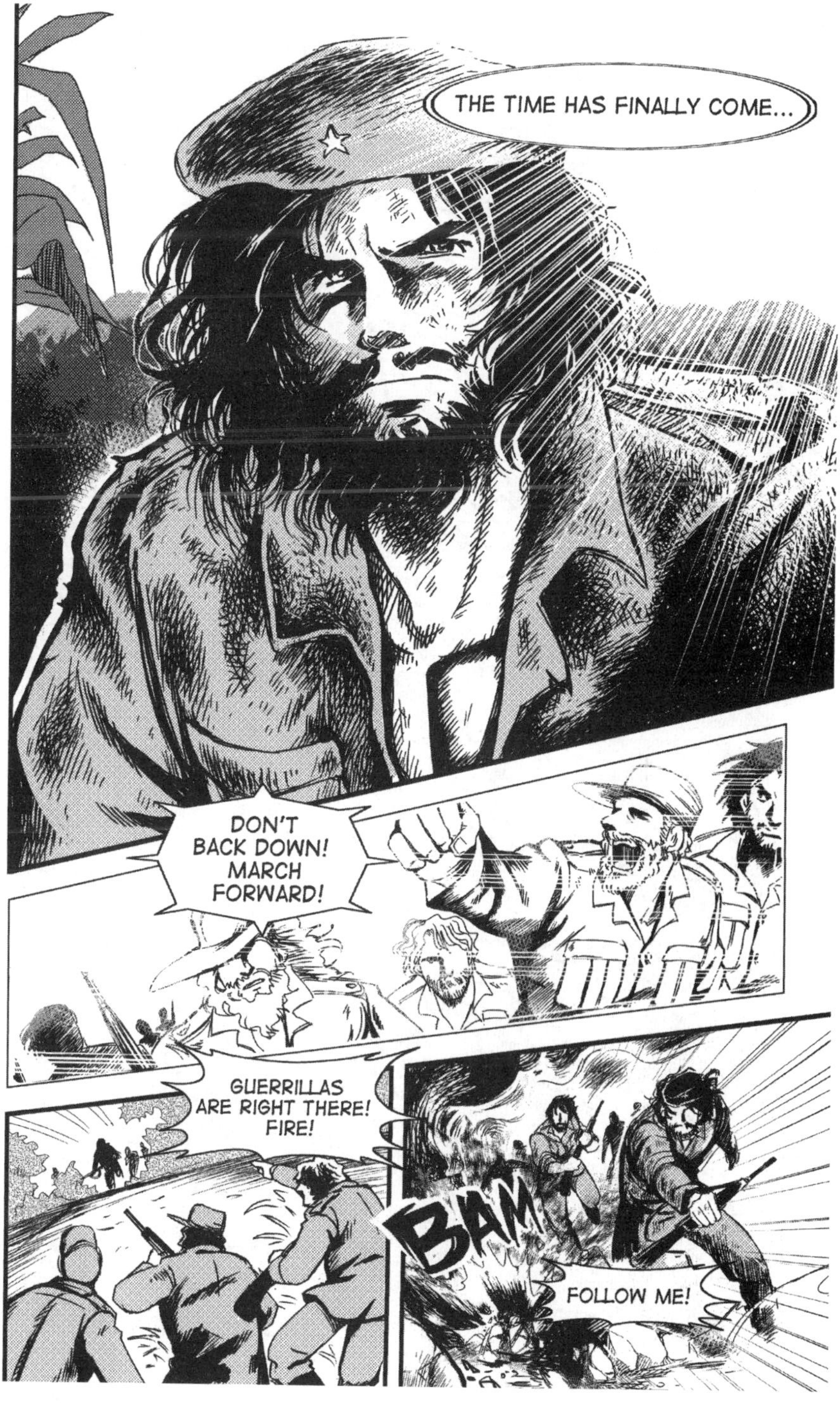

THE TIME HAS FINALLY COME...
DON'T BACK DOWN! MARCH FORWARD!
GUERRILLAS ARE RIGHT THERE! FIRE!
BAM
FOLLOW ME!

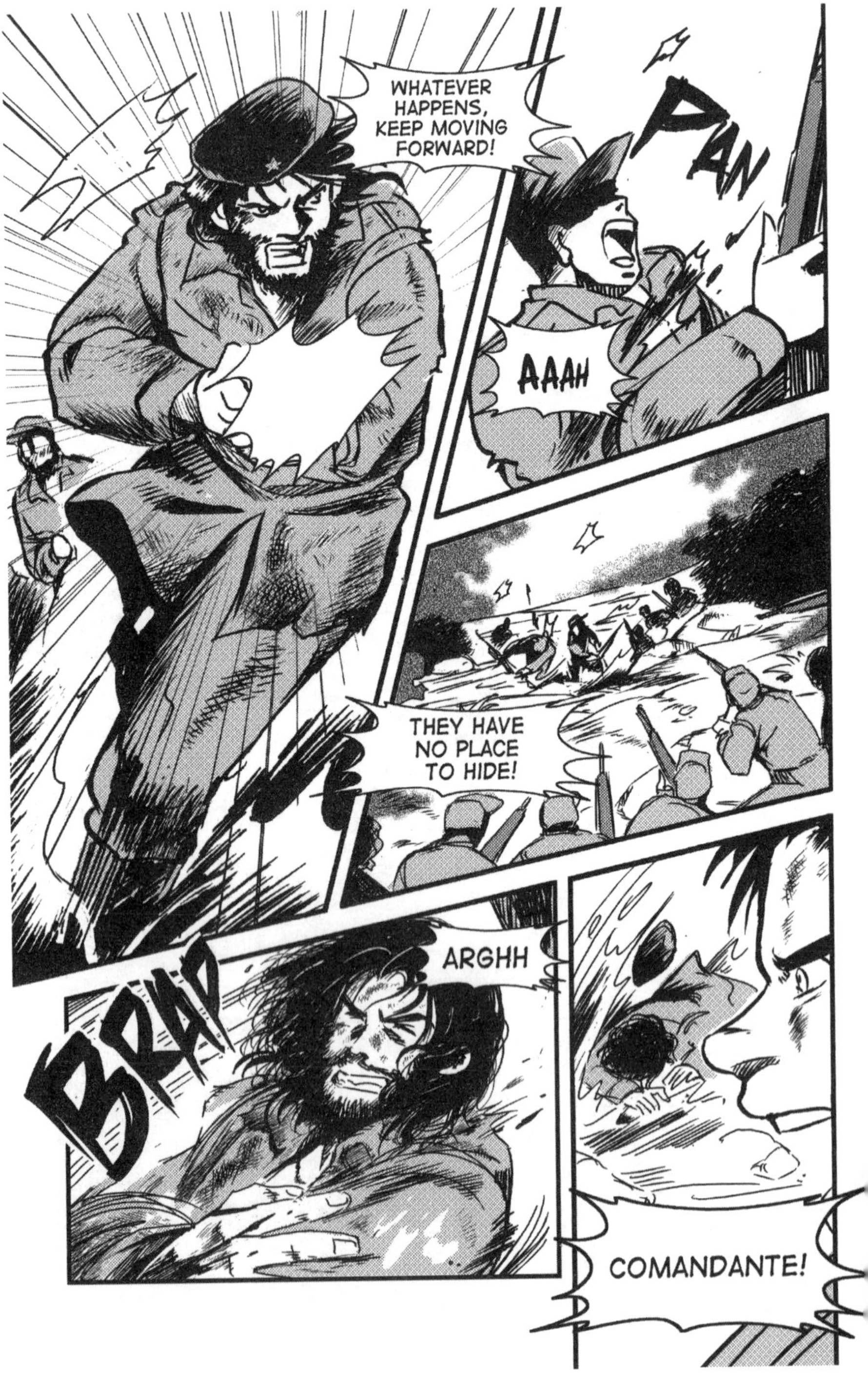
WHATEVER HAPPENS, KEEP MOVING FORWARD!
PAN
AAAH
THEY HAVE NO PLACE TO HIDE!
BRAP
ARGHH
COMANDANTE!

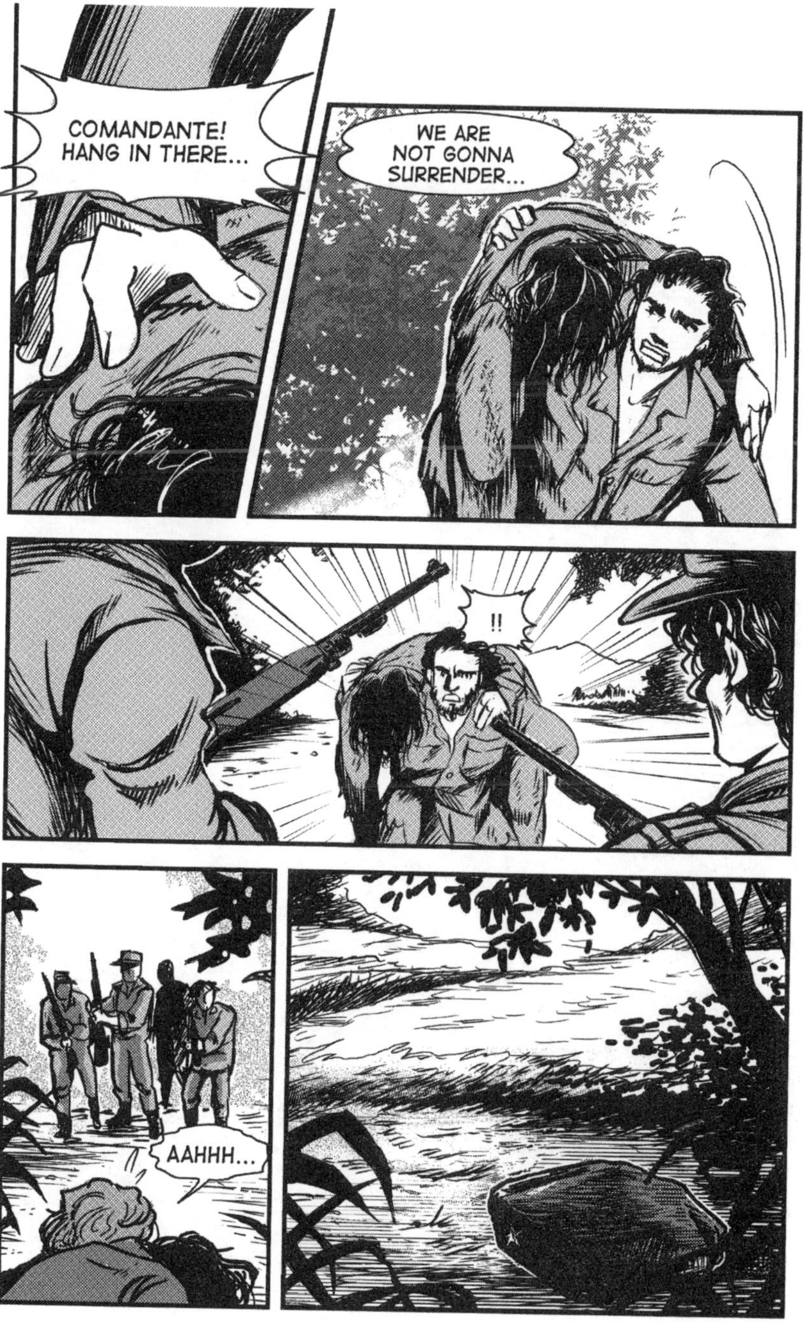
COMANDANTE! HANG IN THERE...
WE ARE NOT GONNA SURRENDER...
!!
AAHHH...

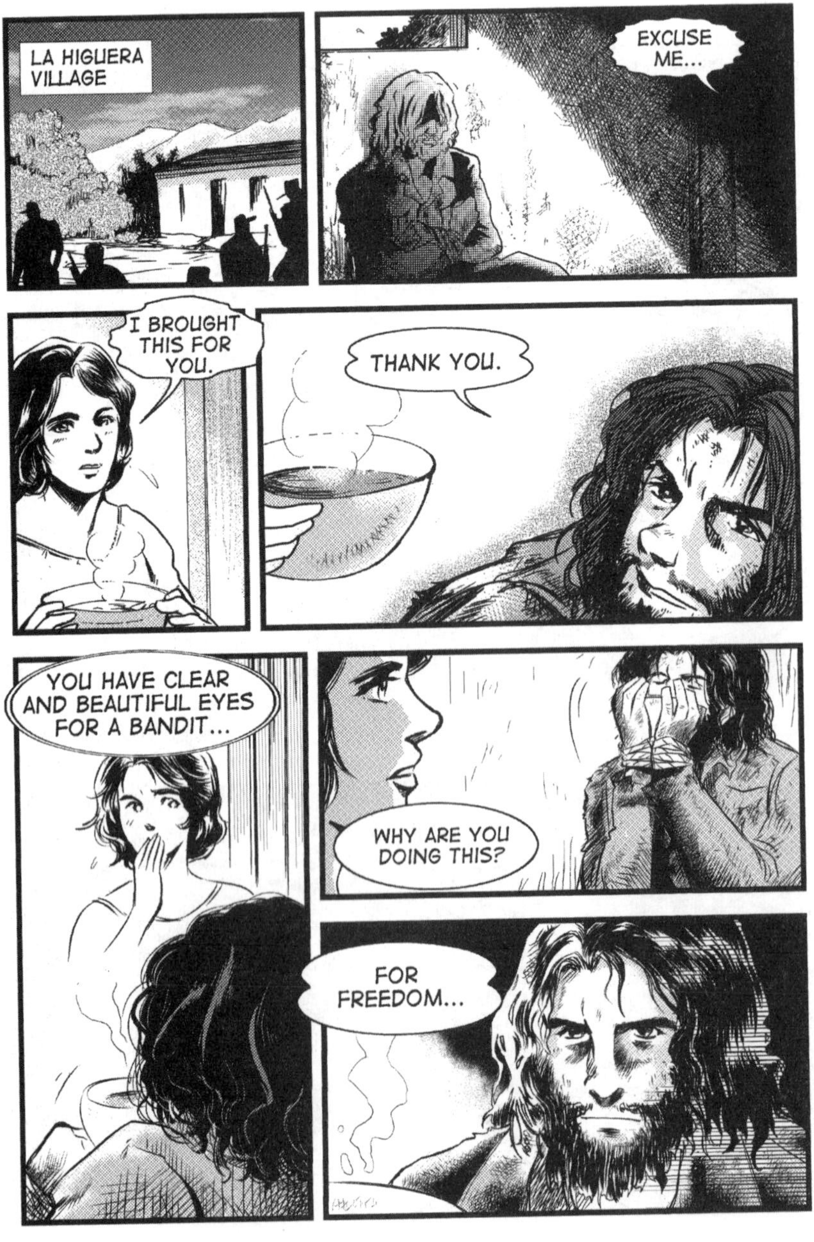
LA HIGUERA VILLAGE
EXCUSE ME...
I BROUGHT THIS FOR YOU.
THANK YOU.
YOU HAVE CLEAR AND BEAUTIFUL EYES FOR A BANDIT...
WHY ARE YOU DOING THIS?
FOR FREEDOM...

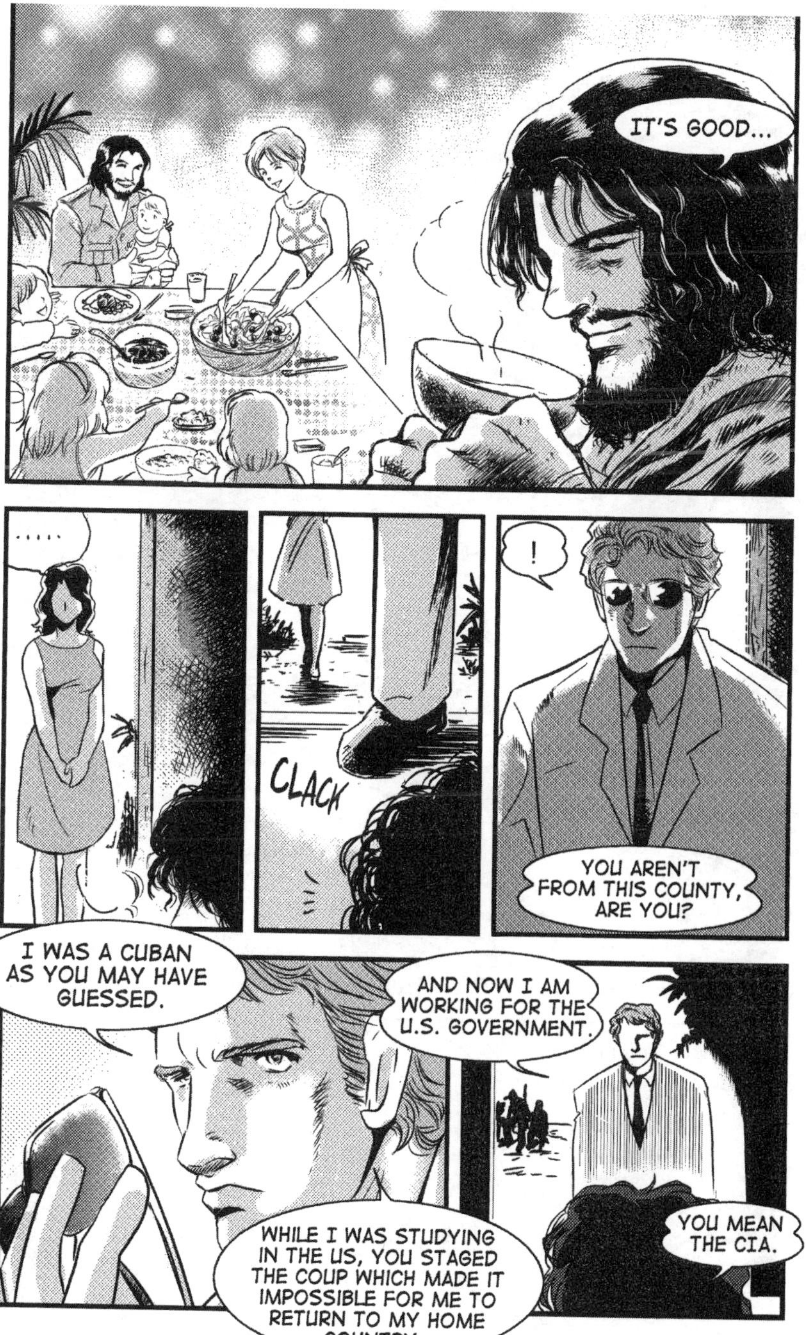
IT'S GOOD...
.....
CLACK
!
YOU AREN'T FROM THIS COUNTY, ARE YOU?
I WAS A CUBAN AS YOU MAY HAVE GUESSED.
AND NOW I AM WORKING FOR THE U.S. GOVERNMENT.
YOU MEAN THE CIA.
WHILE I WAS STUDYING IN THE US, YOU STAGED THE COUP WHICH MADE IT IMPOSSIBLE FOR ME TO RETURN TO MY HOME COUNTRY...

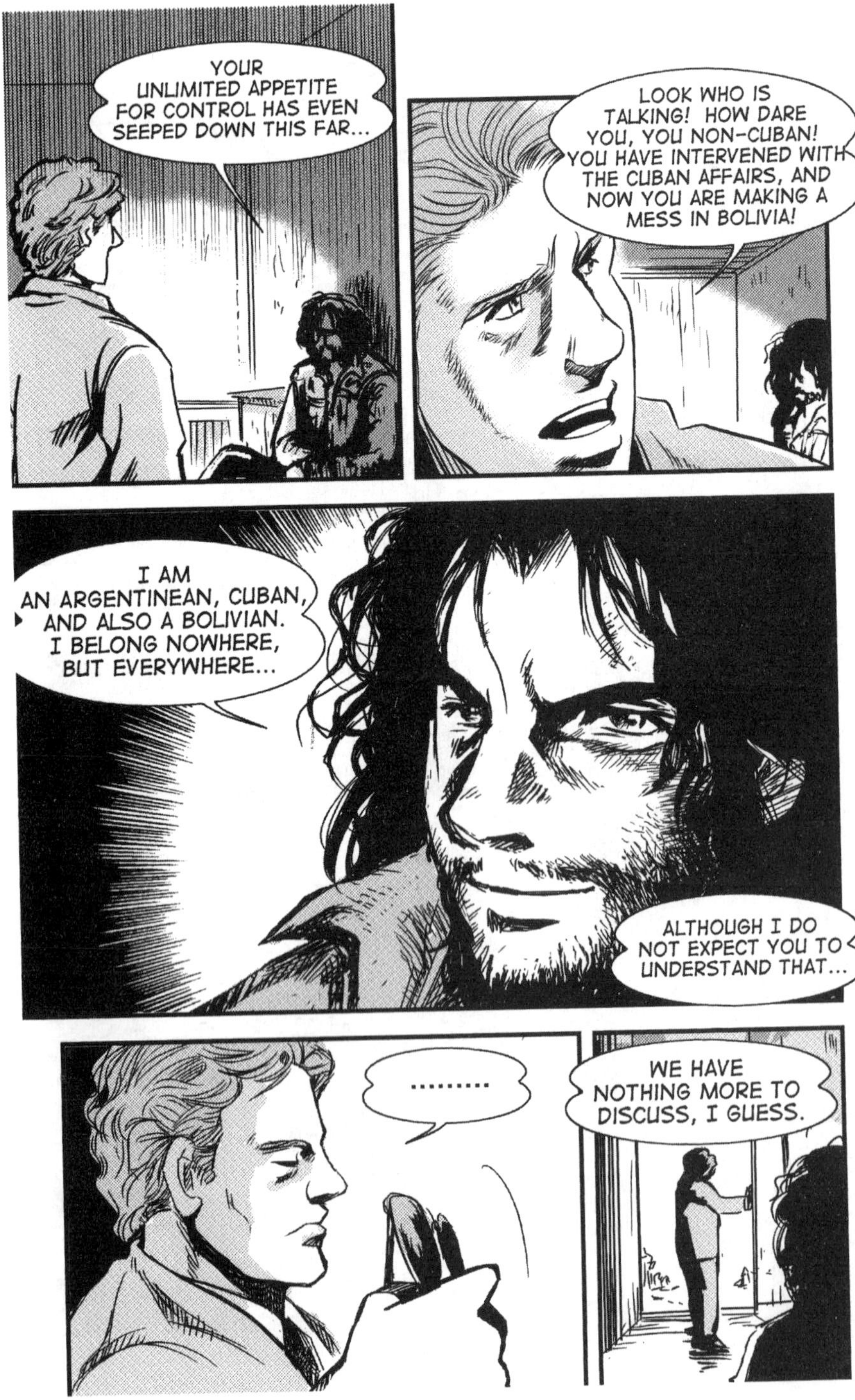
YOUR UNLIMITED APPETITE FOR CONTROL HAS EVEN SEEPED DOWN THIS FAR...
LOOK WHO IS TALKING! HOW DARE YOU, YOU NON-CUBAN! YOU HAVE INTERVENED WITH THE CUBAN AFFAIRS, AND NOW YOU ARE MAKING A MESS IN BOLIVIA!
I AM AN ARGENTINEAN, CUBAN, AND ALSO A BOLIVIAN. I BELONG NOWHERE, BUT EVERYWHERE...
ALTHOUGH I DO NOT EXPECT YOU TO UNDERSTAND THAT...
....
WE HAVE NOTHING MORE TO DISCUSS, I GUESS.

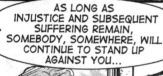

I WILL SEE YOU AGAIN.

?

AS LONG AS INJUSTICE AND SUBSEQUENT SUFFERING REMAIN, SOMEBODY, SOMEWHERE, WILL CONTINUE TO STAND UP AGAINST YOU...

YOU PEOPLE WILL BE GREETED BY THOSE WHO ARE ANGRY AGAIN SOMEDAY.

. . . . .

161

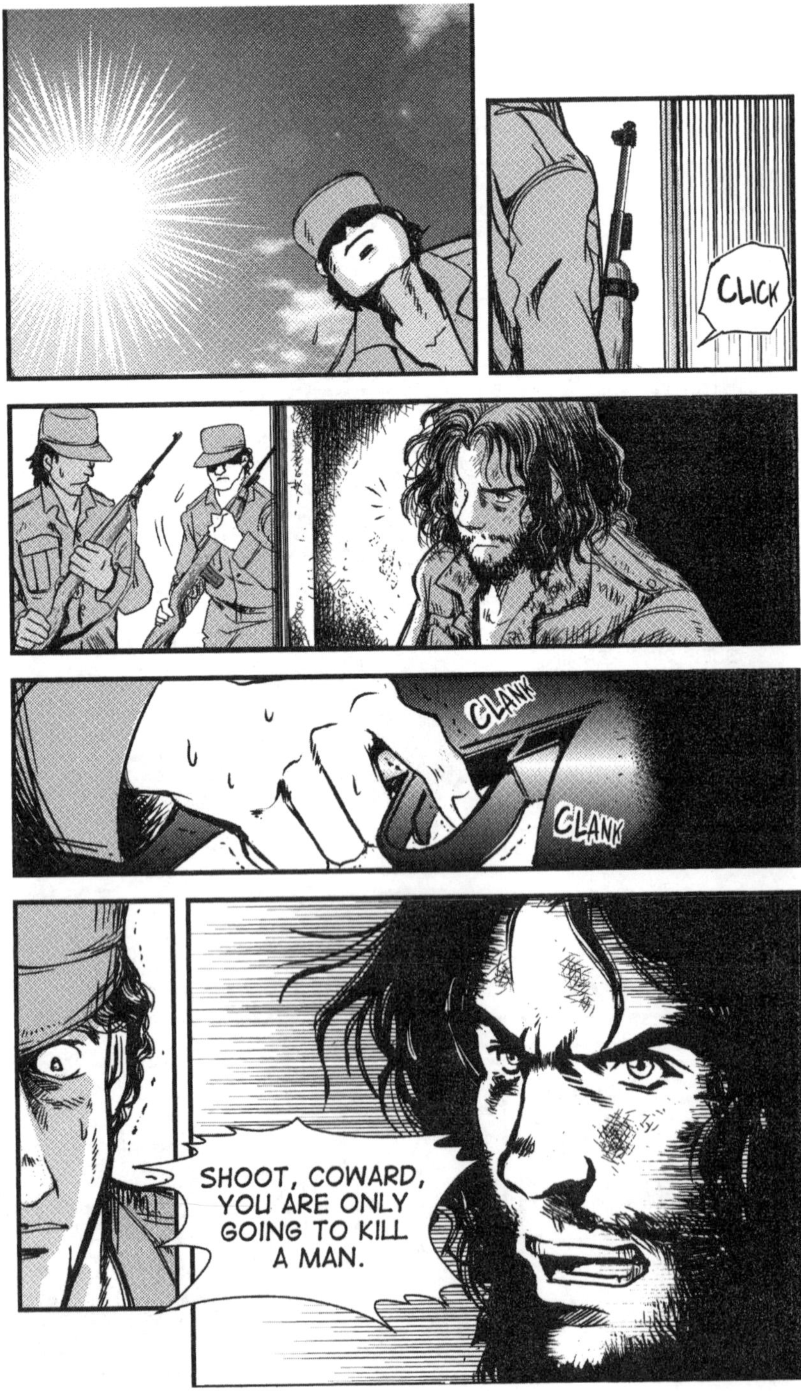
CLICK
CLANK
CLANK
SHOOT, COWARD, YOU ARE ONLY GOING TO KILL A MAN.

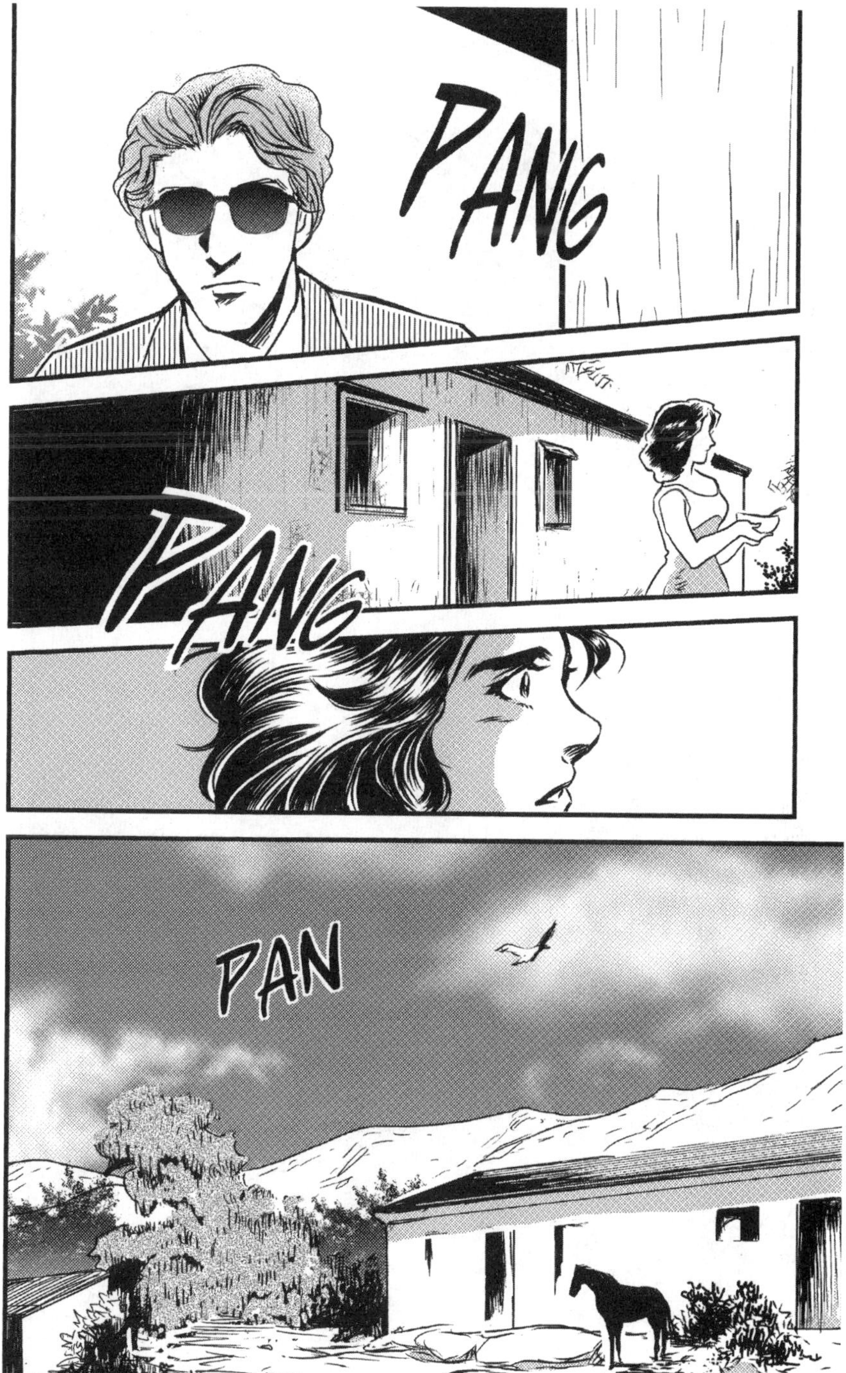
PANG
PANG
PAN

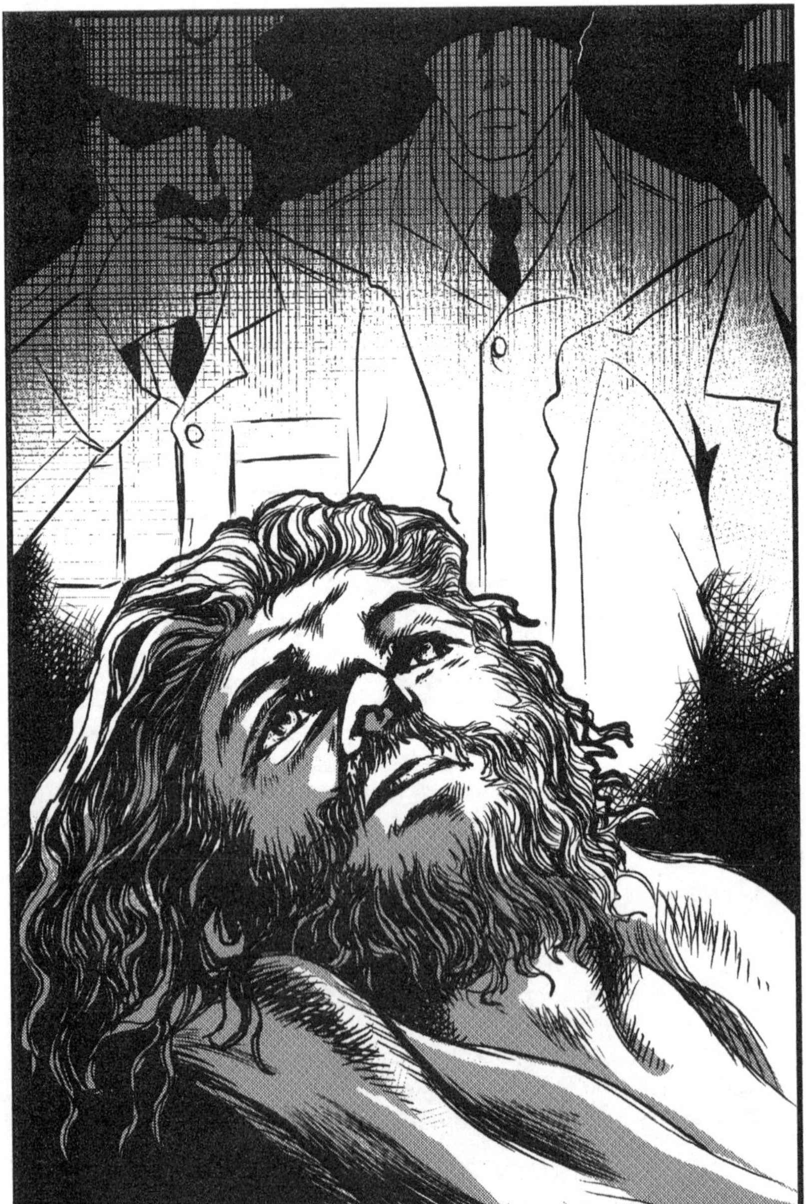

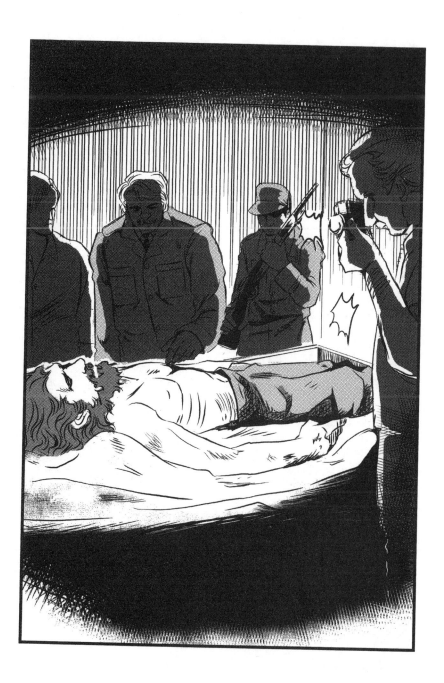

165

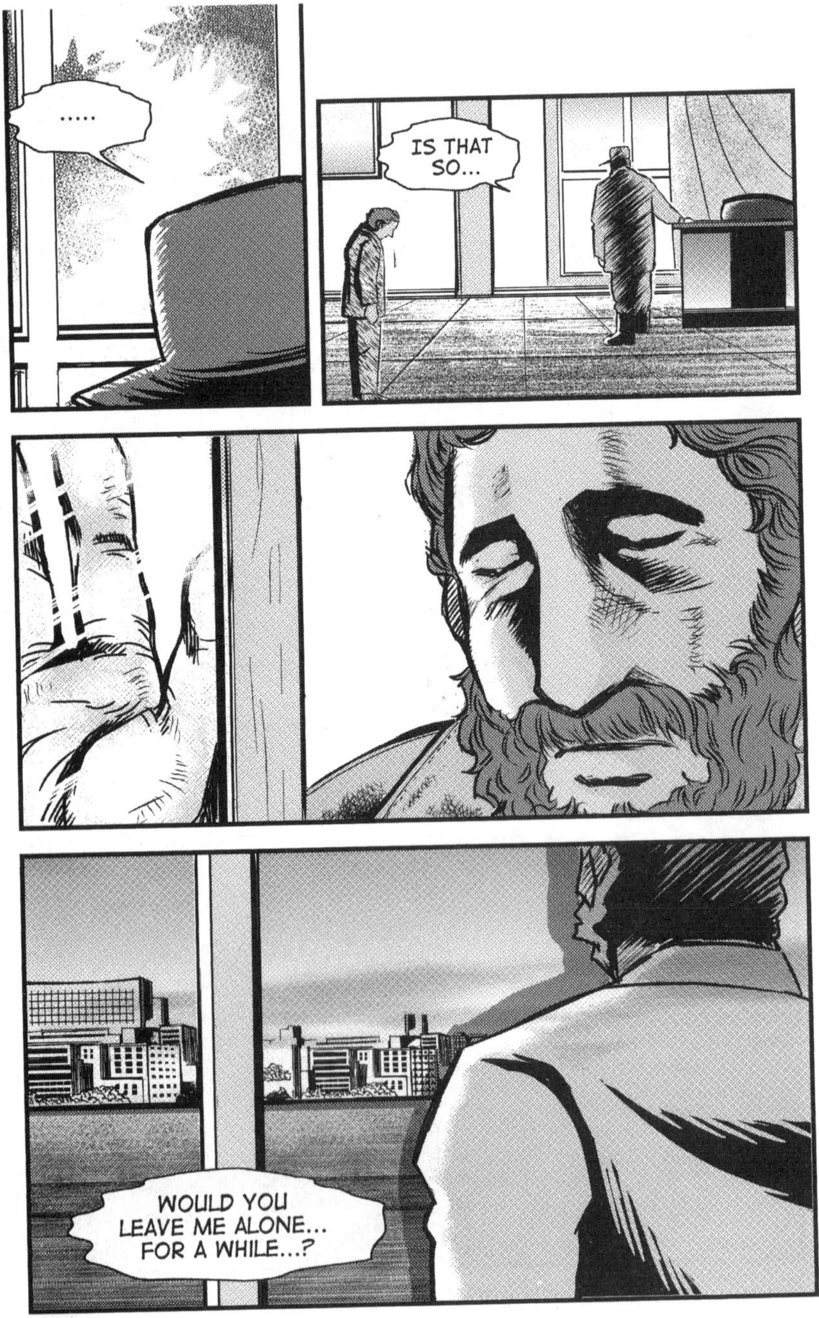
IS THAT SO...
.....
WOULD YOU LEAVE ME ALONE... FOR A WHILE...?

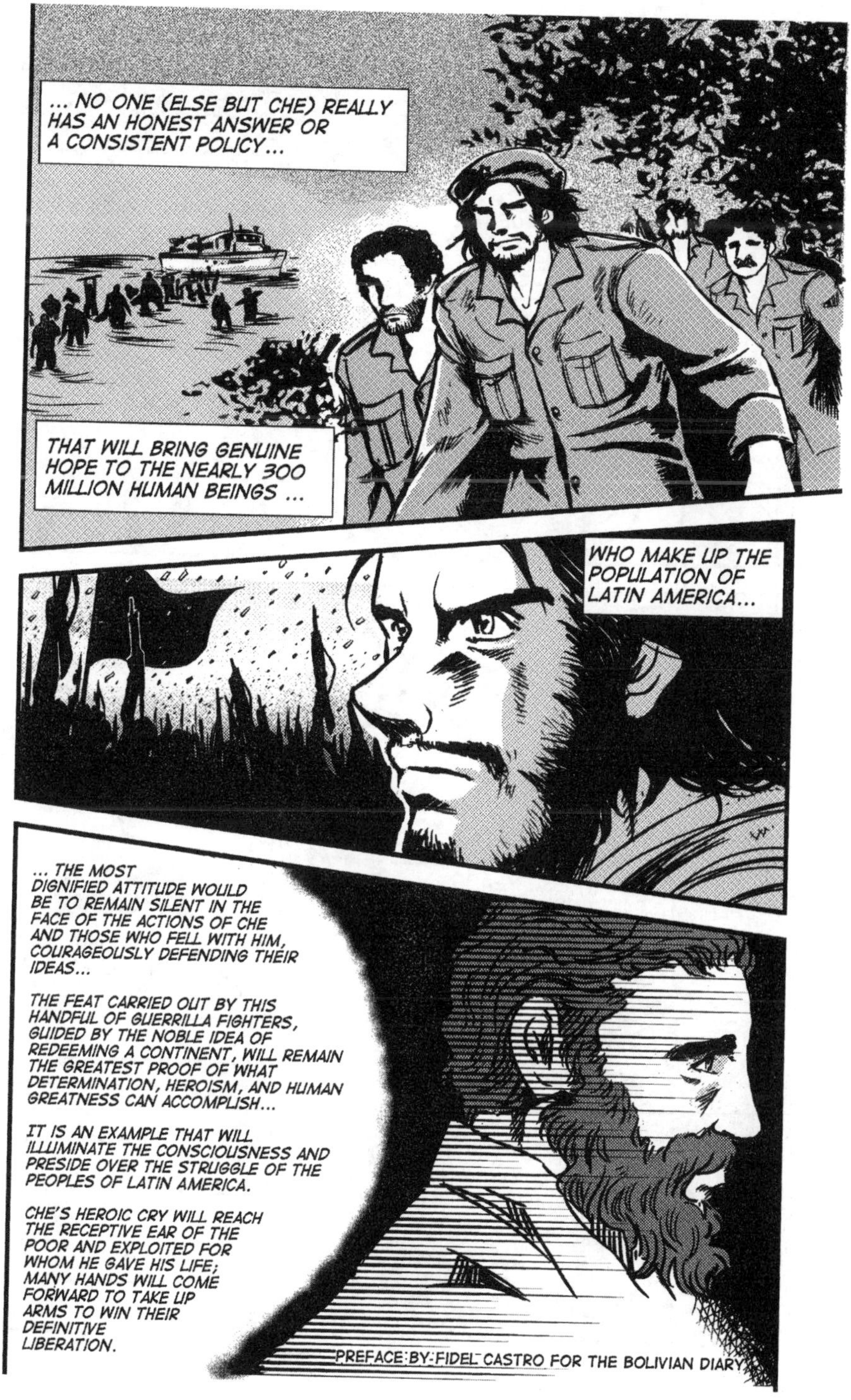
... NO ONE (ELSE BUT CHE) REALLY HAS AN HONEST ANSWER OR A CONSISTENT POLICY...
THAT WILL BRING GENUINE HOPE TO THE NEARLY 300 MILLION HUMAN BEINGS ...
WHO MAKE UP THE POPULATION OF LATIN AMERICA...
... THE MOST DIGNIFIED ATTITUDE WOULD BE TO REMAIN SILENT IN THE FACE OF THE ACTIONS OF CHE AND THOSE WHO FELL WITH HIM, COURAGEOUSLY DEFENDING THEIR IDEAS...
THE FEAT CARRIED OUT BY THIS HANDFUL OF GUERRILLA FIGHTERS, GUIDED BY THE NOBLE IDEA OF REDEEMING A CONTINENT, WILL REMAIN THE GREATEST PROOF OF WHAT DETERMINATION, HEROISM, AND HUMAN GREATNESS CAN ACCOMPLISH...
IT IS AN EXAMPLE THAT WILL ILLUMINATE THE CONSCIOUSNESS AND PRESIDE OVER THE STRUGGLE OF THE PEOPLES OF LATIN AMERICA.
CHE'S HEROIC CRY WILL REACH THE RECEPTIVE EAR OF THE POOR AND EXPLOITED FOR WHOM HE GAVE HIS LIFE; MANY HANDS WILL COME FORWARD TO TAKE UP ARMS TO WIN THEIR DEFINITIVE LIBERATION.
PREFACE BY FIDEL CASTRO FOR THE BOLIVIAN DIARY

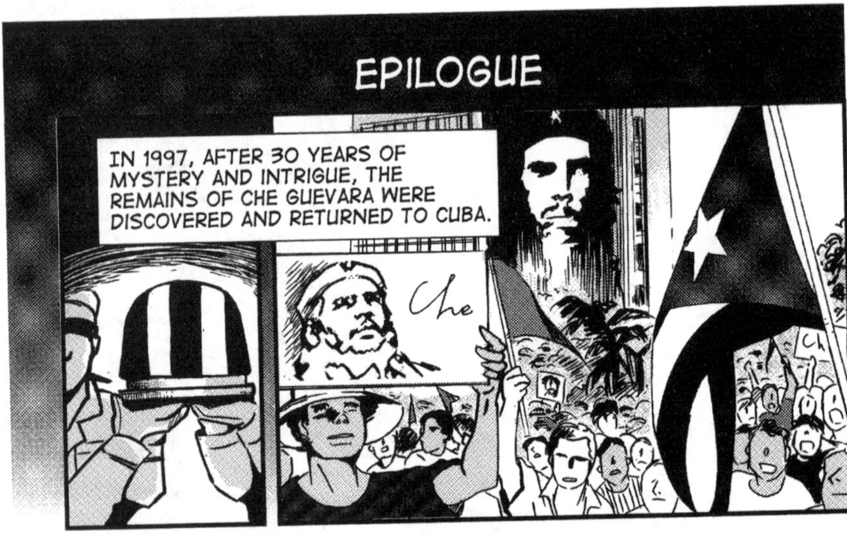
EPILOGUE
IN 1997, AFTER 30 YEARS OF MYSTERY AND INTRIGUE, THE REMAINS OF CHE GUEVARA WERE DISCOVERED AND RETURNED TO CUBA.
Che

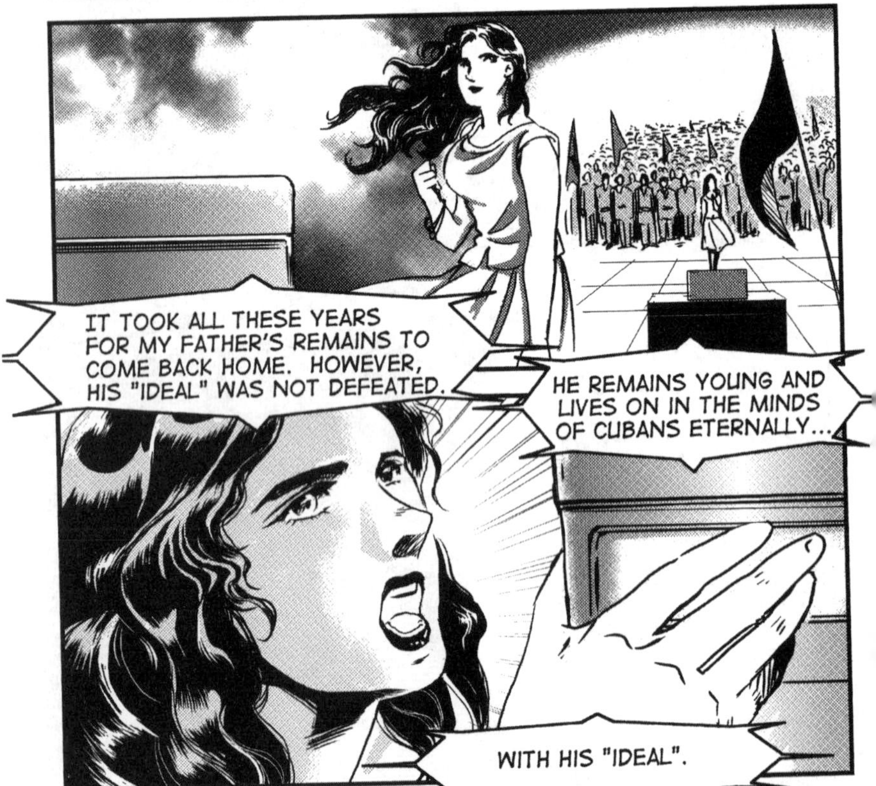
IT TOOK ALL THESE YEARS FOR MY FATHER'S REMAINS TO COME BACK HOME. HOWEVER, HIS "IDEAL" WAS NOT DEFEATED.
HE REMAINS YOUNG AND LIVES ON IN THE MINDS OF CUBANS ETERNALLY...
WITH HIS "IDEAL".

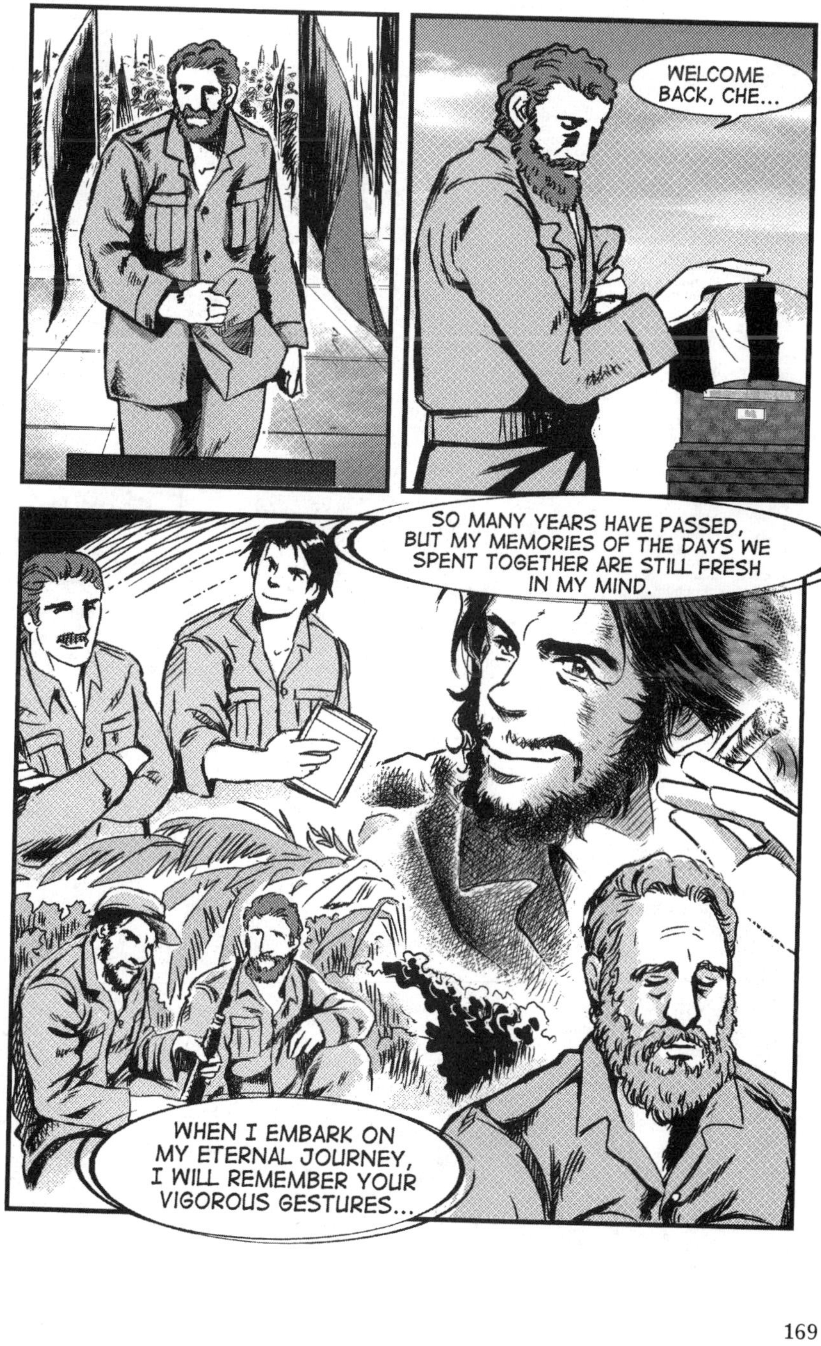
WELCOME BACK, CHE...
SO MANY YEARS HAVE PASSED, BUT MY MEMORIES OF THE DAYS WE SPENT TOGETHER ARE STILL FRESH IN MY MIND.
WHEN I EMBARK ON MY ETERNAL JOURNEY, I WILL REMEMBER YOUR VIGOROUS GESTURES...

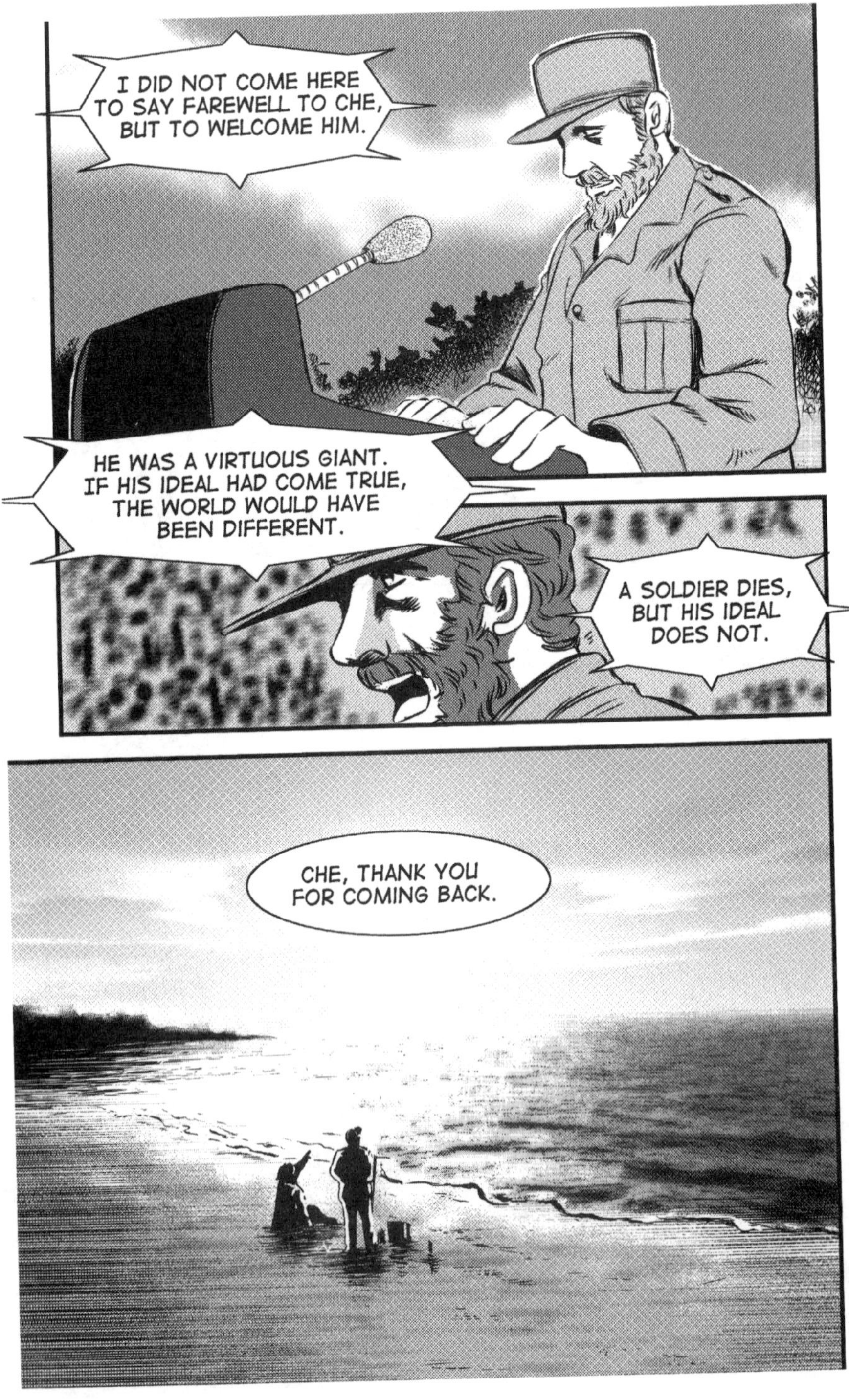
I DID NOT COME HERE TO SAY FAREWELL TO CHE, BUT TO WELCOME HIM.
HE WAS A VIRTUOUS GIANT. IF HIS IDEAL HAD COME TRUE, THE WORLD WOULD HAVE BEEN DIFFERENT.
A SOLDIER DIES, BUT HIS IDEAL DOES NOT.
CHE, THANK YOU FOR COMING BACK.

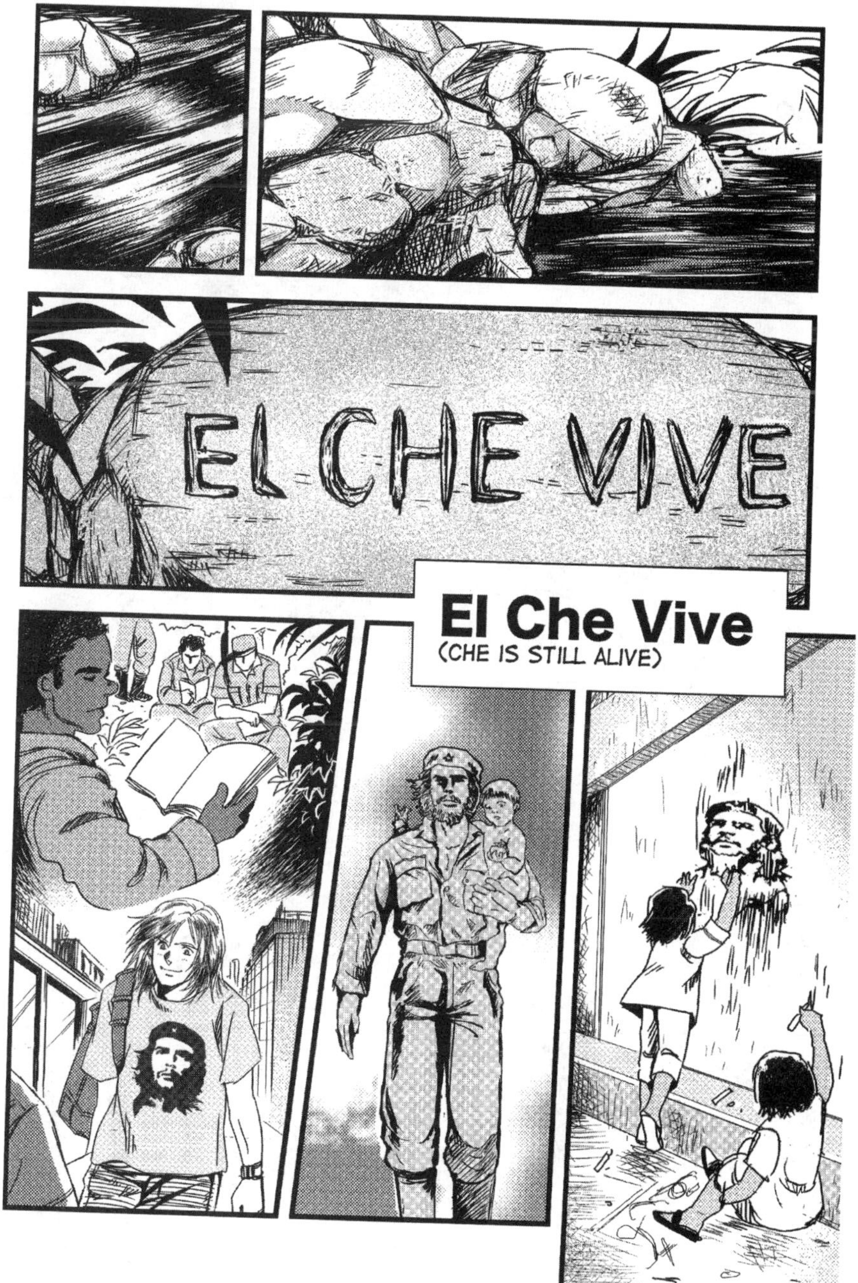
EL CHE VIVE
El Che Vive
(CHE IS STILL ALIVE)

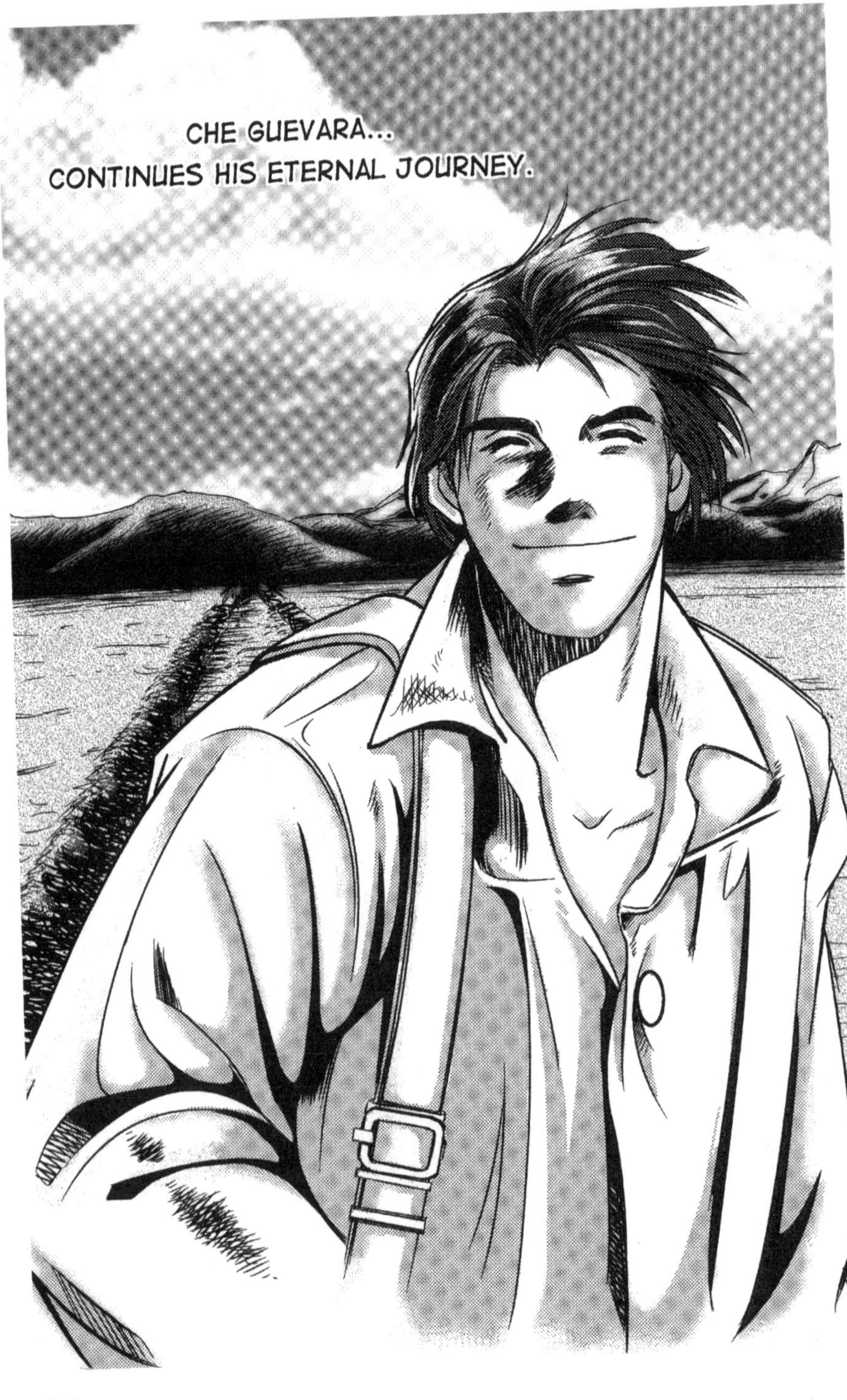
CHE GUEVARA...
CONTINUES HIS ETERNAL JOURNEY.

AUTHOR'S NOTE

After finishing this book, I had an opportunity to meet Aleida March Guevara, a daughter of Che Guevara, when she visited Tokyo. In her eyes and in her speech I could see her resolute will, keeping part of her father vigorously alive.

On October 9, 1967, Che Guevara breathed his last. However, his ideas are increasing in popularity, and it seems his soul will never rest "Hasta la Victoria Siempre" ("Forever, until victory").

In the world of materialism, where we see imperialism in economic terms, his vision and ideas will keep challenging us and shed light on an alternative way to live.

I would like to express my deepest gratitude to Camilo Guevara and Daily Pérez Guillén of Centro de Estudios Che Guevara for their kind understanding of the project and generous support. Without their insightful advice, the book could have never depicted the historical events as accurately as it does.

In closing, I would like to borrow Guevara's words from his farewell letter to his children:

> . . . try always to be able to feel deeply
> any injustice committed against any person
> in any part of the world.

Hoping that more people follow his ideal.

Chie Shimano
Tokyo, Japan

Bibliography

Interviews

1. Guevara, Camilo. Centro de Estudios Che Guevara, "Hisorieta del Che." 20 Dec. 2006.
2. Pérez, Daily Guillén. Centro de Estudios Che Guevara, "Hisorieta del Che." 20 Dec. 2006.

DVDs

1. *Che: Rise and Fall.* Documentary on Che Guevara. Directed by Eduardo Montes-Bradley. Produced by Patagonia Film Group LLC, 2005.
2. *El Che—Ernesto Guevara: Enquete sur un homme de legende.* Directed by Anibal D. Salvo and Maurice Dugowson. Produced by Dutch Film Works.
3. *Fidel: The Untold Story.* Directed by Estela Bravo. Produced by First Run Features.
4. *The Motorcycle Diaries.* Directed by Walter Salles. Produced by Universal Studios, 2005.
5. *Thirteen Days.* Directed by Roger Donaldson. Produced by New Line Home Video, 2001.

Books

1. Ammar, Alain. *Che Guevara, El Cristo Rojo/Che Guevara, Red Christ.* Mexico City: Editorial Diana Sa.
2. Barrio, Hilda, Gareth Jenkins, and Andres V. Castillo. *The Authentic Che Handbook.* Minneapolis: M Q Publications, 2003.
3. Chiteki Koukishin Kenkyu Kai. *Genki ga Deru Guevara Goroku.* Tokyo: Leed, 2007.
4. Cormier, Jean. *Che Guevara: Compagnon de la revolution.* Gallimard.
5. Guevara, Ernesto Che, Aleida Guevara, and Cintio Vitier. *The Motorcycle Diaries: Notes on a Latin American Journey.* New York: Ocean P, 2004.

6. Guevara, Ernesto C., Fidel Castro, and Camilo Guevara. *The Bolivian Diary: Authorized Edition.* New York: Ocean P, 2005.

7. Guevara, Ernesto. *Guerrilla Warfare.* Madrid: Editorial Benei Noaj, 2007.

8. Guevara, Ernesto L. *Che Guevara America Houro Shokan Shu.* Tokyo: Gendai Kikaku Sha, 2001.

9. Matsumoto, Jinichi. *Kalashnikov.* Tokyo: Asahi Shinbun Sha, 2004.

10. Miyoshi, Toru. *Che Guevara Den.* Hara Shobo, 2001.

11. Neruda, Pablo. *Neruda Shishu.* Tokyo: Shinchosya, 2004.

12. Sandison, David. *Che Guevara.* London: Hamlyn, 1998.

13. Salas, Osvaldo, and Roberto Salas. *Fidel's Cuba: A Revolution in Pictures.* New York: Running P Book, 1999.

14. Sarusky, Jaime, and Alberto Korda. *Ernesto Che Guevara to Sono Jidai.* Trans.

15. Masakuni Ohta. Tokyo: Gendai Kikaku Sitsu, 1998.

16. Sasaki, Jo. *Bokensya Castro.* Tokyo: Shueisya, 2002.

17. Toi, Jugatsu. *Rocinante no Abara.* Tokyo: Shueisya, 2000.

18. Yokohori, Yoichi. *Guevara Seishun to Kakumei.* Tokyo: Sakuhin Sha, 2005.